FAMILY WAR STORIES

THE NORTH'S CIVIL WAR
Andrew L. Slap, series editor

Family War Stories

*The Densmores' Fight to
Save the Union and Destroy
Slavery*

Keith P. Wilson

FORDHAM UNIVERSITY PRESS
NEW YORK   2024

Copyright © 2024 Fordham University Press

All rights reserved. No part of this publication may be reproduced, stored in a retrieval system, or transmitted in any form or by any means—electronic, mechanical, photocopy, recording, or any other—except for brief quotations in printed reviews, without the prior permission of the publisher.

Fordham University Press has no responsibility for the persistence or accuracy of URLs for external or third-party Internet websites referred to in this publication and does not guarantee that any content on such websites is, or will remain, accurate or appropriate.

Fordham University Press also publishes its books in a variety of electronic formats. Some content that appears in print may not be available in electronic books.

Visit us online at www.fordhampress.com.

Library of Congress Cataloging-in-Publication Data available online at https://catalog.loc.gov.

Printed in the United States of America

26 25 24   5 4 3 2 1

First edition

Contents

Preface   ix

Introduction | *1*

1 "May his 'soldier life' be as good as the cause he will represent": Orrin Densmore and the Beginning of the Civil War | *11*

2 "I wish Old Abe had a son or some kin or kine up here in danger": The Brothers' War against the Dakota | *19*

3 "Dont give up my Son": Benjamin on Duty at Fort Halleck | *38*

4 "The glorious, new temple of Liberty": Daniel Joins the United States Colored Troops at Benton Barracks | *48*

5 "Kind acts went directly to their hearts": Martha Serves on the Home Front in Red Wing | *61*

6 "Faces of flint": Campaigning against Major General Nathan Bedford Forrest | *72*

7 "The child was 'right glad' to get home": Young Orrin's Military Adventure | *86*

8 "Move the camp down to the grave yard": Camp Life in Memphis | *98*

9 "Christmas with us here promises to be quite a season": Rejoicing and Celebrating | *110*

	10	"She walks off with the work": Service and Friendship: Elizabeth, Mary, and Martha	*122*
	11	"Do come up Martha": Anna and Martha	*134*
	12	"They all fought like Minnesotians": The Mobile Campaign	*145*
	13	"The curse of slavery": Occupation Duty in Alabama	*156*
	14	"They've got money, let them buy their own biscuit": Departure and Homecoming	*166*
		Conclusion	*179*
Characters		*191*
Genealogical Tables		*197*
Notes		*201*
Bibliography		*243*
Index		*257*

Preface

In 1980 I was working as a high school teacher in Melbourne, Australia, when I had an opportunity to spend a year in the United States on a teaching exchange at Episcopal High School. After a long journey I arrived in Virginia with my wife and two very excited young children just before the semester was about to begin. It was a great adventure for all of us, an opportunity to live in a new environment which was radically different from our homeland. The challenge of teaching in an American high school in Virginia appealed to me. Only a few years before I had enrolled in a PhD program at La Trobe University and had begun researching the role of African American soldiers in the Civil War.

I greatly enjoyed my time teaching at Episcopal High School. Living on campus was a marvelous experience for my whole family. The students were hardworking and keen to learn, the staff, most welcoming and helpful. As well as teaching, I had some opportunity to further my interest in the Civil War. As a family we visited battlefields and National Parks and, on some occasions, I managed to visit the National Archives to gather research material for my dissertation. My research at the National Archives was greatly assisted by the late Professor Ira Berlin, who generously agreed to act as a temporary research supervisor while I was in the United States. Professor Berlin gave me invaluable support, and I remain indebted to him. Whenever possible, I managed to make personal visits to some state archives and historical societies. However, I soon discovered that researching the United States Colored Troops (USCT) posed a unique set of challenges and difficulties. Because the USCT was a federal force, there is no one depository of the officers' personal records. Diaries and personal letters and papers are in archives and historical societies in most Northern states. Since I was unable to visit archives in more remote regions, I wrote to the archivists in these states and asked them to let me know whether their archives had material relating to officers serving in the USCT. The response I received was overwhelming. Invariably the archivists generously sent back comprehensive lists of their Civil War collections that contained relevant material. In some cases, the archivists even sent me small caches of photocopies of an officer's diaries and letters.

The archivists' correspondence assisted my research because it suggested new lines of inquiry and helped me uncover rich primary sources. The most significant body of material I received was from the Benjamin Densmore family papers located in the Minnesota Historical Society. The Densmore collection is extensive, and unlike many collections of Civil War letters, far more than a compilation of letters written by soldiers to the folks at home. The Densmore letters reveal a family fighting a household war. The collection consists of a lively correspondence between the serving sons, Benjamin and Daniel, and the other members of the family living in the family home in Red Wing, Minnesota. Two other members of the family who had established their own households, Margaret and Norman, also wrote to Benjamin and Daniel. The Densmore collection also contains many letters from wider family members, many of whom lived near Norman's farm in Emerald Grove, Wisconsin.

Thanks largely to Orrin's political connections in the local Republican Party and his job as Goodhue County Treasurer, the Densmores were one of the leading families in Red Wing. The family's correspondence reflects this elevated social standing and hence yields insights into how the local community was mobilized to fight the war. As well as these deep family and community connections, the Densmore correspondence ranges over the entire length of the war and includes letters written over a wide geographic area. Benjamin, for example, began his military service in 1861 and ended it in 1866. Few soldiers served over a greater geographic area than Daniel Densmore, whose service ranged from the Dakota Territory to the Louisiana Gulf. Therefore, the family was able to maintain a continual commentary on the ebb and flow of war over a lengthy period time and discover the rich geographic diversity of conquered lands.

Based on the "Benjamin Densmore and family papers," *Family War Stories* extends the boundaries of Civil War research by exploring the way one Northern abolitionist family fought the war. Although it is a book about a family's Civil War experience, it is also a book that focuses on the war stories of individual family members. This bifocal approach has enabled me to discover how the war shaped the lives of individual family members and how the parameters of age, gender, and status within the family affected the family's collective understanding of the war. Individually, each family member has a different story to tell. The Densmores fought the war as a household war by linking the home front to the battlefront. *Family War Stories* also describes how the family's abolitionist ideology was tied to its war effort and how its antislavery convictions had to be continually reconfigured to accommodate the evolving nature of the war and changing family circumstances. The family's commitment to the abolitionist cause was inextricably tied to its belief in the superiority of the white race and preeminence of Anglo-American culture. But during the Civil War these discriminatory beliefs were tested and modified, first during the war against the Dakota, and then by the sons' service with Black troops and officers of Hungarian descent in the USCT, and finally by a refugee from slavery working in the family's kitchen. By analyzing the fluid relationship that existed between the Densmores' racial beliefs and their abolitionist ideology, *Family War Stories* takes the Civil War conflict from the remote battlefields into to the family home.

Like many abolitionists, the Densmores' beliefs were shaped by notions of Anglo-American racial, class, and ethnic superiority that governed the age in which they lived. I have not attempted to hide these beliefs. Nor have I sought to exercise historical hindsight and pass critical judgment on the Densmores from the perspective of the twenty-first century. Instead, my aim has been to understand the family and discuss the family's role in the Civil War. In doing so, I have acknowledged the family's positive achievements, as well as their failings. To this end I have described how the family's sacrificial commitment to the Union, their hatred of slavery, and their advocacy of public schooling were all intrinsically mixed with the family's racial, ethnic, and class prejudices. Retelling the Densmore story has made me aware, not only of my own limitations as a writer, but also of the wise comments made by renowned Australian historian, Sir Christopher Clark. The author of *The Sleepwalkers* reminds historians that even though they may earnestly struggle to be fair-minded and balanced, they remain, like the protagonists in their books, "prisoners of time."[1]

In the years I have spent studying the role of the Densmore family in the American Civil War I have received considerable support from a great range of institutions and individuals both here in Australia and in the United States. I would like to thank Monash University for the critical support they provided. The research funding I received from Monash University enabled me to travel to the United States, share my knowledge with American colleagues, and conduct research at various archives and historical societies. I owe a special debt of gratitude to the Monash University librarians, who did an amazing job of collapsing distance and securing research materials from archives and libraries in the United States.

A vital part of my research involved visiting those locations that touched the lives of the Densmore family. Foremost among these was the Minnesota Historical Society. The Densmore family had a keen sense of history and place. This was evident in the way they lovingly preserved their family records and then generously donated them to the Minnesota Historical Society. I thank the Society for allowing me to access these records, and in particular I thank Jenny McElroy and Colin Dunn for providing research assistance. I owe a special debt of thanks to the late Kathryn A. Johnson. In the very early stages of my research Kathryn generously sent me a large package of officers' letters from the Minnesota Historical Society's archive. Letters from Daniel Densmore formed a significant part of this selection, and after reading these richly descriptive and insightful letters, I was motivated to write this book. I also acknowledge the important assistance I received from my research assistant, Ron Kurpiers, who worked tirelessly at the Society in the initial stages of my project.

I owe a debt to the archivists working in the principal hometowns of the Densmores in the Upper Midwest. Because the home townships of Red Wing, Minnesota, and Emerald Grove, Wisconsin, figure prominently in the lives of the Densmores, I owe a debt to the archivists from the Goodhue County Historical Society, Red Wing, and the Rock County Historical Society, Janesville, Wisconsin. Together they helped me uncover important local history material pertaining to the family. Fort Snelling, Minnesota, also played an important part in the experience of the Densmore family; therefore, I am particularly indebted to Stephen Osman for supporting my project by sharing his extensive knowledge of the Fort's history with me. I am also greatly indebted to Jonathan W. White and Reagan Connelly for generously giving me access to their book manuscript, "'Off to Dixie and Adventure': The Dakota War and Civil War Diaries of George W. Buswell, 7th Minnesota Infantry and 68th U.S. Colored Troops." Since Buswell served in the same regiments as Daniel Densmore, their manuscript was a very valuable research source.

I thank the staff of the Beloit College Archives and Special Collections, particularly Arelle Petroich, for allowing me to access their collection of letters the Densmore boys wrote while they were students there. The Wisconsin Historical has two small but important collections of Densmore Civil War letters written principally to members of Elizabeth Densmore's family. I acknowledge Harry Miller's assistance in accessing these letters. Archivists at the Missouri Historical Society and the Tennessee Historical Society generously shared their knowledge of their historical sources with me. I am also indebted to Eleanor Gillers, New York Historical Society Museum Library, for helping me access a line sketch of Fort Halleck, Columbus, Kentucky. Any study of the Union Army and the Civil War inevitably leads to Washington, D.C. While working at the National Archives, I received invaluable assistance from numerous archivists who helped me uncover research gems hidden in the Bureau of Colored Troops and State Regimental Papers. I also thank the staff of the Library of Congress who assisted me while I worked in the newspaper library and selected photographs for publication in my book.

Preface

While I was writing my book, I presented early versions of my research findings to a number of different audiences. I thank panelists, commentators, and members of the audiences at the Australian and New Zealand American Studies Association Conferences. I am indebted to Barry Crompton, Margaret Lee, Byard Sheppard, and other members of the Civil War Roundtable of Australia and New Zealand, who made insightful comments on the papers I delivered on the Densmores' role in the Civil War. The advice and comments I received from members of the Monash School of Humanities, Communications and Social Sciences Research Forums was also very helpful. I would like to thank Peter Farago for sharing his knowledge about the role Hungarian immigrants played in nineteenth-century America. The opportunity I have had to present my research findings to Monash Research Connections has greatly benefited me. I am indebted to the members of Monash Research Connections for their advice and insightful comments.

The editorial staff at Fordham University Press provided me with excellent support. I am indebted to the Director of the Press, Fredric Nachbaur, for his patience and understanding. I would also like to thank: Assistant Managing Editor, Kem Crimmins, for his very helpful advice and assistance; Copy Editor, Teresa Jesionowski, for her insightful suggestions about revising the text; and Will Cerbone, Rights and Permissions Manager, for expertly reproducing the photographs. Andrew L. Slap, the editor of The North's Civil War series, gave me excellent editorial advice and explained how my manuscript could be reshaped to make it more readable. I am also grateful for the anonymous readers for Fordham University Press for their helpful comments. My mapmaker, Julia Swanson, produced excellent maps that significantly enhance my book.

Finally, I thank those friends and family members who have helped me and sustained me in my project. To my long-standing friends, John, Karen, and Sarah Wires, who always so warmly welcomed me when I visited the United States, I say thank you. My family sustained me in difficult times, when research leads dried up, and writer's block set in. Thank you, Timothy, for critically reading the text and Lydia, Jill, Isobel, and Lachlan for your unfailing support. I dedicate this book to Lachlan and my loving wife, Anne. For many years Anne has shared her life with the Densmores. She read their letters and mulled over their journey through the Civil War. Her faith in my project kept me going, and for this I am deeply grateful.

Family War Stories

Introduction

On June 30, 1861, Norman Densmore wrote to his brother Daniel from his farm at Emerald Grove, Wisconsin. Norman commented on the discomfort caused by his left hand being "puffed up," and the crops "all coming along as well as the drouth [drought] permits." A lack of rain was forcing him to sink new wells and destock his farm. "We have only 5 cattle, *all cows* 2 calves 7 horses and colts, 5 hogs & pigs," he complained. Then toward the end of his letter, Norman alluded to the war. "You speak of taking my place in the Rock Co. Rifles. There will be no necessity as our company was raised under the 3 m[months] and the majority refused to go for a longer term." In an earlier letter Norman had informed his brother that if he volunteered to serve in the army, he would "send for someone to take over affairs here."[1]

Daniel's offer to act as his brother's substitute at a time when his farm was experiencing a severe drought points to the ties of affection that bound the Densmore family together. Although Norman did not join the army, this brief exchange reminds us that the family was at the heart of the Civil War soldier's decision to enlist. Soldiers enlisted because they felt a duty to defend their homes and their local communities, and they negotiated their entry into the army through the debates and conversations they held with their families. Enlistment was not a matter to be taken lightly because issues of life, death, family honor, and family well-being were all at stake. Because the family was the wellspring of Northern and Southern culture, it shaped the way the soldiers understood the war.[2]

From the early years of the Republic, political leaders alluded to the family as a metaphor for the nation. When writing to Hugh Williamson, a signatory of the U.S. Constitution, Thomas Jefferson remarked that "as to myself I sincerely wish that the whole Union may accommodate their interests to each other, & play into their hands mutually as members of the same family, that the wealth & strength of any one part should be viewed as the wealth & strength of the whole." Leaders such as Jefferson and John Adams used the concept of the family to promote national loyalty and commitment to authority. The concept of the nation being a family of citizens endured and gained in strength well beyond the early years of the Republic. Abraham Lincoln appealed to this concept when he warned the nation in 1858 that "a house divided against itself cannot stand." When war finally broke, families in the North and South sought to understand its significance in the discussions they held around their kitchen tables and in their drawing rooms.[3]

Northern families sent their fathers, sons, and brothers into the South to defend the family home and restore the Union. Because these two goals were synonymous, victory had to be won both on the battlefield and on the home front. By its very nature, the Civil War transcended the boundaries between the domestic and the military. Because the war was not fought exclusively on the battlefield but touched the most intimate and private aspects of domestic life, whole families were mobilized. *Family War Stories* recognizes this all-encompassing character of the Civil War by describing how Orrin Densmore, his wife Elizabeth, and their two children, Martha and Orrin Jr., served the Union on the home front in Red Wing, Minnesota, while Orrin's sons Benjamin and Daniel fought against the Dakota and the Southern rebels. The themes of family honor, patriotism, race relations, and gender that recur in this book echoed through the halls of many Northern middle-class family homes.[4]

At the beginning of the Civil War six members of the Densmore family, Orrin, Elizabeth, and four of their children, Benjamin, Daniel, Orrin Jr., and Martha, were living at home in Red Wing, Minnesota. Orrin and Elizabeth's eldest son, Norman, and their eldest daughter, Margaret, lived in their own households. Norman worked a farm in Emerald Grove, and Margaret was married to Otis Smith who farmed near Red Wing. Preoccupied by their own household affairs, they wrote far fewer war letters than those living in the family home, and consequentially they are not the focus of my study. Orrin was a leading citizen of the town, and the fulcrum of family activities. United in their commitment to the abolitionist cause, Orrin and Elizabeth shared a companionate marriage, a partnership of mutual affection. As a Northern middle-class family, the Densmores were in varying degrees committed to the idealized view of the "modern" family as an emotional haven from public life. In this model, which evolved in the late eighteenth century and the early nineteenth century, paternal authority was moderated and to some extent replaced by nurturing love. The family was child-centered, promoting the idea that the family was a haven from the stress of the public world of men and a vehicle for the nurturing of moral values that would promote a virtuous life. Because it was believed that the private world needed to be protected from the public world of politics, industry, and military affairs, the domestic sphere of women and the public sphere of men were to be kept largely apart.⁵

The line between the public and private spheres was never impermeable. Historians have shown that this was particularly the case in wartime. The Civil War intruded into the domestic lives of its citizens and broke down the barriers and conventions separating their public and private worlds. As a fervent abolitionist, Orrin supported Elizabeth as she moved outside the home to wage war for the Union as a member of the Red Wing Ladies' Soldiers' Aid Society. During the war Union and Confederate women discovered new opportunities to exercise influence in a wide range of social and political activities, and sometimes these ventures caused rupture, tension, and a realignment of family relationships. Authority structures were challenged, and new roles had to be learned. Of course, to some extent family structures were always subject to change. Industrialization, religious movements, commercial innovation, and changes in education all influenced the way Northern families evolved. Tension and conflict within the family were essential elements of this process of change. However, the Civil War intruded so radically into the public and private worlds of family members that it greatly increased the rate and extent of change. For example, intergenerational conflict had long been a source of tension within families, but this tension greatly intensified when some young men, such as Orrin Densmore Jr., felt impelled to prove their manhood by defying their parents and enlisting in the Union Army. The war was a life-and-death struggle, a mortal conflict to save the nation and defend the home, and so it required a realignment of family roles and responsibilities. Martha's public and private worlds merged as she labored at the tables of the Red Wing Ladies' Soldiers' Aid Society, dispensing refreshments she had prepared at home to soldiers passing through Red Wing on their way to Southern battlefields.

As well as being a powerful force for familial change, the Civil War radically transformed the nation by heralding an age of emancipation and Black enlistment. The escaped slaves who fled to Union lines became powerful advocates of this change. Slowly the government realized that these former slaves could be enlisted to save the Union by fighting against their former masters. A series of defeats in the summer and spring of 1862 and manpower shortages encouraged the Lincoln administration to adopt both emancipation and Black enlistment primarily as war measures necessary to save the Union. By May 1863 the Bureau of Colored Troops had been established to manage the national enlistment of African Americans and the selection of white officers to command them. In the spring of 1863, Secretary of War Edwin Stanton had authorized some Northern governors to raise Black regiments in their states, and Black recruitment began in Louisiana, North Carolina, and the Mississippi Valley.[6]

Because there are few studies of the families of USCT officers, we have a meager knowledge about how they experienced the war.[7] In particular, we know little about the war experience of the small minority of abolitionist families who had kinfolk serving as USCT officers. The experience of these families was different from that of most Northern families because their concepts of honor and duty were not only linked to saving the Union but also to freeing the slaves. For them equitable treatment for USCT officers and men was a core belief. In contrast, the federal government and most military authorities were at best tardy in upholding the Black soldiers' rights and freedoms. This difference in attitude reflected wider divisions in Northern society, where a small minority of abolitionists, both Black and white, sought to uphold Black rights, but the general population treated African Americans in a discriminatory and marginalized manner. Eventually, most Union soldiers accepted emancipation, but at first they did so mainly because they believed emancipation was an important war measure that would help win the war.[8]

Although abolitionism was important, only a small minority of soldiers joined the commissioned ranks of the USCT solely because they were fervent abolitionists. Even though the majority found slavery abhorrent, they joined the USCT mainly for reasons of self-interest, to further their careers. Yet regardless of their personal motives or preferences, by joining Black regiments, all USCT officers were, by association, exposing themselves to the barbs of Northern racism.[9] Because USCT officers were fighting at the frontier of racial change, their families were aware of the inequitable treatment Black soldiers received. Issues such as unequal pay, excessive fatigue duty, lack of combat training, inferior arms and equipment, inadequate shelter, poor medical service, excessively high mortality rates, barriers to prison exchange, and rebel atrocities had a special resonance for them because they directly touched the lives of their loved ones serving in the South.[10]

Perhaps the most visible group of officers in the USCT were the sons belonging to nationally renowned abolitionist families. For example, William Lloyd Garrison, Frederick Douglass, Theodore Dwight Weld, James Gillespie Birney, Charles Francis Adams, Lyman Beecher, and Harriet Beecher all had kinfolk serving as officers in the USCT. For these young men who had joined the war, abolition became a vital war aim mainly because it was rooted in their family heritage and was, therefore, a formative feature in the development of their identity. The vast majority of abolitionist officers, like the Densmore brothers, came from much more humble and diverse backgrounds. Yet regardless of their origin, most were generally committed to the core body of beliefs. They fought for the complete and immediate abolition of slavery. They considered the impact of slavery on the slaves both evil and inhumane because it destroyed family life, treated humans as property, and reduced them to a state of cruel dependency. Like many other abolitionists, the Densmore brothers joined the USCT to advance their military careers and to undo the work of the slaveholder by linking the act of liberation with that of elevation. In the parlance of the day this process was gender-specific and involved raising the allegedly degraded male slave to manhood. Because they believed that enslaved men could not protect their wives and family members from the exploitation by the slaveholders, they assumed that they had lost their manhood. Yet their manhood had never been lost. Influenced by a distorted view of slavery which masked slave resistance, and unable to understand the unconventional ways enslaved men endeavored to fulfill their family roles, the Densmores, and most abolitionist officers, failed to see this.[11]

All Civil War soldiers' families worried about the impact of army life on their loved ones. In particular, they worried about their kinfolks' ability to uphold family honor by displaying the virtues of true manhood. Therefore, they looked for the character traits of steadfastness, resilience, willpower, emotional control, initiative, charity, protection of the weak, loyalty, and courage in the war record of their soldiers. Since combat was considered the supreme test of a soldier's manhood, both Northern and Southern families used their soldiers' valor to help them display their patriotism. Individual soldiers served as family representatives, and because the soldiers were enlisted from local communities, the regiments became an enlargement of the community. Concerned for their soldiers' welfare, family members and community leaders were worried that the debauched army camp environment where drunkenness and gambling prevailed would turn their men into hard-drinking and brawling "roughs" who were estranged from the moral values of their home and local community. In some ways, estrangement was a natural development, the consequence of young men growing into manhood and establishing their own identities. Yet USCT officers' families were touched by this issue more than others, because the USCT was largely organized nationally and the soldiers in the USCT were former slaves. The men who became officers in USCT regiments came from different states and diverse home communities. Friends and kinfolk were not there to greet or support them when they were mustered in. In these circumstances many families were fearful that the legacy of slavery that had marred the lives of Black soldiers could undermine the moral fiber of their sons and brothers who served as officers.[12]

Although roles changed within the Densmore family, these changes were mediated through the core beliefs they all shared. All family members were bound by their sense of family honor, their commitment to the supremacy of the white race and Anglo-American culture, their love of their community and their state, their commitment to the Republican Party and the Union, and their intense hostility to slavery.[13] These core beliefs underlined their cause and justified their sacrifices. Family members shared their understanding of the war with each other, and because of this, their beliefs and values changed as the war progressed. Each letter writer had his or her own perspective of the war, and each perspective reflected the writer's role in the family, the geographic location, and the recipient's needs and preferences. Above all else, letter writing reflected the personal traits of the writer and his or her role in the Union war effort. Like different cords of a strong rope, the letters tied the family together. To understand just how letter writing helped to maintain the integrity of the Densmore family circle one must examine the writing style of the individuals.

Daniel Densmore's letters had a powerful impact on his family. They compacted time and distance and enabled family members to view the war through the eyes of an eyewitness whom they loved and trusted. His letters bear the hallmarks of a young, well-educated middle-class man who was engaged with community affairs and social activities. They reveal an acute eye for detail, and an earnest desire for his family to discover the military world he was living in. By far the most important and prolific correspondent in the family, Daniel wrote his letters over a four-year period from 1862 to 1865. He wrote letters from different places, and under many conditions, and his letters covered great distances to reach the folks at home. From the parched prairie lands of North Dakota, to the miasmic swamps of Tennessee, to the sandy reaches of the Gulf, and the luxuriant plantation districts of Alabama, he wrote home describing the wonders of his military journey. His vivid descriptions bear many of the hallmarks of a travel writer. This is not surprising, for Daniel knew he was writing to very receptive readers. The Densmores loved learning about exotic places and traveling to distant lands.

Like many soldiers, Daniel discovered that letter writing improved his well-being. It enabled him to escape briefly the loneliness and hardship of military service. The letters he wrote and the letters he received from his family helped him to solicit supplies and comforts from home, encouraged him, and transported him back in time to the comfort of a loving family. The writing process helped Daniel discover more about himself and, by doing so, explain himself to friends and family. Letter writing also helped him understand the war. As he explained the war to others, he began to clarify its personal meaning.[14] When he wrote, he was engaging in a dialogue. His letters helped his family understand the war, and the letters he received from home helped shape his image of the war. The family in Red Wing saw the war from a different perspective. Theirs was a composite image that reflected not just their own personal views but also those from the community and their wider circle of friends.

Benjamin Densmore was more reserved than Daniel. Less socially engaged before the war, he gained a local renown for exploring the remote Otter Trail region and for his work as a pioneering surveyor. During the war Benjamin wrote far fewer letters than Daniel, and those he wrote often consisted of brief reports outlining a calendar of events. Short and to the point, his letters contain complaints about military incompetency, lists of the impediments to his promotion, and requests for tonics to cure his illnesses. Even though Benjamin was an irregular correspondent, with a negative view of army life, his letters showed how the ugly side of war could intrude into family life. Orrin and other family members fretted over Benjamin's health and mental state. Like other family members, Daniel was concerned about Benjamin's well-being. But there was also a pragmatic edge to his correspondence. Benjamin and Daniel were able to share their experiences in the USCT and to learn from each other. Letters between soldiers can reveal insights into how soldiers shared their understanding of the war and gave it meaning. They can also reveal hidden aspects of the war. Many soldiers writing home were unable to describe the horrific nature of the war they were experiencing; others imposed a veil of self-censorship on their correspondence. They just did not want their loved ones to know about the harsh brutality of the war. They also hid incidents that could tarnish the family's honor.[15]

The correspondence of Orrin, Elizabeth, Martha, and Orrin Jr. tied each to the war in different ways. Because each family member saw the war differently, they solicited different responses from Benjamin and Daniel. In part these different approaches reflected their different roles within the family. When Orrin, the head of the family, wrote to his sons, he wanted information on the campaigns they had been on, the alien nature on the land they traversed, the performance of Black soldiers, and the tyranny of slavery. These interests reflected his background as schoolteacher, a New York militia man, and his office within the Republican Party. Like a good "republican mother," Elizabeth wrote about the war being a struggle to defend the Founding Fathers' constitution.[16] In some ways the correspondence of Orrin, Elizabeth, and other members of the family replicated the relationships that had developed before the war. For example, Martha was Daniel's eyes and ears in the Red Wing community because before the war they shared social activities and the same circle of friends. Yet the war brought changes too. Martha gained more authority and influence both in the home and in the town. When she wrote to her brothers, she was able to assume a new persona as a household manager and patriotic woman, and she believed that writing was her war work, an essential part of her war service. Conversely, the changing status of Benjamin and Daniel meant that the family members had to relate to them in new ways; for now, they were not simply sons, but also Union officers and patriotic heroes.[17]

Apart from letter writing other forms of communication were important too. Throughout the war the Densmores managed to stay connected by making personal visits. Both Benjamin and Daniel secured leave to return to Red Wing. These occasions were joyous times of reunion and refreshment. But sometimes when sick leave was taken, the reunions taxed the family's resources and were stressful. On a few occasions family members even managed to visit Benjamin and Daniel in their encampments. Family members also strengthened their relationships by exchanging gifts. In this regard the exchange of photographs was particularly important. Trophies and trinkets of war, Christmas presents, and gifts of food and clothing all played their part in cementing relationships between the home front and the battlefront. Benjamin and Daniel also exchanged gifts with each other. Gifts of money and articles of military uniform helped consolidate their friendship and loyalty.

Caught up in the sweeping events of the Civil War, each Densmore family member had a story to tell. I have deliberately focused on telling the story of the four young siblings, Orrin Jr., Martha, Daniel, and Benjamin, who were living in the family home at the onset of the Civil War, for several reasons. First, the Civil War was a testament to youth. It was essentially the young men and women who were on the front line of the conflict. They had the most to give, but they also had the most to lose. For young soldiers such as Benjamin and Daniel, the Civil War was a life-and-death conflict, a personal struggle for survival. For Orrin Jr. the war offered a pathway to manhood, and for Martha it offered a new civic role as a patriotic woman. Because the war so radically influenced the lives of these young siblings, they became the family's most prolific war correspondents. Second, the war broke upon the siblings at a time when they were shaping their identities. Because the war hastened and amplified this, the siblings are excellent subjects to reveal the impact of the war on family relationships. Finally, by studying the siblings we can discover how the war shaped the private life of this middle-class family. In Victorian America, brothers and sisters developed their own, intimate world within the orbit of the family. They grew up together, they learned together, and they were part of the same generation. Theirs was a world shaped by childhood secrets and deep personal relationships, which continued and developed as the war progressed.

A study of the war service of the Densmore siblings helps us understand how individuals experienced the changing world of the Civil War era. It places slavery and emancipation at the center of the Civil War struggle because those who were actively engaged in the fighting saw it that way. The Densmores coped with this era of change through the new relationships they formed and in the new ways they engaged in the world. Benjamin's efforts to educate his men and Daniel's attendance at a Black soldier's wedding all tell us something about how they adapted to the new world. Because the siblings shared experiences, there was a level of equality between them. However, this equality always had to accommodate differences in gender and age.[18]

Orrin and Elizabeth's personal commitment to the war was different from that of their children. While the war enhanced Orrin's career and his position in the Republican Party, Elizabeth became more engaged outside the family home as a member of the Red Wing Ladies' Soldiers' Aid Society and a campaigner for the temperance movement. However, at home she believed her authority was threatened by an African American servant working in her kitchen. Elizabeth wrote very few family letters. In contrast, Orrin exercised an active, paternal guardianship role. He encouraged his sons to write regularly, and as well as generating correspondence, he helped to direct and coordinate it.

The war stories of the Densmore family reveal their innermost thoughts and feelings, providing a penetrating insight into how one family thought about a war that shaped the course of American history. To preserve the family voices, I have included in the text their forms of spelling and grammar as they appear in their letters and reports. I have made corrections only when it is necessary to avoid confusion. However, I have used italic font to indicate words that are underlined in the original documents. The war stories are told in a chronological narrative. I have adopted this approach because the family members' attitudes changed incrementally as the war intruded on their lives in different ways. To give each sibling an opportunity to tell his or her story, I have narrated their stories as historical episodes linked to each other in a broad chronological framework. This approach, which alternates between the battlefront and the home front, reveals how developments on one front influenced change on the other. *Family War Stories* also has structural coherence because Daniel's story provides the historical spine of the narrative. Daniel was the most prolific correspondent. His story was also particularly interesting to other family members because his theater of operation extended widely, and he was often engaged in battle. Because his letters were so freely circulated, they became the most significant reference point of the family's Civil War experience.

1

"May his 'soldier life' be as good as the cause he will represent"

Orrin Densmore and the Beginning of the Civil War

In the spring of 1857, the residents of the small Mississippi river port town of Red Wing, Minnesota, learned that the Red Wing Sawmill had been sold to Orrin Densmore, Archibald McVean, and Robert N. McLaren, from Wisconsin. Shortly after making the purchase Orrin brought his wife and family to Red Wing. His arrival was the culmination of a westward journey that took almost a decade, and at each stage of his journey, he sought to enhance his family's fortune and reputation by actively engaging in community affairs and local politics.[1]

Born in Washington, New Hampshire, in 1805, Orrin moved with his family to Riga in New York state in 1806. There he began his career as a schoolteacher and developed his lifelong interest in music by joining the band of the 177th New York militia. In 1828 he married Elizabeth Fowle and a year later purchased a farm in Alabama, New York. There he raised his young family of three boys (Norman, Benjamin, and Daniel) and two girls (Margaret and Martha) and made his mark in the Alabama community, working as inspector of Alabama's schools and serving on the County Board of Supervisors, the legislative body that governed Genesee County.[2] In 1848 Orrin and his family moved to Wisconsin, where they settled near relatives on a farm at Emerald Grove, Rock County. There Elizabeth gave birth to her last child, Orrin Jr. An ambitious civic leader, with strong antislavery convictions and a progressive political outlook, Orrin again became active in county governance and educational and community affairs. But unsettled by his restless entrepreneurial spirit, he left for Red Wing, Minnesota, in 1857.[3]

Orrin arrived in Minnesota at a time of great change. Most of the settlers in the sparsely populated land lived on homesteads or in townships located in the southern part of the territory, on the lower reaches of the Minnesota River system, and along the Mississippi River, south of St. Paul. Although approximately two-thirds of settlers were originally from the eastern states, increasing numbers of immigrants were arriving from Scandinavia, the German states, and the

Figure 1.1. Orrin Densmore circa 1863. Minnesota Historical Society.

British Isles. Farming was booming. By the late 1850s sufficient frontier land had been cleared to support over 19,000 farms, and, according to the 1860 census, Minnesota had 172, 023 inhabitants. At the time statehood was granted in 1858, the Ojibwe (Chippewa) were located in the forests north of Little Falls, a settlers' fort located on the Mississippi River. The Dakota (Sioux), deprived of much of their traditional land, lived on reservations along the Upper Minnesota River between Lake Traverse and Milford Township.[4]

Upon arriving in Red Wing, Orrin immediately joined the local branch of the Republican Party. Fortunately, he arrived at a time when the political environment was receptive to his abolitionist views. By the time that Minnesota became a state, the Republican Party was the dominant political party in Minnesota. Although the party was divided on issues such as Black political equality, Black military service, and the resettlement of former slaves in the North, it supported temperance, and was unified in its strong opposition to the spread of slavery into the Territories. This stand made the party the logical political home for Orrin,

Map 1. Location of St. Paul, Red Wing, and Goodhue County, Minnesota.

for he supported temperance, fervently opposed slavery, and had supported Republican John C. Frémont in the 1856 presidential election campaign.⁵

Located approximately fifty miles south of St. Paul, on the Mississippi River near Barn Bluff, the town of Red Wing developed on a Dakota village site. Named after a famous Mdewakanton chief, the town fell on hard times when the Panic of 1857 swept through the nation. Faced with ruin, Orrin was forced to sell his mill. In March 1859 he suffered another blow when almost one million feet of saw logs he owned were washed down the Mississippi River.⁶ But these financial crises did have one positive outcome because they encouraged family members to return home. Benjamin left his failing surveying business in St. Paul and sought to establish himself as Red Wing's town surveyor, and Daniel returned home from a teaching post he held in Tennessee after he had graduated from Beloit College in Wisconsin.⁷

With his family drawing closer, Orrin's fortunes began to improve. He arrived in Red Wing at a time when the town and county were being organized and incorporated. An astute opportunist, Orrin used his local political connections to take advantage of the situation. In 1858 he was elected as one of the three Red Wing representatives to Goodhue County's first Board of Supervisors. Created to manage the organization of townships within the county, the board had the task of organizing a range of municipal services. Representing his support base in the Republican Party, he fought hard against his Democratic opponents. As the chair of the Public Building Committee, he waged a successful battle to have a courthouse and jail built in Red Wing.⁸

Elected County Treasurer in 1861 on a Republican Party ticket, Orrin was well placed to coordinate and encourage the commercial development of Red Wing. With a population of 1,251 residents in 1860, the town had developed into a thriving river port servicing the wheat-growing farmlands of Goodhue County and providing a port of entry for immigrant settlers. To meet the needs of the rising population, industries were developed, and new commercial ventures were begun. By mid-1861 the town could boast of a sawmill, two brick works, three hotels, and two breweries.⁹ Red Wing's social and religious life was also flourishing, and its educational facilities were expanding. The town supported three newspapers, and musical concerts and masquerade balls were held in the Court House or the Philleo Hall in Main Street. The community supported several churches, including Presbyterian, Methodist Episcopal, Episcopal, Lutheran, and Catholic. Some churches also met the needs of the growing Swedish, German, and Norwegian immigrant populations. In 1856, the Methodist Episcopal Church opened Hamline University. The first public school was erected in Red Wing in

Figure 1.2. Red Wing looking toward Barn Bluff. The Court House, with the dome tower, is in the center of the photograph. The Central School is the large two-story building to the right of the Court House, and Hamline University is the smaller two-story building to the left of the Court House circa 1860s. Minnesota Historical Society.

1854. A lifelong advocate of public schooling, Orrin worked hard to promote public education not only in his hometown but also in Minnesota. In 1861 while serving as Judge of Probate, he wrote the "State School Law of 1861."[10]

In every way, Red Wing appeared to be prospering at the onset of the Civil War. This small town was governed by a network of municipal elders who represented the leading families in the town. They were bound together by family ties, commercial interests, political preferences, religious affiliations, and cultural activities. Orrin made his family a part of this governing class. The town's mayor, F. F. Philleo, was his close friend, as was State Senator Robert N. McLaren, a business partner and husband of his niece, Anna.[11] Yet just when the family's future seemed secure, the clouds of war threatened. Orrin now realized that his family's standing could not be secured by political connections alone. He knew that in a time of war its future would depend heavily on the patriotic sacrifices it made in defense of the Union.

Lincoln's victory in the 1860 presidential election and South Carolina's secession brought the sectional crisis to a head. When on April 5, 1861, Lincoln called for 75,000 three-month volunteers to put down the rebellion, Minnesota men were among the first to respond. In the fall of 1861 Benjamin Densmore answered the call to defend the Union by enlisting in the Goodhue County Rifles. This decision received Orrin's hearty endorsement because he believed his son was honoring the family name by clearly affirming their sacrificial commitment to the Union's war. But other less lofty motives were also at work. Orrin also supported his son's enlistment because military service offered Benjamin good pay and opportunities for promotion.[12]

Orrin's high hopes for his son dimmed only a few months after Benjamin had joined the army. After the Goodhue County Rifles was mustered into the 3rd Minnesota Infantry, the regiment was sent to Kentucky to join Major General Don Carlos Buell's Army of Ohio. While traveling to Kentucky the harsh realities of army life first confronted Benjamin. In a letter to his father, he outlined his deep disappointment with army life. He and the officers in his regiment were convinced that the U.S. Army and government were "going to waste and ruin in quick time." While "bad management and corruption" were present everywhere, vigilance and energy were seldom seen.[13]

In February 1862 the 3rd Minnesota Infantry was assigned to Murfreesboro, Tennessee, where on July 13 Major General Nathan Bedford Forrest's cavalry besieged it. Forrest duped the officers of the 3rd into believing he had a vastly superior force, and because of this, they decided to surrender without a fight, despite objections from many enlisted men, such as Benjamin Densmore. After surrendering, the 3rd Minnesota was sent to prison in Madison, Georgia, for three months before being paroled. Shocked by the 3rd Minnesota's meek surrender, news of Benjamin's capture plunged the family into a state of depression. "I hope you have heard from him that he is all right, still I can't help anticipating the worst," Norman commented.[14]

When Benjamin arrived, at Benton Barracks, St. Louis, in mid-August, he wrote home assuring his father that he was in good health. Orrin was pleased to get this good news, but he was disturbed to learn his son's confidence in the army had been severely shaken. Benjamin explained that his fate was uncertain, and his status as a parolee was "neither proud nor flattering." He now felt his time was being wasted in much the same way it had been when he had been incarcerated "in a southern slave pen." He blamed incompetency and corruption in the commissioned ranks for the Union Army's multiple failings and defeats. "We have a thousand Napoleons and their road to renown is by regiments," he complained.

Figure 1.3. Maj. Gen. Nathan Bedford Forrest. Library of Congress.

He questioned the call for 600,000 additional men, and asked if the federal government was seeking "to subdue the traitors by *numbers* instead of steel?" He poured most of his scorn on General Buell, whom he accused of surrendering "on the Tennessee River," and of pursuing the enemy tardily on foot. In contrast, the traitors moved "like egyptian locusts in swarms & hordes and visit our outposts with death and destruction at unexpected moments and in remote places."[15]

When news of Daniel's enlistment in the 7th Minnesota Infantry reached Benjamin, he felt duty bound as a veteran to warn him, via a letter to his father, of the dangers of army life. He pointed to the presence of the many officers who were incompetent and drunk and asked Daniel to look out for the "red tape" of regulation, which could "bind regiments and brigades and even divisions and leave them a sacrifice to southern hordes." Yet despite this negative foreboding, he praised Daniel for manfully accepting the challenges of military service. "May his 'soldier life' be as good as the cause he will represent," he commented to his father. Orrin welcomed these words of encouragement, even though they were moderated by comments on the difficulties and dangers of military service. Fearful that Benjamin's humiliating capture might have undermined his patriotism, he seized upon his son's endorsement as evidence that he remained faithfully committed to the Union Army.[16]

Orrin's enthusiasm for Daniel's enlistment was tempered because he knew issues surrounding Benjamin's parole were surfacing and could work against Daniel. Benjamin complained that since his regiment had been at Benton Barracks, one hundred and forty men had taken "French leave" and many more were "determined to do so." Orrin was troubled by this news. Already the Murfreesboro surrender had tarnished the family's honor. Desertion would only exacerbate this problem. He shared his concerns with Daniel by forwarding Benjamin's letter of August 16, 1862, and adding a postscript. "Can anything be done for the 3rd to save them from desertion?" he inquired. Then he answered his question by suggesting that the regiment could be sent to Fort Ridley without breaching the conditions of their parole. Finally, partly to allay Daniel's fears for Benjamin's welfare, he advised him that he had "written to B advising patience."[17]

In September Orrin finally received good news when he learned that Daniel had been appointed Second Lieutenant and that Benjamin had been promoted to Quartermaster Sergeant in the reorganized 3rd Minnesota. The gods of war were smiling upon him and his family. But he knew these military gods were fickle. Military service offered the family a pathway to honor and glory, but Benjamin's brief military experience had shown the route contained dangers. But despite this, Orrin remained resolutely devoted to the Union cause, and even believed the war was now turning in favor of the Union. On September 18 he informed his sons that the Union Army had won a great victory on the Potomac. Good news had also been heralded in Minnesota where the Chippewa had been supposedly "pacified" and the Sioux had manifest "pacific tendencies." Such news gave "a good cheer to faces upon which gloom was becoming chronic."[18]

Yet Orrin's optimism soon dissipated. Although he did not know it at the time, the day before he penned his letter, Dakota warriors had attacked the Jones family at Acton Township, in the Minnesota River Valley. The Dakota War had begun. At the onset of this war Orrin called upon Benjamin and Daniel to defend their homeland. While their service in this conflict honored the family and enhanced their prospects for promotion, it also brought them close to death and left a legacy which shaped their war against the Southern rebels.[19]

2

"I wish Old Abe had a son or some kin or kine up here in danger"

The Brothers' War against the Dakota

By the early 1860s considerable discontent was growing among the Dakota because settler migration and the loss of hunting lands were undermining their traditional way of life. In August 1862 this discontent flared into conflict when the cumulative impact of treaty violations, postponed annuity payments, and hunger caused by poor harvests created the conditions that resulted in Taoyateduta (Little Crow) leading his Mdewakanton Dakota warriors on raids on settlers in the Minnesota River Valley. During these attacks, over five hundred settlers and military personnel lost their lives; many settlers were held hostage by the Dakota; and considerable property damage was done to southern Minnesota. Upon hearing news of the attacks, Governor Alexander Ramsey commissioned Henry H. Sibley, colonel of the state's militia, and ordered him to raise an expeditionary force to rescue Taoyateduta's hostages and defeat the Dakota. In addition to raising the militia Ramsey appealed to Lincoln for federal assistance.[1]

Ramsey's appeal came at a critical time in the Civil War. In the Western Theater federal forces had won significant successes. General Ulysses S. Grant had wrested control of the Tennessee and Cumberland Rivers, won a decisive victory at Shiloh, and both New Orleans and Memphis had been captured. But in the Eastern Theater the situation was very different. General Thomas "Stonewall" Jackson had repelled Union forces in the Shenandoah Valley. Lincoln's hopes of capturing Richmond and ending the war quickly had all but disappeared with General George McClellan's Peninsula Campaign, which ended in defeat in the Seven Days battle in June and July 1862. Approximately a month later General Robert E. Lee heavily defeated General John Pope at Second Bull Run. With Washington under threat and critics attacking his administration, Lincoln could not afford to have Northern papers full of headlines describing massacres on the Minnesota frontier. To quell the Dakota, he created the Department of the Northwest and appointed Pope to command it. Although Pope's appointment was seen by some as a form of banishment, Pope saw it as an opportunity to resurrect his career.[2]

Figure 2.1. Lt. Daniel Densmore, 7th Minnesota Infantry, circa 1863. Minnesota Historical Society.

Although both Daniel and Benjamin joined Sibley's August 1862 expedition, only Daniel wrote extensively about his Dakota War experiences. The movement of letters between Daniel, located on the remote Minnesota frontier, and family members was difficult because the letters had to travel a great distance and pass through many hands.[3] Because correspondence was intermittent and there were few letters written by the family to Daniel, it is difficult to establish a direct

Figure 2.2. Taoyateduta [Little Crow]. A carte-de-visite, colorization of a black and white card, circa 1860. Minnesota Historical Society.

Figure 2.3. Brig. Gen. Henry Hasting Sibley. Minnesota Historical Society.

dialogue between the correspondents. Therefore, one must look at the framing and content of particular letters in order to discover how Daniel and his family's understanding of the Dakota wars evolved.

On September 19, 1862, Sibley's expedition left Fort Ridgely to begin the pursuit of Taoyeduta. Daniel reported the expedition followed the Minnesota River northward without noteworthy incident until on September 22 it "camped about two miles below the Upper Agency on the mouth of the Yellow Medicine River, and on the south side of a lake called Wood Lake." The next day a battle ensued. In a report on the battle written to Aunt Martha, Daniel celebrated the alleged military and moral superiority of the Union troops. He rejoiced in the one-sided nature of the conflict and, to demean the enemy's resistance, employed racist language to describe Dakota warriors as amphibians. It was "a very tolerable sport for us," he reported, "but death to the frogs." The bottom of the ravine was "strewn with the naked (for so they fight) bodies of the savage rascals." Thoughts of mercy and surrender did not come into his mind because he thought the Dakota had fought with savage brutality; they "fearfully mutilated, scalped & cut into pieces" the corpses of dead soldiers. Because he lacked an understanding of Dakota culture, Daniel could not see that the Dakota mutilated the soldiers' corpses, not only for revenge, but also to prevent them fighting in the inevitable conflict that they believed would occur in the afterlife. In his determination to highlight the Dakota's alleged savagery, Daniel failed to mention reports that some soldiers also scalped and pillaged the slain Dakota warriors. Although Benjamin was wounded, the army's victory was complete, for the soldiers' casualty rate was low, and the Dakota were forced from the field.[4]

Three days after the victory at Wood Lake, Sibley's force received Taoyeduta's captives, who had been in the protective custody of chiefs Wabasha, Red Iron, and Taopi. With the remnant of his force, Taoyeduta retreated north to the Dakota prairies where he wintered in the vicinity of Devil's Lake, located in present-day northeastern North Dakota. Shortly after this departure, a military commission was established to put on trial those Dakota who had allegedly participated in attacks on the settlers. During the trial the judicial process was corrupted by the presentation of distorted evidence and widespread hysterical cries for retribution. When Daniel's sister Martha heard a false rumor that Taoyeduta had been shot in August 1862, she immediately wrote to him commenting that it "was almost a pity for him to die so respectable a death." With his death, and the surrender of the remaining chiefs, all that remained to be done was "to pack up the lovely beings and express them to the 'far West.'" She advised Daniel that she would pray for them in the same way the local preacher prayed for the rebels last

Thursday—"'that they may have short lives, a happy death, and we be rid of them forever.'" "Was that not to the point?" Martha added in a cryptic postscript.[5]

Orrin Jr. called for the Dakota to be severely punished, and he also condemned Lincoln for being kindly disposed to the "savages." "I wish Old Abe had a son or some kin or kine up there in danger," he wrote, and then added, "I guess he would begin to see 'a strong necessity for hanging the loathsome red devils.'" Yet Daniel was not swayed by calls for vengeance, even when they came from his own family. In a letter to Aunt Martha, he accused newspapers of exaggerating the Dakota threat so that the Department of Northwest was created and a major general appointed. He also argued that punishment should not be imposed simply on racial grounds and pointed out that Taoyateduta's followers had "robbed and destroyed the property of friendly Indians as well as whites." Although he welcomed the arrest of some Indians, he acknowledged that many friendly Indians had done much to secure the safety of the prisoners. "We have no right in justice & truth to kill any man or race of men who have done us no injury either in word or deed," he commented.[6]

In her reply Aunt Martha revealed the joy she had felt upon learning that both Daniel and Benjamin had survived the battle of Wood Lake, and that wounded Benjamin "was not seized by the Indians and horribly butchered," and that his grave was not to be among the Dakota. She encouraged Daniel to link the Dakota War to the nation's wider struggle for survival. Like her nephew, she did not demand blind vengeance on the Dakota. As she thought more deeply about the wider conflict engulfing the nation, she concluded that the Dakota were no crueler in their fighting than "our white savages in the south." Such a negative depiction of the rebels implicitly called upon Daniel to defend his nation against Southern rebels, just as he defended his state against the Dakota. She believed that if slavery's shackles were not broken and the "broken and oppressed set free," "our once happy land" would become a great slaughterhouse.[7]

When Orrin wrote to his sons in October 1862, he echoed Aunt Martha's words. "We are glad to hear of your being still alive and as well as you are—which is something of a wonder," he admitted. Proud of his sons' achievements, he informed them that he proposed to use his political contacts to advance their military careers. He planned to secure Daniel a First Lieutenant's appointment by approaching Governor Ramsey and other members of the state legislature with recommendations for promotion from Major Abraham Edwards Welch, a hero at Bull Run, and his father Judge William H. Welch.[8] Orrin tied the issue of family honor to his sons' military performance and praised them for not only defending their Minnesota homeland but also for conquering and dispossessing an allegedly savage and primitive people. He believed their punitive expedition against the Dakota was extending the boundaries of the frontier and colonizing an exotic land that lacked civilization and the rule of law. Other family members were so interested in the Densmore boys' adventures that they circulated their letters widely. When Elizabeth visited Emerald Grove in November 1862, she brought with her a cache of Daniel's letters. Aunt Martha read this correspondence and then read the letters aloud to Daniel's aged grandmother. This process of recycling letters meant that the war itself was intertwined in the personal lives of the correspondents.[9]

Margaret invariably found time to read Daniel's letters and take solace from them when her husband was gravely ill. Orrin also copied "some of the most graphic" of the letters and sent them to Norman. He believed the letters were treasured artifacts, personalized letters of family achievement. Conscious that the letters made a "regular history of the expedition," he "put them in a cover in book form." To expedite his filing system, he recommended that his sons' letters have a "3/8 inch" margin on the left side "for binding." The letters then were not just vehicles for family news. They had a deeper, historical meaning linked to family honor and heritage. Orrin was constructing a family archive, "a ready reference," which would be much "pleasanter than a pack of folded letters." While we have no direct evidence of the sons' response to their father's request, Daniel does appear to have taken on the role of family historian with some enthusiasm. Indeed, later, when on Sibley's second expedition against the Dakota, his letters took the form of adventure narratives rather than brief personal epistles. Some letters were over twenty pages long. In part this can be explained by the irregular mail service. However, evidence suggests that Daniel was writing not just to keep in personal contact with the family but also to compile a historical record.[10]

Letters were not the only way Daniel communicated with his loved ones. The keepsakes and trinkets that he sent back home were important too. While these spoils of war were evidence of colonial conquest, they also pointed to the exotic mystery of the Dakota land. He sent Orrin Jr. shell artifacts from Camp Pope. The gift intrigued him. "Were those made out of clam shells?" he asked his elder brother. The very beauty of the objects inspired Orrin Jr. to replicate their creation. Martha, Margaret, and Belle Webster were delighted to receive the rings Daniel sent them. "They are *very neat* and we prize them highly, as gifts from you & mementos of camp Pope," Martha commented. These keepsakes became heirlooms, and much treasured family "trophies of the 'Indian Massacre.'"[11]

After Sibley's expedition concluded, Daniel was sent to New Ulm to guard Dakota prisoners. Although he disliked this duty, he was encouraged by a letter he received from Martha. Martha wrote to comfort Daniel and to reassure him that the family and community had not forgotten him. Therefore, she embedded in her letter images of community joy and harmony to show that Red Wing was a community well worth fighting for, and that he had a valued place in it. She reported enjoying her skating outings with Belle Webster. In a playful, teasing manner, she informed Daniel that his circle of friends, "the young people," had visited the family home on several occasions to play "muggins." All enjoyed this parlor game, except Mollie Ronable, who was disappointed that Daniel, "the life of that game," was absent. "Poor girl! What can be done for her?" Martha asked. Packed with images of warm friendship and family happiness, Martha's letter made little reference to the war until on the final page where she narrated an incident involving a company of the 25th Wisconsin Volunteers, which had passed through Red Wing early in December 1862.[12]

As the soldiers passed by the Densmore home, Martha and her friend Belle Webster spied Lieutenant Robert Whittleton, a school friend of Daniel. Belle and Martha let Whittleton pass by, but on reflection they "regretted not having called him in—to have taken dinner with us." Keen to make amends for their lack of action, the two friends made their way to the camp of the 25th Wisconsin and sought him out. Whittleton dined with the Densmores and regaled the family with stories of his school days. After the dinner ended Benjamin returned Whittleton to his camp. [13]

The events surrounding Whittleton's dinner at the Densmores' home underline Martha's adventurous spirit, her romantic interests, and her growing independence. In many ways she and Belle had broken social conventions when they independently visited the army camp without a male chaperone. The contingencies of the war provided young women such as Belle and Martha with opportunities to be more independent. Yet what would have appealed to Daniel was not the fact that his sister was becoming more independent, but that by her actions she was caring for a dear friend, an "old school chum." Martha demonstrated her love for her brother not only by writing affectionate letters to him but also by the actions she took. After all, Lt. Whittleton was Daniel's guest when he dined at the Densmore household on an evening in December 1862.[14]

December 1862 was a time of coming and going in the Densmore household. After a period on furlough, Benjamin rejoined the 3rd Minnesota Infantry shortly before it left Fort Snelling, Minnesota, for Fort Heiman in Kentucky. In Kentucky he used his engineering skills to strengthen Fort Heiman's defenses, joined raids against rebel guerrillas, and eventually enlisted in the USCT. In December Daniel returned home for Christmas leave. While he was on leave, his company

Figure 2.4. "Interior of Indian Jail." Adrian J. Ebell, "The Indian Massacre and War of 1862." *Harper's New Monthly Magazine* 27. no. 157 (June 1863). Minnesota Historical Society.

moved from New Ulm to Mankato and assisted with the execution of thirty-eight Dakota prisoners on December 26, 1862.[15] Shortly after the execution Daniel returned to his regiment in low spirits. In the letters he wrote he made a special point of sharing with his family anecdotes gleaned from his experience of guarding Mdewakanton prisoners. Yet these stories were not simply meant to inform and entertain. Laced with ridicule and humor, he used them to reaffirm the family's core belief in the racial and cultural superiority of the white race.

In early January Daniel assured his family that his accommodation was particularly good. He was staying at "the Mankato House." There the table was "set for white folks & white folks sat at table." Then he added that "the idea of living among white people has no small force in it." In contrast Daniel found his time guarding the prisoners tiresome and humiliating. He believed it undermined his martial spirit and besmirched his family's honor. "The care of these Indians & the labor of guarding them is really disagreeable," he commented. In part he was responding to the way the Dakota were imprisoned. It was obvious that "three hundred persons all shut into one room cannot help producing an unsavory stench." When Daniel opened the door to visit the guard stationed in the room, the stench nearly knocked him down. For one hour each day the prisoners were allowed out into the prison yard for exercise, and Daniel observed that the "poor wretches seem to enjoy a little prairie breeze immensely." It took a great amount of effort to force them back to "their holes when the time expires." He described the prisoners as appearing more like animals than humans. For example, he described the prisoners in chains as birdlike creatures coming out of the jail "hopping like a robbin, skip across the yard & plumb themselves on top of the woodpile." Sometimes these hopping prisoners would "keel themselves with a jolly roll over among the bevy of empty cracker barrels." Amid this misery some missionaries made efforts to convert and aid the prisoners. But Daniel believed that many prisoners used conversion as a ruse to escape punishment.[16]

In mid-April 1863 Daniel and his company were rushed to defend Madelia, twenty-four miles southwest of Mankato. The Dakota raid on Madelia hardened his racial attitude. Now, for the first time, he witnessed the brutality of an attack on settlers. Like some middle-class citizens who had displayed empathy toward the Dakota, he changed his attitude. He was particularly disturbed by reports that the outrages were committed by so-called "civilized Indians." He related that "the Indian who had wounded Mrs. Rowland when he was leaving her for dead," "snatched her shawl off and said in perfect plain English: 'Now you may go home.'" Clearly the Indians were "not so 'wild' as supposed." Such reports left him with mixed feelings of revenge and despair. "Up here murderers of white men, women & children are too sacred to merit a murderer[']s doom," he complained.[17]

A month after the Madelia attack Daniel's regiment was ordered back into the Dakota Territory on another expedition commanded by Sibley. Mindful that Taoyateduta was attempting to gather warriors in the vicinity of Devil's Lake, Pope decided to launch a campaign to decisively crush any Indian resurgence and demonstrate that further resistance was futile. Unaware that Taoyateduta was unable able to form a new alliance among the tribes, Pope developed a plan that involved sending Sibley's infantry column northward from Fort Randall to Devil's Lake and Brigadier General Alfred Sully's cavalry up the Missouri Valley to Devil's Lake. He believed this pincer movement would trap Taoyateduta between Sibley's infantry and Sully's cavalry.[18]

Early in June 1863 Daniel's regiment joined other regiments at Camp Pope, on the confluence of the Redwood and Minnesota Rivers. While Daniel was there, he spent some time taking short trips into the surrounding countryside to visit the natural wonders of the area. The Redwood Falls particularly impressed him with its tumbling and cascading water flow. But as he traveled through the countryside his mood rapidly changed from wonder to despair and anger. At the small settlement of Beaver Orssk he discovered the remains of nine German settlers, killed by the Dakota, gathered together in one gruesome mound. Elsewhere strewn around the houses were scattered human bones. As he gazed out across

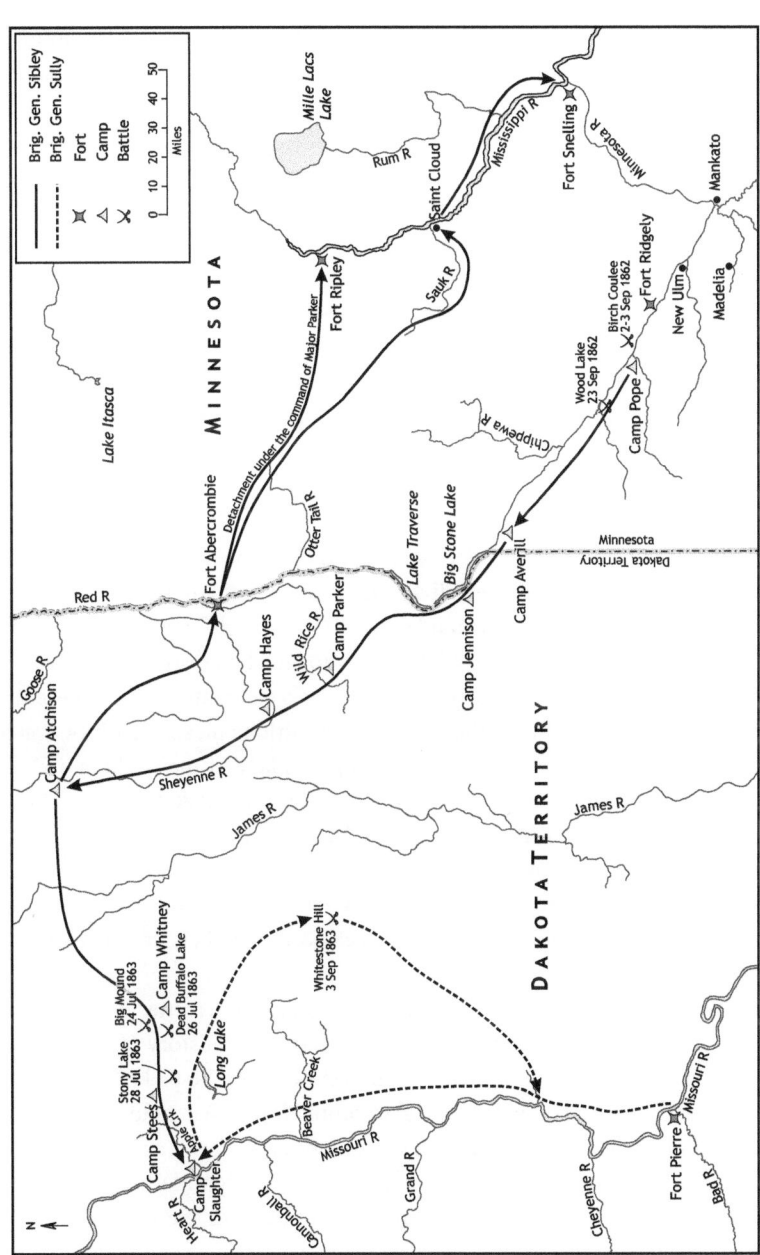

Map 2. Routes of the Expeditions by Brig. Gen. Henry H. Sibley and Brig. Gen. Alfred Sully, June–September 1863.

the prairie he could see the outline of Birch Coulee, the scene of yet another massacre. All these sights revived his memories of the Madelia destruction he had seen only a month before. In a somber mood he returned to Camp Pope galvanized by determination to seek revenge and to defend Minnesotan homes from Dakota attacks.[19]

On June 16 Sibley's expedition left Camp Pope and began its march along the Minnesota River toward Devil's Lake. Even before he began, Daniel informed his folks that he might not "have another opportunity of writing this summer." To overcome this problem, he informed them that he would "always have something written up to date, or nearly, in case we have the privilege at any time of sending back to America." Like pages from a journal, Daniel's letters were often long, detailed descriptions of his journey. From the very moment he left Camp Pope, Daniel felt like an invader penetrating in a mysterious, hostile world. Its climate was particularly exhausting. The sun burned mercilessly down upon the parched Dakota land. "This has been the most tedious, & almost terrible day we have had," commented Daniel from Camp Averill, less than one week into his journey. The sun "rose brazen & was brazen all day in a brazen sky." All day long "scarcely a breath of air stirred," and "not a cloud dared to show itself." As the temperature continued to rise, it became "almost fatal to lie down when resting."[20]

As the expedition advanced deeper into the Dakota territory, it was beset by an increasing number of difficulties. Drought conditions meant that little water was available in the lakes, clouds of grasshoppers plagued the soldiers, fodder was difficult to find, and smoke filled the air because the Dakota set fire to the prairie. Faced with the testing nature of the Dakota land, the expedition crept slowly along its trail hugging close to the larger lakes that contained fresh water. Early in July Sibley reached the Sheyenne River where he established Camp Hayes. There the expedition halted for a week so the soldiers could relax and renew their strength.[21]

Daniel now found time to write home to his folk. In his letter he explained how he could read the land and uncover the rich cultural history of the Dakota imprinted on it. While walking near the Sheyenne River, he picked up "a neat flint arrowhead." As he studied the artifact more closely, he could see that the arrowhead had "scratches or metallic marks on one side." It was as if "Mr. *recruit* Indian" had used "it for the more peaceful purpose of lighting his pipe." Both metaphorically and physically the personal lives of the indigenous Dakota were embedded in the landscape. The soldiers on the expedition were aware of this. George W. Buswell, a private in Daniel's regiment, wrote in his diary that both enlisted men and officers looted Indian graves to acquire artifacts. Shortly before he discovered the arrowhead, Daniel reported to his family on a "fossil" find a soldier had made. In his letter he enclosed a sketch of a "curiosity," "shaped generally like a fish—a pickerel."[22]

It was during this leisure time at Camp Hayes that Daniel had time to carefully read the letters his father had sent him. In his letters Orrin made little comment about Daniel fighting the Dakota. But he did endeavor to identify with his son's campaign by showing an interest in the weather. Red Wing was "so very hot—so very dry," that he appreciated how difficult it was for the "boys who must endure it under military restraint." He also inquired about the men in Daniel's company, the vast majority of whom were from Red Wing. When Orrin wrote to Benjamin, he informed him that the discipline in Daniel's company was very good.[23] Daniel had reported that some of the "troublesome men" had been sent to the artillery battery, and two deserters including "Molloy, a hair brained Irishman," had left the company. The men were "all good, true, and reliable, & will make no officer ashamed of them," Daniel commented. In his mind, and that of his family, military success was closely linked to comradeship and local community ties.[24]

Orrin's letters were full of family and local news. The condition of the family garden, visits by relatives, the deteriorating health of Margaret's husband, Otis, and town gossip were among the common subjects. Family issues that touched on Daniel's personal well-being also featured very prominently in the correspondence. Some of the news was commonplace, for example, reports on the health of Daniel's horse, Turk. But some of the information that Orrin relayed to his son affected his fortune because he acted as Daniel's financial guardian while he was fighting the Dakota.[25] Orrin also looked after Daniel's personal effects. In June 1863 Daniel wrote to his family from Cape Pope and informed them that he wanted to sell "a baritone" and a "Bs Bass." He gave the family instructions to "retain them in possession until the money is paid for them." Not even civic pride could separate Daniel from his money. "If the Red Wing Band wish to use them they must own them," he commented. Two weeks later, Orrin replied that he had the instruments in hand and would carry out Daniel's instructions. On first impressions the sale of musical instruments seems a trivial matter. But given the family's strong musical tradition, it appears more significant. The Densmores prided themselves on being a musical family, and most members could play at least one musical instrument. Family members held their musical instruments close, for they used them to express their personality and affirm their cultural status. Above all else, the sale points to the strong bonds of trust that existed between Daniel and his father.[26]

Conscious of Daniel's remote location, Orrin felt he had a duty to inform his son of the Union Army's progress in the war. Located in the busy Mississippi riverport of Red Wing, Orrin was well placed to gather news on the war that the Union forces were waging in the Mississippi Valley. Because he saw it as his duty to coordinate and collate the correspondence between his two serving sons, his office became a mail clearing house. His reports consisted of brief excerpts describing current developments, highlighting individual generals for praise or condemnation, and then making general optimistic comments on the righteousness of the Union cause. For example, in one letter he commented that the "news from the Southern War" was very mixed, especially in Virginia, Maryland, and Pennsylvania. But he ended by commenting that Generals Ulysses Grant and Nathaniel Banks "so far as heard from are successfully prosecuting the Sieges of Vicksburg and Port Hudson—God speed them both in their terrible work." These comments were made as much to nurture his son's patriotism as to provide news about the war.[27]

Daniel's knowledge of the Civil War was gleaned from his father's correspondence and from letters he exchanged with Benjamin. While he was at Camp Hayes, he wrote a long letter to Benjamin detailing all the trials of the expedition. The locusts, the smoke-filled prairies, the soaring temperatures, and the drought are all described in graphic detail. The expedition was a feat of endurance, and according to Daniel, a fruitless one. "That any Indians have been seen as yet is entirely a matter of guesswork," he commented to his brother.[28]

Daniel's graphic account of his expedition interested Benjamin, but especially interesting were the personal asides and anecdotes in the letters that referred to men with whom he had served. The rumors and gossip surrounding his former comrades made his brother's letters personally appealing. Daniel did not hold back in his criticism of the military and contractors, criticism he knew his brother shared. After explaining that a third of the 90,000 rations of hardtack had been lost due to poor preparation and packaging, Daniel commented that it was "very strange that some of those men having to do with army contracts do not get hung." Finally, and most importantly, Daniel's letters to Benjamin show a deep interest in his brother's welfare. Conscious that Benjamin suffered from bouts of fever, he regularly inquired about his health. Benjamin's career was also foremost in his mind. When he heard news of his promotion to lieutenant, he immediately sent "best wishes for your further success." He assured him that he would "not regret taking the lieutenancy first."[29]

On July 11, Sibley's expedition left Camp Hayes and continued to follow the Sheyenne River northward for eighty miles before establishing Camp Atchison.

After leaving camp Sibley encountered parties of mixed-blood Chippewa hunters who informed him that a large body of hostile Dakota were only a short distance away moving toward the Missouri River. Acting on this information, Sibley set out in pursuit. On July 24 near the summit of Big Mound (northeast of present-day Bismarck, North Dakota), Sibley's scouts came upon two large camps of Dakota from the Sisseton and Wahpeton bands. Although they were close relatives of Mdewakanton, they had not been involved in the earlier war. Keen to stop the advance of the soldiers invading their land, they attempted to parlay. This attempt to stop the advance peacefully failed when one warrior impulsively shot a member of the army's negotiating team. A skirmish followed, which Sibley escalated into a full-scale attack. Pressured by Pope, who accused him of failing to campaign vigorously, and acting on false reports from his scouts about the war preparations of the Dakota, Sibley wanted to win a sweeping victory. Outnumbered and poorly armed, the Dakota were soon driven from the Big Mound battlefield.[30]

Two days after the battle, Sibley broke camp and after beating off attacks at Dead Buffalo Lake and Stony Lake proceeded to Apple Creek, a tributary of the Missouri River, where he established Camp Stees. After leaving camp, at dusk on the evening of July 28, Daniel witnessed the funeral of a cavalry man. This event left a deep impression on him. In a long letter written to his folks describing the battle of Big Mound and the constant skirmishing with the Dakota, his sketch of the funeral stands out. He used the events surrounding the funeral service to remind his family of his own mortality and the honorable sacrifices he was making on their behalf.

The funeral consisted of the "boy's unfortunate comrades" gathered around a grave site located on a bluff, on Apple Creek. In the moonlight, the bereaved comrades slowly and sadly laid the soldier down. The location "seemed like a sweet place for that last, long sleep." Once the burial was completed the loyal friends disguised the site, so it looked like a rifle pit. This ruse led Daniel to reflect upon what he considered was the foreign, forsaken nature of the land in which the dead soldier was interred. He thought about the remoteness of the gravesite, and the abandonment of the dead soldier. He "could but pity him," left "among a race of fiends from whose sacrilegious hands, we had to hide his narrow dwelling place." He could only hope that his own grave, his "narrow house," would be in his family homeland, "where the footsteps of friends might fall."[31]

The folks back home in Red Wing were acutely aware of Daniel's feelings of loneliness and separation. Therefore, in their letters they endeavored to provide solace by reviving old memories and employing humor to restore cherished relationships. Certainly, Orrin Jr. wrote with this purpose in mind. He was very conscious of the fact that since the war against the Dakota had begun, a gulf was opening between him and Daniel. This physical separation pained him, because he had lost not just an elder brother, but his companion, his hunting and fishing partner, and his mentor. The two brothers now lived in different worlds. While Orrin Jr. remained at home under the watchful eye of his mother and Martha, Daniel had entered the world of men. Like many boys of his age, he dreamed of proving his manhood by entering this world.[32]

Unable to join Daniel in the army, Orrin Jr. used his correspondence to maintain his close relationship with his brother. He packed his letters with interesting news and anecdotes about family friends and hunting trips, and he narrated his stories with boyish enthusiasm. His letters to Daniel were full of brotherly banter. Lighthearted in tone, these intimate and engaging letters helped Orrin Jr. reach out and restore the old brotherly relationship. One letter written on June 28, 1863, illustrates this mode of writing. He wrote informing Daniel that the family had not received recent news from Benjamin and that he was puzzled by this. Then he added a small sketch of an African American head with the comment "Ye sable artillery!" which alluded to Benjamin's service in the 2nd Tennessee Heavy Artillery, African Descent. Like other members of his family, Orrin Jr. believed African Americans were a racially inferior people who were defined by their allegedly grotesque racial traits. The small sketch he produced exaggerated, stereotyped racial features, including woolly black hair and large protruding lips. By including this sketch in his letter Orrin was inviting Daniel to indirectly affirm his racist stereotype.

Immediately after mocking Black Americans Orrin turned his attention to ridiculing Southerners resisting the Union siege of Vicksburg. "Heard that the women in the town were getting shot off pretty fast. Too bad to kill them, but they have no business there," he commented. Rebel defenders were having difficulty repairing their works "on account of the cold lead there abouts." Then he concluded, "Bad thing this lead, when taken with a little powder." These comments were followed by a small sketch or doodle of a falling rebel soldier with a large ball of lead in his back.[33]

Orrin Jr.'s letter revived Daniel's spirit because it reminded him of home and the loved ones he was fighting for. Earl J. Hess writes that the letters soldiers received from their loved ones at home formed a "paper tether that kept the soldier from sinking irretrievably into the military environment." They created a psychological link with home, for they constituted a symbolic dialogue that transcended space and time. Above all else the constant flow of letters from

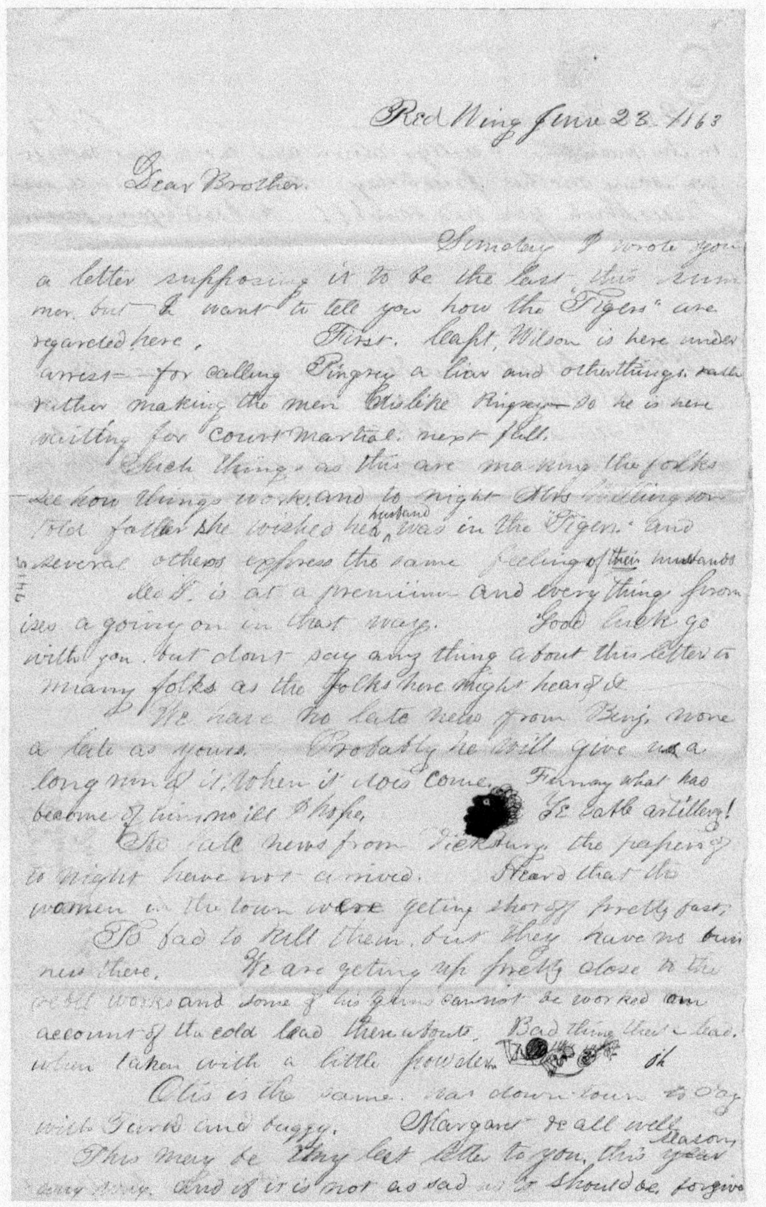

> Red Wing June 28, 1863
>
> Dear Brother,
>
> Someday I wrote you a letter supposing it to be the last this summer, but I want to tell you how the "Tigers" are regarded here. First, Capt. Wilson is here under arrest — for calling Pingrey a liar and other things, rather making the men dislike Pingrey so he is here waiting for court martial next fall.
>
> Such things as this are making the folks see how things work, and to night Mrs. ___ told father she wished her husband was in the Tigers, and several others express the same feeling of their husbands.
>
> Mr. I. is at a premium and everything from us a going on in that way. Good luck go with you, but don't say anything about this letter to many folks as the folks here might hear of it.
>
> We have no late news from Benj, none a late as yours. Probably he will give us a long run of it when it does come. Finney what has become of him no ill I hope. The Late artillery!
>
> The late news from Vicksburg, the papers of to night have not arrived. I heard that the women in the town were getting short off pretty fast. Too bad to kill them, but they have no business there. We are getting up pretty close to the rebel works and some of the guns cannot be worked on account of the cold lead thereabouts. Bad thing this lead when taken with a little powder...
>
> Otis is the same. Was down town to day with Ward and buggy. Margaret & all well. Mason. This may be my last letter to you, this year anyway. And if it is not as sad as it should be, forgive...

Figure 2.5. Extract from Orrin Jr.'s letter to Brother [Daniel], June 28, 1863. Minnesota Historical Society.

home reminded the soldiers that they were not forgotten and in a most powerful way validated the righteous nature of their cause.[34]

In late July 1863 Sibley had established Camp Slaughter on a low bluff on Apple Creek, and there he waited patiently in hot and dusty conditions for Sully to arrive. When Sully did not arrive, Sibley ordered his men to begin the march home. By mid-August, the arduous long journey home severely affected the men's health. Daniel's health declined so much that in early September he was sent directly home to Red Wing on sick leave. A week later Sibley's campaign ended when his expedition reached Fort Snelling.[35]

A would-be author, Daniel loved to tell a story and wanted his story archived. But the family's response to Daniel's Indian war was only partly shaped by the form and content of the letters he wrote. Family members read his story with interest, but remarkably they made few direct references to his war in their letters to him. Although they affirmed his belief in the alleged savagery of the Dakota and strongly supported Sibley's punitive expeditions, they did not comment on the events that highlighted Daniel's involvement. They read his letters like chapters in a book. Perhaps this was because there were few references in Daniel's story which touched on their daily lives, and the long distance the mail traveled disrupted regular correspondence. Moreover, in contrast to the war in the South, the Dakota wars had little relevance to the family's firmly held abolitionist traditions. Family members who wrote to Daniel wrote about the issues and events that personally connected him to them. Except for Aunt Martha, they wrote about musical instruments, Red Wing friends, visits by old school chums, and hunting trips. By sharing their daily lives with him they hoped to revive his spirits and draw him ever closer to home.

Daniel's involvement in the Dakota War left a legacy that foreshadowed his much longer and more extensive service in the Civil War. Although his military service on Minnesota's frontier did not set precise preconditions for his war against the Southern rebels, it influenced the way he and his family viewed military combat and responded to it. Daniel's correspondence during the Dakota War reveals three recurring themes linked to race, landscape, and family honor. First, it reveals an ambivalent attitude to the Dakota. While most members of the family saw the Dakota as a savage race whose attacks needed to be crushed, Daniel's attitude was more complex. A tension existed between his belief in white supremacy, his abhorrence of Dakota attacks on settlers, his admiration of the beauty of Dakota artifacts, and his belief in the just treatment of "friendly Indians."[36] In the South Daniel's ambivalent racial attitudes were also subject to tension and change. Although he considered African Americans to be a racially inferior people whose character was corrupted by slavery, he admired the fighting qualities of his Black soldiers. Second, while he found the Dakota land mysteriously attractive and scientifically alluring, he discovered that traversing its harsh landscape caused him physical exhaustion and serious illness. Similarly, when he invaded the South, he discovered that the landscape and climate appeared as allied combatants of the rebels. Finally, and perhaps most importantly, the family's war correspondence tells a story of heroic conflict in defense of family and home community. The family discovered that no matter where those defending the family's honor fought, whether in the Dakota Territory or in the South, it was essential they receive vital support from home. The ties that bound the family together made the conflict they participated in a household war.

After he had returned home from Sibley's 1863 expedition, Daniel felt a "great temptation" to leave the army and return to civilian life.[37] But gradually, as he recovered from his illness, his sense of duty grew stronger and called him to follow Benjamin's example and return to the army. Imprisoned and paroled by the rebels and wounded at Wood Lake, Benjamin's example shone brightly before him. The family was immensely proud of Benjamin's achievements. Yet they did not foresee the challenges he would face serving in Kentucky. Benjamin's war story, the subject of the next chapter, made them look at the war with new eyes. Over time they realized the war heralded a period of revolutionary change. As they followed Benjamin's service in the South, they discovered the struggle to save the Union had also become a war of African American liberation.

3

"Dont give up my Son"

Benjamin on Duty at Fort Halleck

When Benjamin and the members of the 3rd Minnesota arrived at Fort Heiman, Kentucky, they were pleased to be back fighting the Southern rebels. Their humiliating surrender at Murfreesboro meant that they had a score to settle. Even the acting assistant Inspector General for the District of Columbus noted in his report that this "fine regiment" was keen to "to wipe out the stains of being surrendered at Murfreesboro." Since issues of honor were at stake, Benjamin relished the opportunity to report to his father on the raids he had taken in the vicinity of Fort Heiman. "The rule or order to subsist upon the enemy" was being conducted so effectively that the rebel countryside was being laid waste. He believed the destruction of the "poor man's granaries" was teaching the rebels a "wholesome lesson." One of the consequences of the successful Union raids he observed was a steady flight of formerly enslaved people, commonly known as "contrabands," to the safety of Union lines. Many of these Black refugees found sanctuary in the rapidly expanding contraband camp that had been established in the vicinity of Fort Heiman.[1]

In June 1863 the 3rd Minnesota Infantry moved to Columbus, Kentucky. There Benjamin discovered that the programs being run to aid the contraband refugees offered him opportunities for career advancement. His prospects brightened considerably when the chaplain of his regiment, Benjamin F. Crary, was rewarded for his work among refugees at Fort Heiman by being appointed Superintendent of Contrabands at Columbus. Crary did all he could to ensure that Benjamin gained a position as a clerk working under him. To further promote Benjamin's career, he argued that Benjamin's bravery at the battle of Wood Lake made him a worthy candidate for a commission in a Black regiment he was helping to recruit.[2] While Benjamin was considering his career, his father received some good news from a meeting with Chauncey Hobart, a former chaplain in Benjamin's regiment. With a prejudiced play on words Orrin reported that Hobart considered Benjamin's position "looked decidedly 'Dark.'" Orrin's optimism proved to be well founded, for in June Crary visited Red Wing and joyously informed Orrin that Benjamin was to be appointed a First Lieutenant in the 2nd Tennessee Heavy Artillery, African Descent.[3]

Figure 3.1. Capt. Benjamin Densmore, 4th U.S. Heavy Artillery, African Descent, circa 1864. Minnesota Historical Society.

Crary's determination to employ Benjamin was linked to his friendship with the Densmore family as well as Benjamin's work record. Orrin reported to Daniel that Crary believed Benjamin had done a first-rate job "systematizing the Contraband department" and that his work was the best he had seen. In addition, the engineering skills he had so ably demonstrated at Fort Heiman had impressed the district commander, Brigadier General Alexander Sandor Asboth. Yet friendship and good work habits alone do not explain why he wanted to employ Benjamin. Crary believed the Union Army could be used as vehicle to elevate the slave and raise him to manhood. He also knew that, because Kentucky had been exempt from the Emancipation Proclamation, joining the army was the Kentucky slaves' only pathway to freedom. Above all else, according to Orrin, Crary wanted to employ Benjamin because "he inspired confidence in the *Sable Skins*." Crary, like many abolitionist officers, believed that the institution of slavery had corrupted and demoralized those who had been enslaved, and he looked to Benjamin to restore their self-worth. The fact that Benjamin was being appointed to a heavy artillery unit also pleased him because he believed that service in the artillery would benefit the former slaves. For the first time they would be in a good, stable learning environment with comfortable quarters. He also believed they were motivated to become "the best soldiers" because they were being uplifted from slavery, knew that the war was being fought on their behalf and they hated the "Secesh."[4]

It is difficult to discover just how Crary's attitudes and beliefs influenced the Densmore family's decision to support Benjamin's service in a Black regiment. The fact that Dr. Crary was President of Hamline University, located in Red Wing, and a trusted friend gave considerable weight to his opinions. Also important was a shared commitment to abolitionism. Orrin's letter to Daniel on July 1 clearly indicates that his father held Dr. Crary in high esteem. But earlier correspondence suggests that he was also motivated by less noble considerations. When rumors about Benjamin gaining a position in a Black regiment first surfaced, Orrin wrote to Daniel and reported that "if B. had ever been favored by the Stars I should hope that he might find a place paying him more fairly for his services than theretofore." Orrin was an abolitionist, but he was also strongly influenced by issues of pay and rank.[5]

Although Benjamin's service in a Black regiment was motivated by a variety of factors, ultimately it was made possible by national forces favoring the enlistment of African Americans. Benjamin joined his regiment at a time when Black recruitment in the Mississippi Valley had reached a critical stage. By the spring of 1863 the war had so severely disrupted agriculture that thousands of workers and their families seized the opportunity to flee the plantations and seek refuge in the contraband camps in Union-held territory. A chaotic situation was developing that placed a burden on military commanders. In March 1863 Secretary of War Edwin Stanton sent U.S. Adjutant General Lorenzo Thomas into the Mississippi Valley to coordinate the government's policy of refugee settlement and labor hire with the Treasury Department and to increase Black enlistment. Now for the first time the government was implementing a systematic, centrally controlled policy of Black recruitment.[6]

Army recruiting agents worked hard to implement this policy by enlisting refugees from slavery from contraband camps and abandoned plantations. As Crary's assistant, Benjamin soon discovered that his workload became increasingly focused on military recruitment. In June 1863 he was sent south on a recruiting mission to Fort Pillow, Tennessee. There he was dogged by feelings of frustration and disappointment. The glory of war appeared to have escaped him, for there was nothing to write about except the cold, damp climate, fevers, and bad company. Even his recruiting efforts met with little success because of the opposition from rebel forces. Instead of raising recruits, his expedition brought on attacks of ague. He also felt abandoned, believing that since the fall of Vicksburg, military authorities had shown little interest in the welfare of the men serving in his area. In the face of all these difficulties Benjamin spent his time traversing the countryside around Fort Pillow searching for recruits and traveling back and forth between Fort Pillow and his headquarters at Fort Halleck, Columbus. Slowly he adapted to the mundane duties of his new office. The regular journeys he made upriver to Columbus taught him to put a high value on his good health. On the boats that traveled north he observed, in September 1863, many soldiers looking "emaciated and thin from protracted disease." These invalids looked "as though they were on their last journey." Exhausted by his recruiting efforts, Benjamin's own health began to deteriorate so badly that he was confined to the Post Hospital at Columbus.[7]

Once Benjamin had recovered from his illness and concluded his recruiting duties at Fort Pillow, he settled down with some enthusiasm to life at Fort Halleck. But he soon discovered that adjusting to the fort's military routine was much more difficult than he ever imagined. In part this difficulty reflected the bustling nature of Columbus's role as a thriving riverside port and railway terminal moving goods and troops up and down the Mississippi River. During his whole time in this unsettled environment, he faced a number of challenges, which included training his troops, remaining healthy, and relating to his fellow officers.

Benjamin found the task of training his soldiers arduous, and his negative view of the Black soldier's character compounded his problems. He believed African Americans were an innately inferior race and that slavery had stunted their limited intellectual and moral development. When Sergeant Major William D. Hale, his friend from Red Wing, gained a commission in Benjamin's regiment, he told him

Figure 3.2. "Fort Halleck and Stockade at Columbus, Kentucky. Sketched by A. H. Griffin." *The New York Illustrated News,* May 2, 1863. New-York Historical Society Library, 100210d.

that he thought Black soldiers would make "splendid machines." "Quite true," concurred Benjamin. Because they were "machines" Benjamin believed they had to be driven and controlled. Therefore, since they were incapable of initiative and independent thought, he believed any success they had in soldiering was mainly dependent on the quality of the officers. This negative view of the Black soldiers' character and capabilities differed from that of his friend Benjamin F. Crary. The distinct roles each performed accounts for some of the difference. As Superintendent of Contrabands at Columbus, Crary's relationship with Black refugees was based on principles of Christian philanthropy and his abolitionist beliefs. Although Benjamin shared Crary's ideology and believed that military service could elevate African Americans, unlike Crary, he faced the practical reality of training Black soldiers. When this difficult task of training his soldiers threatened to overwhelm him, he masked his leadership failings by pointing to his soldiers' alleged racial weaknesses.[8]

Benjamin sometimes found routine duties frustrating and exhausting. After his first time on guard duty he returned to camp "drunk with sleepiness." Yet what troubled him most was not the taxing nature of his duties, but the unique challenges he faced training Black troops. The soldiers' illiteracy and cultural differences created difficulties. He complained that the workload required to train Black troops "for any kind of military duty" was "far heavier than with the american troops." In this situation the quality of the officers' leadership was vital. But in Benjamin's regiment there was both an officer shortage and a reluctance by the few officers present to do the duties assigned to them. His company captain, "a broken down merchant with no constitution and a strong appetite for stimulant," was an encumbrance. Benjamin blamed this lack of leadership for demoralizing the Black soldiers and reviving old slave habits.[9]

He was particularly worried about his soldiers' lack of combat training. While on his second assignment of guard duty, his concern heightened because he found it almost impossible to effectively command his inexperienced troops. Wild rumors were circulating in Columbus about an impending assault on the city by an army of 3,000 rebels. Fortunately for Benjamin, the attack did not occur, and he was able to redouble his efforts to provide some combat training while his men were being posted as guards. The racially discriminatory practices of the military authorities at Fort Halleck also limited the amount of combat training Benjamin's men received. Because they were considered racially inferior, Black soldiers were often given inadequate arms, excessive fatigue duty, and poor shelter. Since the military authorities at Fort Halleck did not provide adequate shelter, Benjamin's soldiers had to build their own quarters. The time they spent doing this deprived them of opportunities for drill and combat training.[10]

Benjamin was also deeply concerned about his career prospects. To have his acting appointment confirmed he had to pass a board of examiners. He was keen to prove to his father that he could pass his exams and was more than worthy of his existing rank. At this critical time he called upon his father for help, asking him to send him books "bearing upon the subject of Fortifications." Eventually Benjamin passed the Board of Examiners' examination convened at Columbus. The success of his friend William Hale before the St. Louis Board examining officers of Colored Troops encouraged him to consider undertaking even more study, but bouts of sickness curtailed those efforts.[11]

In the fall of 1863, Benjamin's health declined when the ailments that plagued him at Fort Pillow resurfaced again. To combat these ailments he resorted to a variety of traditional family remedies. In October 1863 he noted that his health had improved, and he pledged to get a bottle of whiskey and some sugar to follow Daniel's prescription. A month later he was promising to follow another family remedy.[12] To eliminate further illness he also relied heavily on "Dr. Shallenberger's Fever & Ague antidote (Pills)." In a war where the death rate from disease was very high, all these references to medicines were issues of vital concern to the Densmores. The family prided itself on its medical expertise and "self-care." Old remedies that had been passed down through the generations were an important part of the family's heritage. Kathryn Shively's research has revealed that during the war, soldiers practiced "self-care" by adapting to the environment and adopting practical measures to eliminate disease and improve their health. A key component of self-care was sharing knowledge and soliciting support from fellow soldiers and the folks at home. This lifted the soldiers' spirits because it enabled them to exercise some degree of control over their fate. The sharing of medical knowledge and cures was one important way the Densmore family members could provide practical support for each other. Since there was a causal relationship between declining mental health and bad physical health, the Densmores' medicines may have reduced Benjamin's feelings of homesickness and improved his physical health. Like photographs, the bottles of medicines were also tangible expressions of the family's affection. Both Benjamin and Daniel had bottles of the family medicines securely located in their quarters. When taken regularly these medicines brought some comfort, and perhaps an occasional cure, but they were always a constant reminder of the ties that bound the family together.[13]

Benjamin carefully explained his health problems by pointing to the challenges he faced, the arduous nature of guard duty during chilly winter nights, and the wide prevalence of illness among other line officers. Above all else he was determined to assure his family that he would remain in the service and that his failing health was not caused by a weak physique or, more important, a lack of willpower. Aware that willpower was the essential requirement of true manhood, he argued that he was so devoted to his duties that he was inclined to neglect his own welfare.[14] He knew that his folks were aware of the difficulties he faced. "All feel the difficulties and unpleasantness that surround you— (That is to the extent one can at this distance) and feel anxious that you may succeed in getting to some more favorable point if nothing else," wrote Orrin. While he feared Benjamin's career path, "might not be right," he was prepared to trust his son's judgment. His concern for Benjamin's career was linked to fears about his health. Such concern was understandable because during the second half of 1863 the Densmore family seemed besieged by illness. Margaret was nursing Otis, her critically ill husband, and taking care of a sick baby. Daniel remained seriously ill at home on sick leave, while Orrin's poor health made his duties as County Treasurer and tax collector tiresome and debilitating. Orrin was so concerned that Benjamin was drifting into a state of depression, that he urged Daniel to write to his brother and encourage him.[15]

While Orrin attributed Benjamin's bleak outlook to his son's poor health and to the incompetence that appeared to be an inevitable part of army life, he also blamed himself for his son's despondency. Both he and Benjamin had entered an unprofitable financial arrangement with an "unprincipled fellow," McVean. Aware that this debt weighed heavily upon Benjamin, Orrin paid it from his own resources. Yet this act of kindness placed an additional obligation on Benjamin because he was now deeply indebted to his father. Moreover, his father's action appeared to demonstrate that he was unable to manage his own affairs. Benjamin now felt circumstances were conspiring against him, so much so that in late July he wrote to Orrin complaining that "the faculty of pushing" himself ahead "always seemed opposed by everything possible to offer opposition."[16]

While Benjamin was in this troubled state of mind, the family placed an additional burden on him. In June 1863 Orrin wrote to Benjamin expressing concern over Margaret's difficulties. Weighed down by the burden of caring for her sick husband, she was bereft of household help. Within the last four months eight helpers had left her service. Worried about Margaret's isolation, Orrin feared that she would be very vulnerable if she experienced an accident. Desperate to solve his family's problems, Otis proposed a radical solution. "Otis has talked of sending for a 'Contraband' to fill the place of transitory Swedes and may well send you an order," he commented. As Otis's health continued to decline, the question of employing contraband labor became more urgent. In September 1863 Orrin again wrote to Benjamin asking him to find a Black worker for the Smith household. Since no hired help was available in Red Wing, Martha was now on duty, assisting Margaret. He informed Benjamin that the family had discussed the idea of "getting a pair of contrabands," "or a woman if a pair could not be had to suit." "What are the chances for such?" he inquired with a note of desperation. Orrin's second request arrived when Benjamin was sick with fever. Upon receiving it, he wrote to Daniel and covertly expressed his lack of confidence in the labor hire venture. Nevertheless, he assured his brother he would continue searching for a helper in the hope he would "hit upon a suitable subject."[17]

Like many Union officers from the Upper Midwest who supported Black emancipation and enlistment, Benjamin had racial prejudices and commitments to white supremacy that were reinforced through his contact with former slaves. In part, his entrenched prejudice was a product of his Upper Midwestern background. His home state of Minnesota had passed laws that severely restricted African American liberties and rights. For example, African Americans were denied the franchise, forced to send their children to inferior, segregated schools, denied the right to serve on juries, to join the militia, to hold public office, or to marry a white person. The cultural milieu of the nation reinforced this restrictive legislation. On the stage, the popular minstrel shows mocked the African American and reinforced a belief in their moral and intellectual inferiority, and in the newspapers African Americans were frequently ridiculed. Influenced by this environment, most officers such as Benjamin and his brother Daniel adopted a very negative view of the African Americans' character. Benjamin's firsthand experience of

African Americans had confirmed for him their alleged animal cunning. He claimed that searching for suitable Black labor was like embarking on a hunting expedition where one was required to look in "nooks and crannies," to find possible candidates. Even then success was not assured because African Americans were "not the most reliable people in the world," and were "apt to be trifling." In addition, the difficulties involved in searching for a worker and arranging transport to Red Wing seemed to weigh heavily against the project. If a suitable worker was to be found, Benjamin believed that a fourteen-year-old girl was likely to be the "right stripe."[18]

Benjamin said nothing about his negative views on Black labor in his reply to his father's second plea for help. Writing from his sick bed in the Post Hospital, Benjamin informed his father that he had placed the issue of Black employment in the hands of Dr. Crary, who was traveling to Red Wing. Dr. Crary had already agreed to find a Black servant for Mr. Hastings of Red Wing, so he was happy to speak to Orrin about finding a domestic helper for Otis and Margaret. This decision to solicit Dr. Crary's help was an astute move. Research by Leslie A. Schwalm has shown that army officers and soldiers played an important role in promoting the migration of refugees from slavery into the Upper Midwest. As well as securing Dr. Crary's assistance, Benjamin assured his father that he would continue to search for a good worker. Although this task was difficult, the wife of one of his soldiers appeared to be a possible prospect. Yet despite all his efforts and Dr. Crary's involvement, as late as March 1864 a Black servant still had not been found.[19]

In addition to grappling with these problems Benjamin had to contend with disputes among the officers in his regiment. Benjamin's commanding officer, Lieutenant Colonel Charles H. Adams, accused a number of his officers of Hungarian descent of incompetence and corruption. Rebuked by a commission appointed to investigate problems within the regiment, Adams had his commission revoked in January 1864. Benjamin sympathized with Adams, mainly because Adams planned to make him a captain, but also because he had an intense dislike of Hungarians.[20] Frustrated by his failure to gain promotion, Benjamin believed his career was being threatened by the increasing number of Hungarian officers joining his regiment. The presence of the 4th Missouri Cavalry composed mainly of German migrants at Columbus between April and December 1863 only exacerbated his fears. Because he did not distinguish between soldiers of Hungarian and German descent, he believed he was surrounded by hostile aliens. He complained to Daniel that the reorganization of his regiment had resulted in several Hungarians gaining commissions, and he feared that if their numbers continued to grow, they would "starve him out." He considered them a "separate class of people" and complained that they could not speak "good de inglish" and that their "own gibberish" was uninviting. He blamed the unwelcome Hungarian presence on his District Commander, General Asboth, and he accused him of ethnic prejudice and of operating a Hungarian clique in his brigade to advance the careers of his fellow countrymen.[21] These complaints received a sympathetic hearing from Daniel who had long held nativist attitudes. When he was a student at Beloit College, Daniel wrote to Benjamin blaming immigrant Irish voters for supporting slavery, corrupting the moral fabric of the nation, and undermining the Republican cause in the 1856 presidential election. During the Civil War he extended the target of his ethnic prejudice to include immigrant officers, particularly those of Hungarian descent.[22]

Like many families that joined the Republican Party, the Densmores' commitment to abolitionism was linked to their temperance beliefs and their dislike of foreigners. Benjamin's strong nativist attitudes reflected these family attitudes and formed one important part of his commitment to the American republic. To encourage their son, Orrin and Elizabeth framed their letters to him in a manner that underscored the nobility of his sacrifice. Aware that he was feeling sharp pangs of separation and dislocation, they did what they could to strengthen his willpower and endurance. While they admitted that service in the United States Colored Troops was dangerous and difficult, they declared the cause was honorable and well worth fighting for. Elizabeth reminded Benjamin that even though he had a hard and unpleasant task training his ignorant men, he was fighting to defend "a just and holy cause." Like his revolutionary forefathers, he too was "struggling to throw off the yoke of oppression." In this struggle perseverance was vital. "I know you often feel as though your work was not appreciated as it should be, Dont give up my Son," she pleaded. She then reminded him that although he was separated from the family by distance and time, he remained within their hearts. "You need not think of being forgotten, that cannot be while you have Father, Mother, brothers and sisters to remember you morning and evening."[23]

Deprived of combat service and confined largely to garrison duty, Benjamin had a challenging time at Fort Halleck. His racism and his nativist beliefs all contributed to the problems he faced training his men and relating to his fellow officers. Yet despite these challenges, he loyally served the Union. His service owed much to the moral support he received from his family who were always ready to fortify his willpower and endurance. While family contact could sometimes be intrusive and even burdensome, ultimately the family's endorsement of his service in the USCT played a vital role in keeping him in the army.

4

"The glorious, new temple of Liberty"

Daniel Joins the United States Colored Troops at Benton Barracks

While Benjamin was facing the challenges of training Black troops in Columbus, Kentucky, in the fall of 1863, Daniel was at home slowly recovering from a fever he had caught in his campaign against the Dakota. By mid-November 1863, with his health restored, he left his home, with some trepidation, to resume his military service at Fort Snelling. He felt as if he were re-entering the storm of war. "I feel like one who has stepped for a moment behind a leeward corner to avoid the wind and storm. Having got warmed up in the home corner I dread to step out again into the cold, rushing blast-out," he commented. Even so, he was confident that he would "rush along with it nicely," with only a "little shivering once in a while."[1] Daniel arrived at Fort Snelling on Thanksgiving Day, and like many soldiers he felt his absence from home keenly at this time. Even so, he had an enjoyable Thanksgiving meal with his old friend, Fort commander Colonel Robert N. McLaren, who was married to his niece, Anna. But the joy of Thanksgiving soon faded when mail from Martha arrived.[2]

Martha reported that the family was facing a crisis because Otis was now gravely ill. This disturbing news was expected, for in August she had informed him that Otis's death seemed to be inevitable. Otis had acknowledged to Margaret all hope had gone, an admission that made Margaret deeply depressed. "It will be a hard trial for her to part with him," commented Martha. This was especially the case because she had a baby to care for. "Poor girl she is realizing some of the 'stern realities' of life," she concluded.[3]

Thanksgiving Day 1863 was a solemn occasion for the Densmores. Only a few days earlier, with relatively little comment, the family had buried Margaret's three-month-old baby. Because of the high infant mortality rate of the time, few family members expected the weak, sickly babe to survive. In these circumstances, the decision to hold the Thanksgiving Day celebrations at Otis's house was disturbing. Mildly critical, Martha admitted to Daniel that "[i]t was Otis' idea entirely." While the occasion caused a good deal of work for Margaret,

Martha acknowledged that the occasion had a higher purpose, because Otis "wanted to see them all together probably for the last time."[4]

Amid the Thanksgiving revelry at Fort Snelling two prisoners jailed for desertion successfully made their escape. McLaren, embarrassed by this escape, appointed Daniel provost marshal of the Garrison. Daniel welcomed his appointment and the associated policing duties, and reported that he had spent a delightful season closing numerous grog shops in the nearby town of Mendota.[5] As well as supporting his family's temperance beliefs, Daniel was keen to assure them that he was being well cared for. He reported he had a youthful, hardworking African American servant, a "dusty angel" named Columbus, who "was an object of note." Daniel derisively called him, "The Jim of the Ocean," and claimed this name suited his catfish-like appearance. Columbus's employment was significant because it set a precedent for his treatment of another young Black servant he had while he was serving in the army. When he reported on his service, he also employed racist stereotyping to remind his servant of his subordinate role. In mid-January 1864 Daniel left Fort Snelling to rejoin his old regiment, the 7th Minnesota Infantry, stationed at St. Louis, Missouri. There he was sent on detached duty at Benton Barracks as assistant provost marshal for colored recruits in the Department of Missouri and promoted to first lieutenant.[6]

Shortly after his new appointment Daniel received news from Martha informing him of Otis's death. In this time of grief, the Densmores provided a protective shield of devotion that sustained Margaret in her time of sadness. The way the Densmores faced death and tragedy at this time highlighted several of the features Drew Gilpin Faust has identified in her study of death in the Civil War. Although death was ever present in the Red Wing community, families such as the Densmores worked hard at ensuring that those who were dying experienced a "Good Death." They did this by practicing the traditions of *ars moriendi* (the art of dying) which laid down protocols and rituals which brought solace to the bereaved and comfort to the dying. These rituals were particularly relevant to Benjamin and Daniel because, like many soldiers, they had seen the rituals of a "Good Death" violated by both the scale and horrific character of the war they were fighting.[7]

Martha played a vital role helping family members facing bereavement. Since the start of the war Margaret had lost her husband and two children, and during each of these tragedies she turned to her younger sister for support. In these crises Martha also played a significant role in organizing the family home and supporting her mother. "We have been together so much of late she is like my right hand," Elizabeth acknowledged as Otis's illness became terminal.[8] Martha also reached out to comfort Daniel. The letter she wrote to Daniel describing the family's tragedy provides insight into their close personal relationship, but more importantly, it also reveals her awareness of the problems soldiers faced when they learned of the death of a loved one. She knew that this news could destroy the soldiers' morale because it pointed to their inability to ameliorate their families' suffering. Therefore, to revive Daniel's spirit, the focus of her letter is not Otis's death, but rather the family's resilience.

Daniel would have drawn some consolation from Martha's letter because it brought news that Otis's suffering had ended, and that he had died honorably at home. He had prepared for death, accepted his fate, and died with courage and calmness in a manner that revealed his manhood. Yet Martha did not simply catalogue the salient features of his "Good Death." She makes no reference to the deathbed or Otis's last hour. Instead, her focus is on the funeral because she knows that Daniel is more interested in Margaret's survival than in his brother-in-law's demise. Since a funeral is an event organized by the living to commemorate the dead, the funeral service reveals much about how the bereaved coped with death. Martha used her emotionally charged and graphic picture of the funeral to honor the deceased, but more importantly, to assuage the grief that Daniel was experiencing. She does this by highlighting the courage of her sister and the devotion of her sister's young son, Gilman.[9]

Martha acknowledged Margaret's tragic circumstances. "How full of trouble this world is! Poor Maggie she is having her full share," was her opening comment. Yet while acknowledging that Margaret was "disconsolate indeed, since Otis' death," and at times overwhelmed by feelings of sadness and loneliness, she drew Daniel's attention to his sister's remarkable courage and determination. She informed him that her sister tried to catch "a glimpse of the silver lining of the cloud that hangs above her." Margaret tried to think it was "alright, and for the best," and knew it would be selfish to wish Otis back to prolong his suffering. Martha's praise for Margaret's stoic forbearance was supported by other family members. Orrin wrote to Daniel to inform him that even though Margaret's "fortitude and bearing failed her," she soon recovered and controlled her emotions. In her letter to Daniel, Aunt Martha Cheney reported that throughout 1863, her "year of trial," Margaret had "shown firmness and strength of mind seldom equaled."[10]

In her description of four-year-old Gilman's mourning, Martha focused on the innocent simplicity of his love for his father. She described how Gilman's response to his father's death exorcised the family's grief and released emotional tension. In some ways Martha's opening comment, "[p]oor little

Figure 4.1. Margaret Seaton Smith (nee Densmore) and Martha Elizabeth Densmore, circa 1863. Minnesota Historical Society.

Gilman realizes his loss keenly for so young a child," is an understatement. She described how, after Otis was "'laid out,' and during the two days his body was in the house," Gilman would "frequently go *alone* into the room where he lay & stand by him & look at him a long time." During the funeral service Gilman was quiet and "very thoughtful and observing" until the coffin cover was lowered. Then he cried out, "'Oh mama I must see papa again! Oh don't let them bury papa as they did little sister.'" This reference to Gilman's baby sister, Margaret Jr., who had died two months earlier was "so innocent that no one present could refrain from weeping." The next day Gilman was struck down with a cold and a fever. Yet a few days later he was "dressed & felt nearly himself again." This revival prompted Martha to consider drawing Margaret and Gilman back to the family home, a move that Margaret declined out of sense of loyalty to her late husband and because she wanted to maintain her independence.[11]

Martha describes a family, not triumphing over death, but through courage, and innocent devotion drawing on inner strength and moving forward into life. The sentimental nature of her description of the funeral also conveyed a deeper meaning. Martha wrote to Daniel not only to comfort him, but also to affirm the family's genteel middle-class status. Her vivid description, which juxtaposed deep grief with self-restraint, would have assured Daniel that the family had not been critically wounded by tragic loss but that Margaret and Gilman would adapt to their new stations and life with piety and determination.[12]

Otis's death magnified the family's desire to secure a Black servant. It was now urgent that domestic help be found to ease Margaret's transition to her new status as widow and sole parent. Furthermore, Elizabeth's health remained frail. Desperate to get a servant the family now changed their approach and made their requests directly to Daniel rather than Benjamin. This change may have occurred because Daniel's new position placed him in a better position to scout for likely candidates.[13] Other factors that may have caused Benjamin to adopt a secondary role in the project included his health problems and his heavy commitment to garrison duties at Fort Halleck.[14]

The arrival of African American refugees in the Upper Midwest occurred at a time when households were undergoing notable change. As the Confederacy began to crumble, former slaves, sometimes aided by sympathetic Union army officers and Freedmen Aid Societies agents, made their way up the Mississippi River to freedom. Prevailing racial prejudice in Minnesota ensured that these refugees from slavery often received a hostile reception. For example, mobs repelled Black refugees when they arrived at the docks at Lowertown, St. Paul, in May 1863. But some citizens welcomed them because they believed they would help overcome a labor shortage the war had created. The introduction of Black labor not only added to a process of societal change, but also contributed to the potential for tension and division within families. Orrin wrote to Daniel informing him that the family had extensively discussed the employment of a Black domestic servant, anecdotally referred to as the "Shady question." He reported that the "fear of getting an unsuitable or unsuited customer" had "induced mother to think unfavorably of the project." However, after some "conversation with others," she had agreed to accept one if Daniel could find one he deemed suitable. "A single woman—tidy and honest—accustomed to *house*work," was thought to be the most desirable prospect.[15]

Orrin believed that a community response would reduce the potential for disruption and conflict, for if other citizens brought Black servants into the town, the servants would support each other, and "they might be better contented." Therefore, he passed on to Daniel the labor requests of other Red Wing citizens, including Mrs. Dr. Jones, Mrs. Pascal Smith, and Mr. Hastings from the "Children's House." He urged Daniel to investigate the wages to be paid and the cost of transportation. If "good help" was available "at fair figures," the venture could proceed. Finally, he reminded Daniel to carefully assess the quality of the potential employees, but he asked him not to go to too much trouble and expense for the neighbors because the family was not yet "authorized to order the commodity." Just a few days after Orrin wrote to Daniel, Martha wrote to him about "'the negro question,'" reinforcing her father's request. Frustrated by the constant turnover of domestic help, Martha declared that the family urgently needed a domestic servant. "You know just what we want," she reminded Daniel, "—a servant that is *neat honest & active*." She earnestly hoped that he would find "'a darkey woman' suited to your mind—and ship her forthwith for Red Wing."[16]

Elizabeth's initial opposition to the employment of African American labor lingered until April 1864 when Orrin wrote to Daniel suggesting that the "Shady" project could be abandoned. He urged him to "[t]ake no particular pains about the Darkey," because Elizabeth had arranged to employ a Swede, Louisa Johnson, as domestic help. Elizabeth did not want to introduce a Black servant into her home because she believed Black and white workers could not labor together, and that a former slave working in her kitchen would undermine her authority in the household. She also believed the proposal devalued white labor, because Louisa "and a darkey would be identified as *help*," and Louisa "would be set aside for the ebony article." These fears were not shared by other members of the family. Perhaps unaware of his mother's fears for her domestic authority, Daniel wrote to

Benjamin in June 1864 and commented that the ideal development would be for Louisa and a "darkey" to labor in the house together. Martha had informed him that the "stranger in the house" [Louisa] was making progress. "If now a good addition of darkey persuasion" could be added to the kitchen "the arrangement [would] be complete."[17] Concerned about Elizabeth's health and heavy workload, Orrin was determined to press on. If Daniel found "an approved article," he advised him to "show her the way towards the North Star." "[W]e will see how the cat will jump," he concluded.[18]

There the issue rested until May when Martha again wrote to Daniel. She assured him that there was no labor crisis in the household, for Louisa Johnson was coming to work at the rate of twelve shillings per week for the summer "(or until our 'Dinah' arrives.)" She acknowledged the whole project of employing a Black servant was full of doubt and uncertainty, but assured Daniel that the family was "ready for the experiment in case a 'subject'" was found. Finally, she urged him not to spend too much time seeking a servant. He was not required to "hunt one out" for service, as he had other more pressing duties to attend to.[19]

As the sadness surrounding his family's tragedy slowly faded. Daniel eased into his provost marshal duties. At first his workload was heavy, but by mid-February he felt like a "clerk of a vacant school district."[20] With time on his hands he had an opportunity to tour the contraband quarters located near the barracks. While he acknowledged that the quarters were occupied by soldiers' families and refugees who had fled from the tyranny of slavery, he described it as "a mammoth robins nest full of blackbirds!!," an allusion which implied that the Black residents had appropriated housing that once belonged to others. The scene violated his sense of order and his spatial sensibilities, for he believed the allegedly chaotic nature of extended families crowding together would make the former slaves ordered transition to freedom very difficult. Like many abolitionists, he believed the refugees from slavery would best make this transition if they lived in well-ordered nuclear families. Yet he found some of the "distinguished characters" living in this "nest" intriguingly amusing. From his standpoint, their allegedly animal-like responses at the morning roll call were particularly entertaining, with responses such as "Geo Washington, heah! Nellie Bly, hee!" and "Andrew Jackson, hyah!" ringing out loud and clear.[21]

Daniel's negative view of the African American character contrasts with his decision in March 1864 to join the United States Colored Troops (USCT). To explain this contradiction, one must look at his experience as a schoolteacher in the South and above all else, his family's history. The Densmores were staunch abolitionists. Orrin Densmore was a prominent Republican Party member in Goodhue County and connected to important state politicians such as the Governor Alexander Ramsey. Although his commitment to the antislavery cause was shared by all members of his family, Daniel was, perhaps, the family's most dedicated abolitionist. As a young college student, he openly espoused the abolitionist cause. While at Beloit College, Daniel wrote a letter to Benjamin outlining his views on slavery and the impending 1856 presidential election. He believed Republican John C. Frémont was "the only man before the people representing the cause of humanity." Further, he welcomed the prospect of war and informed Benjamin that he hoped "to see such a resort to arms as shall tell to our eternal riddance from slavery."[22]

Daniel had an attitude to slavery that was similar to that held by many other Republicans. He believed it was the foundation stone of the Southern planter class that was conspiring to place the whole nation in bondage. Even so, his hostility to slavery became much more intense after he left college and witnessed its impact on African American family life. In the fall and winter of 1858, he taught at a district school in Cotton Wood, near Gallatin, Tennessee. There he witnessed the morbid spectacle of a slave "marriage" and discovered the tragic way slave families could be divided and sold. Daniel never forgot his experience in the South. Because these experiences were so personal, confronting his hatred of slavery became a powerful motivating force leading him into the USCT. Yet like many fellow Republicans his hatred of slavery sat alongside his racially prejudiced view of the African American character. Although he had taught in the South, he had not encountered enslaved people as individuals, and he had little direct understanding of their culture and their resistance to slavery. Influenced by prevailing negative racial stereotypes, he believed African Americans were an inferior people, who were childlike and governed by their emotions. His observations at the contraband quarters confirmed these prejudices because he looked at the scene though a racist lens.[23]

Although Daniel sought to join the USCT to further the cause of abolitionism, other more personal factors also provided powerful motivation. Just a few weeks before Daniel formally made his application to join the USCT he received a disturbing report describing how rebel guerrillas operating in Benton County, Missouri, had plundered the property of Frederick and Mary Hanford, relatives of his dear aunt and uncle, Charles and Susan Hanford. Joining a USCT regiment was one powerful way he could exact revenge on these proslavery insurgents. The glowing letters of recommendation he received from fellow officers also acted as an incentive to join the USCT, and so too did the challenge to his manhood and the lucrative rewards of higher office.[24] "I am tired of playing second fiddle," he confided to Benjamin. "If I cannot handle a man's estate, then I must get me a hoop & top."[25] With these mixed motives fixed in his mind he came before the Board for Examining Officers in the Colored Troops based at St. Louis and successfully secured a promotion to the rank "Major of the 1st Class." Although an immediate appointment was not forthcoming, he was very pleasantly surprised to learn that he was to do detached duty commanding Black soldiers at the Provost General Headquarters in St. Louis. He believed his new appointment was one that "many would probably regard as a very handsome crumb."[26]

Daniel's decision to fight against the slaveholding South by joining the USCT was endorsed by his family. When news that he was applying for a commission in the USCT reached home, Orrin Jr. was quick to offer his support. "You will come out a major at least if you half try. Go in and good luck to you," he commented. Benjamin congratulated Daniel for successfully passing the St. Louis board examinations, commenting that he was "happy to hear of" his promotion to the rank of major, for that rank made him the "*big* second fiddle" in the regiment. While Orrin welcomed news of Daniel's success, he also expressed concern about his fate if he should be captured. Family elders, Russell and Martha Cheney and Charles and Susan Hanford, were also vocal in their support of Black troops and Daniel's commission. Uncle Russell Cheney was keen to see the "poor downtrodden people" advance. Uncle Charles Hanford informed his nephew that he was "truly glad to see the Colored People" fighting so well for their liberty. Like Daniel, he held the rebels in contempt, believing that "we had all become slaves to the South slave holders." Victory all depended on the North being resolute and unified.[27]

Daniel understood the war had reached a critical stage and that resolute leadership was required if the Union was to triumph. In the East Grant, the recently appointed Commanding General of the United States, was preparing for his Overland Campaign. In the West, Major General William T. Sherman was fiercely engaging the enemy during his Meridian Campaign in Mississippi (February 3–March 5, 1864). Early in March Daniel wrote to the Cheneys praising Sherman for waging hard war on the rebels. At the same he condemned Major General William S. Rosecrans for his tardy leadership and Major General John M. Schofield and the late Governor Hamilton R. Gamble for their "treachery." He blamed all three leaders for putting the state of Missouri in the hands of the rebels and for allowing rebel guerrillas to freely roam the land committing "outrages" that allegedly exceeded those of the Dakota Indians. Even Lincoln was not spared criticism. He strongly condemned the president for issuing his Proclamation of Amnesty and Reconstruction, which he believed brought succor to rebel homes while leaving loyal Union men isolated and bereft of support. "Is it not enough to make the loyal men 'radicals?'" he asked the Cheneys.[28]

As well as doing routine provost marshal duties, Daniel was also assigned to special duties associated with the Mississippi Valley Sanitary Fair. On one occasion he distributed a circular issued by the Freedmen's and Union Refugees Department warning of an impending social upheaval caused by the destruction of slavery. To meet this challenge the department promoted the popular abolitionist view that loyal citizens had an obligation to help the freedmen become economically self-reliant. The department was confident of success because the former slaves were now fighting for the nation and had surpassed "all the responsibilities of freedom." Daniel was less sanguine about this prediction. He believed that slavery had so corrupted the freedmen's character that it would take at least ten years before they would become economically self-reliant.[29]

In mid-April Daniel visited the Mississippi Valley Sanitary Fair. In a letter to Aunt Martha, he graphically described the layout of the Fair, and more importantly, he encouraged her to think more positively about the role of African Americans in American society. He was impressed by the immense size of the fair, describing the buildings as being "magnificent—capacious as the heart of the Great West." Much of the construction was done by soldiers who were rapidly completing the building. They worked as if they were building for their own personal benefit, and upon reflection Daniel admitted that "perhaps they are right." Black soldiers were making their contribution too, for each day soldiers from Benton Barracks would come down to assist with the construction. Included in this work detail were men under the command of Lt. George W. Buswell, from the regiment Daniel would soon join, the 68th United States Colored Infantry (USCI). The presence of these former slaves working with white soldiers encouraged Daniel to reflect on the nation's destiny and to call upon imagery associated with building and healing to describe how African Americans would play their part in the new world the war was creating. As he thought deeply about this, his mind turned to the symbolic significance of the Sanitary Fair building. This "superb building" appeared "fitly emblematical of the glorious, new temple of Liberty which the true Americans" were soon to complete. Since all nationalities had helped build the temple, none could be excluded. "[E]ven the despised, downtrodden, black man" could not be forbidden from taking "a freedman's interest, and labor[ing] with a freeman's hands." As fellow builders the freedmen were to enjoy "the ministrations of the temple." Just as during the war the Sanitary

Commission had restored the health of the African American soldier by giving him "cordials to assuage his pains," after the war this new, national temple would sustain his life. No one would be driven from the doors of this temple "hungering for freedom" or because their skin color was black and their rights had "been for generations denied them." Daniel looked forward to the end of the war because he believed a "purer civilization" would emerge from the bloody conflict. Union victory involved more than the military defeat of the South. Above all else it involved rebuilding the nation in a new age of freedom.[30]

Benjamin was less optimistic, for he had a more negative attitude to African Americans. Upon joining the USCT Benjamin had considered the Black soldiers machine-like, and lacking self-direction. In contrast, shortly after he joined a Black regiment, Daniel began to believe that the Black soldiers were capable of self-reliant citizenship. Several reasons account for this difference. First, unlike Benjamin, he had witnessed Black and white soldiers jointly building a project of patriotic significance, the St. Louis Sanitary Commission Fair. Benjamin had never seen such collaboration at Fort Halleck, for there a regime of very rigid racial segregation ruled. Second, the fact that Daniel had a more optimistic outlook, brighter career prospects, and better general health than Benjamin may also partly explain why he was less prejudiced. Benjamin's dark moods encouraged him to adopt a more negative view of army life in the USCT. Finally, Daniel's role as provost marshal meant that he escaped the arduous task of training Black soldiers, a burden that Benjamin found almost overwhelmed him.

Daniel's visit to the Sanitary Fair had a marked impact on his racial attitude. Only a few months before, when visiting the allegedly chaotic contraband quarters, he described the scene by calling upon the racist "bird" imagery that he had previously employed to describe the Dakota prisoners. Now another much more positive image of African Americans was fixed in his mind. At the Sanitary Fair he saw the Black soldiers working as carpenters and builders on a well-planned patriotic project. Daniel still believed Black Americans were inferior, and in that sense racism still haunted him. But now that he was beginning to see them as nation builders, his prejudices were losing much of their luster and some of their potency.

While he was at St. Louis, Daniel's relationship with Benjamin deepened. In some ways their relationship was simply one of brotherly affection, one brother confiding in the other. Yet in other ways it was more than that. In June 1864 Daniel was appointed acting major in the 68th USCI, a recently formed regiment which had many men from Missouri who had been enslaved. Now that both brothers were in the same branch of the military, they were able to function as perceptive counselors and advisers to each other. The bonds between them became particularly strong in the early part of 1864, when Benjamin was trapped in a dark cloud of depression. At this time the letters, goods, and personal effects that Daniel dispatched grew increasingly important to him. In February 1864, Benjamin wrote to Daniel in a state of "despair." He felt like sitting down on his "basket of chips and crying a good old cry." Leave had been denied him, and once again he felt a deep sense of isolation. "Columbus & Fort Halleck are bound to be a theme of great dislike to me," he lamented. Yet Benjamin's letter was not totally enveloped in gloom, for his career prospects had improved. "Today I passed examination before the board appointed to examine officers of the 2nd Tennessee," he reported. In the same letter he reported that he was contemplating further promotion by accepting his brother's advice to go before the Board of Examiners for officers of USCT regiments at St. Louis. To this end, he asked Daniel to supply him with a variety of military texts. Building a military career required brotherly collaboration, and the military texts that moved down the Mississippi river were tangible evidence of this.[31]

The flow of letters between the two brothers enabled them to reinterpret, and some ways moderate, some of the demands that the family correspondence placed on them. Upholding family honor was not any easy task, and sometimes it required a collaborative approach. Less than a month after Benjamin had received good news about his examination, he wrote to Daniel confessing that he had been placed under arrest for striking a sergeant. This was a crisis point in his career, and during this time of trial he exclusively turned to his brother for support. He was aware his career prospects had dimmed. "No doubt the summer of my career may be clouded for a time," he admitted. Yet he had reason to believe that his setback would only be temporary. Shortly after being arrested, he had calls from fellow officers. They pledged their support and "were unanimous in saying that they too would have punished the impudent sergeant the same as I had done." Even the regiment's acting commander, Lieutenant Colonel Peter P. Dobozy, a Hungarian, had regretted "having been obliged to make the arrest." Since he still held Benjamin in high regard as "an officer and gentleman," Benjamin expected the embarrassment of this "untoward event" would soon pass. Release was imminent, and duly occurred on March 8. Yet the whole affair left an indelible mark on him. What he feared most was not the stunting of his military career, but the loss of his family's honor. "I have spoken of this matter confidingly," he wrote. No one else was to be told of his misfortune. He shared his problems with Daniel because, as a fellow officer, Daniel would "appreciate the circumstances" surrounding his arrest.[32]

As well as acting as Benjamin's confidant and giving sound advice, Daniel purchased articles of an artillery officer's uniform and sent them to Benjamin. This action illustrates just how closely their military careers were linked. From February to June 1864, when Benjamin was suffering from depression, arrest, and imprisonment, Daniel worked hard to assemble a splendid uniform. "I must have *those clothes* and since I cannot bother you a *great deal* I will bother you as much as I can," Benjamin wrote to Daniel in February 1864. The whole project depended on Daniel's good judgment. "As to quality & price your judgement will be as good as I could wish," Benjamin commented. Approximately three weeks after Benjamin made his request, Daniel's first assignment arrived at Fort Halleck while Benjamin was under arrest. It provided "perfect satisfaction," and over the next three months the other parts of the uniform arrived. [33]

Daniel's time at St. Louis was a time of change and personal development. There he discovered just how resilient his family was. The fact that Margaret and Gilman had adjusted to the loss of Otis was a comfort to him. He felt the tragic impact of Otis's death too, for in some ways it had changed his relationship with his family. He was now committed to finding a Black worker, and this obligation enmeshed him more deeply in the family's domestic affairs. Daniel welcomed this opportunity to aid the family, for he had much to thank them for. Their support for his decision to join the USCT helped him realize his abolitionist beliefs. But his racial views were also changing and moderating. This change was marked by the visits he made to the contraband quarters and the St. Louis Sanitary Fair. Finally, his relationship with Benjamin changed. Now that he was in the South, fighting the same enemy, and serving in the same branch of the military service, their relationship grew deeper and stronger. The movement of gifts and letters up and down the Mississippi River helped seal this relationship, for it enabled them to not only share their military knowledge, but also their personal problems and family issues. Distance and the contingencies of war kept the Densmore family members apart but did not break the family circle. The folks at home in Red Wing knew this, and so did Benjamin and Daniel.

5

"Kind acts went directly to their hearts"

Martha Serves on the Home Front in Red Wing

A young, patriotic woman, Martha Densmore fought her war for the Union as a member of the Red Wing Ladies' Soldiers' Aid Society. Her defense of the Union was linked to her love of family and her commitment to the community and nation. With two brothers commanding Black troops, and her father actively engaged in Republican Party politics and the abolitionist cause, the war posed its own problems and challenges for her. Yet with these challenges came new opportunities to push against the boundaries of social convention and to achieve new personal goals.

During the war Red Wing became a rendezvous point and refreshment station for Wisconsin and Minnesota regiments traveling to and from the battlefields of the South. The regular sight of young soldiers moving through the town evoked in Martha mixed feelings of compassion and familial concern. When men from the 7th, 9th, and 10th Minnesota Infantry passed through Red Wing, Martha took the opportunity to speak "to two respectable looking ones" as they passed her gate. Although they were very "pleasant," their tired, mud-stained appearance moved her deeply. "Poor boys!" she exclaimed. "I could not help pitying them." These objects of pity also reminded her of her brothers' sacrifices. Every soldier was a link to her brothers' war, and Martha seized upon this link to learn what she could about her brothers' fate. She asked the soldiers whether they knew Daniel who was serving in the 7th Minnesota. A vague affirmative response by one encouraged her to ask him to look out for Daniel.[1]

In several ways Martha's response to the plight of young Union soldiers reveals the general outpouring of philanthropic concern that motivated many young middle-class women during the war. In her study of nineteenth-century benevolent societies, Lori Ginzberg argues that in the antebellum period women became active in charity work by extending their moral authority beyond the domestic domain into the realm of public welfare. Ginzberg believes that the war energized their activities and gave rise to a new generation of women who adopted a new approach to welfare, one that was based on the allegedly male

Figure 5.1. Martha Elizabeth Densmore, circa 1863. Minnesota Historical Society.

values of pragmatic efficiency and science rather than on the so-called female feelings of intuition and empathy. In some ways Martha Densmore represented this new generation. She was well educated, dedicated, assertive, and her capacity to organize and innovate seemed to know no bounds. Yet in other ways Martha's charity work fulfilled the traditional feminine role of benevolence because her home remained the base of her charity work. Even so, she believed aid work involved more than dispensing home-produced products such as refreshments, food, and clothing. Building a strong relationship between the soldiers and the community was also important. Although she believed that it was vitally important for the Red Wing community to demonstrate its support for the soldiers' service in the form of food, clothing, and money, she also believed that the soldiers needed to acknowledge this support in an honorable manner.[2]

One of the most rewarding experiences Martha had during the war was serving meals to the soldiers passing through Red Wing. In mid-February 1864, she informed Daniel that she had a grand time at Sterlings Hall serving refreshments to the men of the 1st Minnesota Infantry, who had recently returned from the South. Yet even though this experience was enjoyable, it was sometimes depressingly sad. The high casualty rate evident in the surviving companies plainly revealed the bloody nature of the war. Company F, which had been recruited in Red Wing, returned with only sixteen men. Because of the high casualty rates many of the returning men decided not to reenlist. In addition, they feared that by returning to the service they would "give the *shirking* ones a chance to stay at home." "I like their decision," commented Martha. She was proud that these men had shown courage under fire. She was equally proud of the way they behaved in Red Wing. Although the war had hardened them, they had retained many of the community values that she and other women had struggled so hard to nurture. Their behavior at the refreshment table was as civil and polite as many of the town's finest citizens. By displaying their good manners these soldiers exemplified their manhood. "Minnesota may well be proud of such soldiers," she reported to Daniel.[3]

In their efforts to provide refreshments for the passing soldiers the women of Red Wing often had to act in an independent, spontaneous manner. This was the case in March 1864 when men of the 2nd Minnesota Infantry passed through Red Wing on their way to Dixie. Arriving at dusk, these men carried rations of "simply coffee, hard-bread & uncooked ham." Immediately upon learning of these meager provisions Martha and a small band of women set to work gathering fresh food for the soldiers' supper and breakfast. Hitching Daniel's horse to a carriage, Martha and Mrs. McInticis called on every house in the street collecting food parcels. These provisions were then taken to a local hall where "refreshments were served by only *six* ladies, without the slightest ceremony." No group of soldiers appreciated the work of these women more than the men of the 2nd Minnesota. The Red Wing women's "kind acts went directly to their hearts," as these men "had been treated with great indifference in St. Paul." Along with a sense of personal achievement, Martha's deep-rooted sense of civic pride sustained her in her labor.[4]

There was a family dimension to Martha's strong commitment to this duty. Early in his military service her brother Benjamin indirectly felt the barbs of parochial rejection when his regiment, the 3rd Minnesota Infantry, had brought shame upon itself by surrendering to Forrest without a fight at Murfreesboro, Tennessee. Courageous service in the 1862 Dakota War restored some of the regiment's honor, but as late as March 1864 Orrin and his family were still calling for community acceptance. Orrin wrote to Benjamin praising the Red Wing ladies for providing meals for passing soldiers. Yet his praise was tempered with disappointment because the men of the 3rd Minnesota had not received the hearty welcome they deserved. "Smarting under the outrageous wrong done to them by cowardly officers," the men failed to gain any solace from the citizens of Red Wing. But Orrin assured Benjamin that this past slackness would spur the citizens on "to promptness on future occasions."[5] Orrin's assurances were not in vain. Almost two weeks later Martha wrote to Daniel that the women of Red Wing had supplied meals for 190 men from the 3rd Minnesota Infantry as well as hundreds more from other Minnesota regiments. "From this you may know that considerable cooking has been done by the patriotic ladies of this town," she proclaimed.[6]

Yet rather than unite the town, the war effort divided it. Martha experienced this division when she began to solicit supplies in March 1864. The mean-spirited nature of Mrs. Northing particularly riled her. "If she cannot furnish a few provisions for our soldiers she should be required to give up her husband" was Martha's response to her intransigence. She flatly rejected arguments made by many other women that men should not serve if they could not live on hardtack and raw pork, and that the men had "'rations good *enough for them*.'" She believed that such unpatriotic citizens would only be brought "to their right senses if they were to live on hard bread and bacon for 'three years.'" Reluctant to waste time condemning these recalcitrant copperheads, she looked forward to a time when they would "be justly dealt with," because their hostile responses betrayed the nation, denigrated the community's spirit, and attacked her family's civic pride. In April 1864, Orrin Jr. wrote to Daniel that Aunt Martha had recently boasted that when the 13th Wisconsin had arrived in Janesville, the Janesville community had fed the whole regiment. Orrin Jr.'s response was, "We can laugh at that here for we have fed the 1st, 2nd, 3rd, 4th and lots of recruits."[7]

Even though Martha's work on behalf of the soldiers was often hard and self-sacrificing, on some occasions it was also immensely enjoyable and entertaining. In April 1864 she was preoccupied with planning a masquerade party to be held at the Court House. The money raised was to be given to the Sanitary Commission. Here was an opportunity to highlight her patriotism and management skills and to give her charity work a direct economic value. While Orrin Jr. believed only fifty partygoers would wear masks, he expected all who attended would pay an entrance fee of fifty cents at the door and then proceed to buy sweet cakes and sugarplums at a very high price. The mystery and intrigue surrounding the party filled Orrin Jr. with excitement. At the party he expected to meet "Ye John Chinaman," John Bull, and "Tom Thumb and fran." He intended to borrow Colonel Robert McLaren's Indian costume and even hoped that Martha would come as his squaw. But a few months later he discovered that not all charity functions were as enjoyable as the masquerade party. In late November he attended a musical evening put on by Mr. Billings and his singing school in aid of the Red Wing Ladies' Soldiers' Aid Society. Although about fifteen dollars was raised for the society, the evening was marred by "large girls (20yrs) who tried to sing music they couldn't learn nor read."[8]

To raise funds for the soldiers the Densmores turned their home into a regular meeting venue for the Red Wing Ladies' Soldiers' Aid Society. In the winter of 1864–1865 Orrin Jr. commented that the family's winter amusements were dominated by attending functions the Soldiers' Aid Society had organized.[9] Visits to Norman's farm at Emerald Grove provided Martha with new opportunities to mix pleasure with service. In August 1864 she attended a "grand soldiers Aid Sociable or Festival" in the neighboring town of Janesville. There she had a pleasant evening of dancing and helped to raise $80 dollars for the Union cause.[10] Yet even though she took pleasure from her aid work, the plight of the Union soldier remained constantly on her mind. Even the changing climate she experienced in Minnesota reminded her of the hardship Union soldiers would experience as they served in the tropical South. When a heat wave struck Minnesota, she informed Daniel that every day she thought about the soldiers in the South dressed in "*woolen* garments,—(those tight fitting uniforms enough to kill a body)," and with little to screen them from the intense sun. The long harsh Minnesota winter also turned her thoughts to the fate of her brothers. "I wish we could know that you and *all* of our soldiers are so comfortable as we," she wrote to Daniel in November 1863.[11]

Martha understood that her volunteering and charity work on behalf of the Union cause was helping to shape the course of the war by tying the defense of the Union to the Northern family home. But her work also had more personal, practical benefits. One way Martha supported her brothers serving in the South was to provide them with small luxuries from home. Gifts of food were particularly important. Yet even in this area of her aid work she moved beyond the traditional feminine cooking role. On some occasions, thanks to her entrepreneurial efforts, the gathering of food parcels became a family affair. In September 1863, while she was visiting her aunts and uncles at Emerald Grove, Martha arranged for a pail of butter to be sent to Benjamin. Originally intended as a gift, Martha bought the butter from her aunts believing that Benjamin would be more likely to ask for more if a payment was made. Martha mailed her gift to Benjamin and urged him to "to take the *benefit* of this nice sweet butter & not to divide it with others until little is left for yourself." "When this butter is used—you may have more from here," she added in a postscript.[12]

Martha knew that letter writing was the most effective way of directly supporting her brothers. She wrote her letters to convey her love and to tie the brothers ever closer to the family and their home community. For these reasons, her letters are full of family news and town stories. But she also wrote them to lift her brothers' morale and protect them from the harsh, destructive elements of army life. Like many middle-class women, she believed that men could lose their self-control and become degenerate if they were removed from the home and the ameliorating presence of women and then subjected to masculine vices so prevalent in military camps. These concerns had some substance, for many soldiers jettisoned their community values as they became hardened by the rigors of army life.[13]

Although Martha wrote to all her brothers, she had a particularly deep affection for Daniel. Perhaps this was because they had common cultural interests and shared social activities with the same group of friends. Her closeness to Daniel enabled her to proffer friendly advice about how he should make the best use of his time. As a resident of Red Wing, Martha believed she was living on a cultural frontier. When Daniel arrived at St. Louis, she admitted that she was envious of his city location which provided occasions for fine music and for sight-seeing. She advised him to seize the opportunity to further his cultural education. "You must listen, see & enjoy as intensely as possible," she advised him, "for no one knows how soon you may be sent to some far-off corner of the union where *music* has perhaps never been thought of."[14] A few weeks after receiving Martha's letter he wrote to her giving an amusing account of an opera he had attended. This report made her even more envious of Daniel's good fortune, and she pleaded for descriptions of further opera visits. Hoping that her brother would appreciate opera as a serious art form, she advised him to change his attitude and learn from his experience. "You may *learn* to be *pleased* with operas, as people *learn to eat lettuce*" was her advice. Yet unperturbed by his young sister's comments, Daniel used her love of music to reward her. Early in March 1864, Martha was thrilled to receive a piano piece, the "Destuque Waltz," from Daniel. To show her appreciation of his gift, she explained just how much music enriched her life. After hearing the 2nd Minnesota Infantry band playing she felt "hungry for more" and believed she "could not exist another day without hearing some good music."[15]

Along with her promotion of good music and the opera, Martha cautioned Daniel against the vice of drinking, which she believed was ruining the army. She warned him that he "must not indulge too freely in the use of 'Lager' [Larger]," or he would be considered "a 'black sheep'" when he returned home. At the time she issued her advice, the family was becoming heavily involved in a temperance movement which was sweeping the town. Meetings had been held throughout Red Wing, pledges had been circulated, and a local temperance society formed. Martha was certain reform was in the air because of the "general interest shown (except by Episcopalians) in the matter." Her news on the temperance movement reinforced the messages Daniel had received a little over a week earlier from his father. Like many Minnesota Republicans, he also believed that temperance reform was sorely needed.[16]

In her letters Martha sometimes adopted the role of matchmaker. Influenced by the notion that romantic love was the basis of all lasting partnerships, she offered Daniel advice on romance and marriage. Among the middle class in mid-nineteenth-century America marriage was increasingly based on the ideal of romantic love rather than economic, religious, and social status alliances. Such notions of love evoked personal reflection and self-revelation. Above all it promoted the idea of a partnership between lovers. Martha also enjoyed giving Daniel courtship advice partly because it encouraged her to reflect on her own romantic prospects and the married life of her cousin and confidant, Anna McLaren. Although Martha's letters to her brother reveal her love of romantic banter and gossip, they also had a serious side. She understood the war disrupted normal courtship rituals and that letters were now an even more important vehicle for establishing serious romantic relationships.[17]

Martha wrote to Daniel constantly teasing him about the young ladies he could court. In March 1864 she affectionately chastised him for ignoring the approaches of girls who were obviously interested in him. When she demurely conveyed to Mary Richter the disappointing news that Daniel would not send her his photograph, it evoked the retort "[J]ust tell that Densmore boy he is big story-teller." A few weeks later Martha reported that two of his former admirers, Mary and Eliza, were now far more interested in a newcomer, a young man named Fleming who worked as a clerk at Smith's Bank. "Now aren't you sorry you didn't send your photographs. It is too late now," she smugly berated him. Daniel had to learn from his mistakes. "[I]t may teach you a lesson for the future," was her final comment.[18]

Daniel was very popular among Martha's female friends and acquaintances. From her letters we learn that Sarah, Aunt Martha's hired girl, had taken a fancy to him. We also learn that, in an act of mindless enthusiasm, she impulsively gave Daniel's photograph to Miss Dewey. Since photographic portraits were widely acknowledged as tangible articles of personal devotion and affection, she asked Daniel to excuse her indiscretion. This exchange between Martha and Daniel suggests that women and men thought differently about photographs. Unmarried women, such as Miss Dewey, believed photographs were given to soldiers as personal objects of affection and romantic commitment. They saw the acceptance of the photograph as a sign that romantic attachment could develop. Men viewed the exchange of photographs differently. Their attitude was less private and personal, and they attached less meaning to implied relationships. To demonstrate that they were attractive to women, some soldiers freely circulated the photographs they received among their comrades. This was not a habit that Daniel adopted. He refused to condone Martha's impulsive action fearing that if he had given his approval he would have encouraged a complicated relationship he did not want. Soldiers fighting in the field found such indiscretion difficult to deal with and depended heavily on family and friends to protect their good name.[19]

Martha's references to Daniel's love life seldom stood alone but were part of a rich commentary on the social world of Red Wing. Overlying gender differences between them was a shared sense of community linked to place and identity. She freely shared the town's scandals with her brother. For example, in 1864 she wrote to Daniel and informed him that Miss Ellen Wilson had eloped with the young son of Mr. Fields. An example of her foolishness was that she started off "without even a change of underclothing." Two weeks earlier, the brother of this boy married a Miss Falls, even though he had a wife back east. "Some queer folks, in this world," was Martha's conclusion. She was even prepared to make light banter over her own unmarried status. When describing her recently constructed walnut bedstead, Martha noted that Mr. Oleson, the builder, claimed he had made it *"long enough* for *any man."* "Think I'm safe," was her response.[20]

The stories of youthful romance that were embedded in Martha's letters only partially concealed some of the significant changes in gender relations that occurred during the Civil War. Even in the small town of Red Wing, in a remote corner of the Union, Martha and her female friends knew that the social changes brought by the war offered opportunities to break from conventional gender roles and gain greater freedom and independence. Her friend Miss Elizabeth Dewey captured some of this spirit in her letter to Daniel when she informed him that in the struggle for the Union "the next call ought to be for *women*." She also questioned the alleged assertion that those left at home were "useless 'samples' of femininity," because they could only watch, wait, and pray for "you—who are 'heroes in the strife.'" To a lesser extent, some of the same spirit that imbued Elizabeth Dewey also influenced her friend Martha in her patriotic work in Red Wing.[21] Although she did not see herself as an ardent advocate of women's causes, Martha was attracted to the new organizing roles the war opened for her. Perhaps this is why she found the writings of Mary Abigail Dodge (Gail Hamilton) appealing. In May 1864 she informed Benjamin, that she was reading *Country Living and Country Thinking* by Gail Hamilton. "It smacks a little of women's rights—but aside from that is really pleasing" was her comment.[22]

It is difficult to understand why Martha had reservations about Hamilton's views on women's rights. Perhaps she may also have believed that Hamilton's views on gender would work against her desire to perform her traditional family duties and responsibilities. We do know that Martha enjoyed her war effort partly because it greatly increased her opportunities to meet attractive young men. From this perspective she may well have felt Hamilton's "women's rights" philosophy would be an obstacle to romance. Yet she enjoyed Hamilton's writing because it described active women managing their own affairs. Hamilton advocated women seeking fulfillment and economic self-reliance through their own creative writing.[23] Finally, Hamilton's support for the abolitionist cause and the Northern women's war effort affirmed Martha's work in soldier aid. Yet Hamilton's political stance had little appeal to Martha. Hamilton opposed female suffrage because she feared the vote would burden women with too many responsibilities and encourage them to act like men. Martha was aware that her labor for the Union had an explicit political dimension, and this new self-awareness increased her feelings of frustration. Aware that she was unable to end the war early by voting for Lincoln, she commented to Daniel, "[h]ow I wish I might cast a vote for him."[24]

Although the war did not create a platform for women's suffrage in the North, it did create a keener awareness of the importance of women's political activities in the defense of the Union. Nevertheless, women such as Martha Densmore who advocated women's suffrage faced considerable opposition from most men. The war created new opportunities for young women to assert their growing independence, but it also created obstacles to women's suffrage. This was because the press and government officials lauded aggressive male values, male military authority and forged a strong link between the right to vote and the right to bear arms. Perhaps the most powerful argument promoted by Black and white advocates of African American equal rights was that Black soldiers had won citizenship and the ballot on the battlefield. In this political environment Elizabeth Dewey's demand that military service be opened for women may be seen, not only as an expression of personal frustration, but also as call for gender equality and equal political representation.[25]

Keen to manage her own finances, Martha taught her own school in the Densmore family home. Her involvement in teaching was supported also by Orrin's strong commitment to education. Orrin did not believe masculinity would be eroded by single women becoming self-supporting. Therefore, he fully supported Martha's work as a schoolteacher and Margaret's becoming a teacher after her husband's death. Labor shortages caused by the war even made him consider the possibility of employing both Martha and Margaret in his tax collecting office. In principle he believed that it was acceptable for women to leave the domestic sphere and earn an income in the public sphere, the world of men. In March 1865 he wrote to Benjamin that he had received news that "the service of ladies in clerkships is becoming common." After citing the evidence of many women working in the provost marshal's office in Janesville, and Mrs. Ford acting as her husband's deputy in the office of the Red Wing City Treasurer, he remarked that he "did not know why there is any impropriety in their so doing." But in his mind some doubts remained about the role of women in the masculine world of commerce and industry, because he concluded his discussion with the comment, "of this further consideration may change our minds." Perhaps Mrs. Ford working in her husband's office disturbed him the most, as he never contemplated Elizabeth working in his office.[26]

By the mid-nineteenth century increasing numbers of young single women entered the teaching profession. Two of Martha's close friends, Belle Webster and Susan Melvina Warner (Daniel's future wife), boarded at the Densmore home while they taught in the Red Wing schools. The teaching profession offered Martha and her friends a degree of middle-class respectability partly because the community generally believed that teaching naturally complemented a woman's feminine nurturing role and moral qualities. Although teaching gave women a degree of freedom and independence, it did not provide executive experience. The management and direction of the school systems remained firmly under the command of men.[27]

The Civil War provided Martha with opportunities to extend her social horizons. In pursuit of her soldiers' aid activities, she moved outside the home, but politically her world remained narrow and limited. From this perspective, when she voiced her desire to vote for Lincoln, she was at once proclaiming her patriotism and venting a protest against gendered laws that denied her the vote. Martha's aid work was never just about meeting the soldiers' physical needs. While she acknowledged that donations of food supplies, medical aid, and funds were important, she also believed that community recognition mattered too. It was this melding of the action of giving with the process of recognition that sustained Martha in her labors. Every meal she dispensed to a hungry soldier and every dollar she raised to aid an infirm veteran made her more committed to the Union cause. By dispensing aid in her refreshment tent, she was serving the Union and honoring her family. Her brothers' war was her war too.

6

"Faces of flint"

Campaigning against Major General Nathan Bedford Forrest

In early 1864 Orrin and Elizabeth Densmore were at ease with the world. Martha was busy working for the Union cause, while Benjamin and Daniel were securely placed as officers in the USCT working on administrative and garrison duties behind the front line. But in April the Densmores' world was suddenly upended when Forrest led his cavalry deep into Union-held Kentucky and massacred Black troops at Fort Pillow, Tennessee. Now for the first time the family faced the unpredictable character of rebel warfare. Jolted by the harsh realities of war in the West, Orrin's ideological commitment to the employment of Black troops wavered. He even began to question whether his sons' decision to serve in the USCT was the right one.

When news of Forrest's raid into Kentucky first broke, the family became anxious about Benjamin's fate. Conscious that Columbus, Kentucky, operated like an outpost of Cairo, Illinois, and that its hinterland harbored many rebel supporters, they feared it could be attacked at any time. They were also very aware that, as a USCT officer, Benjamin stood accused by the Confederate government of the capital offense of inciting servile insurrection. The family, therefore, searched the daily newspapers for news of rebel advances and the fate of colored troops. Early in April, Orrin Jr. reported that the whole family was anxiously awaiting news of Benjamin's fate. The rebels had already burned Paducah, and he feared that if they "*should* get Columbus they would murder all those having any-thing to do with the negroes."[1]

When news of the Fort Pillow massacre broke in Red Wing, Martha immediately wrote to Daniel. "What sad news we hear from Ft Pillow—Isn't it dreadful the way those officers and colored men were slaughtered," she exclaimed. Fearful thoughts of Benjamin's fate constantly haunted her. "Poor Bennie. God preserve *him* from such barbarity," she commented. "We have been very anxious about B's safety for some time," Norman commented. News of the Fort Pillow massacre chilled his blood. Yet he sought comfort in the fact that such disasters might serve to discipline the nation and make it fight harder for total victory.[2]

Orrin was far less sanguine and railed against the apparent injustice of the federal government's inaction. "The recent treatment of prisoners at Fort Pillow does not offer very flattering inducements to enter the colored service," he protested. Until the government developed a policy "to ensure the treatment of the colored soldiers and their white officers according to the rules of war," he would advise against joining a Black regiment. "'A live dog is better than a dead lion,'" was his scriptural advice. Such counsel must have fallen heavily upon Daniel who had only recently received a recommendation for a major's commission in the USCT. Yet Orrin's outburst did not indicate that he had permanently lost his faith in the Union cause. Only a day before Orrin wrote to Daniel, he wrote to Benjamin, echoing the same theme. But while he condemned government inaction, he hoped the situation would change. He advised him to maintain his faith in the government and to keep his powder dry and on hand.[3]

The lightning movement of Forrest's forces encouraged the family to seek constant updates from Benjamin about his location and condition. "Keep us advised of the operations and prospects about the place as you have done," urged Orrin. He particularly bemoaned the wild rumors spread by newspaper editors that confused Fort Pillow with Columbus. Shocked by the "*cruel*, fiendish dispositions" displayed by the rebels at Fort Pillow, Martha also condemned the flying reports of irresponsible newspaper editors. She reassured Benjamin that the family would hide all rumors about rebel massacres from mother until Benjamin's safety was assured. "Words cannot express our thankfulness," she acknowledged, as she praised Benjamin for his reliable letters and reports.[4]

While Benjamin was reporting on Forrest's campaign in Kentucky, Daniel was preparing to fight rebel forces in Tennessee. Early in June 1864 the 68th USCI, under the command of Colonel J. Blackburn Jones, was ordered to Memphis to be attached to Colonel Edward Bouton's First Brigade of U.S. Colored Troops. As Daniel journeyed with his men down the Mississippi River, he had time to write home to his folks and describe the way the river bore the scars of war. When he passed Fort Pillow, he noticed that the site appeared nondescript, with little evidence of the fort remaining or of the Black soldiers' valiant fight for their freedom. It was as if the river itself were removing them from its historical memory, for as well as hiding the fort, the river had washed away most of the rebel water batteries. The true horror of the place was only revealed by the animal world. Buzzards were sailing lazily over the fort, and deeper inland, another group of buzzards surrounded the area where Forrest's men had fallen.[5]

Daniel was captivated by the way Fort Pillow coexisted with scenes of pastoral tranquillity. A half mile below the fort he gazed upon a finely laid out farm and farmstead, with children frolicking around in innocent bliss. This scene upset him, for he saw in the children's play evidence of the South's unrepentant cruelty. Like their fathers, they had "forgotten long ago the fiendish massacre of Fort Pillow." This juxtaposing of childish innocence with the massacre so provoked him that he expressed a desire for immediate revenge. "I felt," he admitted, that "every brat there deserved powder & lead." The children's play appeared to foreshadow their sympathy with murders. It was intolerable that they could be enjoying themselves at a place where once the "cries of the victims, & smell of freemen's blood filled the whole air." For Daniel, the journey south down the Mississippi, with its low banks and dense growth of cottonwood reaching down to the river was a journey into the heart of darkness. The soldiers he commanded felt this too. As the ship glided by the remnants of Fort Pillow, his men gazed intently upon the site of the massacre with grim faces. For these men, Fort Pillow had become an important marker on their march to freedom. "Remember Fort Pillow" became their vengeful battle cry. "I *know*," wrote Daniel, "that Fort Pillow will be held in remembrance when the 68th come to show mercy."[6]

A week after arriving in Memphis Daniel joined Major General Andrew J. Smith's expedition into Northern Mississippi to destroy General Forrest's army. As part of the advance party, Daniel's regiment was sent to guard the Memphis to Charleston railroad. While on guard duty, he had nagging doubts about the success of his new mission. What disturbed him most was the rawness of his troops. Earlier, while traveling down the Mississippi, he had sought to ease the burden on his mind by conveying his concerns to his folks. He reported that his men appeared unprepared for fighting, so much so that he wanted combat duty omitted or delayed. He attributed their lack of combat readiness and their lack of manly pride to the fact that they had previously been the pet regiment of Brigadier General William Pile, commander of USCT troops at Benton Barracks, St. Louis. In this capacity they had been drilled for show, rather than to fight. Recently, several soldiers on guard duty were found carrying guns incorrectly loaded. He had no qualms about the physique or enthusiasm of his men. In fact, he claimed that he had never seen a more able-bodied regiment in the service. They were large, muscular, disciplined soldiers. What they desperately needed was combat training. "I shall be very anxious to get a smell of the powder of blank cartridges before we see any secesh," he wrote to his family.[7]

When Orrin learned about just how fearful Daniel was about going into battle with his raw troops, he immediately wrote to him to boost his morale. While he acknowledged that the "care of colored troops" was onerous, he also reminded him of the opportunities he had to uplift the "poor blacks." Orrin saw service in

Figure 6.1. Maj. Gen. Andrew J. Smith. Library of Congress.

the USCT as a great social experiment, the success of which depended heavily on the officers teaching their soldiers to seize the opportunities the war afforded them. He believed that once they were taught that defeat was "inadmissible" and that "success ranks them among free men with the protection allowed to White men under our law," then they would fight with a determination that would astonish their old masters. According to Orrin the war would bring "mighty consequences" if Lincoln's Cabinet prudently implemented its emancipation policy and Black soldiers were given the same protection as white soldiers. If these goals could be achieved, then the Black soldiers would be "crazy with delight at this opportunity to fight themselves into the condition of men to be rated by merit instead of color, (or rather caste)."[8]

Daniel would have been encouraged by Orrin's empathetic letter which acknowledged the difficulties he faced caring for his men. Caring is the operative word because his letter emphasized the Black soldiers' state of dependency. Further, it reminded Daniel that combat performance was not solely dependent on training, as cultivating a fighting spirit was important too. To this end, he encouraged Daniel to motivate his men by urging them to fight for their freedom and equality before the law. Like his father, and indeed many abolitionists, Daniel also believed that the Black soldiers lacked manhood. Discounting the slaves' long war of resistance against their masters, Orrin believed the Black soldiers needed a protector who would teach them to value freedom and how to fight tirelessly for victory. Orrin's letter would have also reminded Daniel that war also had a political front. The fate of the Black soldier was being decided in Washington as well as on the Southern battlefields. [9]

To allay his family's concern Daniel wrote home asking them not to fear for his safety. To reassure them, he reported that he had good friends who would care for him if he were sick. Better still, the flood of refugees that accompanied the destruction of slavery was working to his personal advantage. He proudly commented that he now had "a small boy" as his "special satellite & man Friday." Daniel's servant proved to be a great help when, a few days after writing to his folks, his regiment was sent to guard two bridges on the Memphis to Charleston Railroad line. There his "man Friday" foraged for food in the wilderness. This was the first time that Daniel had been deep inside rebel-held territory, and in his letters he graphically described the alien and hostile world he was invading. He used these negative descriptions of the South to condemn the rebels, and more importantly, to remind his loved ones of just how much he missed the civilized comforts of his home.[10]

Daniel found this guard duty frustrating and needlessly difficult. It was as if the whole regiment had simply been dumped in a foreign land without logistical support and forgotten. His soldiers eked out an existence by foraging and living off their hardtack rations. Yet these difficulties were relatively minor when compared to the hostility embedded in the Southern landscape. When he was in the Dakota territory, he learned how to read the land to discover the pathology of its inhabitants. Now that he was in the Confederacy, he studied the Southern landscape and found only a wilderness where corruption and sedition flourished. The land appeared to match the people that inhabited it. It was a foreign, desolate place, a country "where nothing thrives but buzzards, southern confederacy, and maggots."[11] He observed that he had acquired some Southern companions. "A regular outfit for one night's sleep here on the ground is three big spiders in each boot, five ants in each shirt sleeve & a wood tick in each ear." "Would I like to eat supper at Densmore's to-night?" he asked, and then with a touch of wry humor answered, "Well, yes if you have anything else than tea & hardtack—or in other words if you have *anything* to eat." But occasionally the wilderness did have some small rewards. He also commented that he was feasting on blackberries three times a day. Even this indulgence brought with it echoes of home, for he reported that his feasts lacked nothing but cream and his family to share it with.[12]

The dull routine of guarding bridges was broken occasionally by minor incursions into enemy territory. Daniel sent Captain William A. Poillon across the Wolf River to seize horses and forage. He was also keen to recover his lost horse, which had slipped its halter. But more importantly, he wanted Poillon to meet a long-standing family request to find an African American servant who could work in the Densmores' home.[13] Help was urgently needed. In early July Orrin wrote to Daniel complaining that Elizabeth would soon have no domestic help. The family "had given up expecting the help" he had promised, but if it finally arrived, Orrin assured Daniel they would gladly employ it because their "Swede," Louisa, proposed to work in the countryside for higher wages during the harvest season. A few weeks later he again wrote, putting more pressure on Daniel: "We do not hear from Capt. Poilons [*sic*] Contraband yet," he complained. Orrin loved his wife and did not want her worn down by hard labor, but he was also aware that a wife that labored as hard as a hired hand diminished the family's status in the community. He faced a dilemma. He knew his wife needed assistance, but he felt unable to cross conventional gender lines and interfere in the running of the household. "I regret that she [Elizabeth] allowed the girl [Louisa Johnson] to leave," commented Orrin, "but I cannot control such matters." In these circumstances he believed that the arrival of a Black servant would not only reduce his wife's workload but also restore a degree of harmony in the household.[14]

As well as receiving urgent pleas from his father, Daniel was also being prevailed upon by Uncle Charles Hanford, who was also seeking to employ a refugee from slavery. Like Orrin, Charles was worried about his wife being overburdened with domestic work. "[S]he is almost determined to do all the work herself as long as she is able and then do more when she is not able," he complained. Reports of African Americans working industriously in his community of Emerald Grove suggested that employment of a Black worker could be a satisfactory solution to his labor problems. Even so, he felt powerless to intervene in domestic affairs by directly asking Daniel to find a Black domestic servant. The problem was that his wife, Susan, opposed his solution. All he could do was hope that her attitude would change. "[P]erhaps if she had one that would do the work to suit perhaps she would try one," he commented in a wistful tone to his nephew. There the matter rested. Daniel never sought a servant for Charles's household.[15]

Poillon was determined to find a worker for the Densmores. His energetic approach reflected both his close friendship with Daniel and his own personal crusade against slavery. His commitment to abolition deepened as he personally discovered the cruelty of slavery. His first attempt to find a servant failed because the owner of a likely prospect sent his slave deep into the Confederacy. Poillon's venture was also impeded because the former slaves had been so badly treated that they were in poor health and had a low resistance to disease. In June he was unable to send a female servant because she suddenly was struck down with the measles.[16] Painstakingly thorough in his approach, Poillon was determined to find a superior servant for the Densmores. This caution was endorsed by Daniel, who was particularly fearful of placing a disruptive servant in his father's home. He had involved Poillon in the project to "insure getting the right stamp of help." If he had not done so, he could have "had some sort of wench booked for Red Wing long ago." Daniel's patience and Poillon's persistence were eventually well rewarded when, in August 1864, Mary Priest left the South for the Densmore household. Like so many refugees from slavery who moved North, Mary's journey was significantly influenced by her desire to secure her freedom and independence. But just how well her aspirations could be reconciled to the Densmores' demand for labor was not directly evident.[17]

Several days after taking up his position on the Memphis to Charleston railroad, Daniel had an encounter with a female refugee from slavery who demonstrated to him the valuable contribution fugitives could make to the Union cause. Carrying a bundle of ragged clothing, a basket full of supplies, and her pockets filled with apples, she had traveled sixteen miles at night to escape her master. Like many slaves escaping to the Union lines, she provided valuable information on the position of rebel forces. Daniel was aware that rebels were in the vicinity because recently four bushwhackers had been captured at brigade headquarters. The woman reported that a force of about five hundred rebels was about to attack the railroad bridges. This timely warning enabled him to prepare for the impending attack.[18]

While he was making his preparations, he received news that his pickets had contacted rebel soldiers and received a bundle of letters written by prisoners from Brigadier General Samuel D. Sturgis's army that had been routed by Forrest at Brice's Crossroads on June 10, 1864. These letters had the marks of humiliation etched into them. Written on scraps of paper and passed from hand to hand until they reached Federal lines, they contained messages of stark survival from soldiers now captive in a foreign land. Daniel knew these letters maintained a chain of hope, love, and assurance between the front line and the home front. If the letters kept arriving, the folks at home knew that their loved ones were alive. Orrin expressed similar feelings just a few days after Daniel had set out on Smith's expedition. He reported the joy and excitement he felt receiving Daniel's letter written on the 22nd of June. While he was disappointed that his letters could reach Benjamin but not Daniel, he acknowledged that it was a wonder that the postal service could operate so efficiently while a war was raging.[19]

Orrin's letters contained news that captured Daniel's imagination and temporarily transported him back to his family. On July 3 Orrin reported on renovations to the family home and that Margaret and her son, Gilman, had joined the local Presbyterian Church. The drought continued, leaving the Mississippi River so low that large ships had been unable to navigate the river. Then, in a concluding paragraph, he noted that he "was reminded of the Cactus you brought from" the Dakota. For a long time it had been dormant, but now it had "come out in a very promising style and we hope to domesticate it as a 'trophy' and memento." Orrin's comments about the cactus appear unremarkable, even trivial, but to Daniel who had brought the plant back from the Dakota Territory under extreme difficulty, it symbolized the conquest of the Dakota and his love of home.[20]

More important than anything else, the July 3 letter expressed the family's concern for Daniel's safety. Orrin was particularly anxious because he feared Black troops would "be likely to find the front," and that "officers of negro troops may not be properly treated if 'gobbled.'" He was also disturbed by reports that he had received from Daniel indicating that his troops were poorly equipped. Discriminated against by the army, Daniel's men would be a tempting target for Forrest. Yet despite these concerns, a week later he wrote to Daniel strongly endorsing his decision to serve in the USCT. He advised him that the process of emancipation had elevated the former slaves. They had been "aroused from the dream of an existence of little value—aimless and fruitless," to a position where they could "assert their right to be men and aid their champions." Now that they had been elevated, "new thoughts and hopes" filled "their dusky minds."[21]

Like most abolitionists, Orrin believed military service had given the former slave a pathway to manhood. Further, he believed that service in the USCT had given Black soldiers such a new sense of self-worth that it was "no wonder they sing the Jubilee." He also believed that once they learned how to use their arms and gained the confidence of their officers, or "champions," their bravery would have no bounds. Their courage would be "a wall of iron and their dusky faces, faces of flint to their foes." While it is not possible to know the extent to which Orrin's advice persuaded his son to think more positively about his military duties, we do know that he sometimes received it at critical times when his belief in the USCT was waning. Yet Orrin's advice had both positive and negative consequences. While it may have renewed Daniel's faith in his military service and his commitment to his abolitionist ideology, it also reinforced the family's negative stereotype of African Americans. This representation depicted those freed from slavery as people who lacked agency, intelligence, and the ability to independently fight for their freedom.[22]

Daniel's racial beliefs were dynamic and evolving. In Minnesota, his attitude to the Dakota changed and became much more negative after he had observed the corpses of settlers killed by Dakota raiding parties. In contrast, in the South his attitude to Black soldiers grew more positive the longer he commanded them, and his empathy for Southern freedmen increased as his personal understanding of slavery deepened. But his racial beliefs were never shaped solely by his personal experiences. They were also influenced by the letters he received from family members, which moderated his empathy and affirmed his family's racist beliefs. This was one important reason his growing commitment to the freedmen never morphed into a belief in racial equality.

As Daniel moved south, he also garnered support from kinfolk and friends attached to other Union regiments serving in the Mississippi Valley. While Pvt. Hanford Fowle, 40th Wisconsin Volunteers, was guarding railroad lines in the vicinity of Memphis, he made every effort to find his cousin Daniel. Although these efforts were unsuccessful, Fowle did manage to write to Daniel. In his letter he admitted that his initial patriotic fervor had waned, but the presence of Daniel's Black troops on the line had deepened his commitment to the Union. As he journeyed south by rail, he observed Black pickets dutifully defending the line. They were impressive troops, "gallant fellows, the most stalwart forms." As Hanford's train was about to pass, these Black soldiers gave three hearty cheers. Hanford's admiration for these troops grew even more when he realized the harshness of the heavy timbered marshland in which they served. Relieved that Daniel and his men had left that region, he was convinced that "you can hardly find a worse place than that."[23]

On June 27, Bouton's Brigade was ordered to report to La Grange, where Smith's army was assembling. Only a few days after Bouton arrived, Smith's army moved south to engage Forrest's cavalry. After crossing the Tallahatchie River

Smith arrived at the small village of Harrisburg near Tupelo on July 13. The next day his army was subject to a heavy frontal attack. During the assaults, Bouton's USCT brigade occupied a position on the Federal left, in the rear protecting Colonel David Moore's 3rd Division. Although heavy losses were inflicted on the enemy, Smith decided to begin withdrawing his forces and return to Memphis. Since he was running short of hardtack for the men and ammunition for his artillery, he considered his army was in no position to pursue the enemy.[24]

Upon returning to Memphis Daniel resumed writing to Benjamin. Troubled by sickness in his camp, he wanted to share this problem with him. He reported that since his return eighteen men had died of disease. In contrast, only two men had died during the expedition. But an analysis of company records reveals that Daniel was mistaken. There was no significant difference in the death rate while the regiment was on Smith's expedition (July 5–July 22) compared to the period when the regiment returned to base (July 22–August 1). In search of an explanation for the alleged difference, he blamed a combination of factors, including a lack of shelter and the impact of slavery. Above all else he blamed slavery for allegedly robbing freedmen of the essential elements of manhood, fortitude and willpower. Therefore, he concluded that "[f]or the Negro sickness is death."[25] Daniel also blamed the Black soldiers for showing a wanton disregard for their own health and shamming illness. According to Daniel, one ruse they employed was to complain of pain in the stomach. If not addressed immediately the complainant was likely to forget the location of the pain. Upon examination, the pain would increase with vehemence until a skillful surgeon administered copious amounts of castor oil, a cure which would "bring the 'misery' to the surface."[26]

In her study of the health of Black soldiers, Margaret Humphreys argues that beliefs like those held by Daniel Densmore were commonplace among many officers in the army. They mistakenly believed the Black soldiers' alleged racial weaknesses were major reasons why they had poor health. In reality, it was the physical suffering caused by slavery that caused major health problems. Many former slaves arrived at Union Army recruiting depots suffering from long-term malnourishment and physical disabilities caused by the hardships of slavery. Since they had come predominantly from a rural setting, they had been isolated from childhood infections and therefore had little resistance to disease. Racial discrimination and maladministration in the army, which resulted in a substandard diet, poor shelter, ragged clothes, excess workload, and poor medical services, also negatively affected the health of Daniel's men. The crowded living conditions of army life may also have been another important condition undermining the soldiers' health. The high death rate in Daniel's regiment in July

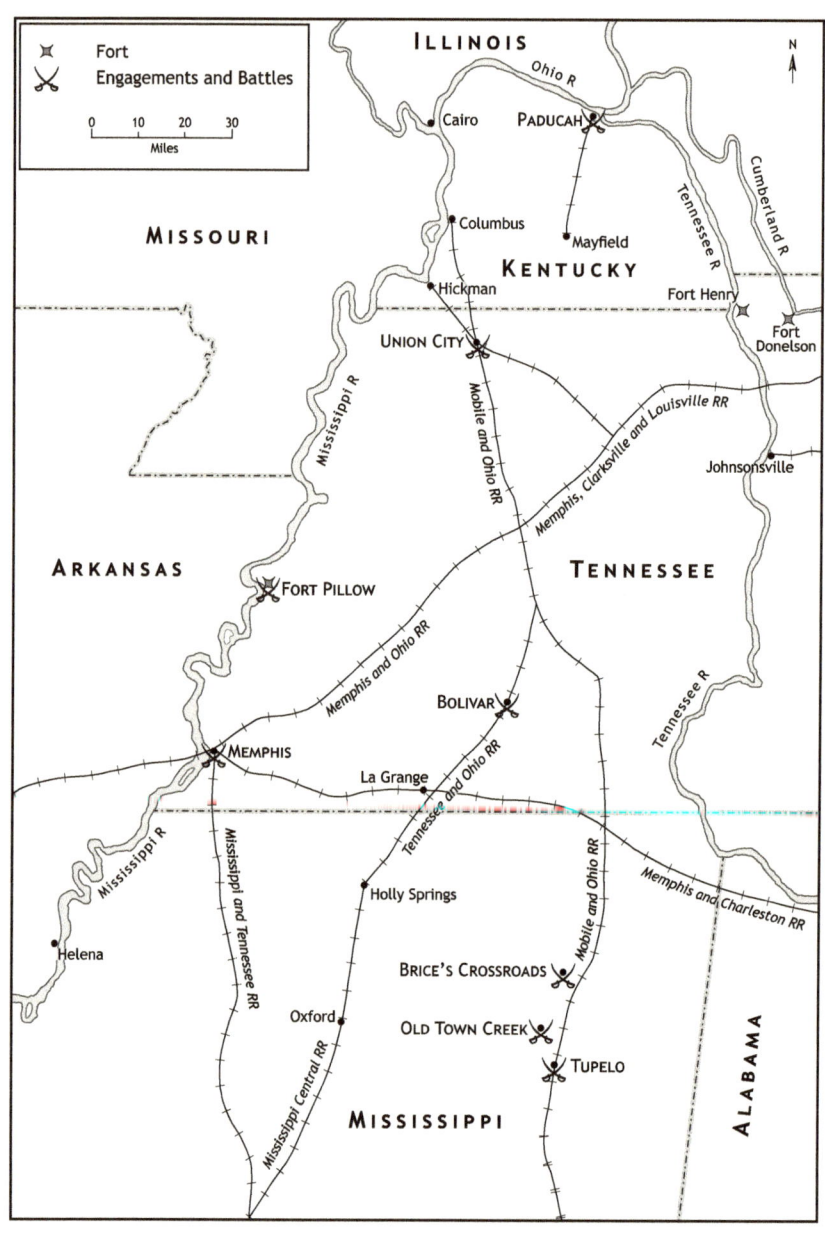

Map 3. Maj. Gen. Nathan Bedford Forrest's Campaign Area, March–August 1864.

1864 may have also resulted from the latent development of contagious diseases first acquired in the crowded quarters of Benton Barracks, St. Louis. The death rate at Benton Barracks reached a peak in the first three months of 1864, when contagious diseases spread among the Black troops. It was during this period that the 65th, 67th, and 68th USCI were shipped down the Mississippi River. It is likely that some of these troops were disease carriers. An analysis of company records of the 68th USCI reveals that during the period the regiment was being organized at Benton Barracks, March to April 1864, sixty-four men died.[27]

Shortly after Smith's soldiers had returned to Memphis they again headed into Mississippi to destroy Forrest's army. By August Daniel's regiment was stationed in the vicinity of Holly Springs, Mississippi, guarding artillery and wagon trains.[28] Although Daniel's time there was largely uneventful, it did provide him with an opportunity to write to Aunt Martha about the strange ways of the rebel folk. Daniel enjoyed writing to his aunt, for he knew that she was intensely interested in the customs and the people of the strange lands he was invading. While he was in the Dakota territory, she had been a faithful and inquiring correspondent. Now that he was in the South she displayed an equally keen interest in his critique of the landscape and its people and the fighting capabilities of his Black soldiers. Daniel wrote about the treacherous nature of Southern civilians. The countryside seemed to be inhabited only by duplicitous widows with bewitching smiles. The only man that could be found was portrayed as both a representative of enfeebled, rustic Southern manhood and a caricature of old age. Dressed in butternut or grey pants, he walked with a stoop, had a silver beard, a thin gaunt face, and a thin and shrunken cadaverous complexion. When arrested for attempting to contact kinfolk in the rebel army, he claimed to be a loyal Unionist.[29]

Daniel's time at Holly Springs gave him an opportunity to comment on the performance of his men under fire, and by doing so confirm his view of the African American's allegedly childlike nature. As rebel shells fell around, he noted that his soldiers responded with jovial enthusiasm and a childlike disregard of death. The "jolly darkies" made lighthearted banter of the fact that the rebel artillery shells were missing their target. The "idea of *'ole secesh done throwing his irons away in de conflile'* [cornfield]" reduced them to laughter. To goad one another, occasionally a soldier would urge his comrades on with shouts of defiance such as "'Gwa you white man [sarcasm] this nigger'll done spite you, sure.'" The battle was real, even though Daniel's racist commentary was laced with comical description. While the comedy in his description exposed views about the childlike character of African Americans widely held in the North, it also revealed his use of humor as a coping mechanism shielding him from the horrors of war. "To be sure," he informed Aunt Martha, "we sometimes have to laugh at what would make the blood of our friends at home seem cold."[30]

While encamped at Holly Springs, Daniel received news that his promotion to the rank of major had been finally confirmed. He was delighted with this news, not only because it marked a personal triumph, but also because it signified the defeat of what he believed was a clique operating under General Pile. In late July he wrote to Benjamin accusing his immediate superior, Lieutenant Colonel James H. Clendening, of being in league with Pile and plotting to have him replaced with another officer. According to Daniel, his promotion was a ruse by Pile and Clendening to placate the "'Minnesota click'" in St. Louis, in whose claws they had unfortunately found themselves. Once the "'Minnesota click'" had been placated, Daniel's promotion was to be withdrawn. Clendening was an unpopular officer. Shortly after first meeting him in May, 1864, Lt. George W. Buswell described him as "a man I cannot bear, a great big pompous chap, more pomp & style than force." In contrast, he described Daniel as "a fine man and steady."

Clendening had been a source of trouble for Daniel for some time. While he was guarding the Memphis and Charleston railroad, Daniel had run up against his harsh command of the regiment. Therefore, he welcomed a breaking rumor that Clendening was going to be court-martialed for cowardly conduct during the battle of Tupelo.[31]

The issues surrounding Daniel's promotion deepened his relationship with Benjamin, because Benjamin also believed he was the victim of clique rule. In Benjamin's case a Hungarian cohort allegedly frustrated his ambition and limited his career. Yet even though promotion conspiracies figured prominently in the brothers' correspondence, they received far less coverage in the letters the brothers sent home. Perhaps this was because Orrin was sometimes quick to give correction and advice in his letters to his sons. For example, when Orrin learned via a letter written by Daniel to Benjamin that Daniel returned late from Smith's expedition, he immediately offered "a word of reproof" for what he thought was his straggling adventure. He accused Daniel of setting such a poor example that in the future it would be difficult for him to punish stragglers. Orrin's accusation of straggling or taking temporary leave without permission was serious because it implied dereliction of duty, even cowardice. But his advice regarding Clendening was more tempered. He advised him to bide his time and to adopt a careful demeanor because Clendening's erratic character would soon lose him the support of the regiment. He believed Clendening was an irrational coward and urged Daniel to avoid a personal confrontation. After all, he was certain that "a coward man was more dangerous than a brave man."[32]

In mid-August Daniel left his regiment and returned to Memphis to be mustered into the 68th USCI as major. This was a time of rejoicing for the whole family, but particularly the youngest, Orrin Jr. "That fixes him [Daniel] from all the Piles and Clendenings on earth can do," Orrin Jr. triumphantly commented when news of Daniel's appointment finally broke. Even Martha could not resist the opportunity to crow about her brother's success. "[H]ow does Br. Clendening feel over it? –Did you have the pleasure of seeing him while in Memphis? He is indeed a gag bird!" she commented ironically. With the congratulatory comments of his family ringing in his ears, Daniel rushed back to his regiment, but upon reaching La Grange, he discovered it had recently departed on Smith's expedition. Disillusioned and bored, he returned to his camp in Memphis which was inhabited by sick and wounded soldiers. Although this unexpected disruption to his service was unwelcome, it gave him time to reflect on his time campaigning in the South.[33]

In many ways, Daniel's time campaigning against Forrest in Tennessee and Mississippi confirmed his long held negative perceptions of the South and its people. In his journey south, Fort Pillow stood out as a symbol of rebel barbarity. The rebel civilians he met appeared to be enfeebled peasant folk who feigned loyalty to the Union, and the African Americans he encountered all bore the marks of slavery on their bodies and on their character. Daniel even observed what he thought was the legacy of slavery in the behavior of his Black soldiers.

Yet as he moved deeper into the South, he discovered that his "jolly darkies" displayed remarkable courage in battle, and a refugee could be a most effective spy. As his empathy toward the freedmen developed, it affirmed his belief that the USCT could be used to destroy the rebels and to restore the Black soldiers' manhood, which had been supposedly lost during slavery. This realization did not come suddenly; rather it was the incremental result of his long military service in the South. Family members contributed too. Staunch abolitionists, they gave him advice which powerfully endorsed his war on slavery and his attempts to elevate his men. But this advice also encouraged Daniel to affirm the family's belief in the myth of Black racial inferiority.

7

"The child was 'right glad' to get home"

Young Orrin's Military Adventure

While Daniel was on General Smith's August 1864 raid into Mississippi, back home Orrin Jr. was becoming increasingly restless and disillusioned. Even though he enjoyed his increasing workload in his father's office, he longed for an opportunity to abandon boyhood and leave home to join the army. Encouraged by his growing feelings of patriotism, he was keen to prove his manhood by campaigning in the South. In the army he believed he could honor his family and demonstrate manly attributes such as self-discipline, courage, endurance, and patriotism. Like many sixteen-year-old boys, he held romantic notions about the glory and honor of war. He searched the newspapers for news of the Union Army's progress in the areas where his brothers served. In April 1864 news that General Forrest had burned the town of Paducah, Kentucky, heightened his concern for Benjamin. Yet rebel barbarity did not intimidate him but only increased his desire to enlist. "If Benj. should be killed I don't think there would be any objection to my going, do you?" he asked Daniel.[1]

In their study of underage enlistment Rebecca Jo Plant and Frances M. Clarke have demonstrated that underage enlistment caused tensions to flare between families and the federal government and within families. In the Densmore family, Orrin Jr.'s desire to join the army brought him into conflict with his father. Although this conflict could be seen as part of the normal pattern of growing up in nineteenth-century America, for the Densmore family it became especially important. Orrin already had two sons serving in the army, and he did not want to send another, especially when his health was frail, and he desperately needed assistance in his office. To ensure that Orrin Jr. continued his valuable work in his office, he devised a plan that he believed would end his son's interest in military service. He proposed to take him on a tour of Benjamin's and Daniel's army camps and expose him to some of the harsh realities of army life. But poor health and the pressure of work forced him to radically alter his plans. He informed Daniel that even though he had been forced to abandon the tour, Orrin Jr. would still go, but he would be shepherded by a family friend, Captain Herman Betcher, who was returning to his regiment after a

Figure 7.1. Martha Densmore and Orrin Densmore Jr., circa 1863. Minnesota Historical Society.

spell on sick leave.[2] Orrin Jr. and Betcher left Red Wing for their journey to Benjamin's camp at Fort Halleck, Columbus, Kentucky, on August 5. First, they traveled to Emerald Grove, then boarded a train at Janesville, traveled to Chicago, and then on to St. Louis, Missouri. Avid tourists, they toured the sights of the city before they boarded a steamer and traveled down the Mississippi River to Cairo, Illinois.[3]

At Cairo, for the first time, Orrin Jr. was confronted by the harsh realities of war when he gazed upon a large ship that had recently come under heavy rebel attack. Bullet holes riddled the hull, and on the gangway evidence of the deceased captain's brain was clearly visible. He was deeply moved as he witnessed the wounded being carried off the ship, and veterans struggling to carry the muskets and knapsacks of their fallen comrades. After laying over in Cairo for the night, Orrin Jr. and Betcher finally reached Columbus. Betcher then continued his journey down the Mississippi River to join his regiment.[4]

When Orrin Jr. arrived at Fort Halleck, he discovered that Benjamin's company was on an expedition in the vicinity of Mayfield. With time on his hands, he dutifully reported to folks at home for the first time. He wrote in detail about his journey, his initial impressions of Black soldiers, and the rebels. Because he knew he was under an obligation to send home regular, well-written progress reports, he labored on his report, even when he felt exhausted. "You will excuse all mistakes for it is awful hot and a person sitting down goes to sleep as easy as he breathes," he commented. Writing at night was difficult because the light attracted mosquitoes. Only four days after he had composed his letter, his father wrote to Benjamin complaining that he needed to write more regularly. Orrin Jr.'s correspondence in the South was shaped by both his personal experiences and the expectations of his parents, particularly those of his father.[5]

The day after Orrin Jr. arrived at Columbus, Benjamin returned to camp. Although he was disheveled, he was "mighty glad," to greet Orrin Jr. In many ways this reunion marked another turning point in Orrin Jr.'s Southern venture. At Cairo he had faced the realities of war and abandoned his role as innocent tourist. At Columbus, the sight of Benjamin and his Black troops triumphantly marching back into camp caused him to reflect more deeply about the meaning of the war itself and the role of the Black soldiers.[6]

Although the Mayfield expedition returned to camp with only one captive and little plunder, Orrin Jr. was so impressed with the performance of the veteran Black soldiers that he believed they were far superior to the white Hundred Days' Men who went with them. Like many of his contemporaries, he was prejudiced against these short-term, lightly trained troops, whose primary function was often to relieve veteran soldiers for frontline combat. Benjamin also shared his younger brother's dislike of the Hundred Days' Men and did not want his Black soldiers associated with them. Orrin Jr. also witnessed the racial divide that existed between the white and Black Union troops, a division that was most clearly seen when the soldiers returned to camp. All the white soldiers were camped outside Fort Halleck, while the Black troops were garrisoned within. He noted that movement between the fort and the outside camp was severely restricted. "[L]ike the fat man of history (Mother Goose) 'they can't come in' while we can go out—with a pass."[7]

While Orrin Jr. admired well-trained Black soldiers, his admiration was mixed with the racial prejudice commonly found in Northern society. "The negroes make queer looking soldiers that is to me," he commented and then added that they were "more like machines than men and more like animals than either." The apparent contradiction between Orrin Jr.'s assessment of the Black soldiers' performance and racial character can be explained by pointing to the great faith he placed in the white officers' ability to train the soldiers, improve their racial character, and undo the work of slavery. Training was important because he believed the Black soldiers lacked initiative and self-direction. It was for this reason he opposed Black soldiers being associated with the Hundred Days Men, as this could mean the impressionable Black soldiers would readily copy their habits and vices. Clearly there was a military edge to the policy of racial segregation operating at Columbus.[8]

His belief in the Black soldiers' capacity for training was reinforced when he observed the daily drill routine conducted at Fort Halleck. He described the fort's daily regime as if he were describing a well-oiled machine set in motion by the regular firing of cannons and guns and the regular beat of drums. Like many young boys with a hunting background, he was also fascinated by the machinery of war, the guns, swords, and armaments that soldiers used to fight with. A visit to the Columbus Ordinance Room persuaded him that the Springfield rifle was the Union soldiers' best weapon. Vigilance was another important feature of army life at Columbus that attracted his attention. Aware that Columbus's hinterland was occupied by rebel sympathizers, he welcomed the punitive raids on rebel farms. He believed these raids yielded valuable plunder, and more important, demonstrated to the rebels that they were a defeated people. But by far the most potent symbol of defeat was the presence of the Black soldier in the South. He informed his father that "the shining face and barrel of a Black sentinel over them show pretty plainly that rebel rule has run out here for some time."[9]

Orrin Jr. believed his parents wanted him to be their eyes and ears while he was in his brothers' camps. Therefore, he gladly wrote to his mother giving her good news about Benjamin's improving health. He had no doubt that his improvement was the work of the herbal medicines he had brought from home. Indeed, Benjamin told him that after he returned from the Hickman expedition, he thwarted oncoming sickness because he used the family's medicine. As well as reporting on Benjamin's physical health, he also commented on the character of his fellow officers.[10]

Orrin Jr. knew that his mother, a zealous temperance campaigner, was particularly anxious that Benjamin should not become a "rough" and indulge in drinking, gambling, and aggressive camaraderie. She wanted Benjamin to hold on to his family values and have sober, morally upright companions to support him in the service. Orrin Jr. reported that Benjamin's messmates were a mixed lot, but those from Minnesota and Red Wing were deemed to be most honorable. The first lieutenant in Benjamin's company, Lieutenant Herman, had ability, but according to Orrin Jr., he was an ethnic outsider, a German and a drunkard. Lieutenant Grant, a Minnesotan, was a sober soldier who always tried to do his best, and Lieutenant Gurney, was a good man, but too learned and bookish. Finally, former Red Wing resident John Winter, the white orderly sergeant, was an excellent companion.[11]

Orrin Jr. believed that Benjamin's mess was particularly fortunate to have two useful African American servants. Ellen, the cook, and the wife of one of the soldiers, did "very well for a wench." Fourteen-year-old George, whom Benjamin liked, was "a first rate boy," who waited on tables, blackened boots, went to market, scoured Benjamin's sword, and ran errands. While he believed some exceptional African Americans could be useful, he also believed that slavery had destroyed the reliability of the Black workforce. Therefore, he doubted whether his family would ever find a trustworthy servant to work in their home.[12]

In mid-August Daniel wrote to Benjamin and Orrin Jr. to report on a disturbing meeting he had with Betcher. Betcher had informed him that Orrin Jr. wanted to enlist. Tormented by this news, Daniel hoped that his young brother would "accept the counsel of us who have been in the mill, and wisely keep out of it." He then went on to list the arguments against Orrin Jr.'s enlistment. These included unremitting hardship of army life, the coarseness of comrades, the lack of empathy toward the suffering, and "the danger of broken down manliness." But far more important than all these was the argument that *"[s]omeone must be at home* and *take care of father and mother."*

Daniel believed that Orrin Jr.'s desire to enlist undermined his and Benjamin's manhood, an integral element of which was the care and protection a son provided for his aging parents. He could not see how he or Benjamin could continue in the army, with a clear conscience, if their parents were "not cared for by one of us boys." Therefore, he believed that if Orrin Jr. enlisted, he or Benjamin would have to resign from the army to take care of them. Without Orrin Jr.'s assistance, he also feared his father would abandon his business and drop into a pitiful dotage. Yet despite his concerns, Daniel welcomed Orrin Jr.'s visit, for he recognized that his young brother needed some respite from small town country life and an opportunity to see the machinery of war. He had no doubt that when he returned home from his Southern tour to care for his parents he would be doing "the very best thing for us all." Finally, Daniel concluded by reiterating the fervent nature of his conviction. "I write this strongly because I feel it," he informed his brothers.[13]

Orrin Jr.'s visit to Daniel's camp was delayed because of Forrest's raid on Memphis on August 21. The raid caused Daniel to be appointed to command the detachment of the First Brigade of United States Colored Troops in Memphis. This new command invigorated him and gave him a new sense of purpose. He noted Forrest's raid was a complete surprise: "everybody was in bed, & the Johnnies charged through several camps without meeting the least opposition." Daniel's camp only escaped invasion because it was hidden by thick fog. But he assured his brothers that if Forrest's men had made another visit, his men "would have given them a jolly round." Even though many of the soldiers in camp were sick and injured, he was confident that they would be "good men for a fight." Daniel reorganized the camp and prepared it for future attack. "I think I shall not prove so useless here after all," he confidently commented [14]

Orrin Jr. finally reached Memphis on August 30. Exhausted and ill, he spent the next three days recovering in camp. "[H]e sleeps as if he thought it a privilege," Daniel informed Benjamin, and then he added, he would take diligent care of him. Daniel was delighted to see his younger brother. "I'm no cannibal, of course, but he looks so good I could almost eat him," he wrote. He had no doubt that if the contingencies of the war permitted, they would have an enjoyable time together. For a long time, he had wanted to introduce him to all the features of army life. Aware that his family would be worried about Orrin Jr.'s safety because of Forrest's raid, Daniel wrote to them and assured them that raid was over and that he would do all he could to protect Orrin Jr.[15]

After he had recovered from his illness, Orrin Jr. immediately wrote home to reassure his folks that he had arrived safely in Memphis. "I wrote you yesterday . . . but Dan'l wants me to write home again although nothing special has occurred since," he complained. Because an embargo had been placed on all letters going north, he believed he was being unjustly accused of being a wayward son for not sending letters home. But gaps in Orrin Jr.'s correspondence may also have occurred because the army mail system lost letters or misdirected them. Early in October Daniel discovered that the chaplain from his regiment had found letters from Benjamin and Orrin Jr. at the headquarters of the Freedmen's Department in Memphis.[16]

Once Orrin Jr. had adjusted to camp life, he enjoyed exploring the social life of Memphis. The pulsating life of this large Southern city was particularly captivating. He observed the city roaring into life on September 9, when one hundred guns were fired from nearby Fort Pickering to celebrate the capture of Atlanta. A few days later he described just how much he enjoyed the "grand illumination" that occurred in downtown Memphis. Lights were placed in the windows of public buildings, with the government prison, the Irving Block, looking the best. Yet most of all he enjoyed the musical performance of the 7th U.S. Colored Heavy Artillery bugle band. He enthusiastically described the band's performance knowing full well that his father had been a member of the 177th New York militia band and loved band music. Like other family members, Orrin Jr. also believed that music appreciation and performance were good indicators of cultural and social development. There was also a gendered aspect to his description of the Black band's performance. In past correspondence he had invariably described the Black soldiers' progress by pointing to their military accomplishments. His father appreciated and understood these descriptions, but Martha and Elizabeth found them much less appealing. However, he knew his mother and sister would find his references to music more interesting. [17]

In his description of the band's performance, Orrin Jr. made a pointed reference to the African American's elevation from slavery and the social revolution that emancipation was bringing to the South. He witnessed the band playing with great gusto in "Court Square a place of resort for the aristocracy." Some of the fine ladies who observed the performance looked quite vexed at what they considered an insult. Such displays of disapproval did not upset the rhythm of the bandsmen. In a celebration of their liberty, "the band played well and showed the difference between the negroes as soldiers now and as slaves a year ago."[18]

Orrin Jr. measured the African Americans' progress in terms of control, performance, and discipline. Whereas the slave was allegedly lazy, emotionally unstable, docile, and slovenly in his dress, the Black Union soldier was the opposite. The well-dressed, disciplined soldiers of the bugle band exhibited all the benefits of military training. Just a few days after arriving in Memphis, he wrote to Benjamin informing him that Daniel's regiment, the 68th USCI, "aint quite as good on the nice things as the 4th Heavy." Further, he had not seen a parade equal to that of Benjamin's regiment. He explained the difference between the two regiments by pointing out that the officers of the 4th U.S. Colored Heavy Artillery had more opportunity to subject their men to intense instruction and training. Since he believed African Americans were naturally irresponsible, he believed this was vital.[19]

The importance of this course of action was apparently demonstrated to him just two days after he had attended the great illumination celebrations. At ten o'clock on the evening of September 12, Orrin Jr. was startled by a very loud series of explosions coming from Fort Pickering, located just one mile from his camp. The explosions, which killed four men, were caused by several shells igniting. He had no hesitation attributing the cause of the explosions to the carelessness of the Black soldiers stationed at the fort. Their disregard of safety totally amazed him. On several occasions, he had witnessed soldiers carrying cartridges for cannons while smoking cigars with ash falling off.[20]

Daniel was pleased that Orrin Jr. was enjoying his time in Memphis, and he did all he could to give his brother a wide range of interesting experiences. Together they visited the New Memphis Theatre, the Navy Yard, the mortar boats, and Fort Pickering. All this activity placed a severe strain on Daniel because it occurred at a time when his own workload was significantly increasing. Colonel Jones's illness required him to assume command of the regiment and manage the movement of the regiment's camp to a new location.[21] Yet regardless of his workload, Daniel remained driven by two prime considerations. First, he was determined to do everything he could to keep his brother healthy. "I shall watch him closely, and cut short his stay immediately if his health should again turn the least unfavorable," he informed Benjamin. Second, he wanted to give Orrin Jr. a good taste of camp life, to relieve his nervousness, and more importantly, convince him that the army was not a place for him. Indeed, he told his parents that he was doggedly determined to convince him "that mother's buttery is a much more comfortable place than 'the ranks' for such as he."[22]

Orrin Jr. found the daily routine of army life difficult, and over time these difficulties wore him down and made military service much less appealing. The discomforts of army life, the unvarying diet of plain, unwholesome food, and the crowded living quarters—all sapped his spirits. Yet these discomforts seldom found a prominent place in his letters home. Instead, they were generally tucked away in passing observations and casual anecdotes. But he did complain openly about the officers' poverty, which resulted in him becoming a principal source of cash for Daniel and his friends. Daniel's lack of money strained his relationship with Benjamin. Embarrassed by the way he had exhausted Orrin Jr.'s funds, Daniel wrote to Benjamin explaining that he expected "to refund him at any moment." He also added that he would also "make right the money" he owed him.[23]

Approximately two weeks after Orrin Jr. had arrived in Memphis, he began to think about his journey home. He was missing his family and friends, and he was keen to return by early October so he could attend both the Wisconsin State Fair at Janesville and the Red Wing Fair. Together he and Daniel planned his return journey. It was decided that he should depart Memphis for Columbus on October 1. As the departure date grew close, Daniel regretted Orrin Jr.'s leaving. Since his military duties had kept him from spending time with him, he wanted him to prolong his visit so the two could share more time together. But Orrin Jr. was keen to set out on his homeward journey because he saw it as a triumph. After spending more than a month in Union Army camps, he looked forward to demonstrating to his family that the South had not broken him, and that his

Southern tour had put a seal on his manhood. He confidently believed he would be welcomed home not as a boy, but as a man.[24]

One week before his planned departure, Orrin Jr.'s travel plans were drastically changed. Rumors of an impending attack on Memphis by Forrest and a rebel river blockade, together with Orrin Jr.'s declining health, all coalesced to force Daniel to act promptly. Even though Orrin Jr. protested that "he had not made his visit out and that he was going to get better," Daniel ordered him to start on his homeward journey immediately. This decisive action strained his relationship with Orrin Jr., who considered he was being treated like a boy being sent to the rear once the fighting started. In a letter to Benjamin shortly after Orrin Jr. had departed, Daniel commented that Orrin Jr. "did not much like being sent to the rear when a fight was threatened & was much afraid of its being thrown in his face." He urged Benjamin to manage the issue of Orrin Jr.'s departure with great sensitivity, so he "would not need to tell his own story" or discuss this potentially embarrassing turn of events. More important still, he warned Benjamin that a "very little indiscreet spurring would send him into the army instanter." Yet despite all the problems, Daniel still believed Orrin Jr.'s visit to Memphis had been a great success because it had changed his attitude to enlistment. According to Daniel, Orrin Jr. now believed he could best serve the family, and the Union, at home.[25]

Orrin Jr. left Memphis on September 24 and reached Columbus, sick and exhausted, two days later. Upon his arrival, Benjamin immediately wrote home, confidently predicting that he would soon recover and depart for home in two days. Yet contrary to this prediction, Orrin Jr.'s health continued to deteriorate, and he remained languishing on his sickbed.[26] This delay caused considerable consternation for the family. On October 9 and 16 Orrin Sr. wrote to remind Daniel that Orrin Jr. had still not arrived home. He felt "unpleasant about it," but recognized that there was little he could do because he could not get him.[27] Daniel's reply only increased his father's anxiety because he recommended that Orrin Jr. stay in Columbus for the winter season. Since he had visited during the worst time to the year, he was certain a winter sojourn would benefit him. This suggestion evoked a pointed response from his father, who was largely unaware of the true state of his son's illness. Orrin explained that he needed Orrin Jr. to work in his office during the winter months and that his Southern tour had not been undertaken to improve his health. He also reminded Daniel of the primary motives behind Orrin Jr.'s visit. He had journeyed south to see his brothers, to see war in the South, and above all to remove his desire to enlist.[28]

Aware of his father's deep unease, Daniel did not raise the issue of Orrin Jr.'s winter sojourn again. As an aside in a letter to Benjamin, he wrote that his father was "getting quite anxious to see Orrin's help," and that "the youth had about staid his time out." The pressure on Benjamin and Daniel continued to mount when Margaret wrote to Benjamin urging Orrin Jr.'s rapid return. She informed him that seasonal change accompanied by the fall of snow had made her parents very anxious about Orrin Jr.'s return. Then she added, "I earnestly hope Orrin may have started today."[29]

While debate raged about his departure, Orrin Jr. remained in Benjamin's camp slowly recovering from "fever and ague." By mid-October he had recovered enough to take care of Benjamin's hunting traps while he was away on detached duty at Paducah. As his health improved, his interest in a military career revived. The threat of a rebel invasion caused him little concern. He reported nonchalantly that recently a scare, "as good as the Memphis one," had occurred in Columbus. With his confidence growing to new heights, he informed Daniel that he might soon have to command the company because John Winter and Lieutenant Grant would be on picket duty and 1st Lieutenant Herman was under arrest. The tension that had existed between the two appears to have largely disappeared, and the friendly repartee surfaced again. In his letter, Orrin Jr. took great youthful delight narrating an amusing battle he had witnessed between a bear named Benjamin and a dog. To capture the hilarity of the conflict, Orrin Jr. included another one of his small sketches of the event. The enthusiastic narrative of the incident together with the childlike simplicity of the sketch suggest that Orrin Jr. had not shed boyhood. Even so, elsewhere in the letter, there were some indications of Orrin's developing manhood. In a postscript he asked Daniel to "remember when Maggie Mitchell comes around to tell her to come to Red Wing for I want to see her."[30]

Gender issues were firmly fixed in Orrin Jr.'s mind as he contemplated his journey home. Many of the threats to his burgeoning manhood that appeared when he departed from Memphis were emerging again as he prepared to leave Columbus. Once again it was the way he was journeying home that most disturbed him. At Memphis he had feared being portrayed as a boy who had been driven from the front line because he was too young to fight. Now he feared being viewed as a sick, dependent boy leaving the South because he lacked robust toughness and endurance, which were important characteristics of mid-Victorian American manhood. These attributes were all exercised by men to honor and protect their families.[31] Another complication also worried him. In late September Benjamin wrote to Martha informing her that he had planned for Lieutenant Dearborn's wife to travel home with Orrin Jr. But Orrin Jr. did not share his brother's enthusiasm for a traveling companion. He complained that

Benjamin's arrangements had placed him in an impossible situation. "It may be ungallant, but I'll be—anyway," he admitted. Then he went on to give the reasons for his opposition. "I don't want travel with charge of a lady when walking twenty rods sets me down for a day," he complained. Physically unable to fulfill the role of an escort offering protection, he feared that if he accompanied Mrs. Dearborn or any other lady, he could be seen as a sick boy who required the tender loving care of a woman. Firm in his convictions, he refused to compromise. Therefore, when he left Columbus, he was accompanied only by Benjamin who traveled with him to Cairo.[32]

Martha finally welcomed Orrin Jr. at Emerald Grove in mid-October. But she welcomed him not as a returning hero, but as her "poor boy," who had narrowly escaped from the savagery of the South. Immediately she wrote to her parents advising them that Orrin Jr. was so ill that he would have to stay in Emerald Grove for an extra four days so he could recover. She was "now so glad" that she waited for him. Why, "the poor boy" looked "as if he needed some-one to care for him on the way."[33]

When Orrin Jr. and Martha finally reached their home in Red Wing in late October, Orrin was pleased to see his son but disturbed to find him very thin and bilious. The day after he arrived home, Orrin Jr. wrote to Daniel. Although his letter contains some home news, there is no direct mention of his time in the South. Yet reading the text carefully, it appears that his enthusiasm for enlisting, and all things military, had waned. He informed Daniel that his health was improving. His yellow complexion was disappearing, but he still had an aching stomach. He missed the companionship of his brothers. "Say—I wish you were home. It is a very comfortable place I can assure you." Yet the final comment on Orrin Jr.'s Southern sojourn was not made by Orrin Jr. but by Martha. In late November, she reported to Daniel on Orrin Jr.'s improving health. "I wish you could see how well Orrin is looking," she commented. She attributed this improvement in health to the Northern climate and decent food. While she knew Orrin Jr. was pleased with his Southern tour, she also knew "the child was 'right glad' to get home." "[P]oor health while South convinces him that 'tis not the place for him," she concluded.[34]

Even though Orrin Jr. was unable to demonstrate his burgeoning manhood in the army, his experience in the South did not dampen his fervor. But he now understood that becoming a man involved more than enduring the hardships of camp and displaying courage on the battlefield. Gender relations were important too. Like most of his contemporaries, Orrin Jr. believed that women were the source of moral authority and civilized living, and that a man's character and reputation could be measured by the way he related to women and how he gained their respect. Anxious to be recognized as a true gentleman, Orrin sought the wise counsel of Daniel. "I have taken your advice to being in ladies company and have succeeded bully so far," he informed him. Then with an air of confidence, Orrin informed him of his plans. "Shall have to postpone operations for a while but shall open the Spring Campaign after the next month," he wrote. Orrin's use of military metaphors, for example reference to "operations" and "Spring Campaign" to describe his romantic liaisons is not accidental. Denied an opportunity to demonstrate to his manhood on the battlefields of the South, he now sought to achieve this goal by conquering the hearts of young ladies at the social functions he attended in Red Wing.[35]

In the world of business and commerce Orrin Jr. sought to demonstrate that he could act independently and responsibly in support of the family. When his parents left for a tour of the South in May 1865, he managed his father's tax-collecting affairs. Noting his growing maturity, Martha observed that he appeared "to realize the responsibility resting upon him."[36] Keen to manage manfully the business alone, he refused to call on Martha for assistance even during the busy season because the office was a "bad enough place for a man let alone a lady." On some days he collected as much as three thousand dollars, a fact that he hid from his father for fear it would "bring him home straight away."[37]

Like all adventures, Orrin Jr.'s time in the South was a journey of self-discovery. At Columbus and Memphis, he discovered how the USCT could be used to elevate African Americans from slavery and help the Union vanquish the South. But this discovery did not change his essentially negative view of the African American character. In many ways his time in the South affirmed it. His determination to use his Southern adventure as a springboard to launch a military career brought him into conflict with his father, who wanted to maintain control over his young son so he could secure the family's fortune, and his brothers who believed his enlistment would curtail their military service. Yet ultimately Orrin Jr.'s time in the South helped resolve the tension within the family. The hardship of camp life moderated Orrin Jr.'s military ambitions and taught him that the South was not a place for him. When he returned home, he discovered that he could demonstrate his manhood in different ways, and that he could best serve both his family and his nation by collecting government taxes, rather than firing bullets.

8   "Move the camp down to the grave yard"

Camp Life in Memphis

After Orrin Jr. departed Memphis, Daniel overcame his sense of loss by throwing himself into routine duties. Life was busy, but his off-duty social activities were so rich and rewarding that he did not feel alone. Friends and kinfolk from neighboring regiments entertained and visited him. Although these visits nurtured networks of friendship that were often built on prewar relationships, the relationships which developed in the army camps took on new forms and meaning. Stripped of the support of their immediate families and involved in a life-and-death struggle, the soldiers became comrades and learned to rely on one another. Daniel, for example, frequently visited the Memphis convalescent camp to support Will Philleo, and he also provided funds for Will's furlough.[1] The Mississippi River became a busy highway, as soldiers from the Upper Midwest functioned as personal couriers carrying letters, articles of clothing, tasty food morsels, and funds to their comrades in the South. Aware that Daniel would be lonely because Orrin Jr. had departed, Martha offered to send him pails of butter. Gifts exchanged between soldiers also strengthened ties of friendship. Even though Daniel found Deacon Love's loud drumming pretentious, he greatly valued the chair Deacon had given him to furnish his rudely equipped tent. Many soldiers also kept a lively correspondence with their comrades in other regiments. Hanford Fowle wrote to Daniel on several occasions from his camp in the 40th Wisconsin, and because this communication occurred in an environment that was considered hostile and alien, the ties of affection between Daniel and his kinfolk and friends grew ever stronger.[2]

Daniel saw his declining health as a marker pointing to the unforgiving nature of the land he occupied. He found fall a particularly testing season, and he welcomed approaching the chilly winter weather, which reminded him of his beloved Minnesota. Although he remained at his post for as long as he could, he was eventually overcome with illness and forced to spend some time in a convalescent tent. Suffering from a kidney infection, he looked as "yellow as the blooming dandelion." Other officers in his regiment also shared a similar fate.

Second Lieutenant George W. Buswell also observed that he was "quite bilious and had 'a yellow look.'"[3] Death and sickness were everywhere about Daniel, reminding him of his own mortality. Indirectly, death even touched his own household. With a heavy heart he wrote to his family and informed them that John A. Johnson, brother of Louisa Johnson, the Densmores' domestic helper, had died of "blood flux."[4]

By early October Daniel's health had deteriorated so badly that Colonel Jones had insisted that he find accommodation in his house. There he had access to a physician and received good, hearty meals. Although he was at ease in his new quarters, he knew that his good fortune and the steady improvement in his health stood in sharp contrast with the suffering of his men, and this contrast disturbed him. Just a few paragraphs after describing his spacious quarters and fine food, he noted that the health of the men was "very poor." He believed that since arriving at Memphis his men had died at the alarming rate of one per day.

Recently, in less than a week, nine soldiers in his regiment had died. Daniel attributed this high mortality rate directly to the inferior quality of the tents the army had provided. Describing the use of these tents as "a puzzle to commonsense," he complained that these "dog tents" had killed "more men than enemy bullets or camp malarias." In addition, the provision of these tents appeared to undermine his standing and that of his men, for it implied that inferior shelter, like that provided to contrabands, would meet the regiment's needs. In frustration he declared the situation had not improved despite the repeatedly strong protests he had made. Other officers shared his concern. For example, Colonel Ignatz G. Kappner, commander of Fort Pickering, defied Daniel's prejudiced assessment of his character and Hungarian lineage by promoting the welfare of the soldiers' families living in the nearby contraband camp. He also wrote to the Memphis military authorities urging that barracks be constructed at the fort. In support of his case, Colonel Ignatz G. Kappner argued that the Black troops had suffered severely in winter because they were supplied with rotten shelter tents. Unmoved by these appeals, army authorities countered dissent by issuing orders that threatened dishonorable discharge for any officer who issued superior tents to their men. Some relief was given to the soldiers by allowing them to build shanties from logs cut from nearby woods. Yet this concession did nothing to allay Daniel's concern for the health of his men. He feared that when winter arrived, he and his fellow officers would "move the camp down to the grave yard, and endeavor to bury the dead as fast as the shelter tents kill them."[5]

Daniel's advocacy on behalf of his men does appear to have been based on solid evidence. An analysis of the company medical records of the 68th USCI indicates that the death rate was particularly high throughout the four-month period from July through October 1864. During this period, each company experienced between three to four deaths each week. Daniel's prediction that the death rate would increase when the winter came is not supported by analysis of the medical records. The quality of Black soldiers' health sometimes improved when the officers and surgeons from their regiments protested against the army's discriminatory policies and supported calls for better medical support. But the experience of Daniel Densmore suggests that even the work of influential supporters could be nullified when it ran hard against higher military authorities.[6] Chance may well have played a part in the quality of health care provided in the 68th USCI. For example, there may be some substance to Daniel's claim that other Black infantry regiments in Colonel Bouton's 1st Brigade USCT received better tents simply because they were organized before regulations requiring the compulsory use of shelter or "dog tents" were issued. The 68th USCI was organized six months later than any other infantry regiment in the brigade. [7]

News of Daniel's declining health and the high death rate in his camp caused considerable consternation to Orrin. To restore Daniel's health, he immediately sent him, by express post, an "oyster can of Jaundice Bitters," a medicine he had previously sent to Benjamin. Daniel was advised to take the medicine three times a day and to increase the dosage until he induced a laxity of the bowels, but not to the extent that he produced a cathartic condition. If the medicine was not needed, Orrin advised him to give it to some poor soul who had the shakes or jaundice. Ever generous with his medical advice, Orrin even suggested that Daniel should cure Colonel Jones's illness by smoking him with saltpeter. Fortunately for Daniel, by late October his health had so improved that the canteen of bitters did not have to be used. Even so, he was very thankful to have a good preventative on hand.[8]

The correspondence which flowed between the family home and the Densmore boys' military camps was shaped by the way the boys' stories and anecdotes touched the individual lives of family members. Orrin saw the suffering of Daniel's men as a political challenge. With Daniel's approval, he was prepared to use his political contacts with Governor Miller and other eminent state politicians to secure adequate shelter for Daniel's regiment. Yet upon further consideration, he believed that there was little chance of success. "The move would perhaps be let alone," was his final comment on the matter. Perhaps no member of the family was more deeply troubled by the suffering in Daniel's camp than Margaret, and she alone wrote thoughtfully and extensively on the subject. In a letter to Benjamin, she claimed that the high death rate in Daniel's regiment pointed to what she considered was one tragic features of the war, men dying from disease and exposure rather than heroically on the battlefield. She considered these deaths shameful because she believed they were caused by widespread government incompetence and neglect.

In *This Republic of Suffering: Death and the American Civil War*, Drew Gilpin Faust reveals that the immense scale of the suffering resulting from the war caused Americans to reevaluate their own view of death and dying. Faust points out that during the war "death's threat, its proximity and its actuality became the most widely shared of the war's experiences."[9] Such was the immense scale of the loss that death was no longer an individually encountered experience. It became a shared experience that transformed the American people and bound them in a "Republic of Suffering."[10]

Although her husband had not fallen for the Union, Margaret Densmore claimed citizenship in this new republic by writing about the way death was cutting through Daniel's regiment. But her empathy for his soldiers was limited because it was moderated by her reflection on her own personal tragedies. She reminded Benjamin that death stalked the streets at home as well as the lines on the battlefield. It seemed "more than ever, busy among those left at home sundering households—scattering families—till the whole land mourns her fallen." In the recent past, death had scarred her own life. In the past year she had lost a child and her husband. Gilman, her remaining child, was now fatherless. The integrity of her closely knit family unit also changed as she was forced, by financial necessity, to take on domestic work and move into her father's home. News of the suffering and death in Daniel's regiment resurrected painful memories of this personal tragedy. Because she felt powerless to help Daniel, she felt compelled to dismiss all thoughts of the illness and the suffering in his regiment from her mind. "I do not like to think of it," she admitted to Benjamin. "I cannot help them and sympathy without works is dead." Margaret coped with death by thinking of life as a journey. She believed that her departed loved ones had reached a new stage on this journey, and that in time they would all would meet again. While news of the suffering and death in Daniel's camp revived this cherished hope, it also evoked in her a sense of sadness and isolation. She did not mourn the fact that her loved ones "had gone from trouble," but the "separation and this *long wait* until we, too may go."[11]

At the end of October 1864, Daniel's life was crowded with a seemingly endless number of competing tasks. When Jones went on leave, Daniel welcomed the opportunity to take sole command of the regiment. His new responsibilities seemed to empower him and drive him to new heights of enthusiasm and confidence.

As well as the normal duties of supervising pickets and strengthening entrenchments, he was responsible for building the regiment's new winter quarters and serving on councils of administration and court-martials. Although he jocularly commented to Benjamin that he was too busy to change his shirt, deep down he felt at ease with the world. "My health is good and my debts are paid up," he wrote to Benjamin, "so I feel free again in stomach and conscience."[12]

By mid-November Daniel was looking forward to completing the building of the regiment's winter quarters. He informed his folks that five companies were already housed in the new barracks, and they were looking extremely comfortable. In mid-December the final additions to the barracks were being made. The new camp was in a beautiful grove, and the trees and buildings sparkled with an ample covering of whitewash. "We are not at all afraid to receive visitors, as we maintain that we cannot be outdone for good looks," Daniel boasted. In many ways the camp was a monument to freedom, visible evidence that former slaves could make the transition from slavery to freedom and self-reliant labor. There was, according to Daniel, much "gratification too of knowing it to be all the fruit of our own industry." Like many officers, Daniel also believed his clean, well-constructed camp was a testament to his own genteel, middle-class values. In addition, he believed the camp's physical presence affirmed his recent promotion and his new authority as acting commander of the regiment. But feelings of pride and accomplishment also developed strongly in the ranks of enlisted men. Recruited from Missouri's refugee camps, they knew that by building their military quarters in a slave state they were staking a claim to their personal freedom.[13]

On the 10th of December, just two hours after the last shelter tent was struck, "and the boys had shut the door on impending death," Daniel received an order from the Major General Napoleon J. T. Dana commanding him to abandon his new camp and transfer his regiment immediately to Fort Pickering. Although this order may have been a routine procedure made in the normal course of military administration, Daniel did not see it in this way. Because he was sensitive to past acts of discrimination, he immediately accused Dana of imposing a new form of tyranny. In a letter to his family written on the day he received the order, he accused Dana of being another pharaoh who was determined to keep his men in servitude and under the constant threat of suffering and death. "Now there arose a King that knew not Joseph, Maj. Gen. N. J. Dana who took command here two days ago," he commented. "And what does that mean?" asked Daniel rhetorically. Then he answered his question by saying that it meant allowing another regiment to march in and enjoy all the benefits of his regiment's labor. In contrast, Daniel's regiment was destined to pitch "*shelter tents* again, on the bleak bluff called Fort Pickering—and *wait for lumber to build barracks.*" This unwelcome news was compounded because he feared falling under the authority of the fort's commander, Colonel Kappner, an officer of Hungarian descent, who was allegedly a strict disciplinarian and no friend of officers from the Midwest. Drawing on Benjamin's alleged experience "under Hungarian rule" at Fort Halleck, Daniel expected a similar fate awaited him at Fort Pickering.[14]

Fort Pickering was an unattractive and unhealthy post. Daniel described it as "a terribly dirty conglomeration of old sheds, unintelligible piles of earth (said to be fortifications, but resembling more the rear slopes of a Scandinavian root cellar) accumulated filth, mud, rats, magazines, mules, and Hungarian muddles." What disturbed him most about the post was the degrading impact he believed it was having on his Black soldiers. Everything about it stood in sharp contrast with his vision of a military post. He believed that service in the Union Army would not only make the former slave a soldier but also eventually a citizen. An important part of the elevation process involved developing in the former slave's habits of pride, discipline, and self-respect. He looked for the development of these personal attributes in the way the soldiers carried themselves about camp, in the way they did their drill, but above all, the way the soldiers cared for their camp environment. A clean, well laid-out camp was symbolically important because it demonstrated that the men were growing in stature and were becoming good soldiers and potential citizens.[15]

To illustrate the negative impact Fort Pickering was having on his men, Daniel took his family on a virtual tour of the Fort. In his travelogue the place-names and the accompanying descriptions he employed all pointed to the corrupting character of the environment. After passing by "Mud Alley," "Mule Street," "the Parapet, an interminable jumble of dilapidated buildings," and "Rat Park," he described "a rusty bevy of boil-less kettles." On one of the piles of rusty kettles sat "an American citizen of African descent clad in military garments," "eating a mince pie made of old cucumber pickles and mince meat." The Black soldier sealed this picture of dejection.[16]

When Daniel's family received news of his regiment's transfer to Fort Pickering, they expressed their outrage. Young Orrin declared that Dana's decision was "decidedly military" in its character, because it demonstrated that both the army and the general lacked common sense. In his youthful fervor he pronounced a curse, "my sgnisselb (backwards) on Gen. N. J. T. Dana," and then went on to add that if curses were effective, Colonel Jones would doubtless have disposed of General Dana long ago. Orrin felt an urge to protest against the relocation of Daniel's regiment but admitted that "any feeling of the kind is of profitless entertainment." He accused the Fort Pickering's commander, Colonel Kappner, of either a lack of common sense or having "his brains addled by elevation." If the latter were the case, he recommended that the family carefully study Proverbs chapter 27, verse 22, which declared: "Though you grind a fool in a mortar, grinding him like grain with a pestle, you will not remove his folly from him."[17]

Orrin was concerned about the long-term impact Dana's decision would have on the Black soldiers. He accused him of teaching the freedmen a "bad lesson," which would cloud the former slave's mind and prevent him from seeing "the difference between his present and his former master," for each was determined to recklessly deprive him of the rewards of his labor. In these circumstances, the only comfort the men of the 68th USCI appeared to have was the hope that "the mighty Gen should sometime meet his glorious destiny by the crack of a brainless skull." He informed Daniel that he would have a challenge convincing his men that they had been fairly treated and that they ought to promptly build their new quarters.[18]

Second Lieutenant Buswell's attitude to the move to Fort Pickering was more optimistic than that of any member of the Densmore family. Less concerned about the physical environment than Daniel Densmore, he was pleased that for the first time since they left Benton Barracks the men in his regiment could sleep inside a barracks. Yet he too was critical of Colonel Kappner's command, because under his leadership the military post was more like a prison than a fort. Only two officers from the 68th USCI could leave the fort at any one time. Buswell believed the fort was "certainly quite like a prison for the men," because it was very difficult for them to leave. Trapped in their new location, the enlisted men were unable to visit loved ones living in the contraband camp in the fort's vicinity. These restrictions were compounded by the strict, prison-like discipline imposed on the regiment by Colonel Kappner. One day after arriving in Fort Pickering Buswell wrote in his diary that the Colonel was "a very strict disciplinarian, we know."[19]

The regiment moved into the Provisional Barracks at Fort Pickering under severe weather conditions. Since the barracks were "no better than dirty cold barns," within two days the men had barking coughs, and the sick list soared. But once the initial shock of the move to Fort Pickering passed, Daniel's attitude became more positive. The Provisional Barracks became more like home as the men settled in, made repairs to their quarters, and the days became warmer. Reports from the Inspector General that the buildings should not be repaired because they could be moved were laughed at by the officers. Daniel even confessed that he thought the change of quarters had been good for the men. "It has weaned them," he wrote. It taught them to be resolute and disciplined, to obey orders and not to be self-centered, but to take a manly pride in their appearance and to labor on regardless of the arbitrary nature of military commands. He even believed that if an order were now given to move camp, the men would hardly raise a murmur.[20]

The whole episode regarding the regiment's movement to Fort Pickering reached a satisfying conclusion on New Year's Day, 1865, when Daniel and several fellow officers left the fort to visit their old camp. The sights he saw on that day confirmed his faith in African Americans as soldiers and the army as a vehicle for their elevation. When he arrived at his old camp, he was "gratified to find its beauty entirely departed." The whole vicinity of the camp was swept clean of fences, trees had been lopped, and the handsome parade ground strewn with rubbish and filth. Daniel commented that he mentioned the derelict camp not "as matter of grief, but as a contrast between the" Black soldiers and white soldiers. The morally responsible and highly disciplined men of the 68th USCI were obviously militarily superior to the unruly mob of white soldiers who succeeded them. The local citizens now bewailed the departure of the 68th USCI a fact that greatly satisfied Daniel, for only weeks previously "they could not find it in their loyal hearts to furnish board for us" USCT officers. Their houses had been so severely damaged by the white troops that they "had their latch strings hanging." He considered it a most enjoyable sight to see these local people searching in vain for their fences, calves, and chickens which the white soldiers had stolen.[21]

There was, perhaps, no better evidence of the discrimination inflicted upon the Black troops than the excessive amount of fatigue duty imposed on them. Daniel and other officers in the USCT found this practice particularly objectionable because it undermined the soldiers' health and limited training. In early October he calculated that of the 524 men fit for duty in his regiment, 380 were daily taken out for fatigue duty. The workload of these men was so exhausting that afterwards they were "hardly fit for picket duty."[22] Daniel believed that he and his regiment were being subject to the arbitrary, authoritarian command of the Hungarian commander of Fort Pickering, Colonel Kappner, and he sympathized with Benjamin who appeared to have his own problems with officers of Hungarian descent at Fort Halleck. "You have spoken of the amenities of a Hungarian rule—A similar prospect hastened (?) our steps, and makes savory our prospects for the future," he commented. To justify his concern, he noted that the first duty given to the 68th USCI when it arrived at the fort was to provide 320 out of 415 men "for guard duty and dirt digging about this old rats' nest." "How in the name of sense are we to bring the instruction of this regiment up to what it should be?" Daniel asked. Given such duties, it was "difficult for any one but a row of incipient I. G's [Inspector Generals] to see" that the regiment could not be brought up to an acceptable military standard.²³ Daniel accused the military authorities of reviving the habits of slavery by working his men like slaves. He even suggested that he and Jones should adopt the terminology of slavery to describe their fatigue duties.

> We have been discussing the propriety of going back to the former nomenclature—as being much more in keeping with our businesses, towit:—Col. to be "Ole Massa," and the remainder of us to be "bosses" numbered 1, 2 &c for convenience,—squads to be "gangs," and all sentences of court-martials to be in terms of "lashes."²⁴

Daniel knew that his soldiers' excessive fatigue duty reinforced prevailing patterns of racial discrimination in the service because it prevented the soldiers from receiving drill and combat training. Denied martial skills and combat opportunities, the Black soldiers had difficulty refuting claims that they were second-class troops. In addition to this altruistic motivation, there were other more personal reasons for Daniel's opposition to excessive fatigue duty. He knew that if his regiment were treated simply as a fatigue detail, then his own career prospects would be tarnished. To make this point he referred to the fate of his commanding officer, Colonel Jones. When, in November 1864, rumors circulated that Paducah was under threat of attack, Jones rushed to headquarters and obtained a promise that if troops were sent from Memphis to defend Paducah, the 68th would be the first to go. An ambitious and competent officer, Jones was keen to become a brigadier general, but knew that a star was much more likely to be won in the heat of battle than by working on a fatigue detail.²⁵ Daniel commented that Jones hated "the idea of being cooped up" in Fort Pickering working as a slave driver."²⁶

Daniel universally despised the frequency and punitive nature of the inspection visits imposed on his regiment.²⁷ He saw them as the culmination of all the injustices imposed on the USCT. Inspecting officers explained the high rate of illness, shoddy clothing, and bumbling drill maneuvers by pointing to alleged weaknesses in the officers' leadership and the inferior quality of the men serving under them. Daniel refused to accept this criticism because he knew these inefficiencies were largely a product of inadequate shelter, a heavy fatigue workload, and the racial prejudice of many officers in the department. On one occasion his regiment was ordered out for inspection on a bitter, windy, Tuesday morning. In stunned silence the men in their dress coats stood for three hours waiting in

Figure 8.1. J. Blackburn Jones. J. Blackburn Jones was appointed colonel of the 68th U. S. Colored Infantry. Jonathan W. White Collection.

line. In the bitterly freezing conditions "the men's hands became so numbed that several dropped their guns in attempting to handle them." In a note of mock self-deprecation, Daniel confessed that "we were disgusted with ourselves, as we had a right to be." Certainly, the inspector "was duly obliged to be disgusted with the pinched up, shivering, dirty nosed, frizzle headed, crowd whose fingers were all thumbs." A few days later another inspection was held. The inspection, which again lasted three hours, consisted of a "green looking Lieut." taking each soldier's gun, giving it a jerk to test the rammer, and then throwing it back to the soldier to catch or cap his knuckles. As the inspecting officer walked down the lines, he uttered a "half audible growl" threatening to have shot or strung up by the thumbs any soldier who had a dirty gun. Such aggressive behavior was not rare in the Union Army. However, Daniel found it particularly offensive because he believed it reinforced prevailing patterns of discrimination toward Black soldiers, and in some degree reproduced the cruel and threatening behavior of the old master.[28]

Although Daniel strongly opposed cruel and unusual punishments being inflicted on his men, he firmly believed that the maintenance of military order was dependent on the imposition of firm and rigorous discipline. Immediately after complaining about the excessive number of inspections imposed on his regiment, he noted, in a casual manner, that the morning inspection on December 16 was to be followed by the public execution of a Black soldier.[29] A week later, he witnessed the execution of Dick Davis, a guerrilla leader. In many ways he believed his Black soldiers were like actors playing roles in a great national tragedy, roles that had to be played out to the bitter end. Public executions were important features of this human drama, for while they pointed to the work of military justice, they also gave the machinery of the military a human dimension by crystallizing, in a moment in time, the human suffering of the war.

Daniel called upon this drama metaphor when he described the execution of Dick Davis. He admitted that it was "hard to see men's lives taken in the cold sullen style of Justice." While from a distance it might appear easy to condemn a man, but when he mounted the scaffold attitudes changed. Then he appeared intensely human, like a friend or neighbor, and in these circumstances, he believed the "the venom against his character oozes out & we see only the man." Yet while the human face of suffering may have moved him, he accepted it as an inevitable part of the conflict. "[D]ead men are a part of the grand play of war," he informed his family. An occasional one seemed quite in place, "an ordinary matter; quite necessary to the occasion."[30]

In his struggle against discrimination Daniel garnered support from friends, fellow officers, and most importantly his family. They endorsed his stand against discrimination and reinforced his views on the role the army could play in elevating the former slaves. The family's main concern, understandably, was Daniel's welfare. They were far more concerned about the way his service was damaging his health, blighting his career prospects, and violating their abolitionist traditions than they were about the suffering of the individual Black soldier. All this is not to suggest that the Densmores had a callous disregard for the men's suffering. They were concerned, but their empathy was moderated by their family relationships and their abolitionist beliefs rather than a comprehensive understanding of the soldiers' plight.

9

"Christmas with us here promises to be quite a season"

Rejoicing and Celebrating

Although the fall and winter of 1864 was a time when Daniel battled for the equitable treatment for his troops, it was also time of celebration and rejoicing. Some of the celebrations had a national significance, marking important military victories and political triumphs. Other celebrations were closely tied to Daniel's regiment and reflected the soldiers' achievements as they passed from slavery into a new age of freedom. Finally, some of the celebrations were traditional, such as the festivities marking Christmas. Celebrations provide a good vehicle to analyze the Densmores' Civil War experience. First, they provide some insight into the shared values and collective experience of the participants. The Densmores rejoiced when they heard news of Union victories on the battlefield because they represented a triumph for their Republican values and abolitionist beliefs. Second, celebrations often involved transition rituals that eased the movement from one state of being to another. For Daniel's soldiers these transition rituals were particularly important because they marked their movement from slavery to freedom. Finally, because celebrations were often held as a reward for goals achieved, studying them helps us comprehend the participants' motivations. Yet all this is not to suggest that all participants celebrated in the same way. Race, class, religion, and antebellum background all shaped the way victories were celebrated and goals acclaimed. Hence, the Christmas celebrations of Daniel's Black soldiers were very different from those he experienced with his fellow white officers.

When Orrin wrote to his serving sons, he often melded his reports of the Union's military progress with political messaging. In September 1864, he wrote to Benjamin conveying the glorious news that Major General Philip H. Sheridan had routed Lieutenant General Jubal A. Early's army in the Shenandoah Valley. This was good news for Orrin, because it marked both a severe reverse for the Confederate Army and a blow against the Democrats who, in his perception, were keen to accept peace on dishonorable terms. He hoped these alleged Northern traitors would get what they deserved, a complete drubbing in the forthcoming presidential election. Conscious of Benjamin's remote location in Kentucky, he felt duty bound to inform him of about the wider progress of the war. By doing so, Orrin hoped to encourage Benjamin by assuring him of the Union's ultimate triumph. Thus, he frequently commented on Union victories, but seldom mentioned Union defeats.[1]

Orrin often melded his reports of the Union's military progress with political messaging. He believed the war to save the Union was being waged on two fronts, on the battlefield and in the political arena. While the main military enemy was in the South, their allies, the traitors who opposed the war, were politically active in the North. Just three weeks after acclaiming Sheridan's victory, he wrote to Daniel bracketing, "cheering political news," about Republican Party victories in Pennsylvania, Ohio, and Indiana, with Sheridan's military advances in the Shenandoah. He expected this news would crush the spirit of the Southern rebels and their Northern supporters and lead them to conclude that their bitter end would "soon to be found in their 'last ditch.'"[2] Later, after describing the defeat of Major General Sterling Price's rebel army in Missouri and the Republican Party's political advances, Orrin again expressed the hope that the rebels in the North and South would surrender in despair.[3]

By describing the war as a seamless military and political conflict, Orrin was also able to portray himself as a combatant, engaged in a political fight at both the local and national levels. As a political combatant, he was more able to freely share his views of the war with his sons. Moreover, his viewpoint had more authority because he was able to discuss both the war and his sons' military service in a political context. The interplay between politics and the military appeared evident when Daniel and Orrin discussed Major General John C. Frémont's role in the war. In September 1864, Daniel wrote home commenting that he felt safe in St. Louis because "Freemont's [sic] forts or 'follies'" provided impassable protection. Then he added as an afterthought that the forts should not be described as "follies," for Frémont comprehended at the beginning the magnitude of the rebellion.[4]

Orrin concurred and in his reply provided a political context. He agreed with Daniel that Frémont had understood the necessity of the war better than any other officer. Then he added that Lincoln's two greatest mistakes were appointing McClellan to command the Army of the Potomac and dismissing Frémont. He believed that in the future these mistakes would be acknowledged, and Frémont's actions would be seen "in their proper light." He supported the appointment of Frémont, antislavery advocate and unsuccessful 1856 Republican Party presidential candidate, as commander of the Department of the West. He also welcomed his declaration of martial law in Missouri and his proclamation freeing the slaves of rebel masters. Because Frémont's proclamation threatened to alienate the Union cause in slaveholding border states such as Kentucky, and because Frémont refused to modify it, Lincoln dismissed him from the Department. But Orrin believed Lincoln's actions pandered to pseudo loyalists in the border states who had only an ambivalent commitment to the Union, undermined the abolitionist cause, and delayed prosecuting hard war against the rebels.[5]

Orrin saw McClellan as Frémont's polar opposite. According to Orrin, McClellan lacked a fighting spirit and was ready to accept dishonorable peace terms. The fact that at the time Orrin penned his letter McClellan was the Democratic Party candidate for the 1864 presidential election would have magnified Lincoln's "mistake" in his eyes. Captivated by the intersection between the world of politics and the military, he prided himself on his ability to apply his knowledge of the political landscape to military developments. Only a few weeks after commenting on political interference in Frémont's downfall, he raised the unwelcome rumor that Senator Charles Sumner was working toward having Major General George Gordon Mead replaced as Commander of the Army of the Potomac by Sheridan. "Sheridan just fits the place he is in . . . why disengage the machinery by the dangerous experiment," he commented.[6]

Lincoln's win in the 1864 presidential election was a time of celebration for the Densmores. On election eve Orrin Jr. wrote to Daniel and predicted Lincoln would take the county, but he feared that the Republicans would lose Red Wing. He found it difficult to understand that so-called enlightened men could support such a "God forsaking crew as McClellan and his retainers." But three days later he wrote joyfully proclaiming the comprehensive electoral victory of Lincoln and the Republican Party at the national and local level. Daniel also welcomed Lincoln's victory, and he noted that in Memphis Lincoln had heavily defeated McClellan. More interested in the military ramifications of Lincoln's victory than anything else, he narrated anecdotal reports that suggested that Lincoln's election victory was encouraging rebel soldiers to contemplate surrender. But then he added that the "South was an extensive country with room for a diversity of opinion—All may not think like them."[7]

Daniel's African American soldiers also shared in the revelry that celebrated Union victories on the battlefield and at the ballot box. But they also celebrated occasions that had a particular relevance to their newly acquired freedom. One such celebration took place in mid-December 1864, when the Black soldiers defeated Memphis's white Union militia in a sword-fighting contest. Daniel described this contest in a letter to his folks with two goals in mind. He wanted to highlight the leadership the officers displayed in the militia's defeat and emphasize the magnitude of the defeat.

In an act of bravado, the local militia had challenged the African American troops to a sword-fighting contest. Although the "militia said they would teach 'them nigger fellows' what's what &c. &c." Daniel was confident that the African American soldiers could "fight on almost any ground." The Black troops made their wager and then proceeded to take up the challenge, causing "Mr. Militia to look black in the face." Although Daniel did not describe how the contest was scored, he rejoiced in the fact that the African American soldiers received the support of General Dana and achieved a decisive victory. In a mood of elation, Daniel was happy to see the militia lose their money and, most important of all, the 68th USCI confounded their critics and performed better than any other Black regiment.[8]

Rich in symbolism, the contest embodied many of the tensions inherent in Black soldiers' service in the Union Army. Drawn from the local region to defend local homes and families, the militia employed the sword, a traditional weapon used to defend Southern honor, in a sporting contest. Although the contest that Daniel described was not a traditional duel, it contained features that shed light on how white Southern racial attitudes were changing in a new age of freedom. Bertram Wyatt-Brown's research has shown that dueling and the defense of honor were intrinsically linked in the communities of the antebellum South. He suggests that dueling was conducted within the rubric of honor and that it enabled the public to recognize a man's claim to honor. Most duels occurred because at least one of the protagonists believed his manliness was being attacked. Dueling also served as a way of venting hidden grievances and feelings. The sword-fighting contest Daniel witnessed was symbolically significant because it demonstrated that white Southerners who were loyal to the Union were prepared to defend the honor of their kin by challenging the Blacks' new status in the South. Yet this challenge was embedded with deep contradictions. According to Southern tradition the white man would not challenge a Black man to a sword fight because a Black man was not his equal and lacked manhood and honor. The fact that the contest took place at all suggests that some Southerners were not only prepared to accept the Black soldiers as men but also to reshape their past cultural practices to find new ways of asserting their claims of white superiority in their state.[9]

This contest was never a simple Black versus white conflict. General Dana supported the African Americans not because he was committed to the abolitionist cause, but because they were his Union soldiers. He saw the Tennessee militia as covert rebels, cotton speculators who used the cover of war to increase their wealth. Daniel also shared this view of the militia and employed rabid, antisemitic stereotyping to condemn them for being "cotton dealing Jews." He believed that these allegedly un-American outsiders appeared to threaten the Union military and the nation's core cultural values. The Black soldiers were different because Daniel believed their experience in the Union Army had made them patriotic. Therefore, they were not fighting for personal gain, but to make the nation a secure home for all its loyal citizens. After the contest had been won, Daniel and his fellow USCT officers ensured that the soldiers' purse of $4,405 dollars was donated directly to the "'Orphans Fair.'" By this unilateral action, they asserted their dominance over their men and made their soldiers' victory over the Memphis militia even more complete.[10]

Some of the celebrations that Daniel attended with his soldiers were more personal. An example of this was a marriage ceremony he attended at Fort Pickering in January 1865. Yet even on this more intimate occasion, the celebration highlighted a significant step the African American soldiers and their wives were making on their march to freedom. Couples living in slavery had long been denied the right to marry and to raise their children in legally binding unions. Because this situation did not make their relationships less meaningful or personally significant, when freedom came, many refugees from slavery had no desire to legally confirm their long-lasting relationships. But others often came before Union chaplains and sought the legal sanction of marriage. The requests of these couples were more than statements of love and personal commitment. For them the marriage certificate, like the military uniform, was also a powerful symbol of their liberated status. Abolitionist officers, such as Daniel Densmore, generally supported their Black soldiers' desire to marry, especially when it did not conflict with their military duties. They saw it as evidence of the Black soldiers' growing manhood and sexual restraint, as well as their desire to establish self-reliant households, a necessary precursor for citizenship. Yet the officers' support for marriage was mediated through their preexisting racial prejudice and social privilege, all of which tore at the marriage union.[11]

Colonel Jones, who was holding the ceremony in his front room, had brought a twenty-cent brass wedding ring for the young couple. When Daniel arrived, the bridal party greeted him, enthusiastically shouting, "'Hurrah, Major, come over!!'" After the "ebony occasion" was over Daniel reflected on its significance, noting that the couple's love for each other was not tarnished by the modest nature of the ceremony. In this respect, "[t]he ring answered just as well as though there had been more brass in it." It was a happy and complete occasion for the couple. But before the newlyweds left the room, the assembled gathering endeavored unsuccessfully to persuade Chaplain A. C. McDonald to kiss the bride. Unable to give a reason for his refusal, the chaplain stood in mock condemnation and in need of correction. "We will have to send him to Missouri to learn that all men are born *free* and *equal*!!" commented Daniel.[12]

At first reading, Daniel's description of the "ebony occasion," appears merely as a prejudiced commentary on a Black soldier's marriage. It was that, and yet it was more than that. Daniel was describing two events that occurred in Colonel Jones's front room. One was the marriage, the other, the challenge issued to the chaplain to kiss the bride. While the first event was mainly, but not exclusively, about personal commitment, the second contained issues with national implications. In his brief description of the marriage ceremony, Daniel highlights the personal devotion of the couple and the paucity of their possessions. A cheap brass ring is used to seal the union. Yet the very simplicity and poverty of the occasion is used to reveal the couple's devotion to one another. They appeared to Daniel oblivious to the racist play and banter inherent in the occasion. Described as caricatures in a comedy, the young couple lack individual identity. When the wedding concluded, Daniel commented, "Pompey departed apparently much delighted with his charcoal-sketched Snowdrop." The use of mock hyperbole is clear here. The soldier is named after the famous Roman general "Pompey" who rivaled Julius Caesar, while his wife to be, "Snowdrop," is given a name that emphasizes the blackness of her complexion.[13]

In his study of humor, Simon Critchley reminds the reader that humor is used to negotiate cultural change by unlocking hidden fears and repressions. Critchley argues that jokes and humorous tales enable individuals to be social anthropologists. Jokes do this by inviting them to speculate on their own lives by becoming spectators in their own world. Jokes encourage them to take a fresh look at the world they take for granted. Jokes and humorous stories pull individuals out of the world of reality to reveal what common sense is. In slave societies, where identity was defined by the presence or absence of freedom, humor played a crucial role in helping individuals fix their place in the world. Mary Beard's research on the humor of the ancient Romans reveals humor acting as a distancing device which helps individuals to authenticate their identity. At Fort Pickering Daniel affirms his identity by writing a letter to his father which confirms his cultural roots by mocking the behavior of the young couple. By employing racist humor, he makes the scene more acceptable both to himself and his father.[14]

Daniel understood he was witnessing history being made. Before the war he had observed slavery's cruel attack on family life and the sanctity of marriage. While working as a schoolteacher in Tennessee, he had been deeply disturbed to discover how a slave sale caused "the destruction of a family circle." During a visit to a plantation, Daniel observed a ritualized slave "marriage" in the dark of the night. There was no joy, laughter, or spontaneous celebration at this ceremony. Indeed, Daniel remarked that the bridal party "seemed enclosed in a globe of darkness." He "could not help thinking how soon the auctioneer's hammer might crush" the hope of building a shared life together.[15]

Almost five years later he was again in Tennessee, but the African American marriage he witnessed was very different. It was performed during the day by an agent of the government and was legally binding. It was an open, public occasion, a celebration of personal commitment. The implications of citizenship and racial equality are clear. This is the challenge issued to the chaplain, to act out the spirit of the marriage law that treated Black and white participants the same. We will never know the real reason Chaplain McDonald refused to kiss the new bride. Perhaps he just never wanted to be seen publicly kissing a Black woman. But Daniel seizes upon this refusal to lightheartedly accuse him of hypocrisy for not accepting the young bride's liberated status. According to Daniel, as a USCT chaplain committed to destroying slavery, he did not practice what he was preaching. Therefore, he needs to go to Missouri, the heartland of John Brown's antislavery struggle, and learn the deep meaning of the abolitionist creed. But Daniel needs to learn this lesson too. By highlighting the chaplain's alleged hypocrisy, he and the others present were masking their own racial fears and prejudices.

With the memories of family Christmases filling his mind, Daniel picked up his pen on Christmas day and wrote to his family. In the opening lines of his letter, he dealt with his deep sense of absence by pretending to be following the social ritual of declining an invitation to his family's Christmas dinner. In his mind's eye he could see the family home with its Christmas decorations and heavily laden table. Christmas 1864 was indeed a time to celebrate because Daniel thought peace was coming, and order was now being restored. "Christmas with us here promises to be quite a season," he exclaimed. He then explained that he had promised to sit at the table of Mrs. Jones, his colonel's wife. Then in a cryptic comment he concluded, "At another time, if you please." Underlying the playful, mock formality of Daniel's rejection is his belief that commitment to duty involved sacrifice. Offered two tables to choose from, he turns away from the family table to sup at the table of Mrs. Jones. The allegorical meaning here is clear. In time of war, national duty takes preference over domestic desires. Daniel would join the family table "at another time," a time of victorious peace.¹⁶

The Densmore family well understood Daniel's resolve. A few days after Christmas had been celebrated, young Orrin wrote to his brother and detailed all the rituals of the family's celebrations. On Christmas Eve all the family's presents were spread on the table. At the invitation of Belle Webster, dressed as Saint Nickolas, each person went forward and received the gifts. Orrin Jr. received a lucrative load, including neckties, slippers, a photograph, and a gold watch key. He noted, "It was a jolly time and only lacked 'the boys.'" He did not dwell on the notable, painful absence of his two older brothers. Instead, he simply commented that "'when Johnny comes marching home,'" there would be Christmas and New Year celebrations "to eclipse all."¹⁷

Although Daniel missed his family, he was intrigued by the Christmas celebrations of his men. To aid these celebrations Brigadier General Augustus L. Chetlain reduced fatigue details and gave each company six daily passes instead of two. Daniel strongly endorsed these measures, for he believed the celebrations would significantly restore the men's health. After casually observing their festivities, he discovered that music was at the heart of their celebrations. When his regiment was finally paid, the musicians brought new fiddles and from sunset to taps the music and dancing never stopped. But formal festivities began on Christmas Eve. They opened with a fine serenade from the band of the 3rd United States Colored Heavy Artillery. This large twenty-four-member band, fully equipped with German instruments, was the proud creation of Colonel Kappner. Daniel appreciated the band's accomplished performance and noted that they played well, "with more than ordinary taste." Then after being plied with beer and apples, they played another tune and moved to another post.¹⁸

After the band moved on, Daniel took the opportunity to move around the men's quarters and observe their informal celebrations. The men were in a jovial mood. Although tired from digging hard all day, a half ration of whiskey and the extension of tattoo until 10:30 p.m. enthused them. What intrigued him most about the celebrations was their emotional exuberance, which he considered had an African quality. The Black revelers seemed to be lost in their own private world, a world that was all absorbing, in some ways graceful, but distinctly different from that of white folks. As he moved from room to room, he noticed a "full orchestra in rapid blast." The soldiers appeared to be at one with the beat of the music. Their "heads were vibrating with an easy, graceful rise and fall," and they appeared to follow the tune much better than white Americans. Like many officers serving in the USCT, Daniel believed that the soldiers' music allegedly affirmed, in a most powerful way, a popular racial stereotype that depicted African Americans as simple people who were governed by their emotional enthusiasm and sense of rhythm.[19]

Daniel was fascinated by the women who had joined the men in their celebration, because their presence underscored the cultural distinctiveness of the festivities. Unlike the white women, these Black women were not following the conventional lead of their male dancing partners. They were driven on by the beat of the music. Daniel saw one woman dancing and observed that "Dinah's head trembled with the rest as she cut the pigeon wing." She became even more frenetic as her father, Sam the musician, who played the bones urged her on with shouts of "golly." To describe the compelling dynamism of the occasion, Daniel again employed racial stereotyping. The woman is given the pejorative generic epithet "Dinah," and she is described performing a slave dance, "the pigeon wing," with robust sexual energy. According to Daniel this dance, which involved waving arms and scraping feet like a pigeon, encapsulated the fervor of the occasion. But finally, as the evening ended, the military world asserted its ascendancy and at 10:30 p.m. tattoo sounded. Then "three strokes on the drum after tattoo left the world to silence & Santa Claus."[20]

The Christmas celebrations of the Black soldiers enabled Daniel to gain insight into the inner world of his men, whose private lives often remained a mystery. On Christmas Eve 1864, he had an opportunity to see his men creating their own world of entertainment. Enslaved African Americans possessed an expressive culture of movement and sound. It was not a written culture. To understand its rich texture, one had to witness the performance and listen to the music. Daniel did this, but the knowledge he gained and shared with his folks at home was infused with his preexisting racial prejudice. The men's celebrations fascinated him primarily because they appeared so alien and primitive. But more importantly, they appeared to confirm his belief that, when they were not subject to white control, African Americans were naturally governed by their emotions. For Daniel nothing more powerfully symbolized this than the dancing he observed. The contrast between the music the men created in their quarters and the military precision of the performance of the 3rd United States Colored Heavy Artillery band was clear. At the close of the evening, military order was restored by the sound of the tattoo, but Daniel believed that old slave ways were not so easily driven away.

When Daniel woke on Christmas morning, he was greeted by a sergeant who called to wish him and his fellow officer, Dr. Andrews, a merry Christmas. In addition to these compliments, the sergeant sought to "claim a Christmas gift,—as per plantation custom." But both Daniel and Dr. Andrews were immediately aware that they were being asked to act as slaveholders. Dr. Andrews, with mock astonishment, sat up right in his bunk and asked whether Daniel liked being addressed as a slave driver. Daniel responded, "How are you, ole boss!'" Suspicious that they were being duped, and aware that masters employed Christmas gift giving to reinforce the slaves' abject status, they devised a plan to teach the sergeant a lesson. Eventually the sergeant departed after being guaranteed a dram, which Andrews promised Daniel "in an undertone, should be eight parts of water and two parts of *water*." Both believed that the plantation owners' festive rituals had no place in a Union Army camp.[21]

Mrs. Jones prepared a sumptuous Christmas dinner for the officers, which even rivaled dinner at home. "Hope your turkey was as jolly, hope you had as good onions and cranberry sauce—& cream pie with as merry a vanguard of oysters," Daniel boasted. The only feature of the dinner that disappointed him was the absence of his good friend, Dr. Andrews, who remained in his quarters with bad lungs. After dinner Daniel returned to his quarters and was pleasantly surprised to find that his friend had not missed his Christmas meal. Mrs. Jones, "the kindest hearted woman in the world,'" had remembered him and had quietly sent a meal to him. Personally indebted to Mrs. Jones and influenced by the prevailing gender roles that attributed to women the ability to make the domestic environment a haven for men, Daniel praised Mrs. Jones's kind act. He assured his parents that Mrs. Jones was making the harsh, military environment more homely and Christmas a most enjoyable occasion. "She is one who loves the chirping of the cricket on the hearth," he concluded. Orrin Jr. also appreciated Mrs. Jones's presence. When he wrote to Daniel in December, he informed him that he was very pleased to learn that "Mrs. Jones is there to smooth over by way of giving a good breakfast."[22]

Daniel enjoyed the camaraderie of his fellow officers. While a racial and social divide separated him from his soldiers, he considered the officers a substitute family. These feelings appeared most noticeably when, on New Year's Day, the officers presented Colonel Jones with the gift of a sword, belt, and gauntlets, as a token of their appreciation of his leadership. A special dinner was held to mark the occasion. Daniel observed that except for his rival, Lieutenant Colonel James H. Clendening, who was facing court-martial charges, "the officers of this regiment might be styled a happy family." Among the officers a "mutual manly courtesy" existed, and in this collaborative environment, Colonel Jones acted as a wise counselor and guardian. In contrast, Daniel considered Clendening a corrupting cancer and therefore strongly supported the colonel's efforts to have him court-martialed.²³ The ubiquitous "Hungarian influence" appeared equally disruptive to the harmonious spirit of the regiment. The strong bonds of comradeship that Daniel forged with Colonel Jones were built, at least partially, on their mutual opposition to Colonel Kappner's rule at Fort Pickering. Only a few weeks after the New Year's Day celebration, Kappner severely reprimanded Jones for failing to submit monthly reports, neglecting the welfare of prisoners, and failing to supervise guard duty. Jones's fighting response, which demanded Kappner "shut up his gibberish, or he would know who was the best man then and there," earned Daniel's admiration. ²⁴

As 1865 began, Daniel looked back at the conclusion of the previous year with mixed feelings. While the discriminatory practices of military authorities in Memphis caused him considerable grief, he had received letters from the family that encouraged him and helped keep him in the service. In this regard, Orrin's letters were particularly important, for his advice went much deeper than normal paternal affection and addressed the unique challenges he faced as an officer in the USCT. Orrin helped both his serving sons develop a philosophical rationale for their service in Black regiments. They had good reasons for serving because pay, promotion, and career opportunities were powerful personal incentives. But by the end of 1864 their military careers had begun to stagnate in the military backwaters of Fort Halleck and Fort Pickering. It was then that Orrin called upon the loftier notions of national patriotism and devotion to the abolitionist cause to sustain them. These motives had always been there, but during times of difficulty they enabled the brothers to portray their service as patriotic sacrifice. Certainly, Orrin viewed Daniel's military service from this perspective when he wrote to him on New Year's Day, 1865.

Orrin commented on how pleased he was to find Daniel in good health and experiencing the "reasonable enjoyment of Soldiers life mixed with its vicissitudes." After congratulating him on his new quarters, he encouraged him to remain in public service. Orrin saw Daniel as a public servant working for the public good by building a more complete Union, and he urged him to remain in his regiment. Although he was serving in a quiet post, it was beneficial to Black soldiers who served under him. He admitted that while commanding Black troops was "perhaps a thankless service," it was nationally important, because it would "aid in the elevation of the blacks—to a capacity they might not have attained in civilian life among the 'chivalry.'" Since he believed Southern society was inherently corrupt, he had no faith in its redemptive powers.²⁵

As a political combatant, Orrin had enjoyed sharing with Daniel his views about the elevation of the former slaves, the triumphs of the Republican Party in the North, and the victories of Union forces in the South. But a notable omission in the correspondence was his lack of engagement with the African American way of life. Orrin made little comment on Daniel's descriptions of slave culture. Perhaps this was because Daniel's descriptions were not controversial but largely endorsed the family's negative views about African Americans. When Orrin did make comments, they were made with reference to slaves making their transition to freedom. This may have been because Daniel, Benjamin, and other USCT officers were considered the architects of this empowering and elevating process. For Daniel, the victory over the Memphis militia, the musical performance of the band of the 3rd United States Colored Heavy Artillery, and even the Black soldier's wedding were all victory markers on the soldiers' progressive journey. But the road he saw them traveling on led to freedom, not equality.

As the year ended, Daniel found time to celebrate in the officers' mess. There amid his "military family" the bonds of comradeship eased the pain of separation and loneliness. But even during the Christmas revelry, some were not welcome. Excluded from the commissioned ranks, Black soldiers could serve the meal, but not partake of it. Lieutenant Colonel Clendening was not invited because he lacked honor, and Colonel Kappner could not find a seat because he had the wrong military traditions and ethnic background. Before celebrations could begin, values had to be shared.

10

"She walks off with the work"

Service and Friendship: Elizabeth, Mary, and Martha

While Daniel was busy serving at Fort Pickering and celebrating Union victories and Christmas, back in Red Wing the pattern of his family's life was being disrupted by the presence of Mary Priest, an African American servant he had sent to the family in the fall of 1864. Chapter 10 examines Mary's work in the Densmores' home, and how she asserted her independence and acquired new skills. It also discusses the way Mary challenged the family's ideas about African Americans and influenced the social dynamics of the household.

The absence of a personal record has made it difficult to compile a historical narrative of Mary's service in the Densmore household. The reader will never know what Mary thought about being emancipated, traveling north to freedom, or serving in the Densmore house. In part, the mystery that surrounds her was a product of her initial illiteracy, the nature of her flight to freedom, and her low status within the Densmore household. Yet even though she left no written account of her experiences, her presence was far more significant than her position would suggest. Mary challenged the family's racial beliefs and was a constant reminder that Benjamin and Daniel were fighting a war against slavery. In many ways she became a representative of the African American race, and her employment by the family, an experiment that could validate or discredit the emancipation process and indirectly the brothers' war service. After all, they had been heavily involved in selecting the very best servant for service in the family's home.

Like that of many former domestic slaves, Mary's employment was influenced by her service within the slave owner's household. Historians who have studied the role of female slaves in the plantation household have long recognized their struggle to resist oppression and win for themselves degrees of independence. The destruction of slavery during the Civil War changed the power relationships between the former slave owners and their freed slaves. In this new age of freedom, those who had been enslaved, such as Mary, defined their freedom on their own terms. This involved negotiating labor contracts, hours of work, and exercising the right to social and financial independence. In short, they claimed all the rights of a free employee.[1]

It is impossible to determine exactly how Mary's service in the Densmores' home was influenced by her experience of slavery, simply because we know nothing about her former master or mistress, or the regime under which she was held. Nor can we speak with any certainty about her immediate post-emancipation experiences as a domestic employee. Even so, Mary's record of service with the Densmores indicates that she had a strong sense of self and a commitment to assert her rights to freedom, privacy, and independence. Elizabeth Densmore and Martha Densmore were not the plantation mistress and daughter in a different guise. Yet these two women, and indeed all members of the Densmore family, called upon the privileges of race and class, and the rituals of deference and condescension, to manipulate Mary's employment. The fact that Mary not only resisted these claims on her service but also challenged members of this abolitionist family to reconsider their negative attitudes to African Americans is testimony to her strength of character and to the resilient spirit she acquired during her time as a slave, as a freed woman in Hannibal, Missouri, and as a household servant in the Densmore home.

We learn of Mary's service by reading extracts from letters that different family members wrote, principally to Benjamin and Daniel, but also to friends and wider family members. These reports, which are generally only a few lines in length, appear intermittently in the correspondence. Although they provide a view of Mary's service over time from several different perspectives, they need to be read carefully. The language used and the personal portraits drawn in the text were influenced not only by prevailing racial stereotypes but also by more immediate family expectations and aspirations associated with Mary's role. One must read the letters with these nuances in mind to understand how the war changed Mary and Mary changed the social dynamics of the Densmore family home. Mary's housework then enables us to understand the meaning of emancipation from several competing and contrasting perspectives grounded in personal, family, and community experience.

A veil of mystery appeared to surround the stranger who entered the Densmore household in August 1864. Mary's arrival at the Densmore family home in mid-August 1864 was the source of great anxiety. However, within a week of her arrival all the tensions that surrounded the "Shady question" and the employment of Black labor appeared to have dissipated. Orrin was particularly pleased that his persistence had been so richly rewarded. He proudly commented that

Elizabeth found Mary satisfactory and that other Red Wing housekeepers were envious of her Black servant. Yet the excitement associated with the arrival of Mary masked several complexities and latent fears that were to influence her continued employment.[2] Uncertain about the outcome, and keen to avoid being labeled as quasi slaveholders or fanatical abolitionists, the Densmores looked upon the employment of Mary as an "experiment." The fact that Mary's complexion was viewed as being almost white added complexity to her relationship with them by blurring the boundaries between race and social status.[3]

Mary's place in the household was significantly influenced by Elizabeth Densmore's attitudes and practices. The kitchen was her domain, and Mary had to find her allotted place in it. Mary's own personality, along with her preferences and attitudes, also significantly influenced the relationships she developed with others. While her capacity for productive work won her the praise of the family, her independent spirit and her work habits, which bore some of the alleged marks of slavery, evoked some criticism and rebuke. The Densmores were not her first employers, and Red Wing was not her first location for freedom. Yet even though Orrin knew that Mary had sustained herself in a state of freedom and had negotiated her wages with a previous employer, he continued to view her as an ignorant fugitive seeking immediate refuge from the tyranny of slavery.[4]

Shortly after Mary arrived, barriers were raised that threatened her continued employment. Her employment was not an act of charity on Orrin's part. On the contrary, his approach was coldly pragmatic. He was seeking a cheap "pair of hands" that would ease the burden of his wife's labor. He was not interested in Mary as a person. Yet even though he was keen to get her conditions of employment settled, he remained uncertain about her prospects. In August he informed Daniel that Mary could leave because she was concerned that there were very few African Americans in the neighborhood. Although there were some living in the vicinity of Red Wing, they were too few to form a community. Sensitive to the privileges of class and race, Orrin never wanted Mary to establish a personal friendship with members of his family.[5]

Mary's reluctance to accept a low wage was another serious impediment to her employment. Described by young Orrin as being "short, fat, white," Mary belied her diminutive stature by doggedly negotiating her terms of employment. Her previous employer had given her two dollars a week, but Orrin, at the insistence of Elizabeth, proposed only one dollar fifty cents a week. In addition, he also sought to recoup the twenty cents he advanced for her fare to Red Wing. He justified the lower wage on the grounds that at Mary's previous place of employment she had "no chance for learning to read as she is having here." The significant wage

Figure 10.1. Elizabeth Fowle Densmore, circa 1865. Minnesota Historical Society.

differential that existed between Mary and her predecessor, the Swede, Louisa Johnson, pointed to Mary's vulnerable situation and the determination of Elizabeth to privilege white labor. Although Elizabeth resented that fact that a Black worker replaced her white housekeeper, she took some comfort in the knowledge that Mary's wage was much lower than the wage Louisa had been paid. In the summer season Louisa had been paid twelve dollars a week.[6]

While Elizabeth's negative attitude to Black labor was influenced by the prevailing climate of racial prejudice in Minnesota, her family history gave her viewpoint more potency. In 1839 Elizabeth's father, Benjamin Fowle, appears to have employed a free African American, or runaway slave, Henry, on his farm in Michigan. Cruelly treated, Henry fled his employer and returned home to Missouri. Upon his return, Henry's sister, Betsy Ann Brockaway, wrote to Mr. Fowle, protesting about her brother's treatment. In defense of the family, "E. D." [Elizabeth Densmore] replied to Betsy's letter, accusing her of being a troublemaker and exaggerating her brother's injury and illness. This family background suggests that Elizabeth's opposition to Mary was more complex than a simple racist response to the employment of Black labor. By opposing Mary, she may have been endeavoring to honor her father's memory.[7]

Because Orrin believed his marriage was a partnership and because he took an active interest in domestic affairs, he wrote to Daniel informing him of Mary's proposed conditions of employment and expressing the hope that an arrangement could be achieved that would suit both the family and Mary. Yet he was also aware that Elizabeth's cooperation and support had yet to be won. He knew that since she jealously guarded her housekeeping duties, she would be reluctant to surrender all the work "to the care of the girl." Further, aware of his wife's critical outlook, he knew that she feared her well-established practices of kitchen management would be replaced, and wasteful expenditures introduced.[8]

Orrin's letter brought an immediate response from Daniel. He advised his father to give Mary two dollars per week rather than lose her, and he assured his mother that a permanent servant was "a great comfort worth fully 50 cents per week," if not to herself, then to the rest of the family who were keen to see a Black servant employed. He even offered to supplement Mary's wage by fifty cents a week from his own funds. Daniel's personal commitment reflected the love he had for his mother, but it was also an attempt to maintain his authority in the household. In his study of Civil War soldiers James McPherson has revealed that men were troubled by their inability to personally fulfill their duties by directly caring for and protecting their families at home. Located deep in the Confederacy, Daniel felt unable to afford his mother the protection and support she deserved. Through the agency of Mary, he could go part of the way to doing this. All family members knew that Mary's presence in the home was the product of Daniel's diligent efforts. When Martha wrote to Daniel, she recorded Margaret's glowing accounts of Mary's service and expressed an ardent desire to have her stay. She commented that such an outcome would benefit the family and reward Daniel for his "untiring perseverance in securing her."[9]

In her letter Martha narrated Margaret's description of Mary's work habits by saying, "she walks off with the work." This pithy epithet was a fair summary of the family's attitude, for as a group they were generally amazed by Mary's capacity for work. From the moment she arrived, Mary labored hard at a considerable number of tasks, including house cleaning, gardening, cooking, and caring for the animals.[10] Yet it was not just the volume of work that pleased the Densmores, particular family members had specific reasons for rejoicing in her labor. Orrin, for example, was greatly pleased to discover that Mary knew how to milk a cow. This meant that he was relieved from having to perform that chore. When news of Mary's hard labor reached Daniel in Memphis, he felt the satisfaction of knowing that he was protecting his mother from hard labor in the kitchen.[11]

Mary's hard work brought with it advantages that extended beyond the family's home. Her labor made the Densmores the envy of their neighbors and friends. A few weeks after her arrival Orrin Jr. commented to Daniel that the neighbors were inquiring if the family could arrange "'contraband help'" for them. He believed that Mary's labor had given "housewives all around the wench fever." Anna McLaren, a close friend of Martha's, also noted Martha's good fortune. "I suppose you are in clover now since you have the house to your mind & a contraband to take care of it," she commented.[12]

The Densmores' praise for Mary derived from the benefits they gained from her labor, but it also reflected their deeply rooted ideological beliefs. Based on their strong antislavery convictions, the family believed that the institution of slavery had so corrupted the African American race that Black labor remained significantly inferior to white labor. They did not understand that many slaves who worked slowly or indifferently were adopting a resistance strategy against their masters' tyranny. Therefore, even before Mary arrived, they had very low expectations about her performance. These negative perceptions derived from a variety of sources. In part they formed from the negative African American stereotypes that pervaded Northern society before the war. They were also the product of the early negative assessments of Black troops that Daniel and Benjamin made during the initial stages of their service in the USCT. Even though these faded once they became more accustomed to commanding Black troops and witnessing their soldiers fighting tenaciously in battle, they helped to set unfavorable preconditions for Mary's arrival.[13] Against this negative background, Mary's achievements shone so brightly that they challenged the Densmores' racist perceptions of the docility and irrationality of African Americans. This was particularly the case because the Densmores were deeply committed to public education and school teaching, and believed they were well placed to assess the educational and moral progress of their servant. [14]

Approximately two months after she had arrived at the Densmores' house, Martha wrote to Daniel informing him that Mary "appears interested in the work, & does remarkably well for one who has been a slave." Mary's work ethic also impressed Orrin Jr. who believed he was well placed to judge the merits of Black labor. While visiting his brothers in Kentucky and Tennessee, he made a special effort to study the impact of slavery on African Americans. In late August 1864 he wrote home to his mother expressing only a faint hope that the former slave woman she was about to employ would be a good worker. Writing from Columbus, Kentucky, "where the institution has reigned," he did not "see how anyone could get a decent woman," and was certain that he could not find one. When he returned home, he used the insights he had gained to assess the quality of Mary's work and was surprised to discover she was an excellent worker. "As far as I have been able to judge Mary is a trump and likely to stay so," he wrote to Daniel. Yet his enthusiastic endorsement of Mary's labor did not signify a revolution in his racial attitudes. [15]

A little over a week after he described Mary as a "trump," he again wrote to Daniel and waxed eloquently about her cooking. He believed Mary's pancakes were glorious and knew Daniel would delight in her cooking. Characterizing himself as "Massa Densmore," he described Mary as being fat, jolly, contented, and eager to please. Orrin Jr.'s fanciful depiction of himself as the contented slaveholder and Mary the contented slave mammy pointed to what he believed was her happy, amenable service and menial status. According to Orrin Jr. service was Mary's natural station in life; lacking self-direction and self-reliance, she had become "one of the institutions of the family." Compliance was not Mary's only alleged virtue. Orrin Jr. observed that she was morally upright; there was "nothing to show any *wench characteristics* about her." Given her upright character, which was matched only by her willingness to faithfully serve, Orrin Jr. concluded that "[m]other and father like her well."[16]

Even though Orrin was very pleased with Mary's work, he took special delight in identifying her faults because he believed they demonstrated the essential inferiority of Black labor, and like Orrin Jr., he called upon class attitudes and racist stereotyping to describe Mary's character. In Orrin Sr.'s case he mixed commendations of Mary's good works with subtle references to alleged character defects supposed to plague African Americans. For example, when writing to Daniel he praised Mary for being "the first one up" and milking the family's two cows and caring for the horses, but he also claimed she was crude and uncouth. Yet despite this alleged character flaw, Orrin was hopeful that she would prove to be a very useful worker. "[S]he may prove coarse but fully meets our expectation and we hope will meet our wants" was his comment.[17]

In mid-October 1864, Orrin again wrote to Daniel that while Mary administered "the kitchen cabinet matters" satisfactorily, she was far too impulsive. To prove his point, he cited an incident that had occurred in the vicinity of Cogels Mill. To water Daniel's horse, Tink, Mary drove him into the Mississippi River near a place that proved to be a quagmire. While struggling to escape from the swamp, the horse harness was cut and Tink lamed. Although Tink fully recovered from his wound, Mary emerged from the swamp allegedly chastened by her experience.[18] Orrin welcomed this outcome, for he informed Daniel in a judgmental tone that "the contraband" was now "too wise to drive again into the marshy margin of the Mississippi." He believed that the incident had taught Mary the important lesson that the habits of slavery, so evident in her allegedly impulsive behavior, had no place in the Densmore household.[19]

While various members of the family proffered moral advice to Mary, by far her most important mentor was not a member of the household. Captain William Poillon took a keen interest in Mary's welfare right from the moment he sent her on her journey to Red Wing. Shortly after she arrived at the Densmores' house, Daniel wrote to his family urging them to relay information on Mary's progress to Captain Poillon, who was languishing in the Officer's Hospital in Memphis. Daniel informed his family that Poillon was "very much interested in getting her sent north," to "show the people what manner of persons are brought under the thrall of the institution of slavery." He believed that since Mary was almost white, she would be a most powerful presentation of the barbaric nature of slavery. In Mary's case the alleged degradation caused by slavery could not be explained simply by pointing to her African racial character. Even those who were nearly white could suffer degradation too. Mary's white complexion may well have also challenged Captain Poillon's belief in the superiority of the white race. From this perspective, his efforts to educate and elevate her may have been motivated by a desire to ensure her behavior suited her physical appearance, and not her slave heritage. [20]

Captain Poillon was very pleased to learn that Mary was making steady progress. Yet Poillon's concept of elevation involved more than simple self-improvement. Essentially, he wanted complete acculturation. As Daniel explained to his family, Captain Poillon was desirous that Mary "break away from her African lineage and raising, and start off a white folk." In order to advance this transition, and act as her mentor, he wrote a letter of advice that was well received by Mary. "She has a high regard for Capt. Poillon & his opinion," commented Martha in a letter to Daniel. Proud of her educational progress, she informed Martha that she would send Captain Poillon "a specimen of her writing."[21] While it is difficult to ascertain the nature of the relationship that existed between Mary and her mentor, there is no doubt that a form of warm affection existed between them which crossed racial boundaries. Yet this friendship was probably based on Mary's sense of personal accomplishment and gratitude, rather than romantic attachment. Mary appreciated Poillon's advice and was keen to demonstrate her educational progress.

For his part, Captain Poillon was less interested in Mary as a person than in her as representative of her race, worthy of reform and elevation. He felt duty bound by his abolitionist beliefs and his belief in white superiority, to raise her up from slavery. "Capt. Poillon was amazed when I told him of Mary's attainments, and wished me to thank you all on his behalf for what you have done for him," Daniel commented to his parents. Because Poillon saw Mary's progress as a personal extension of his own antislavery campaign, he asked the Densmores to retain her in their service and to patiently tolerate her imperfections. To keep Mary at the family home, Daniel passed on to his parents the knowledge both he and Captain Poillon had learned from training Black soldiers. Daniel told them not to ignore Mary's mistakes but to correct her, issuing instructions in a plain, straightforward manner.[22]

Mary developed a close relationship with Martha. Even though this relationship was framed by class and racial differences and governed by the complexities of employer-employee connections, it was closer than any other relationship that Mary had in the household. This situation may have developed because Elizabeth's coldness and overt hostility may have pushed Mary toward Martha. But the closeness may also have developed because Martha took an active interest in Mary's personal development. She endeavored to become her moral guardian and mentor. She believed that Mary's employment placed her in a socially isolated position. In November 1864, she informed Daniel that Mary had often spoken about "being lonesome" and that Mary believed that once she had learned to read this feeling would disappear. To encourage her, Martha spent a considerable amount of time reading and rereading Captain Poillon's advice-laden letters to her. Although she was very pleased that Mary was "really persevering in her efforts to read & write," she believed her progress was ultimately dependent on her sound teaching and guidance. "[W]ith proper encouragement she will be *successful*" was the confident prediction she made to Daniel[23]

In her efforts to portray herself as Mary's guardian and protector, Martha exaggerated Mary's devotion and dependency. She portrayed Mary as a social isolate, a lonely soul who was unwilling to tolerate "colored company," which had infrequently visited her. Yet comments made by Orrin Jr. in a letter three weeks earlier tell a different story. Orrin Jr. noted that Mary attended church and implied that she had little time for the two "negro boys," Jasper and Jim, who called courting her. When bedtime came, they had to immediately leave. Mary was a resourceful and independently minded young woman. If she did have a restless spirit, it was the product of her homesickness and not her alleged dependency on Martha or the legacy of her slave heritage. In fact, Martha admitted as much when she wrote to Daniel in May 1865. "I shall try hard to keep her," but then added "but she says she is growing anxious to see her Father & Mother & would like to go to them next Fall."[24]

Martha tried to keep Mary in her service partly because she was a diligent worker. Yet there were other more personal reasons why Martha wanted Mary to stay. Over time a friendship formed between the two young women. Put simply, Martha enjoyed Mary's companionship. The fact that this relationship was different from that which existed between Martha and Anna McLaren did not mean that it was insignificant. Martha's friendship with Anna was built on family ties, class connections, and shared cultural interests. Martha's relationship with Mary was different, not simply because the connections between class, race, and family were absent, but also because it was more visible and immediate. Mary was there, in the household. In contrast, Martha's dear friend Anna was isolated in Fort Snelling. Even though Martha never treated Mary as an equal or her "dear friend," she enjoyed her company. It is difficult to find evidence of these personal and private moments mainly because most the letters she wrote that contained snippets about Mary were written to Daniel. In this correspondence, Martha attempts to justify Daniel's procurement of Mary by focusing on describing her labor and service to the family.

On one occasion when Martha wrote to her mother about dresses and fashion, she included passing references to Mary that were more personal. She informed her that Margaret had assisted her by trimming her new hat and repairing her old black hat, and "making it look like new." Pleased with her new hat, Martha gave Mary the black hat. Elements of racial paternalism may have been present, since Mary received Martha's old hat, but they were not dominant. While the swapping of hats does not indicate a reversal of roles, it does indicate, that on some occasions class and racial lines could bend when cultural values were shared. Even though Mary received Martha's discarded hat, she was an integral member of the clothing exchange. "So the *hat* question is finally settled" was Martha's concluding remark. At one level Mary could almost be considered a member of the family. Certainly, Martha suggested this when she wrote to Daniel while Orrin and Elizabeth were on their Southern tour. "At present our family is scarcely large enough to deserve the *name*,—only Orrin & myself, besides Mary—Margaret & Gilman are down often to see us," she commented.[25] Like a benevolent employer, Martha considered her servant Mary as part of the household. But even though she appreciated Mary's work, considerations of race, class, and kinship meant that she treated her as a valued servant and loyal companion, but nothing more.

Although Mary fulfilled the primary role of domestic servant, family members related to her in diverse ways. For Orrin, issues relating to her conditions of employment were of primary importance. Elizabeth's relationship with Mary was fraught with difficulty because she saw her as a usurper who threatened her organization of the kitchen and management of domestic affairs. Martha's relationship with Mary was far more positive, and it had a much larger social component. Because Mary was her student and companion, they spent a long time together during Mary's off-duty hours. The contingencies of war meant that Daniel's relationship with Mary was far more distant. Mary was his agent in the house, placed there to ease the work burden on his frail mother. Finally, Orrin Jr. looked upon Mary as a contented, compliant servant and outstanding cook. Yet even though these relationships were expressed differently, all family members believed that slavery was at the core of Mary's identity. Therefore, their dealings with her were built on a desire to exercise power over her so they could control her work and shape her identity. The nomenclature the family used in their correspondence to name and describe Mary clearly points to a differential in power relationships. Some of the names Mary was called included "the contraband," "contraband help," "Dinah," "help," "a subject," "a pair of hands," "the girl," a "trump," and "the institution," and these names reveal the family's sense of superiority, possession, and entitlement. Mary was their "contraband," a prize of war, taken from the seditious Southern slaveholders.[26]

The names given to Mary also functioned as a distancing device, reminding Mary of her place within the family. By "labeling" Mary in this way, the family members reinforced their belief that she was an inferior outsider. Although this nomenclature was based on race, it had a wider function. The Densmores referred to their white domestic worker, Louisa Johnson, as "our Swede," to keep her in her place. Over time, as the family got to know Mary and became impressed with her service, the use of her first name became more frequent. Sometimes Mary was spoken about using terms of affection. For example, when Martha wrote to

Daniel in late November 1864 she referred to "Our Mary." Yet this term of endearment was implicitly associated with the idea of ownership. As late as April 1865, Daniel was still referring to Mary as a "stronger pair of hands." While the Densmores were not her new masters, in their role as her employer they endeavored to control and objectify her. Mary resisted these efforts partly by drawing on her experience of slavery. Perhaps this explains why she adopted the slave survival strategy of hiding elements of her identity. After she had consolidated her position, and three months after she had joined the household, she revealed her true surname, McElroy, but then only to Martha, her companion and teacher. Mary McElroy had her own life, and she wanted to keep parts of it private and free from the family's interference. [27]

11

"Do come up Martha"

Anna and Martha

Although Mary's friendship was important to Martha, her dearest friend was her cousin Anna McLaren, who was the wife of Colonel Robert N. McLaren, the commander of Fort Snelling. Chapter 11 discusses the way this friendship evolved to meet the challenges of the war and how the two friends successfully changed their homes. While Anna changed the social environment of her living quarters, Martha renovated the physical fabric of her home. Although none of Martha's letters to Anna have survived, Anna's letters to Martha provide a penetrating insight into Martha's war effort from a different perspective. They enable us to see how both Anna and Martha met the challenges arising from home environments that were radically changed by the Civil War.[1]

During the Civil War, small numbers of women lived on a semi-permanent basis in Northern army posts and camps. In these military locations, washerwomen, nurses, aid workers, and officers' wives formed the largest group. Women who lived in military posts faced a particularly difficult set of circumstances. Some men welcomed their presence because it reminded them of the finer elements of civilized living and of their loved ones and sweethearts at home. But many others resented the female presence, believing the rough military was no place for a woman and that their presence undermined their masculinity.[2] A vivacious young mother with two children, Archie and Jamie, Anna found her husband's military post inhospitable and secluded. Daniel noted her loneliness when he was stationed at the fort in early December 1863, commenting that "there are only three officers' ladies present making a rather lonely, quiet season for Anna who seemed to enjoy last winter hugely."[3] To some extent Anna's loneliness was ameliorated by Fort Snelling's location close to the state capital, St. Paul. This meant that she was occasionally able to visit St. Paul for shopping and to attend concerts. Even so, she felt very much alone with her husband often absent on long campaigns against the Dakota. Her difficulties were compounded by the fact that Robert seldom corresponded with her while he was on campaigns. While Daniel and Benjamin were campaigning against the Dakota, Orrin wrote to them urging them to encourage McLaren to write home. His young wife pined for his letters. "Give him our good wishes & tell him he must report oftener" was

Figure 11.1. Col. Robert Neil McLaren, 2nd Minnesota Cavalry, circa 1864. Minnesota Historical Society.

Orrin's request. Then in jest he commented that a failure to write would mean that "we shall court martial him or send him to the Po-to-mac where great men are expected to do but little and that with extreme moderation." [4]

The friendship between Martha and her cousin Anna had its origin in kinship ties, but it went deeper than a simple family connection. Anna considered

Martha her soul mate, and she depended on her to help her overcome the isolation of her military environment. "Do come up Martha—I will give you no peace of mind till you come," she pleaded in January 1865. Their friendship was strengthened by their love of good music and the enjoyment they derived from attending concerts and parties. In December 1864, Anna informed Martha that she had recently traveled to St. Paul to attend a party and a concert with a friend. Pleased to escape the drudgery of military life at the fort, she said that her enjoyment was only marred by Martha's absence. "I thought of you many times during the evening & wished you could enjoy it with us," she wrote. This love of music was also linked to a love of literature. Both women enjoyed reading. In the same letter about the concert, she informed Martha that she had managed to get books from the St. Paul library.[5]

Martha's friendship was important to Anna because she faced a difficult domestic environment. The commandant's quarters were not a home of her choosing, and it was not a good place to raise a young family. Moreover, since it was government property, she had only a limited opportunity to remodel it to meet her young family's needs. Although major renovations to the fort had been made in mid-1862 and the fall of 1863, it remained an overcrowded, difficult living environment for the soldiers stationed there. Daniel commented to Martha that the fort was overrun with rats. "Mittie if I should tell you how many rats I saw yesterday you would then have but little idea of the *ratty place* of this place—I counted over fifty in the space of five minutes. That would make a steel trap sweat."[6]

Although there was little Anna could do to change the physical environment of the fort, she seized the opportunity to change her social environment, so it expressed her own cultural values and created a homely atmosphere in her quarters. With Martha's help she did this by organizing social events and gathering female friends and family about her. Sewing and dressmaking were two activities Anna and Martha enjoyed together, and like many middle-class women, they believed that these domestic skills were an essential element of homemaking. Both had a fine eye for superior quality clothing and fashion. The exchange of clothing, material, and dress patterns between the two and other family members strengthened their friendship and consolidated their creative talents. One of Anna's relatives, Mrs. L. C. Meserole, wrote to her informing her of the forthcoming dress styles in New York. "Don't get a large stock of little Quaker hoops on hand for in New York they are commencing to wear larger hoops than have ever been worn," she advised. Shortly after receiving this letter Anna wrote to Martha summarizing this advice and promising to forward to her one of Mrs. Meserole's dress patterns as soon as they arrived in the mail.[7] Yet although Anna saw sewing and dressmaking as essential elements in homemaking, she did not believe inadequate attire should prevent her friends visiting. In January 1864 she wrote to Martha pleading that she ignore preparation and come immediately: "Do not stop to fix up but come & we will fix after you get here," she wrote. In her effort to entice Martha to visit she often listed all the activities they could do together, including sleigh riding and horse riding. Horse riding did not present a problem, for Anna had the attire and the necessary equipment. "If you have a black waist I have a skirt—not much of one—but an apology— & rest of the accoutrements are all on hand."[8]

As well as fostering creativity and kinship, Martha and Anna's interest in dressmaking and fashion served an important social function. By gathering in dressmaking and sewing circles, Anna and her friends socialized and gained comfort from companionship. In these times together they shared stories about the war, celebrated Union victories, and supported each other when tragedy occurred. Anna and Martha knew that the clothes they wore were indicative of their family's social standing. Their dresses revealed their family's wealth and refined cultural values. Like music appreciation, clothing facilitated the entry into middle-class society. Wearing a dress that was admired and generated discussion was a strong indicator of social acceptance. As the wife of Colonel McLaren, the commander of the largest military post in Minnesota, Anna had an important social role to uphold. Active in soldiers' relief, through organizing social functions, Martha also had to be attired in a way that reflected her family's leading status in Red Wing society. But Martha's and Anna's choices of clothing had another purpose too, for it enabled them to reinvent themselves and assert their individuality. For Martha her clothing helped her move outside the home by easing her transition into her new role in the Red Wing Ladies' Soldiers' Aid Society. At some grand charitable events she wore fashionable dresses that reflected her family's status. However, on other occasions, for example when serving at her Soldiers' Refreshment booth, she was dressed more humbly. The working dresses she wore on these occasions may not have appealed to her parents, but they served a practical purpose. Moreover, they helped her form friendships and flirt with the young soldiers she served by diminishing barriers of wealth and class. Confined largely to Fort Snelling, Anna employed her sense of fashion to enhance her social power and physical attractiveness. By wearing beautiful dresses, she was able to distance herself from the drab, rigid military environment that surrounded her.[9]

One way that both women could gain acceptance among their peers was to be seen as leaders of the latest fashion trends. Yet this goal was difficult to achieve

Figure 11.2. Dress worn by Anna McLaren at Fort Snelling, Minnesota. This green brocade and watered silk machine-stitched dress (circa 1860–1865) has a floral design and black velvet stripes and buttons. The photograph depicts an incomplete dress. It should include an 1860s hoop skirt. Minnesota Historical Society.

because both lived in the remote Midwest. Fortunately, Anna's family lived in New York, and sometimes she was able to visit them. These visits reinvigorated the two friends' fashion sense, for when Anna returned to Minnesota she brought the season's latest fashions, new fabrics, and the latest fashion news. Anna also acted as Martha's fashion emissary while she was in New York. On one occasion while she was visiting her parents' home, Anna confessed that after a largely fruitless search she was unable to meet her promise to send Martha the prices of fashionable dresses on sale there.[10] An indulgent shopper, Anna was always on the lookout for a bargain for her friend. "Don't you want me to do something for you in the line of shopping[?]" she enquired of Martha, shortly before she set out for St. Paul on a shopping expedition, adding "the new goods are coming in now & I don't think they are too extravagantly high as I had expected."[11]

For both friends the world of fashion and culture coalesced at parties they attended with the social elite. While being invited to these functions was a sign of social acceptance, attendance could lead to some reflection on one's place in the social hierarchy. In January 1865, Anna reported on one such party she attended with the leading citizens of Rochester, New York. There Anna facilitated her social acceptance by displaying modesty and genteel self-restraint. "Martha—I wished you had been with us last Monday Eve," she exclaimed, adding that "[s]uch splendid music & such beautiful dresses I think I never saw." Perhaps conscious of living in the Midwest, she admitted that she enjoyed being a passive observer viewing the finery, even though it dimmed somewhat her own appearance. "I wore my blue silk & looked very plain—but enjoyed seeing the rest just as well as though," she commented.[12]

Although the friendship between Martha and Anna was maintained by constant letter writing, it was also invigorated by Martha's visits. Although we do not know how Anna's husband reacted to these visits, the comments he made about another relative's visits suggests that he welcomed distractions that entertained his young wife. After one of Aunt Meserole's visits he commented that Anna and her aunt had an enjoyable time making visits to shops and concerts in St. Paul. Robert found it best to tolerate women's alleged indulgences and to "smile on all they did, grant all their requests and go with the current." Rather than protest, the best strategy was to "grieve in silence over the folly of women." His life appears to have been focused on advancing his military career and his entrepreneurial ventures. While he was fond of his wife and valued her role as mother, like many men he did not seek to understand his wife's domestic world because he believed it was a woman's domain. Unable to gain empathy from her husband, Anna looked to Martha and her female friends for emotional support.[13]

To encourage Martha to visit, Anna often included in her invitations references to romantic attachments she could form at the fort. She was aware that the war had widened Martha's social horizons, and she knew that she looked forward to her visits partly because it gave her an opportunity to assert her independence and explore liaisons free from the watchful eye of her parents. In many ways Anna was like a sister to Martha. "Why dont you come up Martha—I have got the most splendid little man picked out for you—unless I conclude to keep him in reserve for *my second*," she wrote in April 1864.[14] Anxious to have companionship, Anna sometimes encouraged Martha to visit with her friend and teaching colleague Belle Webster. Anna even promised to "keep a look out" for Miss Webster. The problem was, as she explained at the time she offered her invitation, "almost all the (otherwise) eligible gentlemen" were "either married or engaged."[15] As the war drew to a conclusion, she warned her friends not to delay their departure. Their failure to visit earlier had caused some consternation. "[W]e ourselves—besides sundry young men were much disappointed that you & Miss Bell failed to make us that visit we expected," she commented.[16]

Although Anna's letters to Martha contained much lighthearted ribbing about her romantic prospects, there was a serious side to her correspondence. Anna was concerned that twenty-eight-year-old Martha would remain unmarried. She also was aware that the war had disrupted traditional patterns of courtship. Fewer young men attended social functions, and more than ever relationships had to be negotiated via mail. In these difficult circumstances Anna was ever ready to help. While men were expected to take the lead in courtship initiation, women were expected to encourage the men of their choice in a subtle manner, without being too forward or being seen as aggressive. Reading the signs of romantic interest was a very difficult task that often required the assistance of a valued friend and confidante.[17]

In November 1864, Anna was disturbed to read in the papers that Lieutenant Davis had married. She announced to Martha, "*Your* Mr. Davis has up & married Mary Graham." This marriage was a disappointment, for she had strong expectations of having Davis as a cousin by marriage. When she learned that Davis had brought his wife to Fort Snelling, she assured Martha that she had "a good mind not to speak to him." On another occasion when she heard that Lieutenant Field had left Fort Snelling to visit Red Wing, she was moved to contemplate a new liaison for Martha and her friends. With the "overflowing generosity" of her heart she thought about how "refreshing to the eyes of you young ladies would be the sight of a whole row of brass buttons." With some regret she thought about the sundry articles she could have retrieved from the Densmore home and "thus make a good excuse for the young man to call." Then in mocking deprecation she exclaimed, "What benevolence—what patriotism! I hear you exclaim (Likewise what writing!!)." Finally, Anna concluded her letter by drawing Martha even more closely into her confidence. "I am *ashamed* of this letter," she wrote. "Don't let anybody see it I beg you. Yours as ever Anna." Such daydreaming enabled Anna to escape from the dreary confines of the fort by entering the imagined romantic world of her close friend. But it also encouraged Martha to rest from her patriotic toil, renew her spirit, and continue her search for a partner.[18]

Although the relationship between Anna and Martha was partly built on a shared interest in Martha's romantic prospects, it also had concrete practical dimensions. While Anna and her husband were living at Fort Snelling, Martha and her family kept a watchful eye on the McLaren property in Red Wing. Martha was continually meeting Anna's requests for items kept in storage to be sent to the fort, and on a few occasions she conducted household cleaning for the McLarens. All this practical help left Anna feeling guilty of exploiting her friend. On one occasion she apologized to Martha saying, "What did you think of me—did you suppose I meant to make a servant of you."[19]

Martha also aided Anna by looking after Anna's children while she was on holiday visiting her parents. Although the presence of Archie in the Densmore household brought the two friends closer together, it was not without its difficulties. On one occasion, while she was away, Anna wrote to Martha informing her that her return would be delayed. "Do you think you can endure it with Archie that length of time?" she asked. Then she advised her to keep him "within bounds" by threatening to take his toolbox. Martha enjoyed the McLarens' visits, but sometimes even their amiable and lively presence was too much for her. Once, when the McLarens were visiting, she complained to Daniel that "[d]uring this siege," she would have liked to have a "'Dinah'" or a good servant for help, but then added "still we have 'got along' very nicely."[20]

In some ways Martha's and Anna's friendship comforted them and shielded them from some of the harsh reality of the war. While she was serving soldiers in her refreshment tent on the Red Wing quayside, Martha had regularly seen maimed and disfigured soldiers shuffling by and others struggling to carry the belongings of deceased comrades. The ugly face of war also confronted Anna at Fort Snelling. In November 1864, Anna was shaken when she heard news that deserters were to be executed at the fort. "[D]on't you think it is dreadful," she inquired of Martha. In their letters to each other the two friends seldom commented on the war. When news from the battlefront was raised, it generally took the form of a passing endorsement on federal success. "Haven't much to say in particular only Hurrah for U. S. Grant & all the rest of them & hope these few lines will find you enjoying the same state of mind," Anna commented to Martha. Only once, when referring to the "terrible battle" of Nashville, did Anna mention the horrific nature of the conflict. Even then the reference was made with an expression of relief that neither Benjamin nor Daniel was caught up in it.[21]

Both friends found the departure of regiments containing friends and loved ones moving occasions and at these times they looked to each other for comfort and support. When the 6th Minnesota Infantry was ordered south, Anna immediately wrote to Martha seeking to comfort her. Referring to her own difficult experience coping with the absences of her husband, she was well "prepared to sympathize." She anticipated that when the 6th Infantry left, Martha would go to the Red Wing dock and cry herself blind because of the departure of her beau, Mr. Potter. Although prone to romantic rhetoric and hyperbole, Anna was heartfelt and prophetic in her concern for Martha. The Civil War severed the relationships of many young lovers, and Martha and her beau also suffered this fate. Approximately two months after Anna wrote to Martha, Assistant Surgeon Augustus O. Potter, 6th Minnesota Infantry, died of disease at Helena, Arkansas.[22]

It has long been recognized that during the Civil War women moved outside their domestic world to work for patriotic causes in the public sphere. But Martha Densmore's war experience suggests that for some women, a diminished male presence at home enabled them to increase their authority and stature in domestic affairs. With two sons away fighting the rebels Martha's aging parents increasingly looked to her to provide direction and authority in the household. Confident in her ability to manage the home, Elizabeth and Orrin took advantage of the cessation of hostilities to go on a Southern tour, during which they visited Benjamin in Columbus.[23] Yet perhaps the most compelling evidence of Martha's growing stature and influence was the way she pressed, successfully, for major renovations to be made to the family home. In her study of the home front, Louise Stevenson argues that Victorian Americans furnished and renovated their homes in ways that imparted their cultural influences and values. Certainly, Martha renovated the Densmore family home in a manner she believed would make it more comfortable, enhance her family's middle-class status, and affirm their genteel values. In June 1864, she wrote to Benjamin outlining the extensive changes to be made, including remodeling mother's bedroom, the kitchen, pantry, dining room, cellar, and wood house. Although she never claimed the architectural plan as her own, she did acknowledge that once the renovations were complete, the whole family would be pleased with the change. Certainly, when Benjamin returned, he would "'see how nice we are.'"[24]

Figure 11.3. Orrin Densmore's Home, 1936. Minnesota Historical Society.

In addition to these major renovations Martha supervised the refurbishing of the house. In late 1864 she informed Daniel that during a visit to Janesville, Wisconsin, she had purchased a carpet for the parlor. The parlor carpet was moved to the sitting room and the sitting room carpet to mother's bedroom. At one level Martha's animated description of all the renovations and improvements had the intended purpose of strengthening the link between the brothers fighting in a foreign land and the home they were fighting for. "I only wish you could step in, & see for yourself—what a *cozy*, yes *delightful* house we have," she wrote to Daniel. Orrin was also proud of Martha's renovations. Both physically and spiritually the Densmore home was a home worth fighting for. It was a home fit for heroes. Yet at another level, Martha's description may have disturbed the brothers because it pointed to their sense of separation. When the brothers opened their mail from home, they discovered their domestic landscape could be significantly changed without their direct involvement. The renovations were so significant that Benjamin suggested to Daniel that "we shall not know the place when we get home again."[25]

Martha shared her ambitious plans for the renovation of her home with Anna. On holiday in New York, Anna wrote to Martha congratulating her on the renovations. "[Y]ou have really succeeded in your purpose of getting the house changed & I congratulate you upon your success," wrote Anna. Then in a further note commenting on Martha's decision not to join her parent's tour she added, "So you did not stay home for nothing. I hope you will be satisfied & more than satisfied with the alterations."[26]

Even though Martha's growing influence at home was somewhat hidden from the public eye, her work for the Union on the home front received public recognition. On the streets of Red Wing she fashioned for herself a new role as a patriotic woman. Her war effort was altruistic and self-sacrificing, but it was also satisfying and personally empowering. Grounded in the life of her family, her patriotic work increased her authority at home by boosting her confidence and advancing her status. But her friendship with her soul mate, Anna, was important too, for it comforted her when she suffered loss and nurtured her inner strength and growing independence by keeping alive her cultural, social, and romantic interests. The Civil War highlighted the important role comradeship could play in securing victory on the battlefront. Perhaps this focus on the soldiers' bonding overshadowed the significant role female friendship played in the fight on the home front. Anna's and Martha's relationship was not unusual or noteworthy, for these two women experienced a strong friendship that was bound by many of the interests and activities shared by other young middle-class women. Yet it was the steadfast nature of the relationship that gave it potency in a war setting.

12

"They all fought like Minnesotians"

The Mobile Campaign

Daniel welcomed news from Martha about her work on the home front, and he took special comfort from the glowing reports of Mary's valuable work in the kitchen. The experiment of employing a former slave appeared to be working well, for the domestic burdens placed on his mother had been considerably lightened. Free from worrying about the situation at home, his mind was now clear to focus on fighting the war. But the problem he faced in December 1864 was that he had little fighting to do. He feared that Memphis was "to be left out in the cold," for the tide of war was turning sharply against the Confederacy. The Shenandoah Valley had been conquered, Petersburg was under siege, and General Sherman had taken Atlanta and concluded his March to the Sea. After General George H. Thomas had defeated General John Bell Hood at Nashville, Daniel had hoped that Hood would turn on Memphis. However, when he learned that Thomas had largely destroyed Hood's army, he commented to his folks that Thomas had "wiped out Hood and our hopes altogether." Uncertain about how far from Memphis he would have to go to fight the Johnnies, he speculated that he would need to go beyond Alabama and perhaps into Georgia. Although he did not know it at the time, his earnest desire to fight the rebels would soon be met in Alabama.[1]

In mid-January 1865, Grant ordered Major General Edward R. S. Canby, commander of the Military Division of West Mississippi, to capture Mobile and conquer Alabama. Daniel's regiment, which was attached to Brigadier General John P. Hawkins's First Division, United States Colored Troops, formed part of Canby's campaigning army. Although he had little knowledge of the Mobile campaign's military objectives, he looked forward to his new military adventure with enthusiasm. While he expected the campaign would test his mettle, he also knew that his journey further into the Confederacy would deepen his understanding of the exotic Southern land, with its cruel institution of slavery and its rebellious people.[2]

Daniel's regiment departed Memphis for Louisiana on February 3, 1865. Three days later when he arrived at Natchez, Mississippi, he received the good news that he would be promoted to the rank of lieutenant colonel once the regiment was enlarged to its minimum size. Pleased at his enhanced career prospects, he nevertheless remained anxious about the future. Once again, he was journeying down the Mississippi river into a strange land which had etched into its landscape lines of hostility and treachery. He had seen these lines of resistance once before as he observed the waters of the Mississippi River lapping the riverbank at Fort Pillow.[3] Now they emerged again as the steamer passed the port of Natchez. Even the weather seemed to turn against the steamer as a severe cold storm swelled up and lashed its decks with driving rain. Finally, a few hours before reaching his destination, the storm abated, and Daniel was able to get out on deck and "view this strange country."[4]

When Daniel arrived in Louisiana he disembarked at the township of Algiers, located on the West Bank of the Mississippi River, opposite New Orleans. The men of the 68th then joined other troops laboring day and night constructing a six-mile railroad across Lake Pontchartrain.[5] Once this work was completed, the regiment rested in the vicinity of Algiers, a town Daniel described as a derelict hellhole, populated by alien outcasts who were given to "gibberish garlic, dirty clothes and the rebellion." Keen to escape from this unattractive place, Daniel decided to go on a tour of the New Orleans battlefield where General Andrew Jackson had defeated the British in 1815. There he discovered a monument to Jackson with General "A. J. Smith's battalions camped as thick as bees all about it." There was nothing magnificent or impressive about the view. In many ways the monument had taken on the undignified appearance of its immediate surroundings. After four days of rain, mud covered everything, so that the "plowed land, mules & men were all the same tint."[6]

The monument consisted of a fifty-foot marble shaft set in a brick base. The fact that it was surrounded by Smith's army gave it some symbolic significance. Federal soldiers were now being called once again to defend national honor and freedom against an alien foe. Even to the casual observer it was obvious that the monument was not complete. Daniel noticed on the top of the monument a hen coop structure in which sat four soldiers gazing upon the old battlefield that stretched out before them. It was clear to him that the construction of the monument had been halted and that national celebration and memorializing would not proceed until the present rebellion had been defeated. Only then could the Union soldiers from Smith's Corps complete the memorial by adding their names to the nation's honor roll.[7]

Approximately two weeks after Daniel's visit to the New Orleans battlefield, Canby's 45,000 strong army moved against Mobile. Canby's plan of attack had three main elements. First, he planned to move several thousand troops to Cedar Point in Southern Mobile County to give the enemy the impression that the attack on Mobile was coming from the West. Second, Canby planned to send Maj. Gen. Andrew J. Smith's XVI Corps from Dauphin Island and Fort Gaines across the Mobile Bay to Dannelly's Mills on the Fish River, Baldwin County. At same time he planned to order Maj. Gen. Gordon Granger's XIII Corps to move from Fort Morgan and Mobile Point to join General Smith at Dannelly's Mills. Once both corps had regrouped under his command, Canby aimed to advance on Spanish Fort and Fort Blakely. The final part of Canby's plan involved a force of 13,200 men under the command of Maj. Gen. Frederick Steele. Steele's column, which included part of Granger's XIII Corps and Brig. Gen. John Parker Hawkins's First Division, USCT, was to move from Fort Barrancas in Western Florida to Pensacola, and then advance toward Montgomery and Selma, destroying railroads as it moved north. After capturing Pollard, it would swing west to join Canby's attack. Once Spanish Fort and Fort Blakely had fallen, it was expected that Mobile and the state of Alabama would fall. The success of Canby's plan depended heavily on naval support to transport troops and provide protecting gun fire.[8]

After sailing from New Orleans, Daniel and his regiment arrived at Fort Barrancas, Florida, on March 11. There he experienced heavy frosts and bleak, cold days. For the first time since he had left Memphis, he and his men fell victims of army discrimination and incompetence. He complained that he had "slept cold for two nights" and "the treat was to be repeated at least for one night more." "[C]ut down" by the military authorities to one wedge tent, Daniel and his fellow officers froze in the cold night air. The plight of the men was even worse. Denied wedge tents by order, and shelter tents by mistake, but for the "Dr's rubber blankets" they would have been "out-of-doors much like cattle." [9]

Daniel was concerned that his regiment would miss the impending fight. He could hear the thunder of the Union guns pounding Mobile's defenses and remarked that somebody was "going to be gloriously thrashed," and he wished his regiment was "there to take a hand." He even speculated that General Andrews's division could be sent directly to the Mobile front when General Hawkins's First Division, United States Colored Troops began their march to Pensacola.

Since he believed, like his father, that the Black soldiers' role in the war was to assist their alleged "champions," the white officers and soldiers, he had no difficulty accepting this possible outcome. "Well, really should not the white troops have the glory in this war in cases where a choice is to be decided between the colors?" he commented to Benjamin. Even so, he hoped that his men would find their "full of fighting" and months of raiding before the conflict ended.[10]

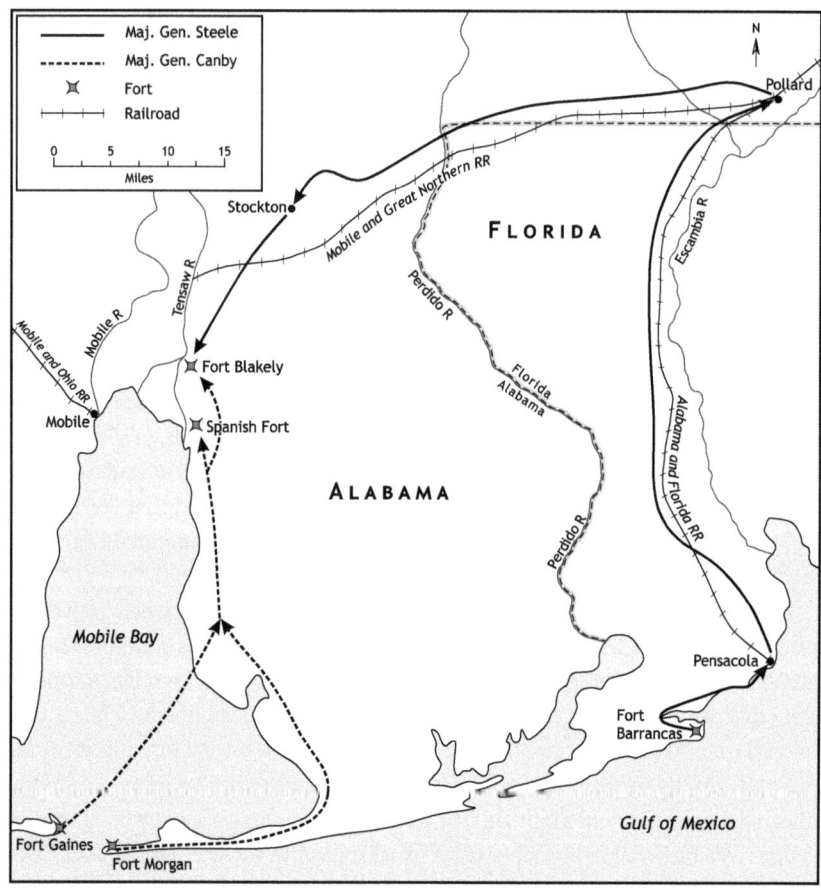

Map 4. Movement of the forces of Maj. Gen. Edward R. S. Canby and Maj. Gen. Frederick Steele during the Mobile Campaign, March–April 1865.

Daniel and his men were pleased to leave Fort Barrancas and escape the sandy blast of the prevailing winds. Indeed, the men complained that they wore down their teeth a "full two inches chewing Barrancas sand." After setting out for Pensacola early in the morning on March 19, they traveled under the cover of a heavy mist until, two miles from the fort, the men removed shoes and stockings, and began to ford Pensacola Bay. As the expedition continued across the bay, the journey took on a somber and foreboding appearance. The men were traveling blind. They felt as if they were attempting to cross the Gulf itself. The fog clung so heavily about them that no one could see the land. In addition, they heard "a doubtfully pleasant roar of breakers somewhere in the distance." Undaunted, the men pushed on, wading through the briny water knee deep all the way. The whole scene impressed Daniel so much that he claimed that, apart from the rebel charge at the battle of Tupelo, it was one of the finest sights he had seen during the war. As a spectacle, it even surpassed the grand scenery found on the plains of Dakota.[11]

The mysterious majesty of an endless army of Black men descending from a dark pine forest, their bayonets glistening in the morning sun, wading through the surging sea, engulfed by heavy mist and the sound of crashing waves, then ascending the opposite shore was a powerful, captivating image for Daniel because it encapsulated the concept of Black soldiers as triumphant heroes. It was as if the soldiers themselves had jettisoned the passive, secondary military service they had at Barrancas and were forging a new role for themselves as Union liberators. Though transfixed by the scene, Daniel was keen to share its significance with others. He wanted friends at home, "sitting in their quiet churches in comfortable and pious inclination," to gaze upon the scene and discover for themselves the trials a soldier was subject to. He believed this dramatic scene would remind these civilians of the "pittance to be 'taken up' for the benefit of the soldier's family," and it would encourage them to sympathize with the soldier "in his privations and hardships."[12]

After this reflection Daniel continued to describe his soldiers traveling for some distance along the beach then cutting inland "wandering through groves of shady pines or skirting along thickets of live-oaks and magnolias." To impress upon his readers the vibrant and exotic nature of the land he was invading, Daniel described in detail the luxuriant nature of the vegetation that surrounded him. It is as if the trees themselves had taken on human form and the forests were the living rooms of this rebel land. There was something surreal about marching through a pine forest and having the tread of so many marching feet "snuffled by the thick carpet of fallen leaves." Scattered on the ground around him were huge pinecones. In the thickets and along the low places there was a luxuriant growth of dwarf or cabbage palmetto. Finally, the march ended at the deserted village of Pensacola. Here images of the vibrant natural world gave way to those depicting the ravages of war. Once the playground of pleasure seekers, Pensacola's prestige and patronage had now gone. Standing in stark contrast to the luxuriant Southern landscape, Pensacola was a burnt wreck, a powerful symbol of rebel intransigence. "Here as in many other places the rebels have found their rights," he commented.[13]

The fast pace and vivid description of Daniel's narrative gives the impression that he was simply crafting his story as he traveled, responding to the changes in the landscape as he marched deeper into enemy territory. Such an impression would be misleading, because he believed he was compiling a personal chronicle of his travels, and at the same time acting as a reporter sending home all kinds of information about a strange land to family and friends. At one level he was writing about what he saw, the tragedy of war, and the beauty of the Southern landscape. At another level he was responding to the needs and desires of his readership. Friends and family regularly wrote to him seeking more information about his travels through the Southern lands. For some the vast extent of the journey was amazing. "I hear from Norman's letter that you are away down in Pensacola—a long way off it seems to me," wrote Aunt Martha. She marveled that his military service had taken him from Lake Superior to the Gulf of Mexico and was surprised that he had had many "narrow escapes that would make your friends tremble if they knew of them." Benjamin also noted that he found Daniel's letters always "full of interest," for they gave "an assurance of good health and an enjoyment of Southern life."[14]

The Densmores had long been interested in the South and were part of a strong antiquarian tradition, a tradition that had been stimulated by Benjamin's and Daniel's involvement in the Dakota wars. This tradition continued long after the immediate family had passed away. Benjamin's eldest daughter, Frances, became a member of the Minnesota Historical Society and a nationally renowned ethnographer famed for preserving the music of Native American tribes. Daniel was a keeper of this tradition. His father commented in March 1865 that his son's expedition would yield new and exciting insights about the South, "aside from the military features and incidents." He had long desired to visit the Gulf region. Now that he was unable to make the journey, he took comfort from the fact that his son could make it, for he knew Daniel had the knowledge and family background to gain from his experiences. "[W]e have read so much of the beauties and wonders of the tropical regions," noted Orrin. He felt certain that, provided Daniel enjoyed good health, he would "be likely to enjoy and profit by the expedition."[15]

Norman echoed his father's sentiments. He advised Daniel that while he was in the South he would discover "many wonders and curiosities that while sitting here in the north 20 years ago about the winter's crackling fire we used to read of in great wonder." Not surprisingly, Norman and his family found Daniel's description of the Southern landscape immensely interesting. Daniel also found the South to be a land of mystery and adventure. Yet it was not a place that was completely foreign to him. He had journeyed there as a young schoolteacher before the war, and long ago in his imagination, as a child, reading books of geographic wonder on cold Minnesota winter evenings.[16]

After Steele's column departed Pensacola, it destroyed the Alabama and Florida Railroad track as it moved north toward Pollard. Heavy rain, flooding, swamps, quicksand, almost impassable roads, and damaged bridges all slowed Steele's progress. The expedition's problems were further compounded by the rebels stripping the countryside of food and supplies. After capturing Pollard, Steele's column followed the Mobile and Great Northern Railroad westward until it diverged from the railroad and arrived at Stockton. From there it moved to Fort Blakely and began siege operations on April 2. During the siege, Hawkins's Division was located on the right of Steele's line, between the Stockton Road and the Tensaw River.[17]

In his official report on operations at Fort Blakely Daniel described the grinding nature of the siege.[18] The 68th USCI were involved in constant heavy skirmishing against an enemy with excellent sharpshooters safely posted in a well-constructed line of rifle pits. Faced with stiff resistance, Daniel's men also suffered from constant shelling by the Confederate gunboats that plied the Alabama River. By April 8, the tide of combat began to turn against the rebels. Late on the afternoon of April 9, the 68th and 76th USCI mounted a charge on the enemies' works. Initially, this assault was successful, with some soldiers almost reaching the enemies' parapet, but lacking support, the attack dissipated, and the men retreated to the safety of their own lines. Undaunted by this failure, they joined the general charge on Fort Blakely ordered at 5:30 p.m. "[I]n less than ten minutes the enemy's works were carried," and Fort Blakely was safely in Union hands.

Daniel reminded his superiors that during the siege his regiment fought courageously, suffering a hundred casualties, including three officers and nine enlisted men killed. In his report he made a special feature of emphasizing men's fortitude, which was an essential element of soldiering. His men had advanced under withering fire and, although exhausted, returned to the field to join in the final assault. Aware that battle performance was the ultimate test of a soldier's ability, he used his report to mark up the Black soldiers' progress. Although he failed to name any of the enlisted men individually, the very non-descript nature of the account made it even more powerful.[19]

As well as writing an official report on the siege of Fort Blakely for his military commanders, Daniel also wrote a second account which was published in the *St. Paul Daily Press* in May 1865. In this account he sought to describe the 68th USCI's performance at Fort Blakely in a manner that celebrated Minnesota's heritage and patriotism. This task was not an easy one, for the 68th USCI was not a Minnesota regiment; it was organized in St. Louis and composed mainly of soldiers from Missouri. Aware of these formative features, Daniel employed several strategies to make his story relevant to Minnesota readers.[20]

In his account Daniel developed a link between his home state and the combat performance of the 68th USCI by focusing on the leadership of the officers. While he acknowledged the bravery of his Black soldiers, his racial attitude led him to believe that they lacked initiative and depended very heavily on the example and direction of their officers when under fire. Right from the start of his account he was at pains to show his regiment was in fact a "Minnesota regiment." He justified this claim by arguing that there were fifteen officers from Minnesota in the 68th USCI. Daniel even made a case for claiming Colonel Jones as a "Minnesotian." Although he enlisted in Illinois, he owned land and estates in St. Peter's, Minnesota, and more important still, "he had the good sense to choose one of her [Minnesota's] fair daughters" for his wife. Long smitten by the "most kind hearted and accomplished" Mrs. Jones, Daniel represented her as epitomizing the noble women of Minnesota. It was as if the rich beauty of the "'[l]and of sky tinted waters'" was reflected in Mrs. Jones's life in the army camp. Mrs. Jones's virtue was such that it encouraged him to ask whether her father, "Alvah Smith, Esq. has yet other daughters?" Conscious of Mrs. Jones's generosity and kindness, he concluded that among Alvah Smith's daughters there could be none braver. Since he believed that wives and mothers were the cornerstones of family life and guardians of civilization, Mrs. Jones's name was deliberately placed at the foot of the honor roll. This strategy enabled him to link his report about the courageous leadership of the Minnesotan officers to the Minnesota home. Mrs. Jones was, after all, identified as Colonel Jones's "chief of staff."[21]

After he introduced the roster of officers, Daniel presented a short history of the organization of the regiment. While acknowledging that most of the men came from Missouri, he claimed that "thirty or more" enlisted in Minnesota. He then turned his attention to the siege of Fort Blakely. At first he gave a general account of the challenges the regiment faced during the siege. In the face of considerable danger, it displayed unflinching steel. For example, as soon as it arrived at the Blakely battlefield, the regiment established a skirmish line within close range of the enemy's rifle pits and held it in the face of intense fire from the rebel soldiers and Confederate gunboats. On the day Fort Blakely fell, the 68th and the other regiments in the 3rd brigade were sent out on to the field one hour before the general assault took place. There they "had an exciting fight over the left of the enemy's earthworks." In the fierce struggle that took place among the felled trees and defensive works, they "created such a diversion as made the general assault much more easy and decisive." By their actions on the battlefield the men of the 68th USCI displayed the valor of veteran Union soldiers. Yet Daniel did not allow the readers' gaze to rest too long on the enlisted men, instead directing their attention to the bravery of the officers.

Beginning with Colonel Jones, Daniel listed several of the officers who were severely wounded or killed and by doing so laid out the stark reality of war in all its brutal simplicity. Colonel Jones was "struck in the hand by a ball cutting an ugly gash." Captain Giger was wounded in the lungs while leading his skirmishers. Yet for Daniel what was most important was not the brutal nature of the wounds themselves, but the way the Minnesota officers dealt with the danger and suffering that surrounded them. His narrative shifts the readers' attention away from the officers' gaping wounds to their resilient fighting spirit. For example, after he described Colonel Jones's wound, he explained how Jones pushed on, leading his men until he was concussed by an exploding shell.

In his tribute to the officer corps, Daniel carefully linked his praise to Minnesota. For example, when describing the death of Lieutenants Talbot and Gleason, he lamented that Minnesota had lost two true men, concluding that "[t]he splendor of her [Minnesota's] bright escutcheon cannot be dimmed by such men." While reluctant to name unharmed soldiers, "whether from Minnesota or other States," he acknowledged their universal bravery, claiming that "they all fought like Minnesotians." He then went on to describe the nature of this Minnesota fighting spirit, which bore hallmarks of true manhood, including self-control and courage under fire. When the "death shots were flying the thickest all were seemingly as cool as on battalion drill. Not a man 'flew off the handle.'" It was as if the battle itself enlivened them and ignited their manhood. At times he described the battle as if he were narrating the events of a game. For example, shortly after being wounded in the hand, Colonel Jones is described as "pocketing the compliment," then pushing on for a few rods until he was hit by an exploding shell which tore his hat, threw him to the ground and made his "'ideas all agog.'" Daniel was so impressed with the displays of bravery "of St. Paul's youngest, latest, soldiers" that he almost thought that "this death-dealing" was "jolly work." Finally, he concluded his report by listing the regiment's casualties.[22]

Issues of class, rank, and gender may partially explain the composition of his newspaper report. Because strong bonds of comradeship bound the 68th USCI officers' mess tightly, Daniel probably wanted to acknowledge the sacrifices of comrades he knew personally. His focus on Colonel Jones's leadership also highlights the manly values he believed the officer class should display. While under heavy fire and even when wounded, Jones displayed resolute self-control and courageous leadership. In this regard, Daniel's report is like many Union officers' reports of their battlefield experiences. But Daniel was not just another Union officer. He was an abolitionist who believed that the Union Army could be used as a vehicle to elevate former slaves and lead them to citizenship. He had expressed these views privately in his letters to his family and friends. But in his public newspaper report he makes no mention of the way his African American soldiers had been transformed into a formidable fighting force. Perhaps this was because he was aware of the racism that pervaded Minnesota, and he knew that the readership of the *St. Paul Daily Press* was keen to receive reports about "their boys." By writing a report about battlefield exploits of the Minnesota officers in the 68th USCI, Daniel believed he was meeting these expectations and publicly proclaiming his loyalty to his home state.

Daniel's attempt to place his regiment within Minnesota's war effort depended not only on the glowing words and phrases included in his military report and his newspaper article, but also on the gaps and silences they contained. In these accounts he made no mention of the events that occurred during the last moments of rebel resistance. This may well have been because some accounts of the battle suggest that the Black soldiers may have attacked and killed rebel soldiers as they attempted to surrender. Two brigade commanders acknowledged that when Fort Blakely fell, rebel soldiers threw down their arms and made frantic attempts to surrender to white Union soldiers because they feared being massacred by Black soldiers.[23] Divisional Commander Hawkins noted that his Black Division captured only 221 prisoners. He explained that "there would have been more men captured but when the rebels saw it was all up with them many ran over to where the white troops were entering the works." While commanders all claimed that their Black troops carried themselves in a soldierly manner, some revenge attacks on unarmed rebel soldiers appear to have taken place.[24]

In a private letter to Brigadier General Christopher C. Andrews, written well over a year after the fall of Fort Blakely, Daniel admitted that soldiers from the Louisiana regiments perpetrated attacks on unarmed rebels who were surrendering. While he did not admit that soldiers from his regiment had committed outrages, he did acknowledge that two officers from his regiment were severely wounded endeavoring to restrain Black troops. After the war, when reflecting on the battle, Andrews admitted that some Louisiana Black soldiers attacked prisoners. The weight of evidence suggests that soldiers from 68th USCI may have been among those perpetrating attacks on unarmed rebels seeking to surrender. In his letter, Daniel describes rebel soldiers huddling together "in mortal fear of the 'niggers' whom they feared would 'remember Fort Pillow.'" Such fears were not without foundation. The soldiers of the 68th USCI were among those Black soldiers who determined to exact revenge for the infamous outrage at Fort Pillow. [25]

We have no way of knowing the impact of Daniel's newspaper report on the people of St. Paul, or Minnesota generally, but we do know that his family members were very pleased to read of his regiment's exploits in the press. The folks back in Red Wing eagerly waited for news of General Steele's campaign in Alabama, and often newspaper reports provided the only extensive commentary. When Martha wrote to Benjamin in mid-April 1865, she welcomed news gleaned from the newspapers that General Steele's force was in the vicinity of Mobile. "Oh! How I long to hear of the capture of the place," she exclaimed. She believed the fall of that city would signify the end of the war. "I do believe the 'good time' is about to come—and have we not waited long enough!" she commented. Benjamin also read the newspaper reports of Steele's progress. Impressed by recent reports in the *Missouri Democrat*, he enclosed a newspaper cutting of these reports about the Mobile campaign in a letter to his father. Yet no newspaper article was received with more enthusiasm than that written by Daniel for the *St. Paul Daily Press*. On May 23 Martha wrote to Daniel that she had spied an article written by "D.D." in the "'Daily Press." She was impressed by the fact that "the *68th* bethought itself to *report*." Then in a casual aside she surmised that "[t]ruly we may almost claim that as a Minn Regt."[26]

For Daniel military service was not exclusively about the clash of arms or battlefield heroics. Recognition and praise of loved ones and the community generally were also important. These themes shone brightly through his description of the Mobile Campaign. His correspondence made a powerful claim for those serving in the USCT to be honored by linking their war effort to the new Republic the war was creating. He saw his Black soldiers as liberators, heralding the death of slavery and a new age of freedom. Yet influenced by prevailing racist attitudes and keen to secure the acclaim of his home state, he promoted the fighting prowess of his officers above that of the Black soldiers. By embellishing some facts and hiding others, he sought to shape his battle narrative so his war effort, and that of his USCT regiment, would be placed in the war annals of his state.

13   "The curse of slavery"

Occupation Duty in Alabama

Daniel came out of the battle of Fort Blakely unharmed and within a week of the conflict he was as hearty as ever. Colonel Jones was not so fortunate. Concussion and a serious hand wound forced him to return home to recuperate. As second in charge, Daniel enjoyed the opportunity to exercise command. After his first battalion drill he received many compliments from his fellow officers, and he was pleased that a competent man, a Minnesotan, had been promoted to the rank of major to act as his second in command.[1] As acting commander, he was mindful of the fact that the war would soon be over. Everywhere pillars of the Confederacy were falling. Lee had surrendered; General Joseph E. Johnston was negotiating surrender terms; and General Edmund Kirby Smith's agents were in Mobile negotiating the surrender of the Trans-Mississippi armies. The collapse of the Confederacy was so fast that Daniel believed there would be no one left to fight. "We have plucked them out of the 'last ditch' in this region. I think we must look for garrison duty from this time on," he commented to his family. Daniel's prediction proved right; his fighting days were over.[2]

Late in April 1865, Daniel was on the move again. As part of Hawkins's First Division, the 68th USCI moved out of Fort Blakely and journeyed to Montgomery.[3] He welcomed the opportunity to serve as a garrison force in this new location. The city was a healthy, pleasant place and much more attractive than the "sand barriers and the stagnant bayous along the Gulf." But Daniel's time in Montgomery was cut short, for he received orders commanding him to march to the river port of Providence Landing and then proceed downriver to Mobile. The men strongly opposed this redeployment, arguing that it was foolish to undertake such a long march in hot weather. "*'[N]ow the war is over I wish to get home'*" was the common refrain. But Daniel dismissed this grumbling. Aware of the rebellious character of the Southern people, he firmly believed the army's policing role was almost as significant as its fighting role.[4]

The march from Montgomery to Providence Landing had a profound effect on Daniel. During the journey he wrote a long letter to his uncle, Russell Cheney, describing it as "one of the most peculiar marches" he had undertaken. For the first time in the war, he felt that he was penetrating the Southern soul and discovering the strange inner life and history of a rebellious people. This experience so overwhelmed him that he felt incapable of adequately describing what he had seen. Yet it was something he would never have missed. What intrigued him about the journey was the diverse array of richly colored images he encountered. The journey was a collage of scenes linking the beauty of the landscape with the dark history of its people. For Daniel, the whole journey had been "an array of magnificent pictures, connected with the most fanciful history of deeds strange, direful, diabolical, horrid, and worse" it was "*true*."[5]

Daniel began his account of his journey by describing the seductively attractive nature of the Alabama landscape. While the hot sun beat down on him and brought some discomfort, he took delight in traveling through what he considered to be one of the most scenic regions of the South. The landscapes he gazed upon were "the very picture of home and happiness," with "fields and groves, hillsides, wooded dales, winding streams, and the clean white villas of the planters." The journey became "a continual feast of loveliness." After describing the beauty of the region, Daniel shifted his attention to one plantation he visited. The alluring beauty of the place drew him in. Close to the plantation house blooming roses climbed over the pillars of the porch, up peach trees, over windows and trellis and through the fences, "where soldiers could pick them, and, (if he had been a *white* man), smell them, and think of home." On trees surrounding the plantation house fruit hung heavily on every branch. The sheer abundance of the land seemed beyond description, so much so that Daniel called upon members of the Cheney family to use their imaginations to visualize its beauty.[6]

At this point in his letter, Daniel abruptly halted his description to remind his readers that on this "most fair and beautiful land is written the curse of slavery." Earlier he alluded to slavery by describing a color line running across the plantation, preventing the Black man from receiving the fruit of his labor, or even picking or smelling the rich perfume of the roses. Now the whole tone of his letter changed. He left behind the persona of the travel writer and adopted instead the role of a fiery preacher intent on exposing the sins of the Southern people. He began his denunciation by framing it with two underlying principles that he believed strengthened his case. First, he clearly stated that his knowledge of slavery in the South was based on personal experience. "What I shall write, I know," he declared. Aware that some would consider his account a "fantastical black republic frenzy," he dismissed this criticism as being ridiculous. Second, he claimed that he was unable to completely describe the evil nature of slavery because "the story of it is too black, too diabolical, to find expression in a human language."[7]

After defending himself from possible criticism, Daniel proceeded to condemn Southerners by employing popular polemic images that cast aside the mythology of Southern manhood by depicting the rebels violating sacred family relationships. He informed his readers that he was not surprised to find slavery emanating from "these *things* called 'southerners,'" for they were a people who rebelled and committed parricide by cutting their parents' throats. Worse still, from the bones of Union prisoners starved to death in their prison camps, these "'*chivalric* people'" fashioned jewelry for their wives and sweethearts. This attack on Southerners was not unique. Indeed, it was part of a Northern polemic that condemned the South for its rebelliousness and its allegedly ghoulish and barbaric practices. Since women were widely seen as the guardians of civilization and high moral culture, Southern women were blamed for being at the heart of the rebellion. They were blamed for being "she devils." Most important of all, Daniel's disparaging criticism of Southern women also attacked the character of Southern manhood because it accused Southern men of promoting the corruption of female innocence and virtue, the very attributes they had pledged to honor and defend. Since Southern social order was founded on white men protecting and caring for their subordinates, women and slaves, Daniel was attacking the basis of Southern society.[8]

Daniel, and many other abolitionists, believed that evidence of the Southerners' uncivilized behavior was found on the slave plantations where family life was destroyed. On the picturesque plantation he visited, his soldiers found five freshly dug graves. When they inquired of an elderly Black woman whose they were, she replied, "'Oh, them's the graves of some of us black u'ns—Tim, and his little brother Sammy and Eliza and her two children.'" The overseer killed them a day earlier with buckshot because they attempted to run away. Daniel believed similar atrocities occurred frequently elsewhere in Alabama and reported that one forage party from Montgomery had found the bodies of twelve slaves within two miles of the city.[9]

Like many Union soldiers, Daniel believed he was waging a war against the Confederacy to save the nation from the thrall of the planter class. Therefore, in his description of his plantation visit, he focused his attention on the depravity of the architect of slavery, "the slave tutored southern man." To probe the depth of his depravity, he believed you had to meet him personally. If this were done, one would discover "nothing but littleness, despicable littleness and meanness." He believed his mind was so distorted by slavery that he was unable to think rationally, and he was so debased by systematic cruelty, that he was "ignorant of the thing called humanity." Daniel employed physiognomy to describe the Southern man as the masculine antithesis of the Union soldier. The rebel's degenerate personal appearance reinforced his depraved intellect. He was "a weazen-faced or a pig-faced animal, white-eyed, sallow, dejected," and "round-shouldered or bloated." As a man he was "in every sense played out, *contemptible.*" To link the Southern man's alleged moral and physical decay to the rebellion, Daniel recalled advice he had received from a Missouri abolitionist. The old man had informed him that when a man became a rebel, he became a reprobate, forsaken by God. Daniel argued the opposite, claiming that depravity was the product of slavery and not rebellion. No amount of Southern preaching or teaching could change this because slavery was the controlling religion of the South. In the North, the situation was entirely different. There he believed the Northern church schools shaped the Northern man's noble character.[10]

Even though Daniel roundly condemned the South, he continued to believe that it could be saved and returned to the Union. He believed that the war had cleansing and redemptive qualities that had changed the lives of those Southerners directly involved in fighting it. In his description of the conquered South, he carefully distinguished between two groups of Southerners he encountered. On the plantations he met the slaveholders who had been corrupted by slavery. But along the roads as well as in Montgomery, he encountered beaten Confederate soldiers, "trudging quietly homeward." These battle-weary veterans evoked some sympathy from him. He admitted that these poor fellows had experienced "a rough time walking all the way from Virginia perhaps."

When he encountered these veterans, he felt encouraged and was convinced that there was some hope for the South. They were cheerful and preoccupied with the thought that they were going home. Their lives had been irrevocably changed for the better by the war. A veil of deception had been lifted from their eyes, for "they had seen the *Yanks* and they were by no means so vile and disreputable a race as they had been told they were, but altogether the contrary." More important still, they now believed they had been duped into fighting for the Confederacy. The planter class had a different story. Because these "stay at homes," had never been whipped, they remained intent on continuing the war and seeking revenge by slipping a dirk into the back of every Yank who ventured into the South. While Daniel took some comfort from his belief that the beaten veterans would "quiet down these fierce men & women of war," he believed the leadership elite was so corrupt that it would continually seek to repress the freedmen.[11]

Although Daniel was aware that many Southerners remained recalcitrant and keen to continue to exercise their authority over their former slaves, he was also aware that defeat and poverty had tempered their rebellious spirit and brought deep feelings of anxiety. Some Southerners were prepared to admit that the war had killed slavery and that they should make the best of their new situation. Stricken by poverty and lacking as little as "five cents to buy a glass of liquor or a chew of *terbackkee*," many were uncertain about how they would make a living. In these uncertain times even the rich planters felt compelled to ingratiate themselves with their victors. They appeared pleased when Daniel and his fellow officers visited them, partook of their hospitality, and talked with them "in a friendly and conciliatory spirit." Such alleged hypocrisy disturbed him, for he believed it was motivated by pure self-interest. Yet what disturbed him more was the planter's attitude to the former slaves. He became incensed when he compared what the planter had made of African American men compared to what the U.S. Army had made of them.[12]

For Daniel, the Black soldier represented not only the triumph of Northern values and civilization, but also a new order in the reconstructed South. In response to the accusation that the North could not make soldiers out of slaves, he cited the times and places when the "valiant and chivalric sons" had been soundly beaten by African American troops. Accusations that Black troops were lawless thieves were countered by marching Black troops through Southern cities and lands to powerfully demonstrate that there was "not a dollar's worth of property molested." The claim that Blacks "can't be taught anything" was dispelled by referring to the Black soldiers' prowess in military training and the rapid progress they had made acquiring literacy. Finally, he threw aside the claim that enslaved men were "animals" by making the declaration that he and his fellow officers in the USCT had proved that they were men "capable of evincing the finest traits of manhood." The only requirement they needed to progress was to "be freed from the damnation of their slave religion."[13]

After reaching Providence Landing, Daniel's regiment traveled down the Alabama River to a camp near Mobile. Daniel now he had time to reflect upon his journey through Alabama and to catch up on his correspondence. He was pleased at the opportunity he now had to command the regiment and admitted that he "would much rather be a chief than 'No 2.'" The discipline of the regiment appeared sound; there had been no disputes with any of the officers, and he could see no problems on the horizon. Yet enjoyable though the privileges of office were, he continued to look forward to the time he would leave the army and exercise his personal freedom. The heavy burdens of army life were beginning to wear him down. "A hard life, a hard fare and a hard-tack" were the features of army life he wished to leave behind.[14]

Daniel welcomed the return of Colonel Jones with mixed feelings. Although he was pleased to see his old friend and knew that his workload would be reduced, he regretted losing his command, and he believed more time was needed to adequately dress and refit the men. However, this situation did not deeply disturb him because he had always believed that the soldier's true home was the field and not the parade ground. Neatly turned out, parade ground soldiers had little appeal to him. He liked to see his Black soldiers coming "out of 'the Field'— worn, rough and out at the elbows." Men dressed this way publicized their veteran status and true manhood. Their torn, besmirched uniforms pointed to the fact that they were "brave fellows who did the work and endured the labors." While the Union government clothed its citizen army in blue military uniforms to foster the nation's collective identity, for the former slaves the uniforms affirmed their aspirations for citizenship. Daniel also shared these aspirations and admitted that it did him "good to see them donning their own clothes, and getting some new, handsome guns."[15]

Some uncertainty surrounded the regiment's fate. The surrender of Kirby Smith's army had ended rumors of a Texas campaign and increased the likelihood that the regiment would remain in Mobile. At this time of uncertainty, Daniel narrowly escaped serious injury when he visited Mobile on the day the city's magazine exploded.[16] While this escape provided some excitement and broke the dull routine of military service, it did nothing to endear him to a career in the postwar army. In part, his feelings of frustration and disillusionment resulted from the fact that he no longer commanded the regiment. But administrative changes and the reorganization of his regiment disturbed him the most. In a letter to Benjamin, who was equally disillusioned with army life, he protested against the officer selection boards that were being established and argued that they would "work a great wrong to many a good, sacrificing deserving officer." He believed that officers who had left book learning behind to fight the enemy in the field would be unable to pass these board examinations and consequently would be "modestly kicked out of the service." A cursory survey of the brave, hardworking officers in his regiment led him to believe that half of them would lose their positions with dishonor. Determined to leave the service with his reputation intact, he informed his brother that he would simply decline to come before the examining board.[17]

As the two brothers grappled with the issue of exiting the service, they forged even stronger bonds of affection. "I see that your thoughts are running over and canvassing the same topics as my own," wrote Daniel in June. He acknowledged that military service did have some advantages. It was a well-paid, honored profession. Moreover, the army had given him some job satisfaction. Recently he had received from the men many unsolicited compliments about the way he commanded the regiment. Yet the arguments for leaving the army seemed much stronger. Military service had lost a lot of its purpose now that the war was over. He also believed that army life was not compatible with his "peculiarly irascible temper." Army bureaucracy and the constant movement from station to post was an intolerable burden to him. More important still, his experience of army life ran hard up against his concept of manhood and his notions of community life.[18]

Daniel's moral and social values had been shaped by his solidly middle-class family upbringing. His concept of manhood reflected his family's belief in individual self-reliance, fortitude, protection of the weak, and community responsibility. Above all else he believed that a man should defend his home and community by showing courage on the battlefield. Honor, duty, and patriotism were the strong motivating forces behind his military service. Notions of manhood that focused on rough masculine dominance and indulgent camaraderie were alien to him. Indeed, he informed Benjamin that he did not enjoy the rough society of military men. He was not and never could become "a roistering 'hell of a fellow,'" for he would not "smoke, drink, chew, gamble, nor play the town gallant." Concerned about the state of his health, he relished physical activity and the habits of muscular manhood. In his search for future employment that would safeguard his health, he was keen to have a career that involved daily exercise. Jealously guarding his independence, he was determined not to be the subject of a "martinet."[19]

Daniel's concept of his manhood was also closely tied to his vision of community life. He believed that for "a man to amount to anything substantial and worthy of the respect in society," he had to be "settled, be known as *a family*, and equally harnessed into the community machinery." Because he believed the family was the foundation of community life, he refused to entertain any idea of marriage until he had a "profession and estate all ready."[20] While he was living a precarious life in the army, he was even reluctant to be engaged in romantic adventures that could lead to marriage. When Benjamin wrote on behalf of an admirer, "Miss G," seeking to acquire his photographic portrait, he declined his request, assuring him that "Miss G" would have his picture "as soon as the *weeds* cease to prevail." He then gently chastised his brother with the questions "What was your idea of Evangelism? 'Coelebs in search of a wife?'" After making this reference to the popular nineteenth-century novel *Coelebs in Search of a Wife* about a devout Christian bachelor's attempt to find a wife, Daniel clearly affirmed his bachelor status by stating "Coelebs is satisfied."[21]

In his search of a postwar career Daniel considered several possible professions and ventures. The thought of being a world traveler attracted him, so too did the idea of establishing a printing business or becoming a newspaper publisher. Business prospects in Red Wing also interested him. The favored ones he listed were banking, timber milling, and warehousing. Yet even while he speculated wildly on his future business activities, one thought remained constant in his mind. He was determined to enter a business partnership with Benjamin, and he assured him that if they could arrange one, it would be much more satisfactory "than mating with strangers."[22]

Benjamin did all he could to encourage Daniel in his pursuit of a suitable career. In his effort to help his brother he involved other members of the family. In a letter to Orrin, he stated he had a responsibility to care for his younger brother. "He is two years my junior," Benjamin wrote, "and to see him established in some position of life both congenial and agreeable would afford me more pleasure than the attainment of any object for self." Shortly after Benjamin had penned this letter, Orrin wrote to Daniel endorsing his decision to leave the army, offering to scout for a position for him at the Red Wing bank and promising to lobby on his behalf at the forthcoming Republican County Convention. Orrin even suggested that Daniel could become a county superintendent of schools, but on reflection admitted the salary would be too low. Full of enthusiasm, Martha took Daniel's career search to heart. She sought an "opening" in the town for him and suggested he could function as his father's deputy while he was looking for more permanent employment.[23]

Although Benjamin's letters and personal banter brought Daniel some relief from the demands of his military service and the uncertainties surrounding his return to civilian life, a developing family crisis at home disturbed him and began to enmesh him in a web of protest and discontent. His authority was waning at home because Mary McElroy's role in the Densmore household had now become a source of contention between mother and son. Even though Mary performed her service very competently, family ties were drawing her home to Hannibal, Missouri. Yet love of family was not the only reason why Mary wanted to leave the Densmores. Elizabeth's growing opposition to her service caused tension to develop until by the spring of 1865 this reached a critical stage. Elizabeth saw Mary as a usurper, someone who was attempting to take her rightful place in the house. The fact that Mary had been enslaved significantly compounded her feelings of displacement and inadequacy. In a letter to Daniel, Orrin admitted that

Mary's service appeared very tenuous because Elizabeth would not leave her to do the hard labor of the kitchen. Even though he knew his wife feared a loss of identity and being "regarded as superannuated," he urged her to accept Mary's help and tolerate her different mode of working.[24]

Orrin's letter brought a sharp reply from Daniel. "So mother talks of getting along without Mary. I shall regard it as unkind in her if she persists in raising the question at all," he asserted. What disturbed Daniel most was his mother's apparently self-centered attitude. By seeking to remove Mary, his mother seemed to be undermining his role as a dutiful, protecting son. Mary was his agent in the household. The positive reports of her service from various family members seemed to suggest that the current moves to dismiss her could be "a mere matter of fancy." In his appeal Daniel commented that the retention of Mary would also please Benjamin. "I hope mother will gratify her children who must be away from home, by permitting them to feel that a stronger pair of hands were carrying the load of the household labor," he pleaded. He then added that he felt greatly comforted knowing that Mary was laboring for his mother and for "Mittie" too. Finally, Daniel rested his case with a forthright statement saying, "I hope all questions as to retaining help will be summarily dismissed."[25]

To strengthen his case for Mary's retention, Daniel informed the family that Captain Poillon was very pleased with Mary's progress and that Poillon earnestly hoped that they would "not sustain this idea of sending her away." Daniel attributed his family's problems to the allegedly unique challenges associated with employing a servant who had been enslaved. Since the family had never employed a Black servant, he decided to give them some guidance on how to manage Mary. "If she does not please in some things, do not stand aloof, but tell her plainly what your wishes are," he advised. This instruction was derived from the knowledge he had acquired commanding Black soldiers. Both he and Poillon were convinced that "this was the only rule to follow with those we have to deal with." To follow orders, soldiers required simple, clear instructions. But there was also racial edge to Daniel's advice, as his counsel reinforced a prevailing stereotype that depicted African Americans as a simple people who were used to following orders. All the family needed to do was to issue firm and clear instructions. He did not realize that the family's labor problems were not rooted in poor labor management practices but in his mother's fears about the way Mary's presence threatened her role and status in the family home. Located deep in the Confederacy, Daniel had little knowledge of these complexities. A dutiful son, he only wanted an African American servant to help his frail mother.[26]

Fortunately for Mary, her difficult situation improved when Orrin and Elizabeth left Red Wing on their five-week Southern tour in early May 1865. While they were away, Mary was more relaxed and her relationship with Martha deepened. In a mild note of criticism Martha commented that Mary was "a *good* help, excepting an inclination to be sulky occasionally." But then she added, "We have had none of these fits since we have been alone." Martha observed that "we are getting along admirably during their absence." Free from Elizabeth's critical gaze, Mary was "thoroughly engaged in cleaning house, making butter, fixing the garden &c, &c."[27] Mary was a competent worker who was proud of her achievements, and she wanted "every thing in order 'if the folks should come home.'" Mary's changed temperament encouraged Martha to mistakenly believe that she was growing dependent on her. In early June she informed Daniel that Mary had "taken a fancy" to her and wanted to be her servant when she set up her own household. Yet two weeks earlier she commented that although she would "try hard to keep her," she wanted to return to her father and mother in the fall. Martha's relationship with Mary went much deeper than the normal employer-employee relationship, for together they shared a supportive friendship. But this friendship was always bound by the parameters of slavery. Martha could never forget that Mary had been a slave, and she believed that slavery was the essence of her being. Therefore, she believed that Mary's natural state was one of dependence and service. She was "indispensable," a "*good* help." It was for these reasons Martha tried "to keep her" even though Mary had wanted to return to parents and shape her own destiny.[28]

A few weeks after Daniel received news that tension within the family home had lessened because his parents were on tour, his regiment was ordered to Carrollton, Louisiana. On arriving at Carrollton, Daniel discovered that wild rumors were circulating about the destination of his regiment. While one group of rumors directed the regiment to Memphis, others pointed to Red River and Shreveport. During this time of uncertainty, he put some of his objections to military service on hold. He was even prepared to submit himself to an examination board, because he did not want his time in the army lengthened by his failure to follow military procedures. The idea of a post-military career attracted him, and he was keen to return home to mediate the conflict between his mother and Mary. Yet before this happened, he had to negotiate his exit from the army. As rumors spread among the ranks about future service on the Red River, his departure appeared to be a very difficult task.[29]

14

"They've got money, let them buy their own biscuit"

Departure and Homecoming

This chapter discusses the closing stages of Daniel's and Benjamin's service in the army and Mary's departure from service in the Densmore household. Departures and homecomings are events that involve the transition from one environment to another. Studying these events has two advantages. First, because they are often emotionally charged, they enable us to probe inner thoughts and attitudes that would otherwise have remained hidden. Second, these events help us discover how journeys were shaped not only by the departees' surrounding environments, but also by the relationships they shared with their families and communities. Although Mary, Daniel, and Benjamin all shared a strong desire to end their service, their journeys home were tortuously difficult. They had to negotiate their departures with employers who exercised considerable authority over them. Moreover, all wanted to exit in good standing.

Rumors that Daniel's regiment was going to be sent from New Orleans to the Red River proved true. Late in June, the 68th USCI journeyed up the Mississippi and Red Rivers and encamped near Pineville, Louisiana. There Daniel remained for a week, ill with fever. Eventually, his condition became so bad that on July 6 he was ordered to begin his journey home on sick leave. At this critical time Benjamin reached out and assisted him. Even though he was also ill and confined to his sickbed, when Daniel passed through Columbus, Kentucky, he arranged to care for his horse and store his equipment. As he journeyed home, Daniel realized his military career was ending in a way he had not contemplated. In all his discussions with his family he had never canvassed the idea of leaving the army because of poor health. In some ways this was an inauspicious end because he was returning home an invalid. Yet even though the battlefield was far behind him, new challenges confronted him at home because controversy still raged about Mary McElroy's position in the Densmore household.[1]

Two months after Daniel arrived home, the turmoil surrounding Mary's service finally dissipated. In September 1865 Daniel informed Benjamin that Mary would soon leave for Hannibal, Missouri. There was no tone of regret or disappointment in his announcement. In fact, he admitted that everyone at home was getting on "swimmingly." He even went as far as saying that Mary, "the institution," had stayed as long as he thought she might, that he was "satisfied with the operation," because it had eased his mother's burdens and helped to restore her health. What had brought about this radical change of attitude was Mary's strong determination to return home to her loved ones. The fact that Daniel was now home and able to placate some of his mother's fears about Mary's service also reduced the level of tension in the household.²

Although the war had brought Mary freedom, she, like many freedwomen, remained economically tied to the white woman's kitchen. Yet through her labor she defied the slave stereotype of a worker who was docile and unable care for work animals. Martha commented that she could handle even the most difficult cows, noting that "the *old red one*, always so frisky, is under *complete subjection.*" Upon further reflection she noted that "Mary takes great pride in this achievement." This sense of accomplishment also shone out in Mary's pursuit of education. As she formed her letters, she could see the progress she was making. While her time in Red Wing was a time of service, it was also a time of personal growth.³

A degree of normality returned to the Densmore household when Daniel returned from the war. Yet his return was not the signal for Mary's departure. She left in her own time and on her own terms with her reputation enhanced. The fact that two white helpers replaced her was evidence of her capabilities and value to the household. Perhaps the most powerful demonstration of her independent spirit can be seen in the way she strove to maintain contact with her family in Hannibal. Mary made such good progress with her studies that before Daniel went on sick leave, Orrin asked Daniel to inform Captain Poillon of her progress. "It may be satisfactory to Capt Poillon to know that Mary has spent most of the winter in School and has done very well," he commented. She was "now able to read consistently," Orrin noted, "and has unaided written letters to her associates in Hannibal." Mary loved her parents, and her family ties were much stronger than any labor contract. In May 1865, she informed Martha that she would like to return home to her parents next fall; then five months later she began her journey. Although she had worked for the Densmore's for only one year, in some ways her presence in the Densmore household was like that of the Black refugees Leslie A. Schwalm has identified moving northward to freedom in the Upper Midwest. These refugees persuaded some Midwestern citizens to positively modify their image of African Americans. Racism may have remained endemic in the region, but the presence of individuals such as Mary McElroy seriously challenged it.⁴

With harmony in the family home restored, Daniel was free to concentrate on recovering from his debilitating illness. For the first few weeks of his sick leave, his difficult lot was made much more bearable by the presence of Benjamin, who had managed to secure twenty days' leave. Although Benjamin was still recovering from illness, the whole family rejoiced at having the boys home together. Yet despite all the loving care lavished upon him, Daniel's recovery was long and slow. Approximately one week after Benjamin had returned to active duty, Daniel wrote him that he got tired easily, vomited frequently, sweated all night, and looked "like a codfish in the face." His feelings of discomfort and weakness were exacerbated by the news he was receiving from his old regiment. A controversy had erupted over the promotion of an officer, and during this dispute Daniel had been made to appear as a "Dammed Rebel" and a snake in the grass. The controversy was sparked by Colonel Jones's passing over the senior captain, James H. McFarlane, and appointing as major a more junior officer. Jones claimed that he was acting on Daniel's recommendation, and that Daniel had requested that McFarlane be placed on the sick list until he returned to the regiment. The controversy resulted in a deluge of letters to Daniel from Jones and McFarlane, and after carefully reviewing all the correspondence Daniel concluded that Jones's account was a lie. To clear his name, he wrote to both Jones and McFarland, clearly stated his position and challenged the officers in his regiment to show a more unblemished record. Although he freely shared the details of his dispute with Benjamin, he warned him against informing other members of the family. Daniel may have kept the controversy hidden so that his parents would not be burdened with his problems. Further, issues of family honor were also implicitly tied to the dispute. In the past Daniel had often informed the family about Colonel's Jones's noble character and able leadership. If he now suddenly depicted Jones as an unprincipled liar, the family could question his judgment and perhaps even his integrity.[5]

In early September he submitted his resignation, and it was duly accepted later that month. His honorable discharge from the service brought him considerable peace of mind. Now he could sleep restfully at night with the assurance that the army could no longer call him "back to the sultry banks of Red River." The controversy that had raged in his regiment also came to a satisfactory resolution. He had received several letters from officers informing him that they believed that someone was trying to deceive him. No guilty party was named, but Daniel had no hesitation in naming Jones. He believed that Jones was counting on him returning to the regiment to clear his name. Once he had returned, he surmised that Jones would be in a much more favorable position to have his resignation application accepted.[6]

The rupture of the relationship between Colonel Jones and Daniel was unexpected. Strong bonds of comradeship had developed between them as they strove to build up the regiment and mold it into a fighting force. The struggle they shared defending their soldiers against racism in the Union Army and their campaigns against a common ethnic enemy, the Hungarians, helped to strengthen these bonds. The rigor of campaigning and the heat of battle had also galvanized their friendship. However, as the war ended, military ambition dulled, and the call of home became stronger, the relationship between Daniel and Jones began to seriously deteriorate. This was no doubt exacerbated by Jones's long absence on sick leave. While demobilization and homecoming evoked aspirations for joyful reunions and prosperous futures, they also placed stresses and demands on soldiers. The friction that developed between Daniel and Colonel Jones demonstrated that in the 68th USCI the attractions of home and civil life sometimes came into conflict with duty and military reputation.[7]

While homecomings were generally times of great celebration, on some occasions community tensions and old grievances surfaced. Daniel witnessed this when the Minnesota regiments returned. When Benjamin's old regiment, the 3rd Minnesota, returned home from the war, members of the regiment voted to boycott the reception the citizens of St. Paul had arranged for them. A legacy of ill feeling existed between the 3rd and the residents of St. Paul. The St. Paul newspapers had roundly condemned the regiment for surrendering at Murfreesboro, and soldiers felt that the residents of St. Paul had not acknowledged their efforts in securing victory at Wood Lake. Deprived of accommodation and pay after their Indian campaign, the 3rd rioted in St. Paul in November 1862. Wounds deepened after the war ended, when one St. Paul newspaper implied that the patriotic service of the 8th Minnesota had mitigated the dishonorable performance of the 3rd Minnesota. The St. Paul reception committee was left bewildered. Daniel reported to Benjamin that "kind hearted and patriotic ladies" saw their piles of pies and cakes go to waste, the band did not play, firemen were unable to light the torches, and the governor and mayor were unable to deliver their welcoming addresses. As a result of this rebuff, the citizens of St. Paul "leaked off home meditating, probably for the first time, upon the possibility of a soldier remembering an insult."[8] In contrast, the 3rd Minnesota's response to the citizens of Red Wing's welcome could not have been more different. At Red Wing Miss Martha Densmore and other patriotic ladies had organized a great mountain of supplies and refreshments for their returning heroes from the 3rd Minnesota, and Daniel's old regiment, the 7th Minnesota Infantry. The men of the 3rd arrived first, and to the satisfaction of the ladies present, they "swept the board to the last crumb and drop." More importantly, "their behavior was in every way particular gentlemanlike and respectful." ⁹

Homecomings sometimes revived prejudices and interregimental rivalries. Daniel was disturbed when he heard that four companies of the 5th Minnesota regiment were soon to descend on Red Wing for refreshments. He accused these "bounty cusses" of enlisting for mercenary motives, of constantly complaining about their duties, and of always pleading to be returned home. These men did not deserve the charity of the patriotic ladies of Red Wing. "They've got money, let them buy their own biscuit" was his response to their requests for refreshments. Daniel condemned men from the 5th Minnesota Infantry for receiving bounties because he believed they lacked manhood and a true patriotic spirit. James McPherson argues that officers from the upper and middle class saw "bounty men" as an inferior and separate group. Motivated by nativism and feelings of class superiority, men such as Daniel Densmore looked down upon immigrants and poor laborers. The fact that the 5th Minnesota had within its ranks several German-speaking officers and a relatively large number of German immigrant soldiers would have provided Daniel with another powerful incentive for opposing refreshments being dispensed to this regiment in Red Wing.¹⁰

Regardless of the personal animosity and regimental rivalry that sometimes surfaced during the soldiers' return, Minnesota communities generally were relieved the war was over, proud of their sons' victory, and touched by a sense of loss for those who did not return. Orrin observed that when discharged, the men of the 3rd Minnesota Infantry had set out for Red Wing with great enthusiasm. They were proud of their accomplishments and could not wait to return home. Daniel noted that Red Wing was equally pleased with them, proclaiming that "there has not been a better regiment in any respect pass up the river, than they." To commemorate the great feats of its fighting men, Goodhue County proposed two projects. One was a community celebration, a grand reception, to be held during the county fair. The other involved the erection of a soldier's monument, on the triangular piece of ground in front of Chilson House. The county's salute to its victorious veterans combined the two common elements found in many homecomings, namely joyous community celebration and solemn civic memorializing. When the veterans returned, the citizens of Red Wing drank to the health of the living and pledged to remember of sacrifices of the dead.¹¹

The wave of celebration and memorializing that swept through most Northern cities and towns in the immediate postwar years often ignored the role of the Black soldiers and their officers in the war. Several factors account for this muted reception. First, even though the role of Black soldiers in the Union Army had to a limited degree tempered racism in the North, strong currents of racial prejudice still ran through the mainstream of Northern society. Aware that service in the Union Army provided African Americans with powerful arguments for citizenship, some racially prejudiced Northerners refused to celebrate or even acknowledge the contribution of Black soldiers to the war effort. Second, while some Black regiments recruited from vibrant Black communities in Northern cities were welcomed home with civic parades and receptions, most regiments did not receive a civic reception. The majority of USCT troops who were recruited from former Confederate states, remained in the South when their officers independently returned to their Northern homes. Although Southern Black communities welcomed their soldiers home as heroes, these Black veterans faced intense hostility from Southern whites and former rebel soldiers.[12]

Because USCT was organized federally, the officers in USCT regiments were drawn from a variety of states. Unlike officers from state-based Union Army units, most officers belonging to USCT regiments had no specific Northern home community to give them aid, honor their service, or welcome them home. When they were mustered out of the military, they returned to their Northern homes as individuals. Their men went in a different direction and returned to their Southern homes. For some officers, such as Daniel Densmore, homecoming became a process of reflective glory. While they, as a group, were unable to share with their men the immediate accolades of their home communities, they were able to reflect in the glory of the old regiments they were drawn from. From this point of view, the achievements of the 3rd and 7th Minnesota took on new meaning for men such as Benjamin and Daniel Densmore who returned to their home communities often well after the war had ended and victory celebrations had ceased. Finally, the United States government's policy of employing Black troops to occupy the reconstructed South muted the reception some USCT officers received when they returned long after the war had ended.[13]

Most of Daniel's immediate postwar correspondence with Benjamin consisted of community gossip and family news. In November he informed Benjamin that the weather had been so wet that the roads had been impassable. A few weeks earlier he reported that their mother had raised a bountiful crop of ripe tomatoes, which would soon be turned into relish or preserved for winter. He also wrote about the romances of Martha and Belle, the impending departure of Mary, selling his horse, the progress he and father had made in extending the family barn, the fire at the Broughton place, and finally, a spate of burglaries which had afflicted Red Wing. The combination of family news and town talk helped affirm Daniel's sense of place. It helped to dull the pangs of army life and reassure him that he had a home in Red Wing.[14]

Slowly recovering from his illness, Daniel was comfortable at home. As he gazed out across the Minnesota landscape, he felt a special sense of belonging, a sense he never felt as he journeyed across the strange lands of the South. He wrote to Benjamin rejoicing that he had experienced the "most beautiful weather throughout the fall season."[15] As the nights grew longer and the days grew colder, Daniel's thoughts turned to the isolation of his elder brother serving in a hostile land. In December he assured Benjamin that all those snugly housed here at home this quiet Sabbath night were constantly "thinking of the boy thats still away." They wondered whether he had good shelter, a warm fire, a fine supper, and congenial company. In the passages that followed these comments Daniel painted for Benjamin a scene of domestic bliss.

He described descending the stairs for supper and finding father, mother, and Martha all reading the latest newspapers. At one end of the lounge he saw the family cat. It yawned and stretched like a jackknife opening up before it curled back to sleep again. As mother peered over her glasses at Daniel who was eagerly devouring his evening meal, she commented that she "wished that Benj had a bowl of bread & milk tonight." These domestic images positioned as they were at the start of the letter were used to convey loving messages of hope and reassurance. Christmas Day was almost upon the family, and while it would be a time of great celebration and good cheer, it would also be a time of sadness. His letter would have been a mixed blessing for Benjamin, for while it would have reassured him of comforts that awaited him at home, it would also deepen the pangs of separation he felt as he served the Union in the South long after the war had ended.[16]

In the first half of 1865, while Daniel was fighting in the siege of Fort Blakely and serving in the army of occupation in Alabama and Louisiana, Benjamin led a largely sedentary existence faithfully carrying out his garrison duties at Fort Halleck. Promoted to the rank of captain in July 1864, he was confident that the Union would triumph over the South, but he was also aware that he was playing only an incidental role in the great national conflict.[17] His limited participation encouraged him to look very favorably upon the exploits of Union heroes. Because they were fighting a war he could not fight, these Union heroes became his representatives and his champions. The exploits of General Sherman greatly appealed to him. In December 1864, he commented that the triumphant march of "Gen. Sherman (the hero of the war) shows well that the Rebellion is rotten at heart." He believed that if Grant could learn from Sherman's victories, he would be able to reduce Richmond to a supply base.[18]

Conscious of his own limited combat experience, Benjamin admitted he had seen the whole war through the newspapers. "'Our Correspondent,'" he acknowledged to his father, "has told me more of it than has been my lot ever to experience." Nevertheless, he justified his contribution to the Union war effort by arguing that if he had not made it, "some *other* would have it to do." He rejoiced that the success of the Union armies meant that the United States had vindicated its reputation as a great nation on the world stage. Although he sometimes thought that the war would end in a whimper, he believed its true significance would be acclaimed in the future when it was known as "The War of Emancipation." While he believed that future generations of Southerners would accept the "retributive justice" imposed on their land, he believed the current generation was so committed to their idol, slavery, that they would "cling to it with the faith of pagans and thus slip away into oblivion."[19]

As the war concluded, Benjamin discovered that his commitment to the Union cause developed in new ways. His service commanding Black troops had so moderated his racial attitudes that he no longer viewed his soldiers as "machines" but as potential citizens. Benjamin believed that the restoration of the rebellious South to the Union would require defeating the Southern armies and raising the allegedly degraded slaves to manhood so that they could become productive, self-reliant citizens. To further this goal, he sought to eliminate racial injustices imposed on his men. For example, in June 1864 he wrote to the U.S. Army Pay Master in St. Louis, unsuccessfully seeking to have his soldiers paid at the same rate as white soldiers.[20] Yet it was his efforts to provide his men with a teacher which most clearly pointed to the desire to prepare his men for their future role as citizens.

Benjamin's interest in the education of his soldiers was stimulated by the death of one of his men. In early May 1864 while making up an inventory of the dead soldier's effects, he discovered sixteen dollars. Perhaps because the soldier's next of kin were unknown, with the agreement of a fellow officer he decided to invest the money in materials for the education of his men. He asked Daniel to purchase slates, books, pencils, and "alphabet cards." The materials were "for the use of the colored soldier, that he may learn something." He left it up to Daniel to make the final selection, with the proviso that the books, "of course be very elementary— of the A.–B. etical [alphabetical] style."[21]

By April 1865 Benjamin was seriously considering appointing a teacher to his company. In search of one he wrote to Martha, who was at the time teaching at the Red Wing School. A belated reply by Martha brought high praise for Benjamin's plans for instructing Black soldiers, good wishes on its execution, but no suggestion of anyone to fill the position.[22] A month later he presented his plan to his father. He was confident that his father would strongly support his proposal because he was an ardent abolitionist with a long-standing interest in public education.

In a spirit of paternalism, Benjamin outlined a comprehensive plan to employ an "Educational Sergeant" who would be paid for by the men out of their wages. The Educational Sergeant would also receive company rations, dine with the officers, and, to avoid disrupting the military routine, harmonize his teaching with the company's military duties. The job would be a growing one, for Benjamin expected the size of his company to increase significantly. He wanted Orrin to speak about the men's character and about his knowledge of army life, "after the manner of an eye-witness." He urged him to emphasize the opportunities military service offered for a good living. Finally, he made it clear that he was looking for a teacher who was of good character, had a fine grasp of the English language, and had excellent teaching skills. The reasons for employing such a teacher were compelling. The soldiers had to learn how to spend their leisure time usefully, and, in this regard, "it could be filled with no better employment than in learning to read, write, cipher, spell &. c." He insisted that it was vitally important that the former slaves were educated because "the time will come when they are thrown on their own resources." More important still, the likelihood of them possessing the franchise and citizenship appeared "no remote possibility." Benjamin believed he had a patriotic duty to prepare them for these responsibilities, and while he did not expect to immediately complete the task at hand, it least he could begin.[23]

Orrin responded enthusiastically to his son's request for help. In June 1865, on his way home from his Southern tour, he asked the ministers attending the Universalist Church Convention at Janesville, and the Congregational minister at Emerald Grove, to name possible candidates. But despite these efforts only one candidate was suggested, an elderly former teacher who was a widower. Although he had poor health, he was "an original abolitionist and ardent friend of the Blacks." Discouraged by this poor response, Benjamin finally abandoned his project when he was separated from his company and appointed District Provost Marshal for Western Kentucky. Yet despite this failure, Benjamin gained from his project in several ways. His commitment to the project reinforced his abolitionist credentials within the family. Confined to garrison duties in Columbus, he had little prospect of striking a blow against slavery. However, his education project offered him this opportunity. Further, his project also enabled him to share his concern for the welfare of his men with his father. As Orrin and Benjamin planned the project, their relationship grew stronger.[24]

As the war concluded, Orrin became increasingly concerned about Benjamin's declining health and his disillusionment with army life. Keen to instill confidence in his son, he encouraged him to think seriously about his future career prospects. Early in January 1865 he informed him that there was a general expectation of a boom in railway construction in Minnesota, and he urged him to seek a transfer to the Engineer Corps so he would be well placed to gain employment when the war ended.[25] In confidence Orrin raised his concerns about Benjamin's career prospects with Daniel in mid-January. He accused Benjamin of being too passive and comfortable, of "settling down too obscurely with his sergeant," and of not seeking to exploit his talents. He urged Daniel to find a promotion for him in his regiment. Daniel's response was anything but hopeful. He informed his father that Benjamin's arrival in his regiment would provoke so much jealousy among the officers that his position would be untenable. Yet despite these gloomy predictions, Daniel unsuccessfully lobbied Colonel Jones on his brother's behalf.[26]

In February, Benjamin seized the initiative and attempted to forge a new career for himself in the navy. On hearing this news Daniel supported Benjamin's action, and in a letter to him written in March, Daniel claimed that the worst challenge he would face was getting his "sea-legs." But his naval prospects disappeared when news broke that half the naval fleet was to be retired and thousands of sailors were to be dismissed from the navy. Benjamin's decision not to pursue a naval career gave some assurance to his parents who, while claiming that Benjamin's career choice should not be made to suit their "particular whim or notion," were concerned about his prospects in the navy.[27]

Although he was concerned about his prospects, Benjamin joined in the celebrations held at Columbus to mark the fall of Richmond. But his time of celebrating was short. When news of Lincoln's assassination broke, loyal Unionists descended into a state of deep mourning. He described the mood of the city of Cairo, Illinois, commenting that once news of Lincoln's death "shot through the heart of the people.—A deep and heavy gloom settled over the place like a funeral pall." He had no doubt that this was the "nation's dark hour." Such an unrestrained display of public mourning convinced him that "*the President lived in the hearts of his people.*"[28] In these dark days he looked forward to a day when peace would settle on the land, a day when the cannon and sword would "be speedily transformed into the plough-shere [*sic*] & pruning-hook." His longing for a peaceful and settled future was reinforced by his boring inactivity. His service in the military had now become an "almost intolerable affair." Yet within a few weeks his outlook improved significantly when news arrived that his parents had set out to visit him during their tour of the South.[29]

Early in May 1865 Orrin and Elizabeth set out on their Southern tour, which included a visit to Benjamin at Columbus. Although they left only a scant record of the tour, their visit encouraged Benjamin. Shortly after their departure he was sent to carry out provost marshal duties first at Hickman and then Paducah. As the pressure of his workload mounted in mid-July, he managed to secure three week's leave.[30] When he returned to Kentucky, his mind was focused on one issue: resignation. But his efforts to secure an early release from the service were unsuccessful. Like all soldiers who had fought a long, hard war, Benjamin wanted to return home to the warm welcome of family and friends. Yet even though the pull of loved ones was very strong, other forces were also at work impelling him to leave.[31]

Benjamin feared that once the federal government's control of Kentucky was loosened, the state would be "rebelized." In despair he commented that "with Martial law removed from the state (an act that may take place at any time) we shall have either to do nothing or to do as the rebels say." He believed that "self-respect would impel any sensible and honest person to avoid such a condition." His regiment now lacked leadership and purpose. "Not literally but in reality *we* might as well be in china as to stay here and try to be loyal to our cause--(if it may be said that we have any cause)." Even the rate of army pay, which was "once honorable," was "now paltry," and he "would not be the worm to gnaw for it."[32]

Family members responded to Benjamin's negative outlook with expressions of compassion and concern. They explained just how much they missed him and how disappointed they were to learn about his failed resignation applications. Margaret felt "strongly inclined to condole with" him on his "dull life and the bad condition of the military government." Aunt Martha also expressed "great disappointment" at his resignation being disapproved. Then she added, "[Y]our last stay with us, when last here was so short, that it seems like a pleasant dream." Packed with warm greetings and images of domestic and community happiness, these letters assured him of his family's love. But they also reminded him of the social adventures he was missing and business opportunities that were being lost.[33]

As well as grieving Benjamin's absence, both Orrin and Daniel were also concerned about his emotional state. Although they did not admit it openly, they were worried that Benjamin would become so depressed that he would act impulsively and perhaps dishonor the family's name. Therefore, in their letters to him they encouraged him to remain steadfast and think positively about his remaining service. In early December 1865, Orrin informed him that the family regretted he was still in the army, but he also expressed their "hope that it may all prove for the best yet." A week later he encouraged him to renew his efforts to establish a school "on the plan he entertained last summer." Daniel assured him that he did not believe in "worrying about matters, (especially military matters) that cannot be helped." He even admitted that after he had considered all Benjamin's trials, he was worried about discouraging him by writing "too blue a letter." While he acknowledged that it was natural for him to "take the first opportunity to come out," he urged him "in the meanwhile to take the matter as quietly as may be, as thereby a man lasts longer." Finally, Daniel reminded Benjamin that he would be earning more money this winter than he would.[34]

The family's concern for Benjamin's welfare significantly increased when they learned that his regiment was to be sent to Arkansas. Orrin was surprised by this news because early in November he had placed his faith in rumors that the USCT regiments in Kentucky would soon be demobilized. A month later he wrote Benjamin bemoaning the regiment's move to Helena, Arkansas. But he expressed the hope that Benjamin's regiment would move up the Arkansas river away from disease-ridden Helena before the spring. "[W]e have learned to regard that as an unhealthy locality from the experience of the 6th Minn while there," Orrin commented. The family's fears subsided when they learned that Benjamin's regiment had moved to Pine Bluff, Arkansas. There conditions became more settled and more akin to civilian life. At Pine Bluff Benjamin managed a government sawmill, an occupation that the family had been heavily involved with in Red Wing. Finally, after several weeks serving at Pine Bluff the 4th U.S. Colored Heavy Artillery was mustered out of the service, and Benjamin began his long journey home to Red Wing.[35]

For many Northern families the return of loved ones from the war was a protracted process fraught with challenges and tension. This was because issues of physical survival, departure, and homecoming were often inextricably linked to family honor and the rigid rule of army law and regulations. Daniel hid the difficulties associated with his departure from the army from his family for fear that his conflict with his former friend and mentor, Colonel Jones, would burden his parents and perhaps tarnish the family's honor. Benjamin's departure from the army was also linked to the family's well-being. The family were primarily worried about Benjamin's health, particularly his mental state. But they were also concerned that he would do his duty and serve his full term so he could return home with his reputation intact. These concerns were very real, for Benjamin's letters home not only complained about his prolonged enlistment, but they also provided a running commentary about the challenges he faced adjusting to the army's changing character as it demobilized and adopted a peacekeeping role in the South.

Homecoming involved important rituals of community endorsement. The celebrations Northern communities held to welcome home their returning boys were expressions of collective appreciation. But sometimes the glare and rhetoric of these festivities concealed tensions that existed within communities and between communities. The contrasting fate of the receptions given to the men of the 3rd Minnesota Infantry by the citizens of St. Paul and Red Wing is indicative of this. Officers, such as Daniel Densmore, from USCT regiments recruited in the South were particularly aware of a lack of local support. Perhaps this lack of community endorsement may partially explain why Daniel felt resentment toward the men of the 5th Minnesota Infantry, a regiment of bounty men. Yet regardless of community rivalries and family tensions, homecoming was an occasion of celebration. Although the war had taken a great personal toll, the bloodletting had now ended; a victorious peace had been heralded; the Union had been saved; and above all else, families such as the Densmores were united once again.

Conclusion

From the moment Benjamin and Daniel enlisted, all family members knew that the family home was at the heart of the conflict. As committed abolitionists, the family condemned slaveholders primarily because their cruel regime destroyed the sanctity of the family, the wellspring of civilized living and Christian life. For the Densmores, the sanctity of family life was clearly accentuated by their sons' involvement in Minnesota's Dakota Wars. When Daniel discovered the destruction wrought by the Dakota on settlers' homes in the summer of 1863, he became increasingly determined to defend the family home. Because the family believed the fight against the Southern rebels was a continuation of their struggle to defend the family home, all family members were mobilized in its defense. Yet ironically, the family failed to see that the defense of their home meant dispossessing the Dakota of their homelands and invading the homes of rebels in the South.[1]

The home was on the front line of the Densmore women's war for the Union. Physically, the large family home embodied many of the Densmores' middle-class cultural and political values, and because of this, it became an important venue for aiding the Union cause. In the spacious kitchen food was cooked and dispensed to hungry soldiers at refreshment booths on the Red Wing quayside. In the drawing room Martha and her mother hosted fundraising meetings of the Red Wing Ladies' Soldiers' Aid Society. Weary soldiers from respectable families, such as Daniel's friend Lt. Robert Whittleton, were also welcome guests. Historians Lisa Tendrich Frank and LeeAnn Whites remind us that the Civil War was a "relational war" that intricately bound the home front and battlefront together in one continuous struggle. Personal correspondence played a vital role in this bonding process. Nothing did more to lift the spirits of Benjamin and Daniel than the letters they received from home, and because the flow of correspondence was reciprocal, a dialogue of concern and commitment was maintained.[2]

While the Densmore boys were receiving help from home, they were also aiding the fight on the home front. The letters the boys sent home gave eyewitness accounts of the war's progress, and they made the family members feel they were actors in the great drama of war. The letters, therefore, encouraged the family to redouble their war effort. Like many parents of USCT officers, the Densmores understood that their sons lacked the companionship of colleagues drawn from the local community. In these circumstances the letters the sons wrote provided welcome assurance that they remained loyal to the family values and had not been negatively influenced by their service with former slaves. Their letters served another function too. Because the boys' letters were circulated among the wider family, they also had the effect of drawing the family net closer.

The war tied the family members together in new ways. At home, a labor shortage caused the family to constantly look to Martha for assistance and guidance, and for Orrin Jr. to take up more work in his father's office. Sometimes old relationships took new forms. For example, while Martha kept Daniel in touch with the social life of Red Wing, Aunt Martha acted as a family elder with whom Daniel could discuss the deeper meaning of the war. On the battlefront, Benjamin and Daniel became increasingly dependent on each other to meet the challenges of serving in the USCT. Yet as well as uniting the family, the war correspondence also caused tension and fractures to occur. Secrets were shared between some members and hidden from others.

The folks at home developed an understanding of the war in the South that underscored their family values and was heavily dependent on the reports they received from their serving sons. But their imagined war was very different from that which their sons personally experienced. Acutely aware of this, Benjamin and Daniel configured their correspondence to preserve the family's honor and hide possible violations of the abolitionist creed. To achieve these goals, they collaborated in deception and exclusion. Their letters home did not mention Benjamin's arrest or Daniel's dispute with Colonel Jones. Deception was also practiced on the home front. To safeguard Elizabeth's well-being, all the family members hid the true horror of Fort Pillow from her. Even efforts to aid the family members sometimes had negative consequences. Mary's presence in the family home caused tension to flare between Daniel and his mother. When Benjamin and Daniel generously hosted Orrin Jr.'s visit to their camps, he became so gravely ill that his visit ended with some recrimination. Yet despite all these difficulties, the integrity of the family not only survived the war but grew stronger. The war was, above all else, a life-and-death struggle for survival. All family knew this, and this knowledge subsumed all the ruptures and difficulties they encountered.

During the war, the Densmores discovered that they had to continually reconcile their abolitionist beliefs with their material self-interest and the military demands the war placed on them. Both Benjamin and Daniel joined the USCT because their personal interests and political ideology coincided. Commissions in the USCT gave them well-paid jobs fighting for a cause they believed in. But the family's commitment to abolitionism remained flexible. When personal circumstances changed, so did their commitment to abolitionism. Hence, toward the end of the war, Benjamin planned to leave the USCT to join the navy. Benjamin's and Daniel's abolitionist beliefs were both constantly evolving, but because Daniel was the most prolific correspondent, his letters became the main medium that helped the family reshape their abolitionist ideology. He invariably asked the family to comment on his experiences and affirm the positions he had taken. In the process of doing this, his family claimed the collective ownership of his experiences.

At the St. Louis Sanitary Commission Fair, Daniel witnessed Black and white soldiers working collaboratively to erect the Fair building. This scene encouraged him to broaden his concept of abolitionism to include the possibility of Black citizenship. This commitment grew even stronger as he journeyed further south and passed Fort Pillow, a site where Black soldiers, prisoners of war, had been slaughtered for fighting to defend the Union. Fort Pillow galvanized his abolitionist faith in the Union cause. Back home the response was different. Orrin blamed the federal government's weak defense of Black prisoners for indirectly allowing the massacre to occur. He did not want his family's honor tarnished or his sons' brave service sacrificed by government neglect or incompetence. For a short time, he even doubted whether his two sons should serve in the USCT.

At Fort Pickering, Memphis, Daniel's abolitionist beliefs were challenged by the racially discriminatory policies of the military authorities and the logistical demands of the army. In the antebellum period the family's abolitionist beliefs had always been directed against the tyranny of the Southern slaveholders. Now the situation was different because Union Army officers appeared to be imposing a new form of servitude on the Black soldiers. To meet this new challenge, Daniel became an advocate for his men. He appealed to his family for support; they believed they could offer empathy, but little else. Orrin urged him to obey the commands of superiors, even if he felt they were unjust. They felt that family honor could not be sacrificed for an ideological creed, no matter how noble it might be.

Both Daniel and Benjamin had a troubled relationship with officers of Hungarian descent who were their commanders at Fort Halleck and Fort Pickering. As a result of this, they aligned their nativism more closely to their abolitionist beliefs by blaming the allegedly corrupt and incompetent officers of Hungarian descent, for many, but not all, of the injustices inflicted on them and their men. Scapegoating the Hungarians helped them reconcile their abolitionist beliefs at least partially with army policies. Despite the problems they faced, they still retained some faith in the Union Army as an institution that embodied the spirit of the nation. While the folks at home generally supported Benjamin's and Daniel's anti-Hungarian position, Orrin once again urged caution.

The most important battleground where the Densmores' abolitionist beliefs were tested was not in the South, but in the kitchen of their family home. Mary McElroy's presence in the kitchen challenged the family's version of abolitionism which denied her agency and control of her own destiny. The Densmores decided to invite Mary into their household because they desperately needed a domestic servant to do housework. They did not employ Mary to validate abolitionism. But over time, as Benjamin and Daniel became more deeply embedded in the USCT, Mary's appointment became more closely aligned with their abolitionist cause. Even before Mary arrived in Red Wing, the Densmores gained considerable status from their efforts to gain contraband labor for their neighbors. When Mary arrived, the family's reputation soared. The Densmores risked a lot of social capital when they employed Mary. Indeed, they called their project an "experiment" because the outcome was so uncertain. If Mary conformed to the slave stereotype and proved to be lazy and disruptive, then the family's reputation would be badly damaged. More important still, a poor performance by Mary would cast a long shadow on the abolitionist cause and indirectly discredit Benjamin's and Daniel's service in the USCT.

As the war concluded, the family acknowledged that their experiment was a resounding success. Mary had worked harder and more efficiently than they had ever imagined. Her ability to work efficiently, learn to read and write, and negotiate her wages shattered the Densmores' slave stereotype. There was nothing of a compliant slave about her, even though members of the family sometimes wrapped criticism of her performance with reference to her slave past. Apart from Elizabeth, the family members valued her industry and efficiency. But none accepted Mary as an equal. The family's response to Mary was always governed by the parameters of race and class. Martha, for example, aided Mary's education and valued her companionship, but her feelings of class superiority and racial prejudice placed limits on their relationship. All members of the family believed that slavery was at the heart of Mary's being. They were convinced it defined her as a person, and because of this they thought dependency and service was her

CONCLUSION 183

natural state. Even Mary's near white appearance could not shake this firmly held conviction.

The Densmores looked at the war through the prism of objects. Perhaps no objects were handled with more loving care than the letters the sons sent home. Orrin collected these as family keepsakes, records of his sons' honorable service. Gifts were important too. The Densmore boys carried with them in their camps objects that reminded them of home. The cans of medicine Orrin sent to his boys may have left a bitter taste, but they were constant reminders of the family's love and devotion. Martha's pails of butter were perhaps more nourishing and symbolized the strong support emanating from the wider Densmore family. But not all the objects came from home. Martha proudly wore the ring Daniel gave her because it was a beautiful jewel and a memento of his war against the Dakota. She was also thrilled to receive the sheet music Daniel sent her. The cactus Daniel planted in the family's garden became a living symbol for the family pointing to the alleged conquest of the Dakota and the exotic mystery of their land. Sometimes the brothers exchanged gifts with each other. For example, Benjamin's spirits were lifted when he donned the new uniform Daniel had sent him. All these objects helped the family members place the war experiences in historical time. But above all else, they were tangible reminders of the family's love for each other and the cause they were fighting for.

The Civil War encouraged the Densmores to look at the natural world with new eyes. The graphically descriptive letters Daniel wrote enabled the family to capture some of the wonder and beauty of the landscapes he traveled through. He did this by exploring the geography of the enemy lands and by describing the relationship that allegedly existed between the land and its people. He described how the hostile landscapes resisted the invader, in a way that matched the rebelliousness of their people. Above all else Daniel's descriptions of the enemy lands affirmed his love for his homeland. His language of place demonstrated to his family that his identity and that of his family was shaped by their place in Minnesota and not by being part of other places. The family's love for their homeland was also deepened by the rich array of material objects sent home. The visible presence in the home of precious stones, fossils, clothing, and plants—all plundered from enemy lands—elevated their feelings of cultural superiority and made them proud of the conquests made in defense of their homeland.

The Mississippi River Valley played a vital role in the Civil War experiences of the Densmore family because it acted as a highway allowing the movement of men, military equipment, and personal supplies. As committed abolitionists, the Densmores were also aware that for African Americans such as Mary McElroy, the Mississippi River could be both a northern pathway to freedom and a southern track to slavery.[3] Yet the river was much more than a highway. For the Densmores, living just a few hundred yards from the levee bank, the river was a participant in the great national tragedy. As a family they had learned to read the river and appreciate the way it could shape the lives of those who traveled or settled along it. During their formative years in Red Wing the flooding Mississippi River had damaged their sawmill business and almost dissipated the family's fortune. On the Red Wing quay the family first encountered the war in all its glory and tragedy. As the brothers journeyed down the river, they observed the horrific nature of the war. Young Orrin lost some of his innocence when he discovered battle-ravaged vessels packed full of wounded soldiers moored at the Cairo wharf. Perhaps more than any of the other family member, Daniel knew that the river had a life that was independent of the rhythms of the war. Sand banks, snags, low water levels caused by drought not only delayed his journey south but also prevented his reunion with Benjamin. As well as revealing the suffering and the vagaries of war, the Mississippi River also had on its banks sites that marked the revolutionary nature of the war. The Densmores looked upon Fort Pillow and Fort Pickering as important sites marking their struggle against slavery. Even after the war ended the river continued to play an important part in the lives of the Densmores. Benjamin and Daniel's manufacturing venture, the Red Wing Iron Works, owed much of its success to servicing shipping in the Port of Red Wing.

The war that changed the nation changed the Densmore family too. The bonds of affection between Elizabeth and Orrin grew stronger. Orrin steadfastly supported Elizabeth as she moved outside the family home and engaged in work as a member of the Red Wing Ladies' Soldiers' Aid Society and the Red Wing Temperance Society. While tension did develop between them over Mary's presence in the household, Orrin never forcibly sought to exercise power over domestic affairs. Motivated by a concern for Elizabeth's health and increasing workload, he offered advice, but nothing more. During the war more responsibility devolved to Martha and Orrin Jr. Martha took a larger role managing the house, and Orrin Jr. took on more duties in his father's office. While some of this change was natural, the result of the parents' advancing age and declining health, the war accelerated the rate and direction of change because it increased the parents' workload and resulted in Benjamin and Daniel leaving the household.

But the end of the war did not signal a return to antebellum domestic normality. While Elizabeth picked up some of her old household responsibilities, Martha's management of domestic affairs continued to grow. Thanks to his family's patriotic service and the connections he had made in the Republican Party, Orrin's public career rapidly advanced after the war. Before he died in 1878 he had served as a Republican Party member of the State House of Representatives from 1870 to 1871, as a trustee on the board of Minnesota's State Insane Asylum, and held the position of clerk in the state education system. At the county level, Orrin acted as the Deputy Collector of U.S. Revenues and Assistant Marshal for the U.S. Census. Elizabeth, who lived on for some time after Orrin, died in Red Wing in 1892.[4]

The lives of Orrin's two children who had established their own households before the war underwent considerable change in the postwar period. An independent widow, Margaret remained in Red Wing, supporting herself by taking in boarders until 1871 when she married James Edwin Smith, the younger brother of her deceased husband, Otis. Norman continued his father's commitment to the Republican Party after he moved from Emerald Grove in 1877 and took up farming in Cerro Gordo County, Iowa. He became a leading voice in the farmers' cooperative movement and the insurance industry, and from 1884 to 1886 he represented the Republican Party as member for the House District of Cerro Gordo in the state legislature.[5]

When their military service ended, Benjamin and Daniel returned as war heroes. This rise in status gave them more authority in domestic affairs, for the whole family was aware they owed them a debt for the sacrifices they had made. Before the war the brothers had lived largely separate lives, Benjamin working as a surveyor in St, Paul and Red Wing, and Daniel studying at Beloit College before working as teacher in Tennessee. But during the war they forged a much closer relationship, which grew even stronger, and developed in new directions in the immediate postwar years, when they jointly established the Red Wing Iron Works. This manufacturing venture appealed to Benjamin because it gave him an opportunity to use the technical skills he had developed during the war while working on fortifications at Fort Heiman and on artillery at Fort Halleck.[6] During the war Red Wing had become an important transit port for shipping men and supplies up and down the Mississippi River, but its importance increased significantly when wheat farming boomed in Goodhue County in the 1870s. The Densmore brothers took advantage of the county's increasing prosperity by supplying machinery to the farmers and equipment to service the Port of Red Wing.

Now the family's standing in Red Wing was not solely dependent on Orrin's political affiliation with the Republican Party because the Red Wing Iron Works anchored it firmly in the heart of the town's business community.

The war left a lasting imprint on the personal life of Benjamin. A few months after he returned home, Benjamin married Sarah Adelaide Greenland and established his own household in Red Wing. One of their children, Frances Theresa, was influenced by her father's involvement in the Dakota wars. She went on to gain national recognition for her work preserving the musical heritage of Native Americans.[7] The war left an imprint on Benjamin's character. The editor of the *Red Wing Morning Republican* alluded to this in his obituary published shortly after Benjamin's death in January 1913. Under a heading "Soldierly Qualities," the editor lauded Benjamin for being able to carry over into civilian life all the all the manly qualities he had developed while serving in the Union Army.[8]

The war helped to make Daniel more politically progressive and racially empathetic than any other member of the family. In November 1865, at a time when debate was raging over Black suffrage, he supported Black voting rights. He believed that the African American man was "entitled to the same means for defending his freedom, that other men employ in protecting theirs." He considered that only "one question" needed to be answered. "Are the negroes loyal to the government?" Like many USCT officers who had led their men into battle against the rebels, his answer was a resounding "yes." For the greater part of his life after the war Daniel lived in Red Wing, in the family home built in 1857 at the corner of Main and Cedar streets. Like Benjamin he became a stalwart of Red Wing's business community. He served on the municipal water board and the cemetery board. Daniel married Susan Melvina Warner late in life, on December 3, 1891, and had no children. After the sale of the Red Wing Iron Works in 1912, he left Red Wing for California on account of his wife's bad health. Susan died in 1914, and a few months later, Daniel died in Los Angeles, California, on March 5, 1915. He was buried in Oakland Cemetery, Red Wing.[9]

The war continued to influence the lives of the two youngest siblings in the household, Martha and Orrin Jr. The war gave Martha opportunities to seek a more active public role outside the family home. It also created a new social environment for her in which she gained a measure of freedom and independence she had never experienced before. But when the boys returned home, her involvement in public affairs declined. Since the Union had been saved, there were now far fewer socially acceptable reasons to bend gender boundaries. Martha's public persona declined even further when, shortly after the war ended, she gave up teaching to devote herself exclusively to the management of the family home. Seven years after the war ended, she married a Red Wing merchant and began to establish her own household. Martha died in Red Wing in 1908.[10]

After one final unsuccessful attempt to join the army in March 1865, Orrin Jr. worked in his father's office.[11] But the allure of military service still haunted him. In May he wrote to Daniel praising him for his valor at the battle of Fort Blakely. As he reflected on his brother's wartime achievements, a sense of loss and disappointment overcame him. "Would that I had a few such experiences to remember in after years," he commented. There was little that was remarkable about Orrin Jr's role in the Civil War. Nevertheless, his war story is important because of the insights it reveals of a family grappling with conflicting goals. Like all families seeking to serve the Union, the Densmores had to weigh the lofty national ideals of patriotism and glory against their personal, pragmatic goal of securing their family's economic health and well-being. To secure the family's future, young Orrin had to help his father in his office. Eventually Orrin Jr. left his father's office and studied for a short time at Beloit College. After college, he returned home to Red Wing, married Theresa Philleo, and worked as an accountant. He died in 1893.[12]

Although the Civil War had a profound impact on the members of the Densmore family, the family's historical legacy is somewhat problematic. Their story is interesting, but does it have historical resonance? I suggest it has, because the family's Civil War experience suggests lines of inquiry that future historians could profitably pursue. As historians, we need to recognize that families who had loved ones serving as officers in the USCT faced distinctive challenges. Their household war was different because the African American soldiers, and by association their officers, were precariously placed in the military. Subject to racism, and lacking full civil rights, the Black soldiers were subject to inequitable treatment. If we are to better understand the role of abolitionist officers in the USCT, we need to know far more about the part their families played in the great national conflict. We need to know how the families nurtured and shaped the abolitionist spirit in their fighting men, and how the levels of discrimination in the army and the war on slavery affected them. We cannot understand what occurred on the battlefront if we ignore the war waged on the home front. The Densmores' stories also suggest that historians need to know much more about the flexible nature of the officers' racial beliefs and abolitionist ideologies. The officers' convictions changed over time to accommodate changing military environments and their encounters with African American soldiers and civilians. But they were also influenced by the way their families at home interpreted their military experiences. More needs to be known about the nature and rate of these changes. Finally, historians need to recognize the tensions that existed between the officers' abolitionist ideologies and their racial beliefs and to discover how the officers' racism set limits on their abolitionist convictions. Since the home is the seedbed of all personal belief systems, perhaps we should begin our study of USCT officers in the family home rather than the officers' mess.

Family War Stories is a book about the Densmore family facing the challenges confronting those who had loved ones serving as officers in the USCT. At the same time, it is a book about individual family members carving out for themselves new roles in the revolutionary war that changed the nation. Yet this time of personal growth was also a time of separation, which the Densmores felt keenly. In December 1863, Daniel wrote to Benjamin and explained just how much receiving family letters meant to him. For Daniel, turning the pages of the letters was like having a quiet conversation with family members. "Your letter of the 6th came in the mail today," he wrote. "So with a letter received from Mittie yesterday, I feel I had visitors today." He asked Benjamin to supply his "reflection," informing him that "I have a little 'family gathering' in the pocket of my Minn book; & was about asking if you could furnish a 'carte' therefore." Hard-pressed by his duties at Fort Snelling, Daniel kept the image of the family firmly in his mind. It sustained him in the darkest days of the war.[13]

When peace came and the Union was restored, the family was reunited. Gradually over time the pangs of separation disappeared. Approximately seven years after Daniel had written to Benjamin asking for his "reflection," the family gathered in a photographic studio to have a portrait taken. As the family members gazed into the camera lens they displayed an aura of middle-class respectability. Orrin and Elizabeth sat in the foreground, and in the background stood their children. Together they convey an image of confidence and prosperity. There is something commonplace about the appearance this family portrait. The Densmores could be any one of the thousands of middle-class families from Northern cities who took part in the Civil War. Yet sometimes the photographic image distorts reality. Despite all the challenges they faced, the Densmores relentlessly fought a long, hard war to honor the family's name, to save the Union, and to destroy slavery. They may have been just one insignificant family from a frontier town in the Upper Midwest, but their Civil War storylines were deeply woven into the fabric of the nation.

Figure C.1. Orrin and Elizabeth Densmore's Family, circa 1870. Back Standing left to right: Martha, Margaret, Norman, Orrin Jr., Benjamin, Daniel. Front Seated, Elizabeth, Orrin Sr. Minnesota Historical Society.

Characters

Adams, Charles H. Lieutenant Colonel Adams commanded the 2nd Tennessee Heavy Artillery, African Descent, when Benjamin Densmore joined it. His commission was revoked for discriminating against officers of Hungarian descent.

Andrews, Christopher C. Brigadier General Andrews commanded the 2nd Division, XIII Corps, which was attached to General Steele's Column during the operations against Mobile. After the war Daniel Densmore wrote to Andrews giving an account of the siege of Fort Blakely in which he claimed that some African American soldiers attacked rebel soldiers who were attempting to surrender.

Andrews, Edwin E. Surgeon Andrews, 68th U.S. Colored Infantry, was Daniel Densmore's close friend and messmate.

Asboth, Alexander Sandor. Brigadier General Asboth commanded the District of Columbia. Benjamin Densmore accused him of unfairly promoting fellow Hungarians to commission in the USCT.

Betcher, Herman. Captain Betcher was a family friend who accompanied Orrin Jr. Densmore when he traveled to Benjamin Densmore's camp in 1864.

Bouton, Edward. Daniel Densmore's regiment was attached to Colonel Bouton's 1st Brigade U.S. Colored Troops, when it fought against General Forrest in 1864.

Buell, Don Carlos. Major General Buell commanded the Army of the Ohio. In his family correspondence Benjamin Densmore criticized Buell for tardily prosecuting the war.

Buswell, George W. Buswell served with Daniel Densmore in General Sibley's expeditions, 1862–1863. He also became an officer in the 68th U.S. Colored Infantry. Buswell kept diaries of his war experiences.

Cheney, Martha Lea and Russell. Martha, Elizabeth Densmore's sister, was married to Russell Cheney and lived on a farm at Emerald Grove, Wisconsin.

Clendening, James H. Lieutenant Colonel James H. Clendening, 68th U.S. Colored Infantry, was Daniel Densmore's archrival. He was cashiered for cowardice.

Columbus. Columbus was an African American servant employed by Daniel when he served at Fort Snelling, Minnesota, in the winter of 1863/1864. Daniel also referred to him as "the *Jim* of the Ocean."

Crary, Benjamin F. Chaplain Crary, 3rd Minnesota Infantry, was a friend of the Densmores who was appointed Superintendent of Contrabands at Columbus, Kentucky. He used his influence to help Benjamin Densmore secure a commission in the USCT.

Dana, Napoleon Jackson Tecumseh. In December 1864 Daniel Densmore blamed Major General Dana, Commander of the Department of the Mississippi, for ordering his regiment out of the camp they had recently constructed to Fort Pickering, Memphis, a place Daniel believed was a rat hole. Daniel praised Dana for supporting his Black soldiers in a sword-fighting contest with the Memphis militia.

Davis, Dick. Davis was a leader of a rebel guerrilla band. Daniel Densmore witnessed his execution in Memphis in late December 1864.

Densmore, Benjamin. Benjamin, the Densmores' second eldest son, joined the 3rd Minnesota Infantry. He was captured at Murfreesboro, Tennessee, in July 1862, paroled, and then served in Sibley's 1862 expedition against the Dakota. He was then commissioned captain in the 4th U.S. Colored Heavy Artillery, at Columbus, Kentucky, where he served until November 1865. He was mustered out in Arkansas in 1866. After the war Benjamin and Daniel managed and owned a successful business in Red Wing, the Red Wing Iron Works.

Densmore, Daniel. Daniel, the Densmores' third eldest son, joined the 7th Minnesota Infantry, served in General Sibley's expeditions 1862–1863, and then served as Provost Marshal at Fort Snelling, Minnesota. In January 1864 he was appointed Provost Marshal of Colored Troops at Benton Barracks, St. Louis. After gaining a commission in the 68th U.S. Colored Troops, he campaigned against General Forrest in the summer and fall of 1864. In 1865 he fought in the Mobile Campaign, and he did occupation duty in Alabama. Promoted to the rank of lieutenant colonel in February 1865, he retired from the army in September 1865 because of poor health. In the decades following the war, Daniel and his brother Benjamin jointly owned and managed the Red Wing Iron Works.

Densmore, Elizabeth. Elizabeth, nee Fowle, was married to Orrin Densmore. She was a member of the Red Wing Ladies' Soldiers' Aid Society and active in the temperance movement.

Densmore, Martha Elizabeth. Martha, the Densmore's second eldest daughter, was a leading organizer in the Red Wing Ladies' Soldiers' Aid Society. She shared a close friendship with Anna McLaren.

Densmore, Norman. Norman, the Densmores' eldest son, farmed at Emerald Grove, Wisconsin.

Characters

Densmore, Orrin. Orrin was a farmer who married Elizabeth Fowle in 1828. He moved his family from New York to Emerald Grove, Wisconsin, in 1845 and then to Red Wing, Minnesota, in 1857. There he became a leading member of the Red Wing Republican Party and Goodhue County Treasurer. After the war Orrin served as a Republican Party member of the State House of Representatives from 1870 to 1871 and worked in the state of Minnesota's education system.

Densmore, Orrin, Jr. Orrin Jr., the Densmores' youngest son, was keen to enlist in the Union Army despite opposition from his family. Some of his enthusiasm dissipated when he became ill after visiting his brothers' camps in 1864. During the war he worked in his father's office.

Dewey, Elizabeth. Elizabeth was a family friend who wrote to Daniel Densmore arguing that the role of women in the Union war effort had been trivialized.

Dobozy, Peter Paul. Lieutenant Colonel Dobozy commanded the 4th U.S. Colored Heavy Artillery. In his family correspondence, Benjamin Densmore criticized Dobozy for favoring fellow Hungarian officers in his regiment and for conspiring with General Asboth to advance the careers of officers of Hungarian descent in the USCT.

Forrest, Nathan Bedford. Major General Forrest captured Benjamin Densmore's regiment in July 1862 at Murfreesboro, Tennessee. In April 1864 the Densmores were shocked to learn that Forrest's forces had massacred Black troops at Fort Pillow, a location Benjamin once used as his USCT recruiting post. In 1864 Daniel Densmore fought in General Andrew J. Smith's army against Forrest.

Fowle, Hanford. Hanford was the son of Elizabeth Densmore's brother, Charles Fowle.

Frémont, John Charles. Major General Frémont, famed explorer and 1856 Republican Party presidential candidate, commanded the Department of the West. Lincoln dismissed him for establishing martial law in Missouri and issuing a proclamation freeing the slaves. The Densmores saw Frémont as an abolitionist martyr.

Gamble, Hamilton Rowan. Gamble was governor of Missouri between 1861 and 1864. In his family correspondence Daniel Densmore criticized Gamble for being sympathetic toward the South and for failing to stem rebel guerrilla raids.

Grant, Ulysses Simpson. General Grant's capture of Forts Henry and Donelson, and Vicksburg, reinvigorated the patriotic fervor of the Densmore family. They rejoiced when they learned of Grant's victories in the Eastern Theater in 1864, but in his family correspondence Benjamin Densmore claimed that Grant's progress would greatly increase once he followed General Sherman's war strategy.

Hanford, Frederick and Mary. The farm in Missouri of these relatives of Elizabeth Densmore's sister, Susan Hanford, was raided by rebels in February 1864.

Hanford, Susan and Charles. Susan, Elizabeth Densmore's sister, was married to Charles Hanford. They lived on a farm at Emerald Grove, Wisconsin. Charles wanted Daniel Densmore to get him an African American servant, but this venture failed because of opposition from his wife.

Hawkins, John P. During the Mobile Campaign Daniel Densmore's regiment was attached to the 3rd Brigade in Brig. Gen. John Hawkins's 1st U.S. Colored Division, General Frederick Steele's column.

Johnson, Louisa. Louisa was a Swedish immigrant who worked for the Densmores as a domestic servant. Her departure spurred the Densmores to continue their search for a "contraband worker." Eventually, Louisa's place in the household was taken by Mary McElroy, a refugee from slavery.

Jones, Joseph Blackburn and Millie M. Colonel Jones, 68th U.S. Colored Infantry, and Daniel Densmore became comrades as they campaigned together against General Forrest, defended their Black soldiers against discrimination by the Memphis military authorities and opposed Col. Ignatz G. Kappner's allegedly tyrannical command of Fort Pickering. Their relationship was severed when the 68th was being demobilized. Millie, the wife of J. Blackburn Jones, visited her husband's camp in the winter of 1864/1865. Daniel believed she epitomized the virtues of Minnesota womanhood.

Kappner, Ignatz, G. A Hungarian immigrant, Colonel Kappner, 3rd U.S. Colored Heavy Artillery, commanded Fort Pickering, Memphis, Tennessee. Daniel Densmore strongly opposed Kappner because of his Hungarian ethnicity and his allegedly authoritarian command.

Lincoln, Abraham. The Densmore family supported President Lincoln's prosecution of the war and his reelection. However, in their family correspondence they criticized him for allegedly sympathizing with the Dakota, for appointing McClellan to command the Army of the Potomac, for dismissing Frémont from the Department of the West, and for issuing the Proclamation of Amnesty and Reconstruction.

McClellan, George Brinton. Orrin Densmore believed Lincoln's appointment of Major General McClellan to command the Army of the Potomac was one of his greatest mistakes. In their family correspondence the Densmores criticized McClellan for tardily prosecuting the war. They rejoiced when Lincoln dismissed McClellan from the Army of the Potomac and defeated him in the 1864 presidential election.

McElroy, Mary. Mary was a refugee from slavery who worked as a domestic servant for the Densmores. Her industry challenged the Densmores' views about slave docility. However, Elizabeth Densmore opposed her presence. Mary was first known as Mary Priest.

McLaren, Anna and Robert. Anna was the daughter of Orrin Densmore's sister, Diana, and the wife of Col. Robert McLaren, the commander of Fort Snelling, Minnesota. Anna was Martha Densmore's close friend.

McVean, Archibald. Archibald McVean was married to Diana, Orrin Densmore's sister. Archibald, his son-in-law, Robert McLaren, and Orrin Densmore invested in the Red Wing Sawmill in 1857. Orrin and Benjamin Densmore appear to have had troubled financial dealings with McVean.

Philleo, William M. Lieutenant Philleo, 7th Minnesota Infantry, was a family friend who was hospitalized in Memphis in 1864. Daniel Densmore aided him.

Pile, William A. Brigadier General Pile supervised the recruitment of Black soldiers in Missouri. In his family correspondence Daniel Densmore accused Pile of turning the 68th U.S. Colored Infantry into a show regiment that lacked fighting capabilities. He also criticized Pile for allegedly conspiring with Lt. Col. James H. Clendening to have him dismissed.

Pope, John. Major General Pope commanded the Department of the Northwest. He had oversight of General Sibley's expeditions, 1862–1863.

Rosecrans, William Starke. Major General Rosecrans commanded the Department of Missouri from January to December 1864. In his family correspondence Daniel Densmore criticized him for supporting Governor Gamble's allegedly pro-Southern policies and for failing to protect Missouri from rebel raids.

Schofield, John McAllister. Major General Schofield commanded the Department of Missouri when Daniel Densmore first arrived in St. Louis, in January 1864. In his family correspondence, Daniel criticized him for failing to resist rebel raids and for supporting Governor Gamble's allegedly pro-Southern policies.

Sheridan, Philip Henry. Major General Sheridan commanded the Army of the Shenandoah. The Densmores were inspired by the victories he gained in the Shenandoah Valley Campaign, August 1864–March 1865.

Sherman, William Tecumseh. Major General Sherman commanded the Military Division of the Mississippi. The Densmores saw Sherman as the hero of the war. They praised him for prosecuting hard war against the rebels during his Atlanta Campaign and his March to the Sea.

Sibley, Henry Hastings. Benjamin and Daniel Densmore took part in Brig. Gen. Henry Sibley's expeditions against the Dakota, 1862–1863.

Smith, Andrew Jackson. Daniel Densmore's regiment formed part of Maj. Gen. Andrew J. Smith's XVI Corps, which campaigned against General Forrest in Tennessee and Mississippi in the summer and fall of 1864.

Smith, Margaret Seaton, Otis, and Walter Gilman. Margaret, the Densmores' eldest daughter, was married to Otis Smith. Gilman was their only child. Otis's suffering and death caused considerable concern for the Densmore family. Otis was the first to suggest the employment a "contraband worker."

Steele, Frederick. During the Mobile Campaign, Daniel Densmore's regiment formed part of Major General Steele's column. Steele's column moved northwest from Pensacola, Florida, and attacked Ft. Blakely from the rear.

Taoyateduta (Little Crow). Taoyateduta, a chief of the Mdewakanton Dakota, led attacks on settlers in the upper Minnesota River region in August 1862. Benjamin and Daniel Densmore joined expeditions led by General Sibley to eliminate him.

Webster, Belle. Belle was Martha Densmore's friend and teaching colleague.

Genealogical Tables

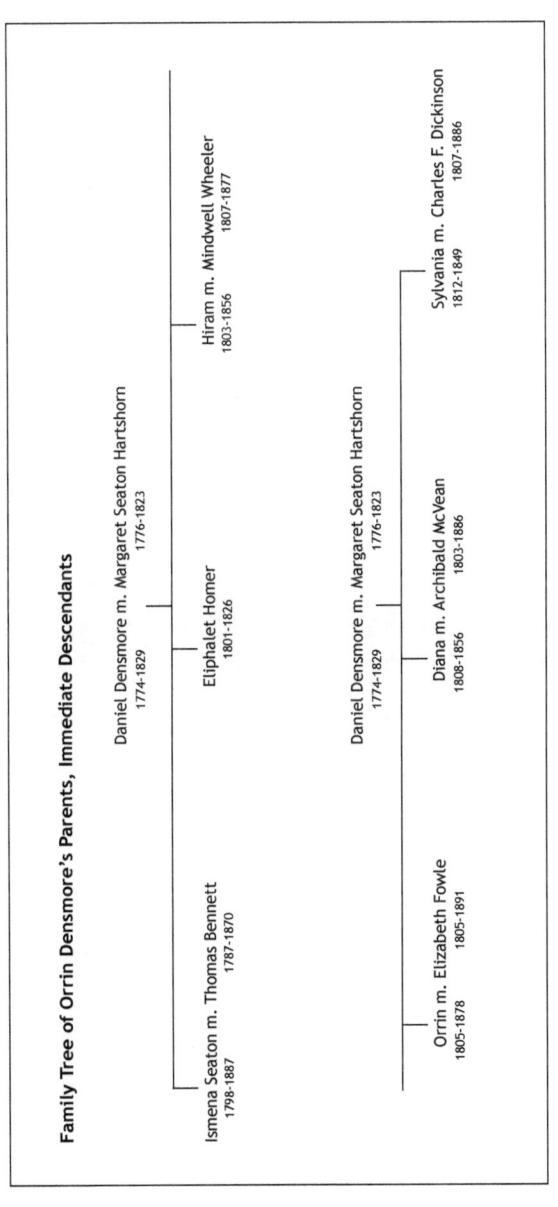

Family Tree of Elizabeth Densmore's Parents, Immediate Descendants

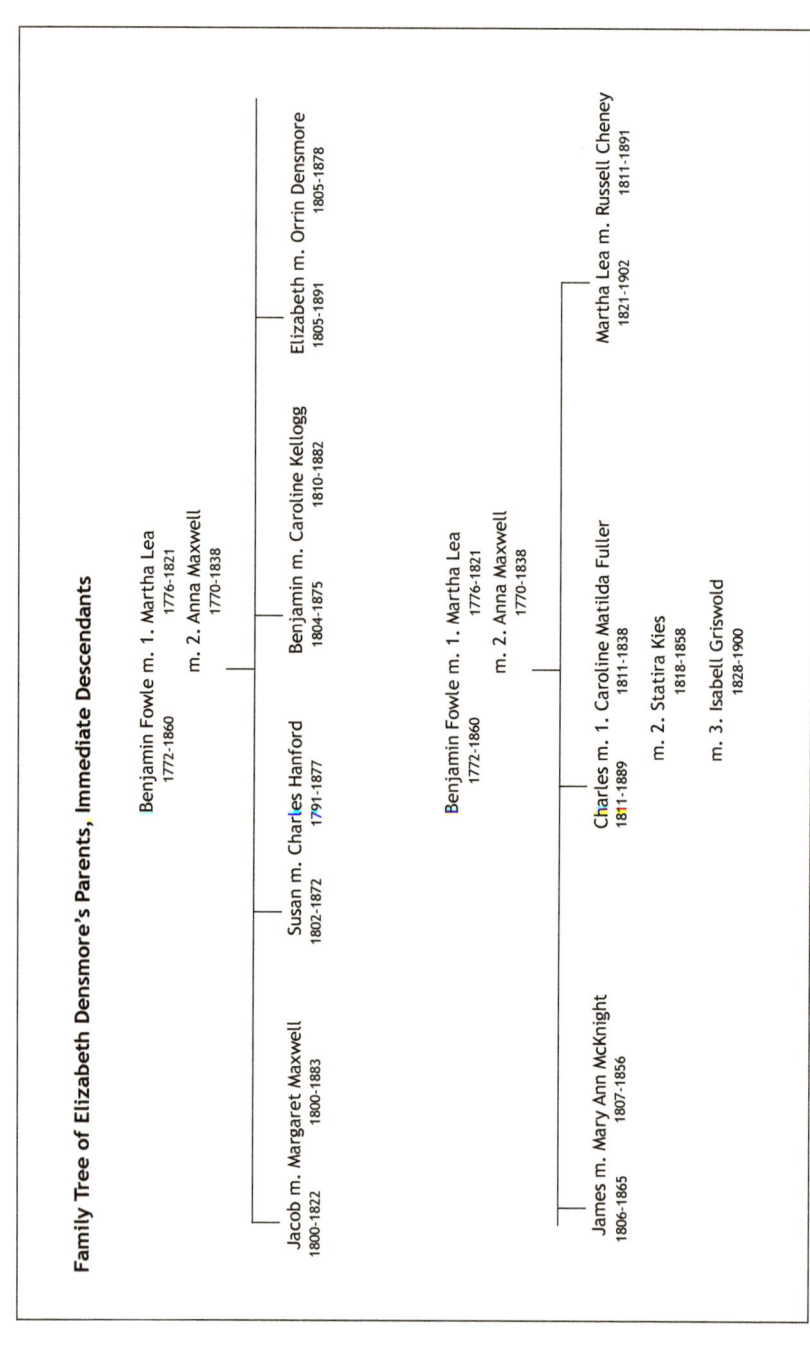

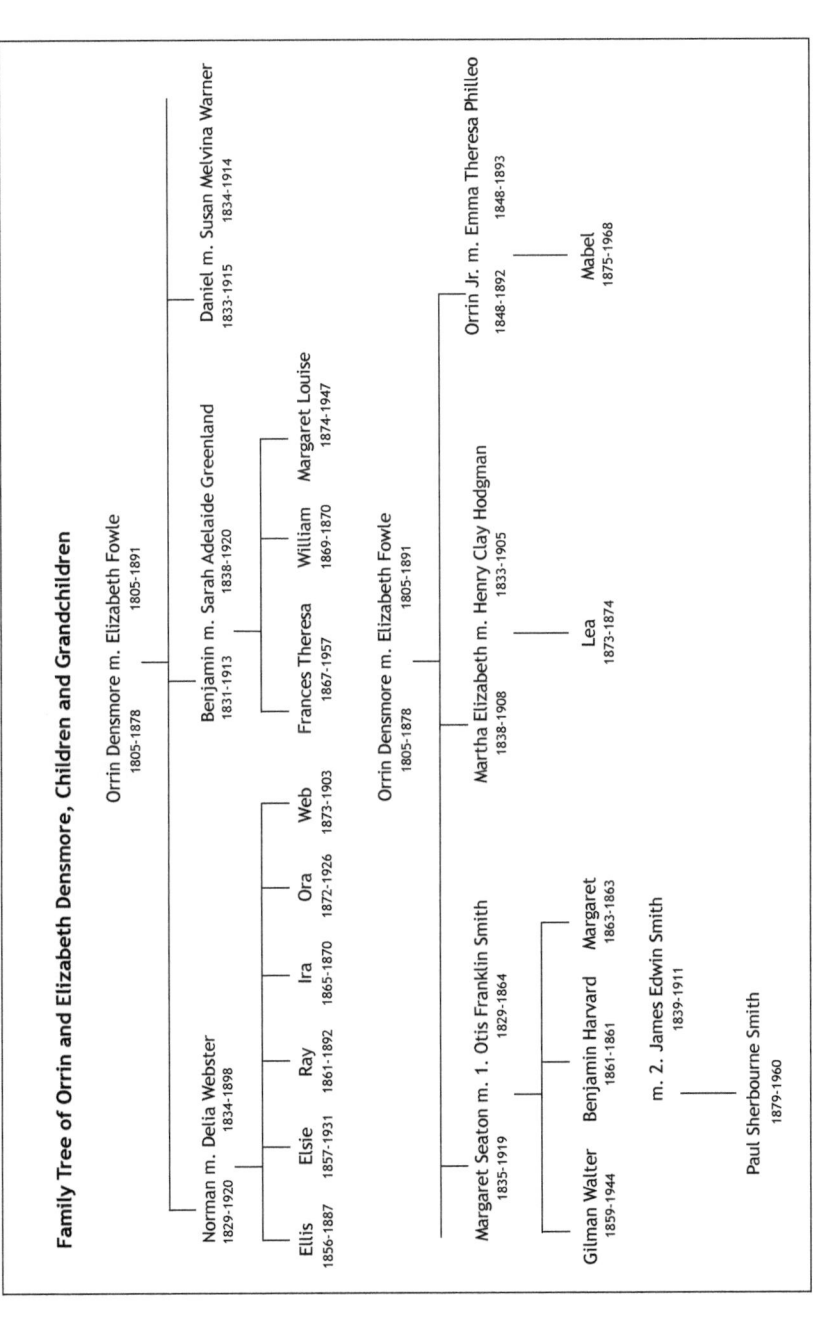

Notes

Preface

1. Christopher Clark, *Prisoners of Time: Prussians, Germans, and Other Humans* (Dublin: Penguin Random House, 2021), xviii; Christopher Clark, *The Sleepwalkers: How Europe Went to War in 1914* (London: Penguin Books, 2013).

Introduction

1. Norman to Daniel, June 30, 1861, Norman to Bro [Daniel], May 12, 1861. Although Norman did not enlist, in 1864 he worked as a clerk in the Provost Marshal's Office in Janesville. Martha to Brother [Benjamin], September 18, 1864, Benjamin Densmore and Family Papers, 1797–1955, Minnesota Historical Society (MNHS).

2. Reid Mitchell, *The Vacant Chair: The Northern Soldier Leaves Home* (New York: Oxford University Press, 1993), 12–15; James M. McPherson, *For Cause and Comrades: Why Men Fought the Civil War* (New York: Oxford University Press, 1997), 22–29; Lisa Tendrich Frank and LeeAnn Whites, "Introduction: The Civil War as a Household War," in *Household War: How Americans Lived and Fought the Civil War*, ed. Lisa Tendrich Frank and LeeAnn Whites (Athens: University of Georgia Press, 2020), 3; Victoria E. Ott, "There's No Place Like Home: Gender, Family, and the Confederate Alabama Household," in *War Matters: Material Culture in the Civil War Era*, ed. Joan E. Cashin (Chapel Hill: University of North Carolina Press, 2018), 181–82.

3. I am indebted to the valuable insights Reid Mitchell and Amy Murrell Taylor have made about how Americans understood the Civil War using the vocabulary of the family. Mitchell, *The Vacant Chair*, 14–16, 37, 52, 116–17, 158; Amy Murrell Taylor, *The Divided Family in Civil War America* (Chapel Hill: University of North Carolina Press, 2005), 1–2, 8–12; "Extract from Thomas Jefferson to Hugh Williamson," in *Jefferson Quotes & Family Letters*, Thomas Jefferson Foundation, accessed September , 2023, https://tjrs.monticello.org/letter/172; Roy P. Basler, ed., *The Collected Works of Abraham Lincoln*, 9 vols. (New Brunswick, N.J.: Rutgers University Press, 1953), 2:462; James M. McPherson, *Abraham Lincoln and the Second American Revolution* (New York: Oxford University Press, 1991), 103–5.

4. McPherson, *For Cause and Comrades*, 134–36; Ott, "There's No Place Like Home," 176–97. Studies that see the Civil War as a conflict that integrates the home front with the battlefront include Frank and Whites, eds., *Household War*; Joan E. Cashin, ed., *The War Was You and Me: Civilians in the American Civil War* (Princeton, N.J.: Princeton University Press, 2002); Paul A. Cimbala and Randall M. Miller, eds., *Union Soldiers and the Northern Home Front: Wartime Experiences, Postwar Adjustments* (New York: Fordham University Press, 2002); Chandra Manning, *What This Cruel War Was Over: Soldiers,*

Slavery, and the Civil War (New York: Alfred A. Knopf, 2007); Stephen W. Berry, *All That Makes a Man: Love and Ambition in the Civil War* (New York: Oxford University Press, 2002); Reid Mitchell, *Civil War Soldiers: Their Expectations and Their Experiences* (New York: Viking, 1988); Mitchell, *The Vacant Chair*.

5. James Marten, *The Children's Civil War* (Chapel Hill: University of North Carolina Press, 1998), 21–22; James Marten, *Children and Youth in the Civil War Era* (New York: New York University Press, 2012), 4–5; Nancy C. Cott, *The Bonds of Womanhood: "Woman's Sphere" in New England, 1780–1835* (New Haven, Conn.: Yale University Press, 1977), 197–206; Patricia L. Richard, *Busy Hands: Images of the Family in the Northern Civil War Effort* (New York: Fordham University Press, 2003), 16–20; Steven Mintz and Susan Kellogg, *Domestic Revolutions: A Social History of American Family Life* (New York: Free Press, 1988), xiv–xv; E. Anthony Rotundo, *American Manhood: Transformations in Masculinity from the Revolution to the Modern Era* (New York: Basic Books, 1993), 22–25; Chris Dixon, *Perfecting the Family: Antislavery Marriages in Nineteenth-Century America* (Amherst: University of Massachusetts Press, 1997), x–xi, 3, 8–9, 22, 82, 179–80.

6. Ira Berlin, Joseph P. Reidy, and Leslie S. Rowland, eds., *Freedom: A Documentary History of Emancipation, 1861–1867*, Series II, *The Black Military Experience* (Cambridge: Cambridge University Press, 1982), 6–10; Joseph T. Glatthaar, *Forged in Battle: The Civil War Alliance of Black Soldiers and White Officers* (New York: Free Press, 1990), 6–10; John David Smith, "Let Us All Be Grateful That We Have Colored Troops That Will Fight," in *Black Soldiers in Blue: African American Troops in the Civil War Era*, ed. John David Smith (Chapel Hill: University of North Carolina Press, 2002), 17–28.

7. Robert F. Engs and Corey M. Brooks, eds., *Their Patriotic Duty: The Civil War Letters of the Evans Family of Brown County, Ohio* (New York: Fordham University Press, 2007); Joseph T. Glatthaar, "Duty, Country, Race, and Party: The Evans Family of Ohio," in *The War Was You and Me*, ed. Cashin, 332–57; Russell Duncan, ed., *Blue-Eyed Child of Fortune: The Civil War Letters of Colonel Robert Gould Shaw* (Athens: University of Georgia Press, 1992); D. Laurence Rogers, *Apostles of Equality: The Birneys, the Republicans, and the Civil War* (East Lansing: Michigan State University Press, 2011).

8. Gary W. Gallagher, *The Union War* (Cambridge, Mass.: Harvard University Press, 2011), 101–4; McPherson, *For Cause and Comrades*, 124–26.

9. Daniel to Benjamin, December 5, 1864, Densmore and Family Papers, MNHS; Berlin et al., *The Black Military Experience*, 406–9; Glatthaar, *Forged in Battle*, 11–12, 36–37, 40–41; Smith, "Let Us All Be Grateful," 37–40; Bob Luke and John David Smith *Soldiering for Freedom: How the Union Army Recruited, Trained, and Deployed U.S. Colored Troops* (Baltimore: Johns Hopkins University Press, 2014), 52–54.

10. Glatthaar, *Forged in Battle*, 169–206; Smith, "Let Us All Be Grateful," 40–52; Keith P. Wilson, *Campfires of Freedom: The Camp Life of Black Soldiers during the Civil War* (Kent, Ohio: Kent State University Press, 2002), 38–58; James M. McPherson, *Battle Cry of Freedom: The Civil War Era* (New York: Oxford University Press, 1988), 565–66.

11. Glatthaar, *Forged in Battle*, 12–15; Wilson, *Campfires of Freedom*, 29–30; Margaret Humphreys, *Intensely Human: The Health of the Black Soldier in the American Civil War* (Baltimore: John Hopkins University Press, 2008), 22–27, 29–31; Mitchell, *The Vacant Chair*, 59–65; Dixon, *Perfecting the Family*, 171.

12. McPherson, *For Cause and Comrades*, 140–43; Mitchell, *The Vacant Chair*, 10–12, 26–27, 32–34; Ross A. Brooks, *The Visible Confederacy: Images and Objects in the Civil War South* (Baton Rouge: Louisiana State University Press, 2019), 187–89; Lorien Foote, *The Gentlemen and the Roughs: Violence, Honor, and Manhood in the Union Army* (New York: New York University Press, 2010), 55–59, 64–65, 178–79; Ginette Aley and J. L. Anderson, eds., *Union Heartland: The Midwestern Home Front during the Civil War* (Carbondale: Southern Illinois University Press, 2013), 5.

13. National, class, and family identity were fostered by emphasizing racial differences both in the North and the South. Brooks, *The Visible Confederacy*, 32–54; David R. Roediger, *The Wages of Whiteness: The Making of the American Working Class* (London: Verso, 1991). For a discussion of the prevalence of racism in the Republican Party see Paul D. Escott, *The Worst Passions of Human Nature: White Supremacy in the Civil War North* (Charlottesville: University of Virginia Press, 2020), 3–4, 11–12, 53, 78, 178–79.

14. David W. Blight, ed., *When This Cruel War Is Over: The Civil War Letters of Charles Harvey Brewster* (Amherst: University of Massachusetts Press, 1992), 9; Randall C. Jimerson, *The Private Civil War: Popular Thought during the Sectional Conflict* (Baton Rouge: Louisiana State University Press, 1988), 5–6; James I. Robertson Jr., *Soldiers Blue & Gray* (New York: Warner Books, 1988), 104–10; Kathryn Shively, *Nature's War: Common Soldiers and the Environment in 1862 Virginia* (Chapel Hill: University of North Carolina Press, 2013), 8, 120–21; LeeAnn Whites, "Written on the Heart: Soldiers' Letters, the Household Supply Lines, and the Relational War," in *Household War*, ed. Frank and Whites, 119–20.

15. Blight, ed, *When This Cruel War Is Over*, 15; McPherson, *For Cause and Comrades*, 11–12; Daniel to Friends at home, October 5, 1864, Benjamin to Brother [Daniel], March 6, 7, 1864, Benjamin to Daniel, March 20, 1864, Densmore and Family papers, MNHS.

16. [Daniel Densmore], "History–Orrin Densmore Senior," in "History and Genealogy of the Family of Orrin and Elizabeth Densmore," 1903, 22–27; Elizabeth to Son [Benjamin], December 30, 1863, Densmore and Family Papers, MNHS; Nina Silber, *Daughters of the Union: Northern Women Fight the Civil War* (Cambridge, Mass.: Harvard University Press, 2005), 4–6.

17. Nancy L. Rhoades and Lucy E. Bailey, eds., *Wanted—Correspondence: Women's Letters to a Union Soldier* (Athens: Ohio University Press, 2009), 18–20, 28–29, 38–39, 43–45; C. Dallett Hemphill, *Siblings: Brothers & Sisters in American History* (New York: Oxford University Press, 2011), 9; Rebecca J. Fraser, *Gender, Race and Family in Nineteenth-Century America* (London: Palgrave Macmillan, 2013), 85–86.

18. Hemphill, *Siblings*, 9; Lee V. Chambers, *The Weston Sisters: An American Abolitionist Family* (Chapel Hill: University of North Carolina Press, 2014); Manning, *What This Cruel War Was Over*, 11.

1. "May his 'soldier life' be as good as the cause he will represent": Orrin Densmore and the Beginning of the Civil War

1. Archibald McVean was married to Orrin's sister, Diana, and Robert N. McLaren was married to McVean's daughter, Anna. [Daniel Densmore], "History—Orrin Densmore Senior," in "History and Genealogy of the Family of Orrin and Elizabeth

Densmore," 1903, 23–25, Benjamin Densmore and Family Papers, 1797–1955, Minnesota Historical Society (MNHS); Kathryn A. Johnson, "Densmore (Benjamin and Family) Papers, 1797–1956," St. Paul, Minnesota Historical Society, 1956, 19. Typescript inventory and description of the Benjamin Densmore and Family Papers.

2. [Daniel Densmore], "History and Genealogy of the Family of Orrin and Elizabeth Densmore," 24, Densmore and Family papers, MNHS.

3. While he was in Rock County, Orrin served on the County Board of Supervisors and the Board of School Inspectors. [Daniel Densmore], "History and Genealogy of the Family of Orrin and Elizabeth Densmore," 24–25, Densmore and Family papers, MNHS; Johnson, "Densmore (Benjamin and Family) Papers," 1–3; Madeline Angell, *Red Wing, Minnesota: Saga of a River Town* (Minneapolis: Dillon Press, 1977), 61–62.

4. B. Horrigan, Introduction to *Minnesota in the Civil War: An Illustrated History*, by Kenneth Carley (St. Paul: Minnesota Historical Society, 2000), xvii–xix; Joseph C. Fitzharris, *The Hardest Lot of Men: The Third Minnesota Infantry in the Civil War* (Norman: University of Oklahoma Press, 2019), 10–11; Paul N. Beck, *Columns of Vengeance: Soldiers, Sioux, and the Punitive Expeditions, 1863–1864* (Norman: University of Oklahoma Press, 2013), 4–5; Gary Clayton Anderson, *Massacre in Minnesota: The Dakota War of 1862, the Most Violent Ethnic Conflict in American History* (Norman: University of Oklahoma Press, 2019), 78.

5. [Daniel Densmore], "History and Genealogy of the Family of Orrin and Elizabeth Densmore," 25–26, Densmore and Family papers, MNHS; Horrigan, Introduction to *Minnesota in the Civil War*, xviii–xix, xxii–xxv; William D. Green, *The Children of Lincoln: White Paternalism and the Limits of Black Opportunity in Minnesota, 1860–1876* (Minneapolis: University of Minnesota Press, 2018), 17; William D. Green, *A Peculiar Imbalance: The Fall and Rise of Racial Equality in Minnesota, 1837–1869* (Minneapolis: University of Minnesota Press, 2007), 77–79, 82.

6. Frederick L. Johnson, *Goodhue County, Minnesota: A Narrative History* (Red Wing, Minn.: Goodhue County Historical Society Press, 2000), 12; Angell, *Red Wing*, 38–40, 47–56, 59–60; James M. McPherson, *Battle Cry of Freedom: The Civil War Era* (New York: Oxford University Press, 1988), 189–91; Horrigan, Introduction to *Minnesota in the Civil War*, by Carley, xxii; [Daniel Densmore], "History and Genealogy of the Family of Orrin and Elizabeth Densmore," 25–26, Densmore and Family papers, MNHS; Fitzharris, *The Hardest Lot of Men*, 11.

7. Johnson, "Densmore (Benjamin and Family) Papers," 7–9; [Daniel Densmore], "History and Genealogy of the Family of Orrin and Elizabeth Densmore," 25, 32, 34, Densmore and Family papers, MNHS.

8. [Daniel Densmore], "History and Genealogy of the Family of Orrin and Elizabeth Densmore," 6–7, 26, 36. Densmore and Family papers, MNHS; Angell, *Red Wing*, pp.76–78; Wood, Alley and Company, *History of Goodhue County: Including A Sketch of The Territory and State of Minnesota* (Red Wing, Minn.: Wood, Alley & Co., 1878; Kessinger Publishing's Legacy Reprints, 2009), 255–68; Johnson, *Goodhue County*, 59 - 60.

9. Johnson, *Goodhue County*, 59–60; Wood, Alley and Co., *History of Goodhue County*, 392–94, 401–2; Angell, *Red Wing*, 119, 121; [Daniel Densmore], "History and Genealogy of the Family of Orrin and Elizabeth Densmore," 26, Densmore and Family papers, MNHS.

10. Angell, *Red Wing*, 79–81, 87–88, 101, 119, 125–26, 132, 136–37; Wood, Alley and Co., *History of Goodhue County*, 348–70, 406–09; [Daniel Densmore], "History and Genealogy of the Family of Orrin and Elizabeth Densmore," 26, Densmore and Family papers, MNHS.

11. "McLaren, Robert N.," in Legislators Past & Present, Minnesota Legislative Reference Library. Accessed July 17, 2014. http://www.leg.state.mn.us/legdb/fulldetail.aspx?ID=13825; Angell, *Red Wing*, 73, 77; Johnson, "Densmore (Benjamin and Family) Papers, 1797–1956," 19; By an Old Settler [Joseph Woods Hancock], *Goodhue County Minnesota, Past and Present* (Red Wing, Minn.: Red Wing Printing Co., 1893; Nabu Public Domain Reprints), 162; [Daniel Densmore], "History and Genealogy of the Family of Orrin and Elizabeth Densmore," 26, 40–41, Densmore and Family papers, MNHS.

12. *Goodhue County Republican*, April 26, 1861; Angell, *Red Wing*, 100–104; Johnson, *Goodhue County*, 62–63; Orrin to Son [Daniel], August 25, 1862, Orrin to Benjamin and Daniel, Densmore and Family papers, MNHS.

13. Service Record of Capt. Benjamin Densmore, 4th US Cld. Hvy. Art, Carded Records, Volunteer Organizations: Civil War, ser. 519, RG 94, National Archives and Records Administration (NARA); Frederick H. Dyer, *Compendium of the War of Rebellion*, 2 vols. (1908; reprint: Dayton, Ohio: National Historical Society in cooperation with the Press of Morningside Bookshop, 1979), pt. 3, 1297; Benjamin to Father, February 3, 1862, Densmore and Family papers, MNHS.

14. Fitzharris, *The Hardest Lot of Men*, 87–102; Carley, *Minnesota in the Civil War*, 68–70; Norman to Daniel, July 27, 1862, Densmore and Family papers, MNHS.

15. Benjamin to Father, August 16, 1862, Densmore and Family papers, MNHS; For comment on the devasting impact of the surrender on the morale of the 3rd Minnesota see Fitzharris, *The Hardest Lot of Men*, 4, 102.

16. Benjamin to Father, August 16, 1862, Densmore and Family papers, MNHS.

17. Ibid.; Orrin to Son [Daniel], August 25, 1862, Densmore and Family papers, MNHS; Fitzharris, *The Hardest Lot of Men*, 105.

18. Orrin to Son [Daniel], August 25, 1862, Orrin to Daniel, September 8, 1862, Orrin to Benjamin and Daniel, September 18, 1862, Densmore and Family papers, MNHS.

19. Kenneth Carley, *The Dakota War of 1862: Minnesota's Other Civil War*, 2nd ed. (St. Paul: Minnesota Historical Society Press, 1976), 7–11.

2. "I wish Old Abe had a son or some kin or kine up here in danger": The Brothers' War against the Dakota

1. At the time of the Civil War, Minnesota had three main tribal bands consisting of the Mdewakantons, Wahpekutes, Wahpetons, and Sissetons (Eastern Dakota), the Yanktons and Yanktonais (Western Dakota), and the Lakotas (Tetons). The Eastern and Western Dakota called themselves the Dakota and saw themselves as one people. Although they were never a united group, the Eastern Dakota bands, especially the Mdewakantons, were held in high regard because they were considered the descendants of the first Dakota people. The Mdewakantons lived on reservations along the upper Minnesota River. Enemy neighboring tribes called the people from the Eastern and Western Dakota the "Sioux," meaning "snakes," and settlers generally adopted this name to refer

to all tribal people in the region. Because the Eastern Dakota bands called themselves "Dakota" and because the U.S. Army was primarily engaged in fighting the eastern tribal bands, particularly the Mdewakanton, Sisseton, and Wahpeton, I have employed the appellation "Dakota" rather than "Sioux." Taoyateduta was called Little Crow by Minnesota's settlers. I have used the name Taoyateduta because that was the name his people called him. Frederick L. Johnson, *Goodhue County, Minnesota: A Narrative History* (Red Wing, Minn.: Goodhue County Historical Society Press, 2000), 10; Gary Clayton Anderson, *Massacre in Minnesota: The Dakota War of 1862, the Most Violent Ethnic Conflict in American History* (Norman: University of Oklahoma Press, 2019), 3, 6–8, 135; Paul N. Beck, *Columns of Vengeance: Soldiers, Sioux, and the Punitive Expeditions, 1863–1864* (Norman: University of Oklahoma Press, 2013), 4–5, 9–14, 21–24; Joseph C. Fitzharris, *The Hardest Lot of Men: The Third Minnesota Infantry* (Norman: University of Oklahoma Press, 2019), 11; Kenneth Carley, *The Dakota War of 1862: Minnesota's Other Civil War*, 2nd ed. (St. Paul: Minnesota Historical Society Press, 1976), 1–7; Linda M. Clemmons, *Dakota in Exile: The Untold Stories of Captives in the Aftermath of the US–Dakota War* (Iowa City: University of Iowa Press, 2019), 19–21.

2. Carley, *The Dakota War of 1862*, 59–61; Beck, *Columns of Vengeance*, 31–32; James M. McPherson, *Battle Cry of Freedom: The Civil War Era* (New York: Oxford University Press, 1988), 392, 395–420, 464–71, 524–33.

3. Daniel to Dear Friends at home, July 9, 1863, Daniel to Dear Sister and Friends at home, July 11, 1863, "Benjamin Densmore and Family Papers, 1797–1955," Minnesota Historical Society (MNHS); Michele Clodfelter, *The Dakota War: The United States Army versus the Sioux, 1862–1865* (Jefferson, N.C.: McFarland, 1998), 90.

4. Daniel to Dear Aunt [Martha], October 5, 1862, Civil War Letters of Daniel Densmore, 1833–1915, and his Family in the Charles V. Hibbard Papers, 1811–1954, Wisconsin Historical Society (WHS); Sibley's expedition was camped at Lone Tree Lake or Battle Lake, not Wood Lake. Carley, *The Dakota War of 1862*, 62–63; Gary Clayton Anderson, *Little Crow: Spokesman for the Sioux* (St. Paul: Minnesota Historical Society Press, 1986), 158–60, 228n60; Beck, *Columns of Vengeance*, 35–36; In his diary, George W. Buswell, a private in the 7th Minnesota Infantry, described the attacking Dakota as "devils, who were hooting and with the most hellish demonical yell." George W. Buswell, Diary, September 23, 1862, in Jonathan W. White and Reagan Connelly, eds., "'Off to Dixie and Adventure': The Dakota War and Civil War Diaries of George W. Buswell, 7th Minnesota Infantry and 68th U. S. Colored Troops," unpublished book manuscript, 45; James T. Ramer, Diary, September 22, 23, 1862, 18–19, James T. Ramer Diary and Letter, 1862 August 14–September 5, 1865, Aug. 16, microfilm M87, MNHS; Fitzharris, *The Hardest Lot of Men*, 114–18; For an account of the battle of Wood Lake through Dakota eyes see Gary Clayton Anderson and Alan R. Woolworth, eds., *Through Dakota Eyes: Narrative Accounts of the Minnesota Indian War of 1862* (St. Paul: Minnesota Historical Society Press, 1988), 219, 234–37, 241–44.

5. Carley, *The Dakota War of 1862*, 65–70; Beck, *Columns of Vengeance*, 36–37; June Namis, *White Captives: Gender and Ethnicity on the American Frontier* (Chapel Hill: University of North Carolina Press, 1993), 251–52; James Madison Bowler to Lizzie, September 27, 1863, Bowler Family Papers, MNHS; Martha to Brother [Daniel], August 12, 1862, Densmore and Family Papers, MNHS.

6. Orrin Jr. to Brother [Daniel], November 27, 1862, Densmore and Family Papers, MNHS; Daniel to Dear Aunt [Martha], October 5, 1862, Civil War Letters of Daniel Densmore, WHS.

7. Aunt Martha to Nephew Daniel, November 16, 1862, Civil War Letters of Daniel Densmore, WHS.

8. Orrin to Sons [Benjamin, Daniel], October 21, 1862, Densmore and Family Papers, MNHS; Johnson, *Goodhue County*, 63, 65.

9. Aunt Martha to Nephew [Daniel], November 16, 1862, Densmore and Family Papers, MNHS; Jeffrey Ostler, *The Plains Sioux and U.S. Colonialism from Lewis and Clark to Wounded Knee* (New York: Cambridge University Press, 2004), 2–5.

10. Orrin to Sons [Benjamin, Daniel], October 21, 1862, Densmore and Family Papers, MNHS.

11. Daniel to Friends, May 7, 1863, Orrin Jr. to Brother [Daniel] June 11, 1863, Martha to Brother [Daniel], June 24, 1863, Orrin to Daniel, December 18, 1864, Densmore and Family Papers, MNHS; Belle Webster was Martha's teaching colleague. For comment on how "feminine objects" reveal cultural and political values during the Civil War, see Joan E. Cashin, "Introduction: The Idea of the Thing," and "Relics from Two Wars: Revolutionary Artifacts in the Civil War," Victoria E. Ott, "There's No Place Like Home: Gender, Family, and the Confederate Alabama Household," in *War Matters: Material Culture in the Civil War Era*, ed. Joan E. Cashin (Chapel Hill: University of North Carolina Press, 2018), 3, 6–7, 37–38, 44–47, 176–97.

12. Martha to Bro. [Daniel], December 7, 1862, Densmore and Family Papers, MNHS; Carley, *The Dakota War of 1862*, 87; Service Record of Lt. Daniel Densmore, 7th Minn. Inf., Carded Records, Volunteer Organizations: Civil War, ser. 519, RG 94, National Archives and Records Administration (NARA).

13. Martha to Bro. [Daniel], December 7, 1862, Densmore and Family Papers, MNHS.; Frederick H. Dyer, *Compendium of the War of Rebellion*, 2 vols. (1908; reprint: Dayton, Ohio: National Historical Society in cooperation with the Press of Morningside Bookshop, 1979), pt. 3, p. 1684; Wisconsin Adjutant General's Office, *Roster of Wisconsin Volunteers, War of Rebellion, 1861–1865* (Madison, Wisc.: Democrat Printing Company, 1866), 2:304.

14. Patricia L. Richard, *Busy Hands: Images of the Family in the Northern Civil War Effort* (New York: Fordham University Press, 2003), 49–50, 69; Nina Silber, *Daughters of the Union: Northern Women Fight the Civil War* (Cambridge, Mass.: Harvard University Press, 2005), 92–96; Elizabeth D. Leonard, *Yankee Women: Gender Battles in the Civil War* (New York: W. W. Norton, 1994), xvii–xxv.

15. Service Record of Capt. Benjamin Densmore, 4th US Cld. Hvy. Art, Carded Records, Volunteer Organizations: Civil War, ser. 519, RG 94, NARA; Daniel to Aunt Mittie [Martha], November 28, 1862, Densmore and Family Papers, MNHS; Namis, *White Captives*, 211, 222–23, 228, 235–36, 251–55; Anderson, *Massacre in Minnesota*, 241–67; Beck, *Columns of Vengeance*, 39–40.

16. Daniel to Friends, January 1, 1863, Daniel to Friends, January 5, 1863, Densmore and Family Papers, MNHS; Clemmons, *Dakota in Exile*, 34, 38–39; Carley, *The Dakota War of 1862*, 71–72.

17. Daniel to Aunt Martha, April 24, 1863, Civil War Letters of Daniel Densmore, WHS; Clemmons, *Dakota in Exile*, 21, 26–27.

18. Carley, *The Dakota War of 1862*, 87–88; Beck, *Columns of Vengeance*, 61.

19. Daniel to Friends at home, June 2, 1863, Daniel to Friends at home, June 7, 1863, Daniel to Friends at home, June 14, 1863, Densmore and Family Papers, MNHS.

20. Carley, *The Dakota War of 1862*, 89; Daniel to Friends at home, June 14, 1863, Daniel to Friends at home, June 22, 1863, Densmore and Family Papers, MNHS.

21. Daniel to Friends at home, June 22, 1863; [Daniel to Father], July 4, 1863, Daniel to Benjamin, July 7, 1863, Daniel to Sister and friends at home, July 9, 1863, Daniel to Friends at home, July 11, 1863, Densmore and Family Papers, MNHS; *Saint Paul Pioneer and Democrat Weekly*, July 24, 1863; Clapp Diary, June 13, 16, 22, 23, 1863, George C Clapp and Family Papers, MNHS; Ramer, Diary, July 2, [1863] p.62, James T. Ramer Diary and Letter, MNHS; Bornarth, Diary, July 17, 1863, Charles Bornarth papers, MNHS; Beck, *Columns of Vengeance*, 81–89.

22. Daniel to Dear Friends at home, July 11, 1863, Densmore and Family Papers, MNHS; Buswell, Diary, July 7, 183, in White and Connelly, eds., "Off to Dixie and Adventure," 113–14.

23. Orrin to Daniel, June 11, 1863, Orrin to Son [Daniel], June 19, 1863, Orrin to Benjamin, June 11, 1863, Densmore and Family Papers, MNHS.

24. Daniel to Dear friends at home, June 7, 1863, Densmore and Family Papers, MNHS.

25. Orrin to Daniel, June 11, 1863, Orrin to Son [Daniel], June 19, 1863, Densmore and Family Papers, MNHS.

26. Daniel to Dear Friends at home, June 7, 1863, Orrin to Son [Daniel], June 19, 1863, Densmore and Family Papers, MNHS.

27. Orrin to Daniel, July 1, 1863, Densmore and Family Papers, MNHS.

28. Daniel to Benjamin, July 7, 1863, Densmore and Family Papers, MNHS.

29. Ibid; Daniel to Brother [Benjamin], August 16, 1863, Densmore and Family Papers, MNHS.

30. Daniel to Dear Friends at home, July 11, 1863, Daniel to Brother [Benjamin], August 16, 1863, Densmore and Family Papers, MNHS; Buswell, Diary, July 24, 183, in White and Connelly, eds., "Off to Dixie and Adventure," 118–21; Beck, *Columns of Vengeance*, 99–116; Anderson, *Massacre in Minnesota*, 279–80.

31. Daniel to Friends at home, August 9, 1863, Densmore and Family Papers, MNHS.

32. Orrin Jr. to Brother [Daniel], June 21, 1863, Orrin Jr. to Brother [Daniel], June 28, 1863, Orrin Jr. to Brother [Daniel], July 8, 1863, Densmore and Family Papers, MNHS; Reid Mitchell, *The Vacant Chair: The Northern Soldier Leaves Home* (New York: Oxford University Press, 1993), 12–13, 16–18; James M. McPherson, *For Cause and Comrades: Why Men Fought the Civil War* (New York: Oxford University Press, 1997), 25–26, 31, 78; James Marten, *The Children's Civil War* (Chapel Hill: University of North Carolina Press, 1998), 165–66.

33. Orrin Jr. to Brother [Daniel], June 28, 1863, Densmore and Family Papers, MNHS.

34. Earl J. Hess, *The Union Soldier in Battle: Enduring the Ordeal of Combat* (Lawrence: University Press of Kansas, 1997), 123–24; McPherson, *For Cause and Comrades*, 133; Richard, *Busy Hands*, 119–24, 189; Nancy L. Rhoades and Lucy E. Bailey, eds., *Wanted—Correspondence: Women's Letters to a Union Soldier* (Athens: Ohio University Press, 2009), 38–39.

35. Daniel to Benjamin, August 16, 1863, Daniel to Dear Friends, August 25, 1863, Daniel to Dear Friends, August 30, 1863, Orrin to [Benjamin], September 10, 1863, Densmore and Family Papers, MNHS; Carley, *The Dakota War of 1862*, 90.

36. Walter L. Hixson, *American Settler Colonialism* (New York: Palgrave Macmillan, 2013), 3–4.

37. Daniel to Brother [Benjamin], October 13, 1863, Densmore and Family Papers, MNHS.

3. "Dont give up my Son": Benjamin on Duty at Fort Halleck

1. Inspection Report, Maj. Thomas J. Newsham, A. A. Inspector General, District of Columbus, Department of Tennessee, May 13, 1863, Inspection Reports, ser. 245, RG 393, Pt. 4, National Archives and Records Administration (NARA); Benjamin to Father, May 3, 1863, in *Goodhue County Republican*, May 22, 1863. Joseph C. Fitzharris, *The Hardest Lot of Men: The Third Minnesota Infantry in the Civil War* (Norman: University of Oklahoma Press, 2019), 155. In August 1861, Lincoln signed the First Confiscation Act, which authorized the seizure of all property, including slaves, which had been used to give military support to the rebellion. Refugees from slavery who sought the sanctuary of Union lines were classified by the government and military authorities as "contraband of war," or captured enemy property. The term "contraband" was a generic term commonly used to referred to all enslaved people who had fled slavery. In their pursuit of freedom, refugees from slavery established camps, "contraband camps," close to Union lines. The military authorities and freedmen aid societies often assisted in the establishment of these camps. Many inhabitants from the contraband camps aided the war effort by working as military laborers, washerwomen, cooks, and nurses. Thousands from the camps also joined the Union Army. Chandra Manning, *Troubled Refuge: Struggling for Freedom in the Civil War* (New York: Vintage Books, 2017), 32–33; James M. McPherson, *Ordeal by Fire: The Civil War and Reconstruction* (New York: Alfred A. Knopf, 1982), 267–68.

2. Orrin to Daniel, July 1, 1863, "Benjamin Densmore and Family Papers, 1797–1955," Minnesota Historical Society (MNHS); B. F. Crary to Capt. I. H. Harris, Asst. Adj. Gen. District of Columbus, Department of Tennessee, June 4, 1863, Service Record of Capt. Benjamin Densmore, 4th US Cld. Hvy. Art, Carded Records, Volunteer Organizations: Civil War, ser. 519, RG 94, NARA; Frederick L. Johnson, *Uncertain Lives: African Americans and Their First 150 Years in the Red Wing, Minnesota, Area* (Red Wing, Minn.: Goodhue County Historical Society Press, 2005), 19; Frederick H. Dyer, *Compendium of the War of Rebellion*, 2 vols. (1908; reprint Dayton: National Historical Society in cooperation with the Press of Morningside Bookshop, 1979), pt. 3, p. 1297; No refugee camps were established for Kentucky slaves until the last year of the war. The refugee camps that were established at Paducah and Columbus were for refugees from other slave states. Officially these camps could not provide sanctuary for Kentucky slaves. However, Kentucky slaves did manage to shelter in them because officials had difficulty determining a slave's place of origin. Amy Murrell Taylor, *Embattled Freedom: Journeys through the Civil War's Slave Refugee Camps* (Chapel Hill: University of North Carolina Press, 2018), 180, 292n10; Fitzharris, *The Hardest Lot of Men*, 156, 158.

3. Orrin to Daniel, July 1, 1863, Densmore and Family Papers, MNHS; Crary assisted in the recruitment of the 2nd Tennessee Heavy Artillery, African Descent. This regiment was organized at Columbus, Kentucky, between June 16, 1863, and April 19, 1864. On March 3, 1864, its designation was changed to 3d U.S. Colored Heavy Artillery, and then on April 26, 1864, it changed again to the 4th U.S. Colored Heavy Artillery. United States Adjutant General's Office, *Official Army Register of the Volunteer Force of the United States Army*, 8 vols. (Washington, D.C.: Adjutant General's Office, 1867), pt. 8, p. 151; Special Orders No. 111, Hd. Qrs. District of Columbus, Columbus, Kentucky, May 13, 1863, Orders, 3rd Minn. Inf., Regimental Books and Papers, U.S. Vol. Org., RG 94, NA.

4. Orrin to Daniel, July 1, 1863, Densmore and Family Papers, MNHS. "Secesh" refers to secessionist who supported the Southern states succeeding from the Union." https://www.merriam-webster.com/dictionary/secesh; Fitzharris, *The Hardest Lot of Men*, 160; Slavery remained legally intact in Kentucky during the war, but slaves could gain their freedom by enlisting in the Union Army. In March 1863, Congress passed legislation that allowed the wives and children of African American soldiers to claim their freedom once they reached Union Army camps. Taylor, *Embattled Freedom*, 180–81, 186–87, 206.

5. Orrin to Daniel, July 1, 1863, Orrin to Son [Daniel], June 19, 1863, Densmore and Family Papers, MNHS.

6. Ira Berlin, Joseph P. Reidy, and Leslie S. Rowland, eds., *Freedom: A Documentary History of Emancipation, 1861–1867*, Series II, *The Black Military Experience* (Cambridge: Cambridge University Press, 1982), 116–19; William A. Dobak, *Freedom by the Sword: The U.S. Colored Troops, 1862–1867* (Washington, D.C.: Center of Military History United States Army, 2011), 173–77; Michael T. Meier, "Lorenzo Thomas and the Recruitment of Blacks in the Mississippi Valley, 1863–1865," in *Black Soldiers in Blue: African American Troops in the Civil War Era*, ed. John David Smith (Chapel Hill: University of North Carolina Press, 2002), 251–61; Taylor, *Embattled Freedom*, 110–15.

7. Benjamin to Friends, July 19, 1863, Benjamin to Brother [Daniel], September 20, 1863, Benjamin to Brother [Daniel], September 22, 1863, Densmore and Family Papers, MNHS. Ague was a common term used during the Civil War for a form of malaria fever. Andrew M. Bell, "Trans-Mississippi Miasmas: Malaria & Yellow Fever Shaped the Course of the Civil War in the Confederacy's Western Theater," *East Texas Historical Journal* 47, no. 2 (2009): Article 6, p.5, Accessed July 21, 2021. https://scholarworks.sfasu.edu/ethj/vol47/iss2/6.

8. Benjamin to Brother [Daniel], October 25, 1863, Densmore and Family Papers, MNHS.

9. Ibid., Benjamin to Mother, November 3, 1863, Densmore and Family Papers, MNHS.

10. Benjamin to Mother, November 3, 1863, Benjamin to Brother [Daniel], November 14, 1863, Densmore and Family Papers, MNHS; Smith, "Let Us All Be Grateful," in *Black Soldiers in Blue*, ed. Smith, 42–43, 46–52; Joseph T. Glatthaar, *Forged in Battle: The Civil War Alliance of Black Soldiers and White Officers* (New York: Free Press, 1990), 160, 166–76, 182–85, 190–92, 201–5.

11. Benjamin to Father, September 22, 1863, Benjamin to Brother [Daniel], February 18, 1864, Densmore and Family Papers, MNHS.

12. Benjamin to Brother [Daniel], October 25, 1863, Benjamin to Brother [Daniel], November 14, 1863, Densmore and Family Papers, MNHS.

13. Benjamin to Brother [Daniel], March 20, 1864, Benjamin to Brother [Daniel], April 15, 1864, Densmore and Family Papers, MNHS; Lt. Benjamin Dinsmore [sic], 2nd Tenn. H. A. A. D., Carded and Medical Records, ser. 534, RG 94, NARA; Kathryn Shively, *Nature's War: Common Soldiers and the Environment in 1862 Virginia* (Chapel Hill: University of North Carolina Press, 2013), 2–3, 12; Susan J. Matt, "You Can't Go Home Again: Homesickness and Nostalgia in U.S. History," *Journal of American History* 94 (September 2007): 481.

14. Benjamin to brother [Daniel], October 25, 1863, Densmore and Family Papers, MNHS; Michael C. C. Adams, *Living Hell: The Dark Side of the Civil War* (Baltimore: Johns Hopkins University Press, 2014), 128; Frances M. Clarke, *War Stories: Suffering and Sacrifice in the Civil War North* (Chicago: University of Chicago Press, 2011), 24–25; Frances Clarke, "So Lonesome I Could Die: Nostalgia and Debates Over Emotional Control in the Civil War North," *Journal of Social History* 41 (Winter 2007): 257.

15. Orrin to Son [Benjamin], July 30, 1863, Orrin to Daniel, August 10, 1863, Densmore and Family Papers, MNHS.

16. Benjamin to Father, July 24, 1863, Orrin to Son [Daniel], August 10, 1864, Densmore and Family Papers, MNHS. Orrin was probably referring to his sister Diana's husband, Archibald McVean. Kathryn A. Johnson, "Densmore (Benjamin and Family) Papers, 1797–1956," St. Paul, Minnesota Historical Society, 1956, 19. Typescript inventory and description of the Benjamin Densmore and Family Papers.

17. Orrin to Benjamin, June 11, 1863, Orrin to Benjamin, September 9, 1863, Benjamin to Brother [Daniel], September 20, 1863, Densmore and Family Papers, MNHS.

18. Benjamin to Brother [Daniel], September 20, 1863, Densmore and Family Papers, MNHS; The ideology of "white supremacy" asserts that the white race is innately superior to other races and that this superiority is evident in social, cultural, political, and economic development. Leslie A. Schwalm, *Emancipation's Diaspora: Race and Reconstruction in the Upper Midwest* (Chapel Hill: University of North Carolina Press, 2009), 27, 29, 270n28; Kristopher A. Teters, *Practical Liberators: Union Officers in the Western Theater during the Civil War* (Chapel Hill: University of North Carolina Press, 2018), 83–84; Ross A. Brooks, *The Visible Confederacy: Images and Objects in the Civil War South* (Baton Rouge: Louisiana State University Press, 2019), 43–45, 53 -54.

19. Benjamin to Father, September 29, 1863, Densmore and Family Papers, MNHS; Schwalm, *Emancipation's Diaspora*, 68–72.

20. Martin W. Öfele, *German-Speaking Officers in the U.S. Colored Troops, 1863–1867* (Gainesville: University Press of Florida, 2004), 125–26; Lt. Col. C. H. Adams to Maj. C. W. Foster, November 23, 1863, Lt. Col. C. H. Adams to Capt. F. H. Harris, December 12, 1863, Hd. Qrs. 2nd Tenn. Hvy. Art., Letter Book, 4th U.S. Cold Heavy Art., Regimental Books and Papers USCT, RG 94, NARA; *Official Army Register of the Volunteer Force*, pt. 8, p. 151; Benjamin to Brother [Daniel], September 20, 1863, Daniel to Friends at home, August 5, 1863, Benjamin to Brother [Daniel], November 14, 1863, Densmore and Family Papers, MNHS.

21. William L. Burton, *Melting Pot Soldiers: The Union's Ethnic Regiments* (Ames: Iowa State University Press, 1988), 108–9; Benjamin to Brother [Daniel] April 7, 1864, Densmore and Family Papers, MNHS; Öfele, *German-Speaking Officers in the U.S. Colored Troops*, 100, 105, 131; Murray M. Horowitz, "Ethnicity and Command: The Civil War Experience," *Military Affairs* 42 (December 1978): 182–89.

22. Daniel to Brother [Benjamin], November 19, 1856, Densmore Family Papers, Beloit College Archives and Special Collections, Unprocessed; Daniel to Father, January 28, 1864, Densmore and Family Papers, MNHS.

23. Elizabeth to Son [Benjamin], December 30, 1863, Densmore and Family Papers, MNHS; Christian B. Keller defines nativism as "an anti-immigrant attitude espoused by long-term residents of a certain geographic area, strongly influenced by xenophobic and nationalistic sentiments." For comment on the close association between temperance, nativism, and the rise of the Republican Party, see Christian B. Keller, *Chancellorsville and the Germans: Nativism, Ethnicity, and Civil War Memory* (New York: Fordham University Press, 2007), 7, 12, 143; William E. Gienapp, "Nativism and the Creation of the Republican Majority before the Civil War," *Journal of American History* 72 (December 1985): 529–59; James M. McPherson, *Battle Cry of Freedom: The Civil War Era* (New York: Oxford University Press, 1988), 133–44. For comment on the significant way dislocation and separation negatively affected the mental health of Union soldiers, see Clarke, "So Lonesome I Could Die," 253–82; David Anderson, "Dying of Nostalgia: Homesickness in the Union Army during the Civil War," *Civil War History* 56 (January 2010): 249–56.

4. "The glorious, new temple of Liberty": Daniel Joins the United States Colored Troops at Benton Barracks

1. Daniel to Brother [Benjamin], November 11, 1863, Benjamin Densmore and Family Papers, 1797–1955, Minnesota Historical Society (MNHS); George C. Rable, "Hearth, Home, and Family in the Fredericksburg Campaign," in *The War Was You and Me: Civilians in the American Civil War*, ed. Joan E. Cashin (Princeton, N.J.: Princeton University Press, 2002), 85–111.

2. Daniel to Friends at home, November 27, 1863, Martha to Brother [Daniel], November 28, 1863, Densmore and Family Papers, MNHS; Stephen E. Osman, *Fort Snelling and the Civil War* (St. Paul: Ramsey County Historical Society, 2017), 100.

3. Martha to Brother [Daniel], November 28, 1863, Martha to Brother [Daniel], August 10, 1863, Densmore and Family Papers, MNHS.

4. Martha to Brother [Daniel], November 28, 1863, [Daniel Densmore], "Family of Margaret Seaton Densmore & Otis Franklin Smith," in "History and Genealogy of the Family of Orrin and Elizabeth Densmore," 36, Densmore and Family Papers, MNHS; Drew Gilpin Faust, *This Republic of Suffering: Death and the American Civil War* (New York: Alfred Knopf, 2008), xii; Frederick L. Johnson, *Goodhue County, Minnesota: A Narrative History* (Red Wing, Minn.: Goodhue County Historical Society Press, 2000), 144; Philip S. Paludan, *"A People's Contest": The Union and the Civil War* (Lawrence: University Press of Kansas, 1996), 364.

5. Daniel to Dear Friends at home, December 2, 1863, Daniel to Brother [Benjamin], December 2, 1863, Daniel to Friends at home, December 9, 1863, Densmore and Family Papers, MNHS; Osman, *Fort Snelling*, 197.

6. Daniel to Dear Mother, [undated], Densmore and Family Papers, MNHS; Osman, *Fort Snelling*, 100–101; Daniel to Friends, June 17, 1864, Densmore and Family Papers, MNHS; Service Record of Lt. Daniel Densmore, 7th Minn. Inf., Carded Records, Volunteer Organizations: Civil War, ser. 519, RG 94, National Archives and Records Administration (NARA).

7. Martha to Brother [Daniel], February 8, 1864, Densmore and Family Papers, MNHS; Faust, *This Republic of Suffering*, 7–29; John R. Neff, *Honoring the Civil War Dead: Commemoration and the Problem of Reconciliation* (Lawrence: University Press of Kansas, 2005), 22–39; Reid Mitchell, *The Vacant Chair: The Northern Soldier Leaves Home* (New York: Oxford University Press, 1993), 142–43.

8. Elizabeth to Son [Benjamin], December 30, 1863, Martha to Brother [Daniel], February 8, 1864, [Daniel Densmore], "Family of Margaret Seaton Densmore & Otis Franklin Smith," in "History and Genealogy of the Family of Orrin and Elizabeth Densmore," 36, Densmore and Family Papers, MNHS

9. Martha to Brother [Daniel], February 8, 1864, Densmore and Family Papers, MNHS.; Faust, *This Republic of Suffering*, 10–11, 147–53; Neff, *Honoring the Civil War Dead*, 22–23.

10. Martha to Brother [Daniel] February 8, 1864, Orrin to Daniel, January 30, 1864, Martha Cheney to Daniel, February 8, 1864, Densmore and Family Papers, MNHS.

11. Martha to Brother [Daniel], February 8, 1864, [Daniel Densmore], "Family of Margaret Seaton Densmore & Otis Franklin Smith," in "History and Genealogy of the Family of Orrin and Elizabeth Densmore," 36, Densmore and Family Papers, MNHS; It was considered undesirable for a woman to manage a household alone. Nicole Etcheson, "No Fit Wife: Wives and Their In-Laws on the Indiana Home Front," in *Union Heartland: The Midwestern Home Front during the Civil War*, ed. Ginette Aley and J. L. Anderson (Carbondale: Southern Illinois University Press, 2013), 97–124.

12. Karen Halttunen, *Confidence Men and Painted Women: A Study of Middle-Class Culture in America, 1830–1870* (New Haven, Conn.: Yale University Press, 1982), 124–26, 130–34, 144, 146.

13. Orrin to Son [Daniel], March 24, 1864, Martha to Daniel, March 25, 1864, Densmore and Family Papers, MNHS.

14. Benjamin to Daniel, March 20, 1864, Benjamin to Mother, November 3, 1863, Densmore and Family Papers, MNHS.

15. William D. Green, *The Children of Lincoln: White Paternalism and the Limits of Black Opportunity in Minnesota, 1860–1876* (Minneapolis: University of Minnesota Press, 2018), 72–74, 79; David Vassar Taylor, *African Americans in Minnesota* (St. Paul: Minnesota Historical Society, 2002), 7–8; Leslie A. Schwalm, *Emancipation's Diaspora: Race and Reconstruction in the Upper Midwest* (Chapel Hill: University of North Carolina Press, 2009), 68–72, 97–99; Leslie A. Schwalm, "'Overrun with Free Negroes': Emancipation and Wartime Migration in the Upper Midwest," *Civil War History* 50, no. 2 (2004): 169–71; Orrin to Son [Daniel], March 24, 1864, Densmore and Family Papers, MNHS.

16. Orrin to Son [Daniel], March 24, 1864, Martha to Brother [Daniel], March 27, 1864, Densmore and Family Papers, MNHS; Frederick L. Johnson, *Uncertain Lives: African Americans and Their First 150 Years in the Red Wing, Minnesota, Area* (Red Wing, Minn.: Goodhue County Historical Society Press, 2005), 20; Schwalm, *Emancipation's Diaspora*, 98.

17. Orrin to Son [Daniel], April 28, 1864, Daniel to Benjamin, June 22, 1864, Densmore and Family Papers, MNHS; Schwalm, *Emancipation's Diaspora*, 99.

18. Orrin to Son [Daniel], April 28, 1864, Densmore and Family Papers, MNHS; Johnson, *Uncertain Lives*, 20.

19. Martha to Daniel, May 1, 1864, Densmore and Family Papers, MNHS.

20. Daniel to Uncle and Aunt [Russell Cheney, Martha Cheney], February 1, 1864, Daniel to Aunt Martha, February 14, 1864, Civil War Letters of Daniel Densmore, 1833–1915, and his Family in the Charles V. Hibbard Papers, 1811–1954, Wisconsin Historical Society (WHS).

21. Daniel to Aunt Martha, February 14, 1864, Civil War Letters of Daniel Densmore, WHS; Amy Murrell Taylor, *Embattled Freedom: Journeys through the Civil War's Slave Refugee Camps* (Chapel Hill: University of North Carolina Press, 2018), 72–82.

22. Daniel to Brother [Benjamin], November 2, 1856, Densmore Family Papers, Beloit College Archives and Special Collections, Unprocessed.

23. David R. Roediger, *The Wages of Whiteness: Race and the Making of the American Working Class* (London: Verso, 2007), 170; Paul D. Escott, *The Worst Passions of Human Nature: White Supremacy in the Civil War North* (Charlottesville: University of Virginia Press, 2020), 3–5, 11–12, 20–21, 53, 78, 178–79; Daniel to Cousin Susie, March 1, 1859, Civil War Letters of Daniel Densmore, WHS

24. Uncle Charles and Aunt Susan Hanford to Daniel, February 14, 1864, Densmore and Family Papers, MNHS; Lt. Col. W. R. Marshall to Col. Daniel Huston, March 26, 1864, Col. R. N. McLaren to Col. Daniel Huston, March 13, 1864, Governor S. Miller, to Col. Daniel Huston, March 12, 1864, in Service Record of Lt. Col. Daniel Densmore, 68th USCI, 68th USCI, Carded Records, Volunteer Organizations: Civil War, ser. 519, RG 94, NARA.

25. Daniel to Benjamin, March 26, 1864, Densmore and Family Papers, MNHS.

26. Daniel to Benjamin, April 3, Densmore and Family Papers, MNHS.

27. Orrin Jr. to Brother [Daniel], April 5,1864, Benjamin to Brother [Daniel], April 7, 1864, Orrin to Son [Daniel], April 28, 1864; Aunt Martha [Cheney] to Daniel, April 4, 1864, Uncle Charles Hanford, Aunt Susan Hanford to Nephew Daniel, February 14, 1864, Densmore and Family Papers, MNHS. Martha Cheney and Susan Hanford were sisters of Elizabeth Densmore. Kathryn A. Johnson, "Densmore (Benjamin and Family) Papers, 1797–1956" (St. Paul: Minnesota Historical Society, 1956), 20. Typescript inventory and description of the Benjamin Densmore and Family Papers.

28. Daniel to My Dear Friends, [Russell Cheney and family], March 13, 1864, Civil War Letters of Daniel Densmore, WHS; James M. McPherson, *Battle Cry of Freedom: The Civil War Era* (New York: Oxford University Press, 1988), 718; Eric Foner, *Reconstruction: America's Unfinished Revolution, 1863–1877* (New York: Harper and Row, 1988),

35–37; Ira Berlin, Joseph P. Reidy, and Leslie S. Rowland, eds., *Freedom: A Documentary History of Emancipation, 1861–1867*, Series II, *The Black Military Experience* (Cambridge: Cambridge University Press, 1982), 187–90.

29. Daniel to Benjamin, March 26, 1864, Densmore and Family Papers, MNHS; "The Freedmen's and Union Refugees' Department of the Mississippi Valley Sanitary Fair, Circular," enclosed in Daniel to Benjamin, March 26, 1864; Nina Silber, *Daughters of the Union: Northern Women Fight the Civil War* (Cambridge, Mass.: Harvard University Press, 2005), 244; Leon F. Litwack, *Been in the Storm So Long: The Aftermath of Slavery* (New York: Vintage Books, 1979), 399–406; James M. McPherson, *Ordeal by Fire: The Civil War and Reconstruction* (New York: Alfred A. Knopf, 1982), 399.

30. Daniel to Aunt and Friends [Martha Cheney], April 19, 1864, Civil War Letters of Daniel Densmore, WHS; George W. Buswell Diary, May 19, 1864, George W. Buswell Papers, 1862–1888, The Huntington Library, San Marino, California; Louis S. Gerteis, *Civil War St. Louis* (Lawrence: University Press of Kansas, 2001), 230–33.

31. The 68th USCI was organized at Benton Barracks, Missouri, between March and April 1864 as the 4th Missouri Volunteers, African Descent. Its designation was changed to the 68th USCI on March 11, 1864. United States Adjutant General's Office, *Official Army Register of the Volunteer Force of the United States Army*, 8 vols. (Washington, D.C.: Adjutant General's Office, 1867), pt. 8, p. 241; "68th USCT Infantry Roster," *Columbia Daily Tribune*, March 11, 2014. Accessed August 7, 2023. https:www.columbiatribune.com/story/news/2014/03/11/68th-infantry-roster/21717060007/; Service Record of Lt. Daniel Densmore, 7th Minn. Inf., Carded Records, Volunteer Organizations: Civil War, ser. 519, RG 94, NARA; Benjamin to Brother [Daniel], February 18, 1864, Densmore and Family Papers, MNHS.

32. Benjamin to Brother [Daniel], March 6, 7, 1864, Benjamin to Daniel, March 20, 1864, Densmore and Family Papers, MNHS; Special Orders No. 29, March 5, 1864, Special Orders No. 30, March 7, 1864, Hd. Qrs., 2d Tenn., Hvy. Art., A. D., Orders, 4th USCHA, Regimental Books and Papers USCT, RG 94, NARA.

33. Benjamin to Brother [Daniel], February 18, 1864, Benjamin to Brother [Daniel], March 6, 7, 1864, Benjamin to Brother [Daniel], April 7, 1864; Benjamin to Daniel, May 11, 1864; Benjamin to Brother [Daniel], June 4, 1864, Densmore and Family Papers, MNHS.

5. "Kind acts went directly to their hearts": Martha Serves on the Home Front in Red Wing

1. Martha to Daniel, March 11, 1864, Benjamin Densmore and Family Papers, 1797–1955, Minnesota Historical Society (MNHS).

2. Reid Mitchell, *The Vacant Chair: The Northern Soldier Leaves Home* (New York: Oxford University Press, 1993), 131–73, esp. 135, 144, 155–56, 172–73; Lori D. Ginzberg, *Women and the Work of Benevolence: Morality, Politics, and Class in the Nineteenth-Century United States* (New Haven, Conn.: Yale University Press, 1990), 131–73, esp. 135, 144, 155–56, 172–73. Jeanie Attie and Nina Silber argue that during the war, aid work remained localized and strongly influenced by the home environment. Jeanie Attie,

Patriotic Toil: Northern Women and the American Civil War (Ithaca, N.Y.: Cornell University Press, 1998), 3–5; Nina Silber, *Daughters of the Union: Northern Women Fight the Civil War* (Cambridge, Mass.: Harvard University Press, 2005), 163–78.

3. Martha to Daniel, February 16, 1864, Densmore and Family Papers, MNHS; Mitchell, *The Vacant Chair*, 24–31; Lorien Foote, *The Gentlemen and the Roughs: Violence, Honor, and Manhood in the Union Army* (New York: New York University Press, 2010), 55–59, 64.

4. Martha to Brother [Daniel], March 11, 1864, Densmore and Family Papers, MNHS.

5. Orrin to Benjamin, March 14, 1864, Densmore and Family Papers, MNHS.

6. Martha to Daniel, March 27, 1864, Densmore and Family Papers, MNHS.

7. Ibid; Orrin Jr. to Daniel, April 5, 1864, Densmore and Family Papers, MNHS.

8. Orrin Jr. to Daniel, April 5, 1864, Orrin Jr. to Daniel, November 21, 1864, Densmore and Family Papers, MNHS; Silber, *Daughters of the Union*, 192–93.

9. Orrin Jr. to Daniel, November 26, 1864, Orrin Jr. to Daniel, December 11, 1864, Orrin to Son [Daniel], January 1, 1865, Orrin to Son [Daniel], January 18, 1865, Densmore and Family Papers, MNHS.

10. Martha to Daniel, August 19, 1864, Aunt Martha to Daniel, August 19, 1864. Martha's August 19 letter was enclosed in Aunt Martha's August 19 letter. Densmore and Family Papers, MNHS.

11. Martha to Daniel, June 5, 1865, Martha to Brother [Daniel], November 28, 1863, Densmore and Family Papers, MNHS.

12. Martha to Brother [Benjamin], September 6, 1863, Densmore and Family Papers, MNHS; Steven Mintz, *A Prison of Expectations: The Family in Victorian Culture* (New York: New York University Press, 1983), 31–33; LeeAnn Whites, "Written on the Heart: Soldiers' Letters, the Household Supply Line, and the Relational War," in *Household War: How Americans Lived and Fought the Civil War*, ed. Lisa Tendrich Frank and LeeAnn Whites (Athens: University of Georgia Press, 2020), 121–23, 130–31.

13. Mitchell, *The Vacant Chair*, 24–27, 74–75; Earl J. Hess, *The Union Soldier in Battle: Enduring the Ordeal of Combat* (Lawrence: University Press of Kansas, 1997), 154; Foote, *The Gentlemen and Roughs*, 55–59, 64–65, 178–79.

14. Martha to Daniel, February 8, 1864, Densmore and Family Papers, MNHS; Patricia L. Richard, *Busy Hands: Images of the Family in the Northern Civil War Effort* (New York: Fordham University Press, 2003), 18, 76–77, 98–99, 112; Mitchell, *The Vacant Chair*, 24–27.

15. Martha to Daniel, March 4, 1864, Martha to Daniel, March 11, 1864, Martha to Daniel, February 24, 1864, Densmore and Family Papers, MNHS.

16. Martha to Daniel, February 8, 1864, Densmore and Family Papers, MNHS; James I. Robertson Jr., *Soldiers Blue & Gray* (New York: Warner Books, 1988), 96–101, 131; Bell I. Wiley, *The Life of Billy Yank: The Common Soldier of the Civil War* (Baton Rouge: Louisiana State University Press, 1978), 252–54; Mitchell, *The Vacant Chair*, 5–7; Foote, *The Gentlemen and the Roughs*, 29–39; Orrin to Daniel, January 30, 1864; William D. Green, *A Peculiar Imbalance: The Fall and Rise of Racial Equality in Minnesota, 1837–1869* (Minneapolis: University of Minnesota Press, 2007), 78.

NOTES TO PAGES 67–72

17. Karen Lystra, *Searching the Heart: Women, Men, and Romantic Love in Nineteenth-Century America* (New York: Oxford University Press, 1989), 28–35; Nancy L. Rhoades and Lucy E. Bailey, eds., *Wanted—Correspondence: Women's Letters to a Union Soldier* (Athens: Ohio University Press, 2009), 7–8, 51–55; Richard, *Busy Hands*, 144–46, 154–56.

18. Martha to Daniel, March 11, 1864, Martha to Daniel, March 27, 1864, Densmore and Family Papers, MNHS.

19. Martha to Daniel, October 21, 1864, Martha to Daniel, June 28, 1864, Densmore and Family Papers, MNHS. Rhoades and Bailey, eds., *Wanted—Correspondence*, 65–70, 73; Shawn Michelle Smith, *American Archives: Gender, Race, and Class in Visual Culture* (Princeton, N.J.: Princeton University Press, 1999), 6, 51–54.

20. Martha to Daniel, undated [1864], Martha to Daniel, March 4, 1864, Densmore and Family Papers, MNHS.

21. Elizabeth Dewey to Daniel, June, 27, 1864, enclosed in Martha to Daniel, June 28, 1864, Densmore and Family Papers, MNHS; Lystra, *Searching the Heart*, 141–43.

22. Martha to Benjamin, May 9, 1864, Densmore and Family Papers, MNHS; Gail Hamilton, *Country Living and Country Thinking* (Boston: Ticknor & Fields, 1861). *Country Living and Country Thinking* is a collection of essays in which Hamilton derides, in a humorous manner, the efforts made by herself and males to make gardens.; Susan Coultrap-McQuin, "Legacy Profile: Gail Hamilton (1833–1896)," *Legacy* 4, no. 2 (1987): 53–58; Judith E. Harper, *Women during the Civil War: An Encyclopedia* (New York: Routledge, 2004), 186–89.

23. Rhoades and Bailey, eds., *Wanted—Correspondence*, 38–39; Silber, *Daughters of the Union*, 2–4, 36.

24. Martha to Daniel, October 5, 1864, Densmore and Family Papers, MNHS; Coultrap-McQuin, "Gail Hamilton (1833–1896)," 55.

25. Elizabeth Dewey to Daniel, June 27, 1864, enclosed in Martha to Daniel, June 28, 1864, Densmore and Family Papers, MNHS; Silber, *Daughters of the Union*, 10–12, 262–64; Mary Nina Silber and Mary Beth Sievens, eds., *Yankee Correspondence: Civil War Letters between New England Soldiers and the Home Front* (Charlottesville: University of Virginia Press, 1996), 20–22. Attie, *Patriotic Toil*, 45–46.

26. Orrin to Son [Benjamin], March 7, 1865, Densmore and Family Papers, MNHS.

27. Orrin Jr. to Brother [Daniel], November 7, 21, 1864, Orrin to Daniel, December 18, 1864, Orrin to Son [Benjamin], March 7, 1865, Densmore and Family Papers, MNHS; Rhoades and Bailey, eds., *Wanted—Correspondence*, 73–82. Frances B. Cogan, *All American Girl: The Ideal of Real Womanhood in Mid-Nineteenth-Century America* (Athens: University of Georgia Press, 1989), 63–100; Jackie M. Blount, *Destined to Rule the Schools: Women and the Superintendency, 1873–1995* (Albany: State University of New York Press, 1998), 11–38.

6. "Faces of flint": Campaigning against Major General Nathan Bedford Forrest

1. Orrin Jr. to Daniel, April 5, 1864, Benjamin to Daniel, April 7, 1864, Benjamin Densmore and Family Papers, 1797–1955, Minnesota Historical Society (MNHS); John David

Smith, "Let Us All Be Grateful That We Have Colored Troops That Will Fight," in *Black Soldiers in Blue: African American Troops in the Civil War Era*, ed. John David Smith (Chapel Hill: University of North Carolina Press, 2002), 44–46; Joseph T. Glatthaar, *Forged in Battle: The Civil War Alliance of Black Soldiers and White Officers* (New York: Free Press, 1990), 201; Jack Hurst, *Nathan Bedford Forrest: A Biography* (New York: Vintage Books, 1994), 161–62; Eddy W. Davison and Daniel Foxx, *Nathan Bedford Forrest: In Search of the Enigma* (Gretna, La.: Pelican, 2007), 219–20.

2. Martha to Brother [Daniel], April 18, 1864, Benjamin to Brother [Daniel], April 15, 1864, Norman to Daniel, April 26, 1864, Densmore and Family Papers, MNHS; John Cimprich, "The Fort Pillow Massacre: Assessing the Evidence," in *Black Soldiers in Blue*, ed. Smith, 150–68.; Kenneth B. Moore, "Fort Pillow, Forrest, and the United States Colored Troops in 1864," in *Trial and Triumph: Essays in Tennessee's African American History*, ed. Carroll Van West (Knoxville: University of Tennessee Press, 2002), 128–44; Glatthaar, *Forged in Battle*, 156–58.

3. Orrin to Son [Daniel], April 28, 1864, Orrin to Son [Benjamin], April 27, 1864, Densmore and Family Papers, MNHS; *The Bible* (New York: Thomas and Sons, American Standard Version, 1901), Ecclesiastes 9:4.

4. Orrin to Son [Benjamin], April 27, 1864, Martha to Brother [Benjamin], May 9, 1864, Martha to Brother [Daniel], May 1, 1864, Densmore and Family Papers, MNHS.

5. Daniel to Friends at home, June 2, 1864, Daniel to Benjamin, May 30, 1864, Densmore and Family Papers, MNHS; Pension Application, Civil War Pension File, Daniel Densmore, 68th U. S. Colored Infantry, RG 15, NARA; Frederick H. Dyer, *Compendium of the War of the Rebellion*, 2 vols. (1908; Dayton, Ohio: National Historical Society in cooperation with the Press of Morningside Bookshop, 1979), pt. 3, p. 1734.

6. Daniel to Friends at home, June 2, 1864, Densmore and Family Papers, MNHS; Fellow officer, 2nd Lt. George W. Boswell, 68th USCI, was also deeply moved by emotion as he passed Fort Pillow. George W. Buswell Diary, April 12, June 4, 1864, George W. Buswell Papers, 1862–1888, The Huntington Library, San Marino, California; William A. Dobak, *Freedom by the Sword: The U.S. Colored Troops, 1862–1867* (Washington, D.C.: Center of Military History United States Army, 2011), 205–9; Maj. Gen. N. B. Forrest to Maj. Gen. C. C. Washburn, June 19, 1864, in U.S. War Department, *The War of the Rebellion: A Compilation of the Official Records of the Union and Confederate Armies*, 128 vols. (Washington, D.C.: Government Printing Office, 1880–1901), ser. 1, vol. 32, pt. 1, p. 586.

7. Frank J. Welcher, *The Union Army, 1861–1865*, 2 vols. (Bloomington: Indiana University Press, 1989), 2,:225–26, 842–48; Daniel to Friends at home, June 2, 1864, Daniel to Friends, June 17, 1864, Densmore and Family Papers, MNHS; Buswell Diary, May 22, 1864.

8. Orrin to Daniel, June 26, 1864.

9. Ibid.

10. Daniel to Friends, June 17, 1864, Densmore and Family Papers, MNHS; Buswell, Diary, June 20, 1864; Welcher, *The Union Army*, 2:842–43.

11. Daniel to Benjamin, June 22, 1864, Densmore and Family Papers, MNHS.

12. Ibid.

13. Ibid.

14. Orrin to Daniel, July 10, 1864, Orrin to Son [Daniel], August 1, 1864, Densmore and Family Papers, MNHS.

15. Charles Hanford to Nephew [Daniel], May 29, 1864, Densmore and Family Papers, MNHS.

16. Daniel to Benjamin, May 5, 1864, W. A. Poillon to Lt. D. Densmore April 29, 1864, Daniel to Benjamin June 22, 1864, Densmore and Family Papers, MNHS.

17. Daniel to Father, May 12, 1864, Orrin to Son [Daniel], August 20, 1864, Densmore and Family Papers, MNHS; Frederick L. Johnson, *Uncertain Lives: African Americans and Their First 150 Years in the Red Wing, Minnesota, Area* (Red Wing, Minn.: Goodhue County Historical Society Press, 2005), 20; Some USCT officers sent former soldiers and their camp servants home to work in their households and on farms. Kristopher A. Teters, *Practical Liberators: Union Officers in the Western Theater during the Civil War* (Chapel Hill: University of North Carolina Press, 2018), 98–101; Leslie A. Schwalm, *Emancipation's Diaspora: Race and Reconstruction in the Upper Midwest* (Chapel Hill: University of North Carolina Press, 2009), 72–73; Amy Murrell Taylor, *Embattled Freedom: Journeys through the Civil War's Slave Refugee Camps* (Chapel Hill: University of North Carolina Press, 2018), 28.

18. Daniel to Friends, June 22, 1864, Densmore and Family Papers, MNHS. Refugees from slavery proved valuable to scouts and spies for the Union Army. Taylor, *Embattled Freedom*, 29–30; Glenn David Brasher. *The Peninsula Campaign and the Necessity of Emancipation* (Chapel Hill: University of North Carolina Press, 2012), 82–84, 119–21, 127–31.

19. Daniel to Friends, June 22, 1864, Orrin to Daniel, July 3, 1864, Densmore and Family Papers, MNHS.

20. Orrin to Daniel, July 3, 1864, Densmore and Family Papers, MNHS.

21. Ibid.; Orrin to Daniel, July 10, 1864, Densmore and Family Papers, MNHS.

22. Orrin to Daniel, July 10, 1864, Densmore and Family Papers, MNHS; Reid Mitchell, *The Vacant Chair: The Northern Soldier Leaves Home* (New York: Oxford University Press, 1993), 4–18; James M. McPherson, *For Cause and Comrades: Why Men Fought the Civil War* (New York: Oxford University Press, 1997), 25–26. Gerald F. Linderman, *Embattled Courage: The Experience of Combat in the American Civil War* (New York: Free Press, 1989), 7–8.

23. Hanford Fowle to Dear Cousin [Daniel], June 19, 1864, Hanford Fowle to Dear Cousin [Daniel], July 2, 1864, Densmore and Family Papers, MNHS. Hanford Fowle was the son of Elizabeth Densmore's brother, Charles Fowle. Kathryn A. Johnson, "Densmore (Benjamin and Family) Papers, 1797–1956" (St. Paul: Minnesota Historical Society, 1956), 20. Typescript inventory and description of the Benjamin Densmore and Family Papers.

24. Hurst, *Nathan Bedford Forrest*, 200–11; Davison and Foxx, *Nathan Bedford Forrest*, 281–302; Welcher, *The Union Army*, 2:842–48; Dobak, *Freedom by the Sword*, 215–19.

25. Daniel to Benjamin, August 1, 1864, Densmore and Family Papers, MNHS; Register of deaths for companies A, C, F, G, H, I, and the Descriptive Roll of Company K. Descriptive Book, 68th USCI, Regimental Books and Papers, USCT, RG

94, National Archives and Records Administration (NARA); Margaret Humphreys, *Intensely Human: The Health of Black Soldiers in the American Civil War* (Baltimore: Johns Hopkins University Press, 2008), 10, 69–72, 88–91, 94; Record of Events, Co. D, 68th USCI, roll 212, Microfilm M594, Compiled Records Showing Service of Military Units in Volunteer Union Organizations, RG 94, NARA; Ira Berlin, Joseph P. Reidy, and Leslie S. Rowland, eds., *Freedom: A Documentary History of Emancipation, 1861–1867*, Series II, *The Black Military Experience* (Cambridge: Cambridge University Press, 1982), 633–34.

26. Daniel to Aunt Martha, August 8, 1864, Civil War Letters of Daniel Densmore, WHS; Humphreys, *Intensely Human*, 18, 69–73; Frank R. Freemon, "Detecting Feigned Illness during the American Civil War," *Journal of the History of the Neurosciences: Basic and Clinical Perspectives* 2 (July 1993): 239–42.

27. Humphreys, *Intensely Human*, 69–72, 94; Paul E. Steiner, *Disease in the Civil War: Natural Biological Warfare in 186–1865* (Springfield: Charles C. Thomas, 1968), 20; Register of deaths for companies A, C, F, G, H, I, and the Descriptive Roll of Company K. Descriptive Book, 68th USCI, Regimental Books and Papers, USCT, RG 94, NARA.

28. Welcher, *The Union Army*, 2:707–10; Hurst, *Nathan Bedford Forrest*, 210–12; Dobak, *Freedom by the Sword*, 219.

29. Daniel to Aunt Martha, August 8, 1864, Civil War Letters of Daniel Densmore, 1833–1915, and his Family in the Charles V. Hibbard Papers, 1811–1954, Wisconsin Historical Society (WHS).

30. Daniel to Aunt Martha, August 8, 1864, Civil War Letters of Daniel Densmore, WHS; Humphreys, *Intensely Human*, 24–26; Randall C. Jimerson, *The Private Civil War: Popular Thought during the Sectional Conflict* (Baton Rouge: Louisiana State University Press, 1988), 77–78, 81–82, 89–92; Reid Mitchell, *Civil War Soldiers: Their Expectations and Their Experiences* (New York: Viking, 1988), 63–64.

31. Daniel to Benjamin, July 24,1864, Daniel to Benjamin, August 11, 1864, Daniel to Benjamin, June 22, 1864, Daniel to Benjamin, July 1, 1864, Daniel to Benjamin, July 24, 1864; Densmore and Family Papers, MNHS; Col. J. Blackburn Jones to Brig. Gen. L. Thomas, July 30, 1864, Daniel Densmore to Brig. Gen. L. Thomas, August 11, 1864, D–282 1864, ser. 360, CTD, RG 94, NARA; Buswell Diary, May 15, November 21, 24, 26, December 5, 1864; Clendening was found guilty and cashiered. United States Adjutant General's Office, *Official Army Register of the Volunteer Force of the United States Army*, 8 vols. (Washington, D.C.: Adjutant General's Office, 1867), pt. 8, p. 251.

32. Orrin to Son [Daniel], August 1, 1864, Orrin to Son [Daniel], August 7, 1864, Densmore and Family Papers, MNHS; Michael C. C. Adams, *Living Hell: The Dark Side of the Civil War* (Baltimore: Johns Hopkins University Press, 2014), 119–21; Kathryn Shively, *Nature's War: Common Soldiers and the Environment in 1862 Virginia* (Chapel Hill: University of North Carolina Press, 2013), 126–46.

33. Orrin Jr. to Mother, August 23 [1864], Martha to Brother [Daniel] August 29,1864, Daniel to Brothers [Benjamin and Orrin, Jr.], August 20, 1864, Densmore and Family Papers, MNHS. By claiming Clendening is a "gag bird," Martha is stating that he is a sham, or person to be laughed at.

7. "The child was 'right glad' to get home": Young Orrin's Military Adventure

1. Orrin Jr. to Brother [Daniel], April 5, 1864, Benjamin Densmore and Family Papers, 1797–1955, Minnesota Historical Society (MNHS); Rebecca Jo Plant and Frances M. Clarke, "Studying Underage Enlistment in the American Civil War," *Journal of the History of Childhood and Youth* 2 (Winter 2018): 48–50; Emmy E. Werner, *Reluctant Witnesses: Children's Voices from the Civil War* (Boulder, Colo.: Westview Press, 1998), 2; James Marten, *The Children's Civil War* (Chapel Hill: University of North Carolina Press, 1998), 165–66; Reid Mitchell, *The Vacant Chair: The Northern Soldier Leaves Home* (New York: Oxford University Press, 1993), 4, 11–13; James M. McPherson, *For Cause and Comrades: Why Men Fought the Civil War* (New York: Oxford University Press, 1997), 25–26, 31; E. Anthony Rotundo, "Boy Culture: Middle-Class Boyhood in Nineteenth-Century America," in *Meanings for Manhood: Constructions of Masculinity in Victorian America*, ed. Mark C. Carnes and Clyde Griffen (Chicago: University of Chicago Press, 1990), 30, 32.

2. Plant and Clarke, "Studying Underage Enlistment in the American Civil War," 49–50; Amy E. Murrell, "Union Father, Rebel Son: Families and the Question of Civil War Loyalty," in *The War Was You and Me: Civilians in the American Civil War*, ed. Joan E. Cashin (Princeton, N.J.: Princeton University Press, 2002), 346; Benjamin to Daniel, June 27, 1864, Orrin to Son [Daniel], August 1, 1864, Orrin to Son [Daniel], August 7, 1864, Orrin to Son [Benjamin] August 7, 1864, Orrin to Daniel, August 21, 1864, Densmore and Family Papers, MNHS.

3. Orrin Jr. to Father, August 16, [1864], Densmore and Family Papers, MNHS.

4. Ibid.

5. Ibid.

6. Ibid.

7. Ibid.; Benjamin to Brother [Daniel], June 18, 1864, Densmore and Family Papers, MNHS; Kylie Nappi, "When Johnny Comes Marching Home: One Hundred Days in the Ohio Volunteer Infantry during the Civil War," Ohio History Connection, Accessed August 29, 2023. https://www.ohiohistory.org/when-johnny-comes-marching-home-one-hundred-days-in-the-ohio-volunteer-infantry-during-the-american-civil-war/.

8. Orrin Jr. to Father, August 16 [1864], Densmore and Family Papers, MNHS; Joseph T. Glatthaar, *Forged in Battle: The Civil War Alliance of Black Soldiers and White Officers* (New York: Free Press, 1990), 12–13; John David Smith, "Let Us All Be Grateful That We Have Colored Troops That Will Fight," in *Black Soldiers in Blue: African American Troops in the Civil War Era*, ed. John David Smith (Chapel Hill: University of North Carolina Press, 2002), 37–39; George M. Fredrickson, *The Inner Civil War: Northern Intellectuals and the Crisis for the Union* (New York: Harper Torchbooks, 1968), 170–72.

9. Orrin Jr. to Father, August 16, 1864, Densmore and Family Papers, MNHS; Earl J. Hess, "The Material Culture of Weapons in the Civil War," in *War Matters: Material Culture in the Civil War Era*, ed. Joan E. Cashin (Chapel Hill: University of North Carolina Press, 2018), 117, see also 99–122.

10. Orrin Jr. to Mother, August 23, [1864], Orrin to Son [Benjamin], August 7 [1864], Densmore and Family Papers, MNHS.

11. Orrin Jr. to Mother, August 23, [1864], Densmore and Family Papers, MNHS; Mitchell, *The Vacant Chair*, 7, 24–27; McPherson, *For Cause and Comrades*, 25–26; Lorien Foote, *The Gentlemen and the Roughs: Violence, Honor, and Manhood in the Union Army* (New York: New York University Press, 2010), 6, 71, 77–80, 90–91.

12. Orrin Jr. to Mother, August 23, [1864], Densmore and Family Papers, MNHS.

13. Daniel to Brothers [Benjamin and Orrin Jr.] August 17, 1864, Densmore and Family Papers, MNHS.

14. Daniel to Brothers [Benjamin and Orrin Jr.], August 22, 1864; *Official Records*, ser. 1, vol. 34, pt. 1, pp. 477–78; Michael B. Ballard, *Civil War in Mississippi: Major Campaigns and Battles* (Jackson: University Press of Mississippi, 2011), 25–60.

15. Orrin Jr. to Friends, August 27, 1863, Orrin to Daniel, August 29, 1864, Daniel to Friends at home, August 30, 1864, Daniel to Benjamin, August 30, 1864, Densmore and Family Papers, MNHS.

16. Orrin Jr. to Friends, September 2, 1864, Orrin Jr. to Friends at home, September 4, 1864, Daniel to Brother [Benjamin], October 1, 1864, Densmore and Family Papers, MNHS.

17. Orrin Jr. to Brother [Benjamin], September 9, 1864, Orrin Jr. to Friends at home, September 13, 1864, Densmore and Family Papers, MNHS.

18. Orrin Jr. to Friends at home, September 13, 1864, Densmore and Family Papers, MNHS.

19. Ibid., Orrin Jr. to Benj, September 6, 1864, Densmore and Family Papers, MNHS.

20. Orrin Jr. to Friends at home, September 13, 1864, Densmore and Family Papers, MNHS.

21. Daniel to Brother [Benjamin], September 18, 1864, Daniel to Benjamin, September 22, 1864, Densmore and Family Papers, MNHS.

22. Daniel to Brother [Benjamin], September 18, 1864, Daniel to Friends at home, September 19, 1864, Densmore and Family Papers, MNHS.

23. Daniel to Brother [Benjamin], September 18, 1864, Orrin Jr. to Brother [Benjamin], September 9, 1864. Daniel comments on his debts to Orrin and Benjamin are enclosed in a special note attached to Orrin Jr.'s September 9, 1864, letter. Densmore and Family Papers, MNHS.

24. Orrin Jr. to Friends at home, September 13, 1864, Daniel to Benjamin, September 22, 1864, Daniel to Friends at home, September 30, 1864, Densmore and Family Papers, MNHS.

25. Daniel to Friends at home, September 24, 1864, Daniel to Brother [Benjamin], October 1, 1864, Densmore and Family Papers, MNHS.

26. Daniel to Friends at home, September 24, 1864, Benjamin to Father, September 26, 1864, Benjamin to Father, October 2, 1864, Daniel to Friends at home, September 30, October 12, 1864, Densmore and Family Papers, MNHS.

27. Orrin to Son [Daniel], October 9, 1864, Orrin to Son [Daniel], October 16, 1864, Densmore and Family Papers, MNHS.

28. Daniel to Friends at home, October 12, 1864, Orrin to Son [Daniel], October 21, 1864, Densmore and Family Papers, MNHS.

29. Daniel to Dear Brother [Benjamin], October 29, 1864; Margaret to Bennie [Benjamin], October 14, 1864. Densmore and Family Papers, MNHS.

30. Orrin Jr. to Dear Brother [Daniel], October 13, 1864, Densmore and Family Papers, MNHS.

31. McPherson, *For Cause and Comrades*, 25–26, 31; Mitchell, *The Vacant Chair*, 4, 11–12; Reid Mitchell, *Civil War Soldiers: Their Expectations and Their Experiences* (New York: Viking, 1988), 17 -18; Gerald F. Linderman, *Embattled Courage: The Experience of Combat in the American Civil War* (New York: Free Press, 1989), 7–8.

32. Benjamin to Sister [Martha], September 22, 1864, Orrin Jr. to Brother [Daniel], October 13, 1864, Densmore and Family Papers, MNHS; United States Adjutant General's Office, *Official Army Register of the Volunteer Force of the United States Army*, 8 vols. (Washington, D.C.: Adjutant General's Office, 1867), pt. 8, p. 151.

33. Martha to Parents, October 19, 1864, 1864, Martha to Brother [Daniel], October 21, 1864, Densmore and Family Papers, MNHS.

34. Orrin to Daniel, October 27, 1864, Orrin Jr. to Brother [Daniel], October 27, 1864, Martha to Brother [Daniel], November 27, 1864, Densmore and Family Papers, MNHS.

35. Orrin Jr. to Brother [Daniel], January 15, 1865, Densmore and Family Papers, MNHS; Mitchell, *The Vacant Chair*, 74–75; Foote, *The Gentlemen and the Roughs*, 79–80.

36. Martha to Mother, May 6, 1865, Densmore and Family Papers, MNHS; Mitchell, *The Vacant Chair*, 12.

37. Orrin Jr. to Brother [Daniel], May 13, 1865, Martha to Daniel, June 5, 1865, Densmore and Family Papers, MNHS.

8. "Move the camp down to the grave yard": Camp Life in Memphis

1. Daniel to Benjamin, September 22, 1864, Daniel to Friends at home, September 19, 1864, Daniel to Brother [Benjamin], September 18, 1864, Benjamin Densmore and Family Papers, 1797–1955, Minnesota Historical Society (MNHS); Civil War Pension File, William M. Philleo, 7th Minn. Vols., RG 15, National Archives and Records Service (NARA); Service Record of 2nd Lt. William M. Philleo, 7th Minn. Vols., Carded Records, Volunteer Organizations: Civil War, ser. 519, RG 94, NARA; Reid Mitchell, *Civil War Soldiers: Their Expectations and Their Experiences* (New York: Viking, 1988), 17; Reid Mitchell, *The Vacant Chair: The Northern Soldier Leaves Home* (New York: Oxford University Press, 1993), 158; David W. Blight, ed., *When This Cruel War Is Over: The Civil War Letters of Charles Harvey Brewster* (Amherst: University of Massachusetts Press, 1992), 11–13.

2. Martha to Daniel, October 5, 1864, Daniel to Benjamin, October 10, 1864, Daniel to Friends at home, August 30, 1864, Orrin Jr. to Benjamin, September 13, 1864, Hanford Fowle to Dear Cousin [Daniel], June 19, 1864, Hanford Fowle to Dear Cousin [Daniel], July 2, 1864, Hanford Fowle to Cousin Daniel, October 10, 1864, Densmore and Family Papers, MNHS; Randall C. Jimerson, *The Private Civil War: Popular Thought during the Sectional Conflict* (Baton Rouge: Louisiana State University Press, 1988), 124–79; Mitchell, *Civil War Soldiers*, 131–35.

3. Daniel to Brothers [Benjamin and Orrin Jr.], August 26, 1864, Daniel to Benjamin, October 1, 1864, Daniel to Friends at home, October 5, 1864, Densmore and Fam-

ily Papers, MNHS; Buswell Journals, September 22, 1864, George W. Buswell Papers, 1862–1888, The Huntington Library, San Marino, California.

4. Daniel to Friends at home, October 8, 1864, Daniel to Benjamin, October 10, 1864, Densmore and Family Papers, MNHS; Minnesota Board of Commissioners on Publication of History of Minnesota in the Civil and Indian Wars, *Minnesota in the Civil and Indian Wars, 1861–1865*, 2 vols. (St. Paul: State of Minnesota, 1890–93), 1:381.

5. Daniel to Friends at home, October 5, 1864, Densmore and Family Papers, MNHS; John D. Billings, *Hardtack and Coffee; or, The Unwritten Story of Army Life* (Boston: George M. Smith, 1887), 51–53; István Kornél Vida, *Hungarian Émigrés in the American Civil War: A History and Biographical Dictionary* (Jefferson, N.C.: McFarland, 2012), 157–58; Col. I. J. Kappner to Maj. W. H. Morgan, July 16, 1864, Letters Sent, ser. 2818, RG 393, Pt. 2, NARA; Colonel Kappner to Col. Herman Lieb, December 24, 1864, Letters Sent, ser. 2818, RG 393, Pt. 2, NARA; Daniel to Friends at home, October 5, 1863, Densmore and Family Papers, MNHS.

6. Register of Deaths, companies A, C, F, G, H, I, Descriptive Roll of Company K, Descriptive Books, 68th USCI, Regimental Books and Papers, USCT, RG 94, NARA; Buswell Journals, September 22, 23, 1864; Margaret Humphreys, *Intensely Human: The Health of Black Soldiers in the American Civil War* (Baltimore: Johns Hopkins University Press, 2008), 6, 10–11, 68–69, 77–79, 94; Joseph T. Glatthaar, *Forged in Battle: The Civil War Alliance of Black Soldiers and White Officers* (New York: Free Press, 1990), 76, 185–87; Richard M. Reid, ed., *Practicing Medicine in a Black Regiment: The Civil War Diary of Burt G. Wilder, 55th Massachusetts* (Amherst: University of Massachusetts Press, 2010), 18–19, 25–26. Paul E. Steiner believes disease peaked in the South in the hot, humid summer months. Paul E. Steiner, *Disease in the Civil War: Natural Biological Warfare in 1861–1865* (Springfield, Ill.: Charles C. Thomas, 1968), 21; Bell I. Wiley, *The Life of Billy Yank: The Common Soldier of the Civil War* (Baton Rouge: Louisiana State University Press, 1978), 56.

7. Daniel to Friends at home, October 5, 1863, Densmore and Family Papers, MNHS; Col. Edward Bouton's 1st Brigade, U.S. Colored Troops consisted of the 59th, 61st, 68th USCI, and Battery "I" 2nd U.S. Colored Light Artillery. The 59th and 61st USCI were organized between June and September 1863, and the 68th USCI was organized between March and April 1864. United States Adjutant General's Office, *of the Volunteer Force of the United States Army*, 8 vols. (Washington, D.C.: Adjutant General's Office, 1867), pt. 8, pp. 167, 232, 234, 241; Frank J. Welcher, *The Union Army, 1861–1865*, 2 vols. (Bloomington: Indiana University Press, 1989), 2:848.

8. Orrin to Son [Daniel], October 21, 1864, Orrin to Son [Daniel], October 16, 1864, Daniel to Father, October 25, 1864, Densmore and Family Papers, MNHS.

9. Orrin to Son [Daniel], October 21, 1864, Margaret to Bennie, October 14, 1864, Densmore and Family Papers, MNHS; Drew Gilpin Faust, *This Republic of Suffering: Death and the American Civil War* (New York: Alfred Knopf, 2008), xiii.

10. Faust, *This Republic of Suffering*, xii–xvi.

11. Margaret to Bennie, October 14, 1864, Densmore and Family Papers, MNHS.

12. Daniel to Benjamin, October 29, 1864, Daniel to Benjamin, November 7, 1864, Densmore and Family Papers, MNHS.

13. Daniel to Friends at home, November 13, 1864, Densmore and Family Papers, MNHS; Lorien Foote, *The Gentlemen and the Roughs: Violence, Honor, and Manhood in the Union Army* (New York: New York University Press, 2010), 52–53; Amy Murrell Taylor, *Embattled Freedom: Journeys through the Civil War's Slave Refugee Camps* (Chapel Hill: University of North Carolina Press, 2018), 70–72, 76, 78–80.

14. Daniel to Friends at home, December 10, 1864, Densmore and Family Papers, MNHS; Robert F. Engs and Corey M. Brooks, eds., *Their Patriotic Duty: The Civil War Letters of the Evans Family of Brown County, Ohio* (New York: Fordham University Press, 2007), 296, 298; Martin W. Öfele, *German-Speaking Officers in the U.S. Colored Troops, 1863–1867* (Gainesville: University Press of Florida, 2004), 131.

15. Daniel to Brother [Benjamin], December 15, 1864, Densmore and Family Papers, MNHS.

16. Undated and unsigned letter written by Daniel probably to his folks in late December 1864. The content of the letter is about the 68th USCI moving to Fort Pickering and adjusting to life in the fort. The letter has been incorrectly catalogued as being written on March 20, 1865, Densmore and Family Papers, MNHS.

17. Orrin Jr.'s curse, "sgnisselb," is "blessings" spelled backwards. Orrin Jr. to Daniel, December 28, 1864, Orrin to Son [Daniel], December 18, 1864, Densmore and Family Papers, MNHS; The Bible (New York: Thomas and Sons, American Standard Version, 1901), Proverbs 27: 22.

18. Orrin to Son [Daniel], December 18, 1864, Densmore and Family Papers, MNHS.

19. Buswell Diary, December 12, 13, 1864. George W. Buswell was severely criticized by Colonel Kappner for failing to instruct his men on their duty to salute superior officers. Buswell Diary, December 24, 1864.

20. Daniel to Friends at home, December 18, 1864, Daniel to Brother [Benjamin], December 15, 1864, Daniel to Father, January 1, 1865, Densmore and Family Papers, MNHS; Buswell Journals, December 26, 29, 1864.

21. Daniel to Father, January 1, 1865, Densmore and Family Papers, MNHS.

22. Daniel to Friends at home, October 5, 1864, Densmore and Family Papers, MNHS.

23. Daniel to Brother [Benjamin], December 15, 1863, Densmore and Family Papers, MNHS; Reid, ed., *Practicing Medicine in a Black Regiment*, 25–26; Donald M. Murray and Robert M. Rodney, "Colonel Julian E. Bryant: Champion of the Negro Soldier," *Illinois State Historical Society Journal* 56, no. 2 (1963): 277–79.

24. Daniel to Brother [Benjamin], December 15, 1864, Densmore and Family Papers, MNHS.

25. Daniel to Brother [Benjamin], November 7, 1864, Densmore and Family Papers, MNHS.

26. Daniel to Brother [Benjamin], December 15, 1864, Densmore and Family Papers, MNHS.

27. Ibid.

28. Daniel to Dear Friends at Home, December 18, 1864, Densmore and Family Papers, MNHS.

29. Daniel to Brother [Benjamin], December 15, 1864, Densmore and Family Papers, MNHS. George W. Buswell noted that three African American soldiers were executed on

December 16, 1864. In contrast, Daniel Densmore claims only one was executed and that the execution took place on Thursday, December 15. Buswell Diary, December 16, 1864. Jonathon W. White and Reagan Connelly claim that the three soldiers were from Colonel Kappner's regiment, the 3rd U.S. Colored Heavy Artillery. They were convicted of murdering a Black civilian and plundering his home in January 1864. Jonathon W. White and Reagan Connelly, eds., "'Off to Dixie and Adventure': The Dakota War and Civil War Diaries of George W. Buswell, 7th Minnesota Infantry and 68th U.S. Colored Troops," unpublished book manuscript, n324, 299; Robert I. Alotta, *Civil War Justice: Union Army Executions under Lincoln* (Shippensburg, Pa.: White Mane, 1989), 138–39, 200–201.

30. Daniel to Friends at home, December 25, 1864, Densmore and Family Papers, MNHS; Buswell Diary, December 21–23, 1864.

9. "Christmas with us here promises to be quite a season": Rejoicing and Celebrating

1. Orrin to Son [Benjamin], September 23, 1864, Benjamin Densmore and Family Papers, 1797–1955, Minnesota Historical Society (MNHS); James M. McPherson, *Battle Cry of Freedom: The Civil War Era* (New York: Oxford University Press, 1988), 777.

2. Orrin to Son [Daniel], October 16, 1864, Densmore and Family Papers, MNH.

3. Orrin to Son [Daniel], October 23, 1864, Orrin to Daniel, October 27, 1864, Densmore and Family Papers, MNHS; McPherson, *Battle Cry of Freedom*, 786–88.

4. Daniel to Friends at home, September 30, 1864, Densmore and Family Papers, MNHS.

5. Orrin to Son [Daniel], October 9, 1864, Densmore and Family Papers, MNHS; Elbert B. Smith, "Frémont, Jessie Benton (1824–1902), Political activist," and "Frémont, John Charles (1813–1890), Union general, politician," in *Encyclopedia of the Civil War: A Political, Social and Military History*, ed. David S. Heidler and Jeanne T. Heidler (New York: W. W. Norton, 2000), 785–88; Kristopher A. Teters, *Practical Liberators: Union Officers in the Western Theater during the Civil War* (Chapel Hill: University of North Carolina Press, 2018), 9–10; James M. McPherson, *Ordeal by Fire: The Civil War and Reconstruction* (New York: Alfred A. Knopf, 1982), 95–96, 158, 269; McPherson, *Battle Cry of Freedom*, 352–54.

6. Orrin to Son [Daniel], October 23, 1864, Densmore and Family Papers, MNHS; McPherson, *Ordeal by Fire*, 213–14, 300–301, 440–42; McPherson, *Battle Cry of Freedom*, 348–50; 771–72.

7. Orrin Jr. to Brother [Daniel], November 7, 1864, Orrin Jr. to Brother [Daniel], November 10, 1864, Daniel to Folks at home, November 13, 1864, Densmore and Family Papers, MNHS.

8. Daniel to Friends at home, December 18, 1864, Densmore and Family Papers, MNHS; Ernest Walter Hooper, "Memphis, Tennessee: Federal Occupation and Reconstruction, 1862–1870," Ph.D. diss., University of North Carolina, 1957, 30–31.

9. Daniel to Friends at home, December 18, 1864, Densmore and Family Papers, MNHS; Bertram Wyatt-Brown, *Honor and Violence in the Old South* (New York: Oxford University Press, 1986), 142–53; Bertram Wyatt-Brown, *The Shaping of Southern Culture: Honor, Grace, and War, 1760s–1880s* (Chapel Hill: University of North Carolina Press,

2001), 43–44, 69; Kenneth S. Greenberg, *Honor and Slavery: Lies, Duels, Noses, Masks, Dressing as a Woman, Gifts, Strangers, Humanitarianism, Death, Slave Rebellions, The Proslavery Argument, Baseball, Hunting, and Gambling in the Old South* (Princeton, N.J.: Princeton University Press, 1996), 7–9, 58, 62–64, 81–82; Lorien Foote, *The Gentlemen and the Roughs: Violence, Honor, and Manhood in the Union Army* (New York: New York University Press, 2010), 78.

10. Daniel to Friends at home, December 18, 1864, Densmore and Family Papers, MNHS.

11. Daniel to Father, January 28, 1864 [1865]. Daniel wrote this letter on January 28, 1865, but mistakenly dated it January 28, 1864, Densmore and Family Papers, MNHS; Amy Murrell Taylor, *Embattled Freedom: Journeys through the Civil War's Slave Refugee Camps* (Chapel Hill: University of North Carolina Press, 2018), 34–35; Ira Berlin, Joseph P. Reidy, and Leslie S. Rowland, eds., *Freedom: A Documentary History of Emancipation, 1861–1867*, Series II, *The Black Military Experience* (Cambridge: Cambridge University Press, 1982), 659–61; Keith P. Wilson, *Campfires of Freedom: The Camp Life of Black Soldiers during the Civil War* (Kent, Ohio: Kent State University Press, 2002), 193–201; Richard M. Reid, *Freedom for Themselves: North Carolina's Black Soldiers in the Civil War* (Chapel Hill: University of North Carolina Press, 2008), 252–53; Chandra Manning, *Troubled Refuge: Struggling for Freedom in the Civil War* (New York: Vintage Books, 2017), 36.

12. Daniel to Father, January 28, 1864 [1865], Densmore and Family Papers, MNHS.

13. Ibid.; Robin Seager, *Pompey the Great: A Political Biography* (Oxford: Blackwell, 2002), 152–68; Like "Sambo," "Sam" and "Tambo," "Pompey" was a pejorative, generic name used to control African American men and convey their alleged inferiority. Randall M. Miller and John David Smith, eds., *Dictionary of Afro-American Slavery* (Westport, Conn.: Praeger, 1997), 655–56.

14. Daniel to Father, January 28, 1864 [1865], Densmore and Family Papers, MNHS; Simon Critchley, *On Humour* (London: Routledge, 2002); Mary Beard, "What Made the Romans Laugh?" Background Briefing, Radio National, Australian Broadcasting Corporation, broadcast, April 19, 2009.

15. Daniel to Cousin Susie, March 1, 1859, Civil War Letters of Daniel Densmore, 1833–1915, and his Family in the Charles V. Hibbard Papers, 1811–1954, Wisconsin Historical Society (WHS).

16. Daniel to Friends at home, December 25, 1864, Densmore and Family Papers, MNHS. For a discussion of the way Christmas and Thanksgiving Day celebrations evoked feelings of nostalgia, separation, loneliness, and romantic visions of home see George C. Rable, "Hearth, Home and Family in the Fredericksburg Campaign," in *The War Was You and Me: Civilians in the American Civil War*, ed. Joan E. Cashin (Princeton, N.J.: Princeton University Press, 2002), 85–111.

17. Orrin Jr. to Daniel, December 28, 1864, Densmore and Family Papers, MNHS.

18. Daniel to Friends at home, December 25, 1864, Densmore and Family Papers, MNHS.

19. Ibid.

20. Ibid. "Rhythm bones" or the "bones" are folk percussion instruments. Originally, they were made from a pair of animal bones, but sticks of wood or metal may also be

used. The striking of the "bones" causes clicking sound. Although playing the bones was a common slave pastime, it is believed that bone playing may have been brought to America by the Irish or other European migrants. In the nineteenth century playing the bones was popularized by the minstrel shows. Robert E. McDowell, "Bones and the Man: Toward a History of Bones Playing," *Journal of American Culture* 5, no. 1 (1982): 38–43. For a discussion of the way USCT officers' understanding of African American music was influenced by racial prejudice and stereotypes, see Wilson, *Campfires of Freedom*, 147–75. The Pigeon Wing was a challenge dance. In challenge dances, dancers attempted to surpass their rivals by performing more intricate steps. Mark Knowles, *Tap Roots: The Early History of Tap Dancing* (Jefferson, N.C.: McFarland, 2002), 44; Miller and Smith, eds., *Dictionary of Afro-American Slavery*, 173–74; Lynne Fauley Emery, *Black Dance: From 1619 to Today*, 2nd ed. (Princeton, N.J.: Princeton Book Co., 2017), 90; Dinah was a pejorative, generic name for both enslaved and freed African American women. Union soldiers often used the name Dinah to refer to all African American women. "Testimony of Lizzie McCloud," Federal Writers' Project: Vol. 2, Arkansas, Part 5, McClendon-Prayer, 1936. Accessed July 26, 2021. https://www.loc.gov/item/mesn025/. The view that slave women had unrestrained sexual energy and were promiscuous was common in the Union Army and American society generally. Deborah Gray White, *Ar'n't I a Woman: Female Slaves in the Plantation South*, rev. ed. (New York: W. W. Norton, 1999); Taylor, *Embattled Freedom*, 85–87; Leslie A. Schwalm, *A Hard Fight for We: Women's Transition from Slavery to Freedom in South Carolina* (Urbana: University of Illinois Press, 1997), 102–3, 141–42.

21. Daniel to Friends at home, December 25, 1864, Densmore and Family Papers, MNHS; Greenberg, *Honor and Slavery*, 51, 65–67; Charles Joyner, *Down by the Riverside: A South Carolina Slave Community* (Urbana: University of Illinois Press, 1984), 134–36; Eugene D. Genovese, *Roll, Jordan, Roll: The World the Slaves Made* (New York: Vintage Books, 1976), 573–75.

22. Daniel to Friends at home, December 25, 1864, Orrin Jr. to Daniel, December 11, 1864, Densmore and Family Papers, MNHS. Mrs. Jones only stayed with the regiment during the winter season. Patricia L. Richard, *Busy Hands: Images of the Family in the Northern Civil War Effort* (New York: Fordham University Press, 2003), 19–20. A cricket on the hearth was an omen that was thought to bring happiness and good fortune to the home it resided in. Daniel may also have been alluding to Charles Dickens's popular but sentimental Christmas book, *The Cricket on the Hearth: A Fairy Tale of Home*. It is the story of true love and family affections triumphing over difficulties. Heather Anne Tilley, "Sentiment and Vision in Charles Dickens's *A Christmas Carol* and *The Cricket on the Hearth*," *19: Interdisciplinary Studies in the Long Nineteenth Century* 4 (April 2007): 12–17.

23. Daniel to Father, January 1, 1865, Densmore and Family Papers, MNHS.

24. Daniel to Father, January 28, 1864 [1865], Densmore and Family Papers, MNHS; Col. I. G. Kappner to Col. Blackburn Jones, December 12, 1864, Col. I. G. Kappner to Col. Blackburn Jones, December 14, 1864, Col. I. G. Kappner to Col. Blackburn Jones, January 10, 1865, Col. I. G. Kappner to Col. Blackburn Jones, February 1, 1865, Fort Pickering, Memphis, Letters Sent, ser. 2818, RG 393, pt. 2, National Archives and Records Service; Blight, ed., *When This Cruel War Is Over*, 11–13; Reid Mitchell, *Civil War Soldiers: Their Expectations and Their Experiences* (New York: Viking, 1988), 17; Reid Mitchell, *The*

Vacant Chair: The Northern Soldier Leaves Home (New York: Oxford University Press, 1993), 158.

25. Orrin to Son [Daniel], January 1, 1865, Densmore and Family Papers, MNHS.

10. "She walks off with the work": Service and Friendship: Elizabeth, Mary, and Martha

1. Elizabeth Fox-Genovese, *Within the Plantation Household: Black and White Women of the Old South* (Chapel Hill: University of North Carolina Press, 1988); Brenda E. Stevenson, *Life in Black and White: Family and Community in the Slave South* (New York: Oxford University Press, 1996), 195–96, 203–4; Deborah Gray White, *Ar'n't I a Woman: Female Slaves in the Plantation South*, rev. ed. (New York: W. W. Norton, 1999); Thavolia Glymph, *Out of the House of Bondage: The Transformation of the Plantation Household* (Cambridge: Cambridge University Press, 2008), 1–11; Leslie A. Schwalm, *A Hard Fight for We: Women's Transition from Slavery to Freedom in South Carolina* (Urbana: University of Illinois Press, 1997), 177–78, 207–11.

2. Orrin to Daniel, March 24, 1864, Orrin to Son [Daniel], August 20, 1864, Orrin to Son [Daniel], August 21, 1864, Daniel to Friends at home, August 30, 1864, Orrin Jr. to Brother [Daniel], October 27, 1864, Benjamin Densmore and Family Papers, 1797–1955, Minnesota Historical Society (MNHS).

3. Martha to Brother [Daniel], May 1, 1864; Orrin Jr. to Brother [Daniel], October 27, 1864, Densmore and Family Papers, MNHS.

4. Orrin to Son [Daniel], August 21, 1864, Densmore and Family Papers, MNHS.

5. Orrin Jr. to Brother [Daniel], October 27, 1864, Orrin to Son [Daniel], August 21, 1864, Densmore and Family Papers, MNHS; Frederick L. Johnson, *Goodhue County, Minnesota: A Narrative History* (Red Wing, Minn.: Goodhue County Historical Society Press, 2000), 231.

6. Orrin to Daniel, August 21, 1864, Martha to Daniel, May 1, 1864, Densmore and Family Papers, MNHS; Frederick L. Johnson, *Uncertain Lives: African Americans and Their First 150 Years in the Red Wing, Minnesota, Area* (Red Wing, Minn.: Goodhue County Historical Society Press, 2005), 20.

7. Caroline Fisher to Miss Brockaway, April 29, 1839; Betsy Ann Brockaway to Sir [Benjamin Fowle], May 6, 1839; E. D. [Elizabeth Densmore] to [Betsy Ann Brockaway] undated, Densmore and Family Papers, MNHS; Kathryn A. Johnson, "Densmore (Benjamin and Family Papers, 1797–1956," St. Paul, Minnesota Historical Society, 5, Typescript inventory of the Benjamin Densmore Family Papers; Leslie A. Schwalm, *Emancipation's Diaspora: Race and Reconstruction in the Upper Midwest* (Chapel Hill: University of North Carolina Press, 2009), 27, 29.

8. Orrin to Daniel, August 21, 1864, Densmore and Family Papers, MNHS.

9. Daniel to Friends at home, August 30, 1864, Martha to Brother [Daniel], August 29, 1864, Densmore and Family Papers, MNHS; James M. McPherson, *For Cause and Comrades: Why Men Fought the Civil War* (New York: Oxford University Press, 1997), 134–36; Reid Mitchell, *The Vacant Chair: The Northern Soldier Leaves Home* (New York: Oxford University Press, 1993), 14–15.

10. Martha to Brother [Daniel], August 29, 1864, Orrin to Daniel, August 29, 1864, Orrin to Son [Daniel], October 16, 1864, Orrin Jr. to Benjamin, September 6, 1864, Martha to Mother, May 6, 1865, Densmore and Family Papers, MNHS.

11. Martha to Brother [Daniel], August 29, 1864, Daniel to Friends at home, August 30, 1864, Daniel to Friends at home, September 19, 1864, Densmore and Family Papers, MNHS.

12. Orrin Jr. to Brother [Daniel], October 27, 1864, Anna to Martha, November 18, 1864, Densmore and Family Papers, MNHS.

13. John Hope Franklin and Loren Schweninger, *Runaway Slaves: Rebels on the Plantation* (New York: Oxford University Press, 1999), 2–4; Peter Kolchin, *American Slavery, 1619–1877* (New York: Hill and Wang, 1993), 157; John W. Blassingame, *The Slave Community: Plantation Life in the Antebellum South* (Oxford: Oxford University Press, 1979), 288, 313–14; Randall C. Jimerson, *The Private Civil War: Popular Thought during the Sectional Conflict* (Baton Rouge: Louisiana State University Press, 1988), 81–82, 89–92; Joseph T. Glatthaar, *Forged in Battle: The Civil War Alliance of Black Soldiers and White Officers* (New York: Free Press, 1990), 81–85; Benjamin to Brother [Daniel], October 25, 1863, Benjamin to Mother, November 3, 1863, Daniel to Aunt Martha, February 14, 1864, Daniel to Friends at home, June 17, 1864, Densmore and Family Papers, MNHS.

14. Martha was a schoolteacher, and Orrin and Daniel had worked as schoolteachers. Some of Martha's teaching colleagues boarded with the Densmores. Orrin Jr. to Daniel, November 21, 1864, Orrin to Daniel, December 18, 1864, [Daniel Densmore], "History and Genealogy of the Family of Orrin and Elizabeth Densmore," 1903, 23–24, 34, Benjamin Densmore and Family Papers, MNHS; Like the Densmores, teachers working in the slave refugee camps were often amazed by the progress made by their students because they grossly underestimated their students' innate ability and lacked knowledge of the level of education in slave communities. Amy Murrell Taylor, *Embattled Freedom: Journeys through the Civil War's Slave Refugee Camps* (Chapel Hill: University of North Carolina Press, 2018), 194–95.

15. Martha to Daniel, November 27, 1864, Orrin Jr. to Mother, August 23, 1864, Orrin Jr. to Brother [Daniel], October 27, 1864, Densmore and Family Papers, MNHS; Orrin Jr. left Red Wing on his tour of the South on August 3, 1864, a little more than two weeks before Mary arrived at the Densmore household. He arrived home in Red Wing in late October 1864.

16. Orrin Jr. to Brother [Daniel], November 7, 1864, Densmore and Family Papers, MNHS.

17. Orrin to Daniel, August 29, 1864, Densmore and Family Papers, MNHS.

18. Orrin to Son [Daniel], October 16, 1864, Orrin to Son [Daniel], October 23, 1864, Densmore and Family Papers, MNHS.

19. Orrin to Son Daniel, October 27, 1864, Densmore and Family Papers, MNHS.

20. Daniel to Friends at home, August 30, 1864, Densmore and Family Papers, MNHS.

21. Daniel to Friends at home, November 13, 1864, Martha to Daniel, May 23, 1865, Densmore and Family Papers, MNHS.

22. Daniel to Friends at home, April 17, 1865, Densmore and Family Papers, MNHS.

23. Martha to Brother [Daniel], November 7, 1864, Densmore and Family Papers, MNHS.

24. Ibid.; Orrin Jr. to Brother [Daniel], November 27, 1864; Martha to Daniel, May 23, 1865, Densmore and Family Papers, MNHS; The 1865 Minnesota census lists Red Wing as having three African American residents, two of whom, James Perry and Jasper Thompson, may have courted Mary McElroy. See Johnson, *Uncertain Lives*, 142.

25. Martha to Mother, May 6, 1865, Martha to Daniel, May 23, 1865, Densmore and Family Papers, MNHS; One important reason why masters allocated clothing to their slaves was to exercise control over them. Eugene D. Genovese, *Roll Jordan Roll: The World the Slaves Made* (New York: Random House, 1974), 555–57; For comment on how former slaves used clothing to express their self-determination see Taylor, *Embattled Freedom*, 167–172.

26. Orrin to Daniel, April 28, 1864 ("Darkey"), Orrin Jr. to Brother [Benjamin], September 6, 1864 ("the wench"), Orrin to Daniel, October 16, 1864 ("the contraband", "the girl"), Orrin Jr. to Brother [Daniel], October 27, 1864 ("contraband help," "a trump"), Orrin Jr. to Brother [Daniel], November 7, 1864 ("nigger"), Martha to Daniel, November 27, 1864 ("Our Mary"), Daniel to Friends at home, April 17, 1865 ("pair of hands"), Martha to Daniel, May 1, 1865 ("Dinah"), Daniel to Benjamin, September 13, 1865("the institution"), Densmore and Family Papers, MNHS.

27. Orrin to Daniel, July 10, 1864, Martha to Daniel, November 27, 1864, Daniel to Friends at home, April 17, 1865, Densmore and Family Papers, MNHS; Herbert G. Gutman, *The Black Family in Slavery and Freedom, 1750–1925* (New York: Random House, 1977), 236–37.

11. "Do come up Martha": Anna and Martha

1. United States Adjutant General's Office, *Official Army Register of the Volunteer Force of the United States Army*, 8 vols. (Washington, D.C.: Adjutant General's Office, 1867), pt. 7, p. 304; Frederick H. Dyer, *Compendium of the War of Rebellion*, 2 vols. (1908; Dayton: National Historical Society in cooperation with the Press of Morningside Bookshop, 1979), pt. 3, pp.1293–94; Kenneth Carley, *Minnesota in the Civil War: An Illustrated History* (St. Paul: Minnesota Historical Society, 2000), 213; Colonel Robert N. McLaren commanded the 2nd Minnesota Cavalry which was organized at Fort Snelling between December 1863 and January 1864. Colonel McLaren was stationed at Fort Snelling until he was discharged with his regiment in November 1865. Anna McLaren was probably resident at Fort Snelling between December 1863 and November 1865.

2. Nina Silber, *Daughters of the Union: Northern Women Fight the Civil War* (Cambridge, Mass.: Harvard University Press, 2005), 92–96; Richard H. Hall, *Women on the Civil War Battlefront* (Lawrence: University Press of Kansas, 2006), 43–45; Michele Nacy, *Members of the Regiment: Army Officers' Wives on the Western Frontier, 1865–1890* (Westport, Conn.: Greenwood Press, 2000), 2, 4, 6–7.

3. Daniel to Brother [Benjamin], December 2, 1863, Benjamin Densmore and Family Papers, 1797–1955, Minnesota Historical Society (MNHS).

4. Anna to My dear Martha, December 7 [1864], Daniel to Brother [Benjamin], December 2, 1863, Orrin to Sons [Daniel, Benjamin], October 21, 1862, Benjamin Densmore and Family Papers, 1797–1955, Minnesota Historical Society (MNHS).

5. Anna was the daughter of Orrin's sister, Diana. Diana was married to Archibald McVean. [Daniel Densmore], "History and Genealogy of the Family of Orrin and Elizabeth Densmore," 1903, p. 25, Densmore and Family papers, MNHS; Kathryn A. Johnson, "Densmore (Benjamin and Family) Papers, 1797–1956," St. Paul, Minnesota Historical Society, 1956, p. 19. Typescript inventory and description of the Benjamin Densmore and Family Papers; Anna to My dear Martha, December 7 [1864], Anna to My dear Martha, August 6, [1865], Densmore and Family Papers, MNHS; Anna to Dear Cousin [Martha], January 16, [1865], Densmore and Family Papers, MNHS.

6. Stephen E. Osman, *Fort Snelling and the Civil War* (St. Paul: Ramsey County Historical Society, 2017), 27–30, 38–39; Daniel to Dear friends at home, December 2, 1863, Densmore and Family Papers, MNHS.

7. A. C. Meserole to Dear McL [Anna McLaren], May 11, 1865, Anna to My dear Martha, May 20, [1865]; Anna to Dear cousin Martha, April 11, [1864], Anna to Dear Martha, July 7, [1864]; Anna to Dear Martha [December 1865], Densmore and Family Papers, MNHS; Clifford Edward Clark Jr., *The American Home, 1800–1960* (Chapel Hill: University of North Carolina Press, 1986), xii–xv, 4, 12.

8. Anna to My dear cousin, January 29 [1864], Anna to My dear Martha, March 16, [1865], Densmore and Family Papers, MNHS.

9. A. C. Meserole to Dear McL [Anna McLaren], May 11, 1865, Anna to My dear Martha, May 20, [1865]; Anna to Dear cousin Martha, April 11, [1864], Anna to Dear Martha, July 7, [1864]; Anna to Dear Martha, [December 1865] Densmore and Family Papers, MNHS; Silber, *Daughters of the Union*, 168–69; Amy Murrell Taylor, *Embattled Freedom: Journeys through the Civil War's Slave Refugee Camps* (Chapel Hill: University of North Carolina Press, 2018), 367, 170–71; Victoria E. Ott, "There's No Place Like Home: Gender, Family, and the Confederate Alabama Household," in *War Matters: Material Culture in the Civil War Era*, ed. Joan E. Cashin (Chapel Hill: University of North Carolina Press, 2018), 178–79.

10. Anna to Dear cousin Martha, July 7, [1864], Densmore and Family Papers, MNHS.

11. Anna to Dear Martha, April 11 [1864], Densmore and Family Papers, MNHS.

12. Anna to My dear little boy, January [1865], Densmore and Family Papers, MNHS; Karen Halttunen, *Confidence Men and Painted Women: A Study of Middle-Class Culture in America, 1830–1870* (New Haven, Conn.: Yale University Press, 1982), 61–63, 96–98.

13. Robert N. McLaren to Dan [Daniel Densmore], February 4, 1864, Densmore and Family Papers, MNHS; Patricia L. Richard, *Busy Hands: Images of the Family in the Northern Civil War Effort* (New York: Fordham University Press, 2003), 15–22; Mary P. Ryan, *Cradle of the Middle Class: The Family in Oneida County, New York, 1790–1865* (New York: Cambridge University Press, 1981), 195–198; Karen Lystra, *Searching the Heart: Women, Men, and Romantic Love in Nineteenth-Century America* (New York: Oxford University Press, 1989), 42, 154.

14. Anna to My dear Martha, April 10 [1864], Densmore and Family Papers, MNHS.

15. Anna to My dear Martha, March 16, [1865], Densmore and Family Papers, MNHS.
16. Anna to My dear cousin [Martha], January 16, [1865], Densmore and Family Papers, MNHS.
17. Lystra, *Searching the Heart*, 9–10, 186–91.
18. Anna to My dear cousin [Martha], November 18, 1864, Anna to My dear cousin [Martha], December 17, [1864], Densmore and Family Papers, MNHS.
19. Anna to Dear Martha, April 11 [1864], Densmore and Family Papers, MNHS.
20. Anna to My dear Martha, [1864 undated], Anna to My dear Martha, May 20, [1865], Martha to Brother [Daniel], May 15, 1865, Densmore and Family Papers, MNHS.
21. Anna to Dear cousin [Martha], November 18, 1864, Anna to My dear Martha, April 10, [1864], Anna to Dear cousin [Martha], December 17, [1864], Densmore and Family Papers, MNHS. Because of public protest the deserters were not executed. Osman, *Fort Snelling*, 210.
22. Anna to Dear cousin Martha, July 7, [1864], Orrin to Sons, [Daniel, Benjamin], October 15, 1863, Densmore and Family Papers, MNHS. Martha's "beau" was probably Assistant Surgeon Augustus O. Potter, Companies F, and S, 6th Minnesota Infantry. Company F, known as "The Goodhue Guard," was recruited in Red Wing. Augustus O. Potter died on September 13, 1864. Carley, *Minnesota in the Civil War*, 208; Madeline Angell, *Red Wing, Minnesota: Saga of a River Town* (Minneapolis: Dillon Press, 1977), 105.
23. The parents' trip began in mid-May 1865 and finished early in June 1865. Orrin Jr. to Daniel, May 13, 1865, Martha to Daniel, May 23, 1865, Densmore and Family Papers, MNHS.
24. Martha to Brother [Benjamin], June 27, 1864, Densmore and Family Papers, MNHS; Louise L. Stevenson, *The Victorian Homefront: American Thought and Culture, 1860–1880* (Ithaca, N.Y.: Cornell University Press, 2001), xxiv, xxxiv, 1–29; Richard L. Bushman, *The Refinement of America: Persons, Houses, Cities* (New York: Alfred A. Knopf, 1992), 267–79; Built in 1857, Orrin Densmore's family home was located on the corner of Main and Cedar Streets. [Daniel Densmore], "History and Genealogy of the Family of Orrin and Elizabeth Densmore," 35; Pryor & Co's *Red Wing City Directory*, 1876/77, 59.
25. Martha to Daniel, November 27, 1864, Benjamin to Daniel, June 18, 1864, Orrin to Daniel, June 26, 1864, Densmore and Family Papers, MNHS.
26. Anna to My dear cousin Martha, July 7, [1864], Densmore and Family Papers, MNHS.

12. "They all fought like Minnesotians": The Mobile Campaign

1. Daniel to Friends at home, December 25, 1864, Daniel to Benjamin, December 26, 1864, Benjamin Densmore and Family Papers, 1797–1955, Minnesota Historical Society (MNHS).
2. Daniel to Benjamin, February 4, 1864 [1865]. Daniel incorrectly dated this letter 1864. Daniel to Benjamin, February 7, 1865, Densmore and Family Papers, MNHS; William A. Dobak, *Freedom by the Sword: The U.S. Colored Troops, 1862–1867* (Washington, D.C.: Center of Military History United States Army, 2011), 142–54; John S.

Sledge, *These Rugged Days: Alabama in the Civil War* (Tuscaloosa: University of Alabama Press, 2017), 171–76; Daniel's regiment was part of Col. Charles W. Drew's Third Brigade. Frank J. Welcher, *The Union Army, 1861–1865*, 2 vols. (Bloomington: Indiana University Press, 1989), 2:689–97; United States War Department, *The War of the Rebellion: A Compilation of the Official Records of the Union and Confederate Armies*, 128 vols. (Washington, D.C.: Government Printing Office, 1880–1901), ser. 1, vol. 49, pt. 1, 780–81.

3. Daniel to Benjamin, February 4, 1864 [1865], Daniel to Benjamin, February 7, 1865, Benjamin to Father, February 19, 1865. Daniel's appointment was confirmed when his regiment reached New Orleans. Daniel to Benjamin, February 12, 1865, Densmore and Family Papers, MNHS.

4. Daniel to Benjamin, February 7, 1865, Densmore and Family Papers, MNHS.

5. Daniel to Benjamin, February 12, 1865, Daniel to Friends at home, February 19, 1865, Densmore and Family Papers, MNHS.

6. Daniel to Benjamin, February 26, 1865, Densmore and Family Papers, MNHS.

7. Ibid.; National Park Service, "The Chalmette Monument," accessed August 20, 2022, https://www.nps.gov/parkhistory/online_books/jela/hrs12.htm.

8. Sledge, *These Rugged Days*, 172–73; Welcher, *The Union Army*, 2:693–97.

9. Welcher, *The Union Army*, 2:697; Frederick H. Dyer, *Compendium of the War of the Rebellion*, 2 vols. (1908; Dayton, Ohio: National Historical Society in cooperation with the Press of Morningside Bookshop, 1979), pt. 3, p. 1734; Daniel to Benjamin, March 11, 1865, Densmore and Family Papers, MNHS. Union soldiers were issued with a canvas ground sheet, which was covered with a rubber gum. Dorothy Deneen Volvo, *Daily Life in Civil War America* (Westport, Conn.: Greenwood Press, 1998), 143.

10. Daniel to Benjamin, March 11, 1865, Orrin to Daniel, July 3, 1864, Densmore and Family Papers, MNHS; All nine USCT regiments in General Steele's column were attached to General Hawkins's First Division. Welcher, *The Union Army*, 2:697.

11. Daniel to Dear friends, March 19, 1865 [long letter], Densmore and Family Papers, MNHS. Daniel wrote two accounts of his journey to Pensacola both addressed to "dear friends." Both were dated March 19, 1865, the day he made the journey from Barrancas to Pensacola. One account is two pages long, and the other account is four pages.

12. Daniel to Dear friends, March 19, 1865 [long letter], Densmore and Family Papers, MNHS.

13. Ibid.

14. Aunt Martha to Daniel, April 9, 1865, Benjamin to Father, April 6, 1865, Densmore and Family Papers, MNHS.

15. Orrin to Benjamin, March 26, 1865, Densmore and Family Papers, MNHS; Nina Marchetti Archabal, "Frances Densmore: Pioneer in the Study of American Indian Music," in *Women of Minnesota: Selected Biographical Essays*, ed. Barbara Stuhler and Gretchen Kreuter (St. Paul: Minnesota Historical Society Press, 1998), 94–115.

16. Norman to Daniel, March 28, 1865, Densmore and Family Papers, MNHS.

17. Welcher, *The Union Army*, 2:694–95; Dobak, *Freedom by the Sword*, 145; Sledge, *Rugged Days*, 172–73; *Official Records*, ser. 1, vol. 49, pt. 1, 279–87.

18. *Official Records*, ser. 1, vol. 49, pt. 1, 297–99.

19. Ibid., 298–99.

20. Undated newspaper extract, of a letter signed by "D. D." The letter was addressed to the "Editors St. Paul Press," and was written from Mobile, Alabama, April 20, 1865. 1865 Scrapbook, vol. 29, Densmore and Family Papers, MNHS. For comment on the importance of state affiliation to Union veterans, see Paul A. Cimbala, *Veterans North and South: The Transition from Soldier to Civilian after the American Civil War* (Santa Barbara, Calif.: Praeger, 2015), 20.

21. Undated newspaper extract, Densmore and Family Papers, MNHS.

22. Ibid. Self-control, or coolness, was considered an essential manly virtue. Lorien Foote, *The Gentlemen and the Roughs: Violence, Honor and Manhood in the Union Army* (New York: New York University Press, 2010), 56–58.

23. *Official Records*, ser. 1, vol. 49, pt. 1, 286–87; Dobak, *Freedom by the Sword*, 153.

24. *Official Records*, ser. 1, vol. 49, pt. 2, p. 306; Dobak, *Freedom by the Sword*, 152–53; Gregory J. W. Irwin "Introduction: Warfare, Race, and the Civil War in American Memory," in *Black Flag Over Dixie: Racial Atrocities and Reprisals in the Civil War*, ed. Gregory J. W. Irwin (Carbondale: Southern Illinois University Press, 2004), 9; John Johann Diary, April 10, 1865, John Johann Civil War Diary April 1864–1865, 2008. Typescript, Wisconsin Historical Society.

25. D. Densmore to C. C. Andrews, August 30, 1866, Andrews Papers, MNHS; C. C. Andrews, *History of the Alabama Campaign: Including the Cooperative Operations of General Wilson's Cavalry in Alabama* (New York: D. Van Nostrand, 1889), 201; Dobak, *Freedom by the Sword*, 153–54; Sledge, *These Rugged Days*, 188; Daniel to Friends at home, June 3, 1864, Densmore and Family Papers, MNHS.

26. Martha to Benjamin, April 14, 1865, Benjamin to Father, April 16, 1865, Martha to Brother [Daniel], May 23, 1865, Densmore and Family Papers, MNHS.

13. "The curse of slavery": Occupation Duty in Alabama

1. Daniel to Friends at home, April 17, 1865, Daniel to Father, May 27, 1865, Benjamin Densmore and Family Papers, 1797–1955, Minnesota Historical Society (MNHS); Daniel's second in command was Major Oliver H. Holcomb. United States Adjutant General's Office, *Official Army Register of the Volunteer Force of the United States Army*, 8 vols. (Washington, D.C.: Adjutant General's Office, 1867), pt. 8, p. 241.

2. Daniel to Friends at home, April 17, 1865, Daniel to Friends at home, April 27, 1865, Densmore and Family papers, MNHS; J. G. Randall and David Donald, *The Civil War and Reconstruction* (Boston: D. C. Heath, 1961), 526–29.

3. Daniel to Friends at home, April 27, 1865; Daniel to Dear Brother Benjamin, May 21, 1865, Densmore and Family papers, MNHS; Frank J. Welcher, *The Union Army, 1861–1865*, 2 vols. (Bloomington: Indiana University Press, 1989), 2:695–96.

4. Daniel to Uncle, Aunt & Friends [Uncle Russell Cheney, Aunt Martha Lea Cheney, and Friends], May 12, 1865, Civil War Letters of Daniel Densmore, 1833–1915, and his Family in the Charles V. Hibbard Papers, 1811–1954, Wisconsin Historical Society (WHS).

5. Ibid.

6. Ibid.

7. Ibid.

8. Ibid.; Simon Harrison, *Dark Trophies: Hunting the Enemy Body in Modern War* (New York: Berghahn Books, 2012), 97–102; Chris Dixon, *Perfecting the Family: Antislavery Marriages in Nineteenth-Century America* (Amherst: University of Massachusetts Press, 1997), 39; Reid Mitchell, *The Vacant Chair: The Northern Soldier Leaves Home* (New York: Oxford University Press, 1993), 89–113; Chandra Manning, *What This Cruel War Was Over: Soldiers, Slavery, and the Civil War* (New York: Alfred A. Knopf, 2007), 62–64, 71–72. LeeAnn Whites claims that Southern men saw abolition not only as an attack on the slave system, but also as an attack on their manhood. LeeAnn Whites, "The Civil War as a Crisis of Gender," in *Divided Houses: Gender and the Civil War*, ed. Catherine Clinton and Nina Silber (New York: Oxford University Press, 1992), 9–10.

9. Daniel to Dear Uncle, Aunt & Friends [Uncle Russell Cheney, Aunt Martha Lea Cheney, and Friends], May 12, 1865, Civil War Letters of Daniel Densmore, WHS; Frances M. Clarke, *War Stories: Suffering and Sacrifice in the Civil War North* (Chicago: University of Chicago Press, 2011), 21–22.

10. Daniel to Dear Uncle, Aunt & Friends [Uncle Russell Cheney, Aunt Martha Lea Cheney, and Friends], May 12, 1865, Civil War Letters of Daniel Densmore, WHS; Russell Duncan, ed., *Blue-Eyed Child of Fortune: The Civil War Letters of Colonel Robert Gould Shaw* (Athens: University of Georgia Press, 1992), 190, 195; Randall C. Jimerson, *The Private Civil War: Popular Thought during the Sectional Conflict* (Baton Rouge: Louisiana State University Press, 1988), 133–35; Bell I. Wiley, *The Life of Billy Yank: The Common Soldier of the Civil War* (Baton Rouge: Louisiana State University Press, 1978), 96, 98–99; James M. McPherson, *For Cause and Comrades: Why Men Fought the Civil War* (New York: Oxford University Press, 1997), 118–19; Manning, *What This Cruel War Was Over*, 48–49, 71–72. Confederates also demonized Yankees and depicted them as a brutally inferior people. George C. Rable, *Damn Yankees: Demonization and Defiance in the Confederate South* (Baton Rouge: Louisiana State University Press, 2015). In his richly penetrating study of Confederate images and objects Ross Brooks describes how Confederates used physiognomy to depict Yankees as a morally degenerate, rapacious people, the opposite to noble Southerners. Ross A. Brooks, *The Visible Confederacy: Images and Objects in the Civil War South* (Baton Rouge: Louisiana State University Press, 2019), 33–34.

11. Daniel to Dear Uncle, Aunt & Friends [Uncle Russell Cheney, Aunt Martha Lea Cheney, and Friends], May 12, 1865, Civil War Letters of Daniel Densmore, WHS.

12. Ibid.; Reid Mitchell, *Civil War Soldiers: Their Expectations and Their Experiences* (New York: Viking, 1988), 112–17; Wiley, *The Life of Billy Yank*, 102–3.

13. Daniel to Dear Uncle, Aunt & Friends [Uncle Russell Cheney and Aunt Martha Lea Cheney & Friends], May 12, 1865, Civil War Letters of Daniel Densmore, WHS.

14. Daniel to Benjamin, May 21, 1865, Densmore and Family papers, MNHS.

15. Daniel to Father, May 27, 1865, Daniel to Benjamin, May 29, 1865, Densmore and Family papers, MNHS; For comment about the military uniform fostering national identity, especially in the South see Brooks, *The Visible Confederacy*, 115, 130–31.

16. Daniel to Father, May 27, 1865, Densmore and Family papers, MNHS; *New York Times,* May 30, 1865.

17. Daniel to Benjamin, May 29, 1865, Densmore and Family papers, MNHS.
18. Daniel to Benjamin, June 2, 1865, Densmore and Family papers, MNHS.
19. Ibid.
20. Ibid.
21. Daniel to Benjamin, June 25, 1865. The phrase, "as soon as weeds cease to prevail" may be an allusion to the Garden of Eden Bible story found in Genesis, chapter 3, verses 17–18. When God expelled Adam and Eve from the Garden of Eden God punished Adam by cursing the land so it would always produce weeds. Since weeds would never stop growing, "Miss G" would never receive Daniel's photographic portrait. The Densmores sometimes alluded to Bible stories in their letters, see Orrin to Son [Daniel], April 28, 1864, Daniel to Friends at home, December, 10, 1864, Orrin to Son [Daniel], December 18, 1864, Daniel to Dear friends, March 19, 1865, Densmore and Family papers, MNHS; Hannah More, *Coelebs in Search of a Wife: Comprehending Observations on Domestic Habits and Manners, Religion and Morals* (London: T. Cadell and W. Davis, 1808); Anne Scott, *Hannah More: The First Victorian* (Oxford: Oxford University Press, 2004), 274–82. The Miss G was probably a family friend, Sarah Adelaide Greenland. Benjamin Densmore married Sarah Greenland in 1866. Sarah A. Densmore, "Declaration for Widow's Pension," Pension Application, Civil War Pension File, Benjamin Densmore, 4th U.S. Colored Hv. Arty., RG 15, National Archives and Records Administration.
22. Daniel to Benjamin, June 2, 1865, Densmore and Family papers, MNHS.
23. Benjamin to Father, June 17, 1865, Orrin to Son [Daniel], June 25, 1865, Martha to Daniel, June 5, 1865, Densmore and Family papers, MNHS.
24. Orrin to Daniel, March 19, 1865, Densmore and Family papers, MNHS.
25. Daniel to Friends at home, April 17, 1865, Densmore and Family papers, MNHS. Daniel often called his sister, Martha, "Mittie."
26. Ibid.
27. Martha to Daniel, May 23, 1865, Densmore and Family papers, MNHS.
28. Martha to Daniel, June 5, 1865, Densmore and Family papers, MNHS.
29. Daniel to Benjamin, June 21, 1865; Daniel to Benjamin, June 25, 1865; Densmore and Family papers, MNHS.

14. "They've got money, let them buy their own biscuit": Departure and Homecoming

1. Daniel to Benjamin, June 21, 1865, Daniel to Benjamin, June 25, 1865, Benjamin to Father, July 15, 1865, Benjamin Densmore and Family Papers, 1797–1955, Minnesota Historical Society (MNHS); U.S. War Department, *The War of the Rebellion: A Compilation of the Official Records of the Union and Confederate Armies*, 128 vols. (Washington, D.C.: Government Printing Office, 1880–1901), 1st ser., vol. 49, pt. 1, 136–37; Lt. Col. Daniel Densmore, 68th USCI, Carded and Medical Records, ser. 534, RG 94, National Archives and Records Administration (NARA).
2. Daniel to Benjamin, September 13, 1865, Densmore and Family papers, MNHS.
3. Martha to Daniel, May 23, 1865, Densmore and Family papers, MNHS; LeeAnn Whites, "The Civil War as a Crisis of Gender," in *Divided Houses: Gender and the Civil*

War, ed. Catherine Clinton and Nina Silber (New York: Oxford University Press, 1992), 3–21; Randall M. Miller and John David Smith, eds. *Dictionary of Afro-American Slavery* (Westport, Conn.: Praeger, 1997), 636; John Hope Franklin and Loren Schweninger, *Runaway Slaves: Rebels on the Plantation* (New York: Oxford University Press, 1999), 2–3.

4. Martha to Daniel, May 23, 1865, Orrin to Son [Daniel], March 19, 1865, Daniel to Benjamin, September 13, 1865, Densmore and Family papers, MNHS; Leslie A. Schwalm, *Emancipation's Diaspora: Race and Reconstruction in the Upper Midwest* (Chapel Hill: University of North Carolina Press, 2009).

5. Daniel to Benjamin, August 14, 1865, Densmore and Family papers, MNHS. McFarland did not become a major. He was mustered out of the service on October 22, 1865. United States Adjutant General's Office, *Official Army Register of the Volunteer Force of the United States Army*, 8 vols. (Washington, D.C.: Adjutant General's Office, 1867), pt. 8, p. 241.

6. Daniel to Benjamin, September 13, 1865, Daniel to Benjamin, September 27, 1865, Densmore and Family papers, MNHS; Lt. Col. Daniel Densmore, 68th USCT, Carded and Medical Records, ser. 534, RG 94, NARA; Service Record of Lt. Col. Daniel Densmore, 68th USCI, Carded Records, Volunteer Organizations: Civil War, ser. 519, RG 94, NARA.

7. Daniel to Benjamin, September 27, 1865, Densmore and Family papers, MNHS; Paul A. Cimbala, *Veterans North and South: The Transition from Soldier to Civilian after the American Civil War* (Santa Barbara, Calif.: Praeger, 2015), 52–58.

8. Daniel to Benjamin, September 13, 1865, Benjamin to [Family], November 17, 1862, Orrin Jr. to Brother [Daniel], November 27, 1862, Daniel to Aunt Mittie [Martha], November 28, 1862, Martha to Daniel, March 27, 1864, Densmore and Family papers, MNHS; Joseph C. Fitzharris, *The Hardest Lot of Men: The Third Minnesota Infantry* (Norman: University of Oklahoma Press, 2019), 129–30, 221–22.

9. Daniel to Benjamin, September 13, 1865, Densmore and Family papers, MNHS.

10. Daniel to Benjamin, September 13, 1865, Densmore and Family papers, MNHS; James M. McPherson, *For Cause and Comrades: Why Men Fought the Civil War* (New York: Oxford University Press, 1997), 8–9; Dorothy O. Pratt, "Bounty System," in *Encyclopedia of the Civil War: A Political, Social and Military History*, ed. David S. Heidler and Jeanne T. Heidler (New York: W. W. Norton, 2000), 256–57; Michael Thomas Smith, "The Most Desperate Scoundrels Unhung: Bounty Jumpers and Recruitment Fraud in the Civil War North," *American Nineteenth Century History* 6, no. 2 (2006): 153, 164–65; Kevin J. Weddle, "Ethnic Discrimination in Minnesota Volunteer Regiments during the Civil War," *Civil War History* 35 (September 1989): 255, 259. Ethnic German soldiers were accused of acting cowardly at the battle of Chancellorsville and blamed for causing the Union defeat. Christian B. Keller, *Chancellorsville and the Germans: Nativism, Ethnicity, and Civil War Memory* (New York: Fordham University Press, 2007), 125, 127, 137.

11. Daniel to Benjamin, September 13, 1865, Densmore and Family papers, MNHS.

12. Joseph T. Glatthaar, *Forged in Battle: The Civil War Alliance of Black Soldiers and White Officers* (New York: Free Press, 1990), 253–55; Forrest G. Wood, *Black Scare: The Racist Response to Emancipation and Reconstruction* (Berkeley: University of California

Press, 1968), 13–14; For a discussion on the way the public memory of the Black soldier was repressed in the decades following the Civil War, see W. Fitzhugh Brundage, "Race, Memory, and Masculinity: Black Veterans Recall the Civil War," in *The War Was You and Me: Civilians in the American Civil War*, ed. Joan E. Cashin (Princeton, N.J.: Princeton University Press, 2002), 136–56; David W. Blight, *Race and Reunion: The Civil War in American Memory* (Cambridge, Mass.: Harvard University Press, 2001), 1–5, 194–98; Donald R. Shaffer, *After the Glory: The Struggles of Black Civil War Veterans* (Lawrence: University Press of Kansas, 2004), 31, 59–60, 168–70, 173–74, 177–78; Cimbala, *Veterans North and South*, 20; Ira Berlin, Joseph P. Reidy, and Leslie S. Rowland, eds., *Freedom: A Documentary History of Emancipation, 1861–1867*, Series II, *The Black Military Experience* (Cambridge: Cambridge University Press, 1982), 733–36.

13. Cimbala, *Veterans North and South*, 18; Berlin et al., *The Black Military Experience*, 734–36.

14. Daniel to Benjamin, September 13, 1865, Daniel to Benjamin, September 27, 1865, Daniel to Benjamin, November 7, 1865, Densmore and Family papers, MNHS.

15. Daniel to Benjamin, November 28, 1865, Densmore and Family papers, MNHS.

16. Daniel to Benjamin, December 17, 1865, Densmore and Family papers, MNHS.

17. Special Orders No. 13, July 10, 1864, Hd. Qrs., 4th USCHA, Orders, 4th USCHA, Books and Papers USCT, RG, NARA; Capt. B. Densmore to Brig. Gen. L. Thomas, July 11, 1864, D–244 1864, ser. 360, CTD, RG 94, NARA.

18. Benjamin to Father, December 17, 1864, Densmore and Family papers, MNHS.

19. Benjamin to Father, March 28, 1865, Densmore and Family papers, MNHS.

20. Paymaster Jeremiah Ferno to 1st Lt. B. Densmore, June 15, 1864, Benjamin Densmore Papers MNSH. At first Black soldiers were paid $10 per month, three of which was for clothing. In contrast white soldiers received $13 per month. In mid-June 1864 equal pay was granted to all soldiers. Black soldiers who had been free on April 19, 1861, were granted back pay at the same rate as white soldiers. This restriction officially prevented many 68th USCI soldier from gaining back pay. In March 1865, equal pay from the date of enlistment was granted to all Black soldiers who had been enlisted under the promise of equal pay. Glatthaar, Forged in Battle, 169–75.

21. Benjamin to Daniel, May 11, 1864, Densmore and Family papers, MNHS.

22. Martha to Benjamin, April 14, 1865, Densmore and Family papers, MNHS.

23. Benjamin to Father, May 17, 1865, Densmore and Family papers, MNHS.

24. Orrin to Son [Benjamin], June 15, 1865, Densmore and Family papers, MNHS; Special Orders No. 142, Hd. Qrs., Post of Columbus, Kentucky, 20 June 1865, Orders, 4th U.S. Cold Heavy Art., Regimental Books and Papers USCT, RG 94, NARA.

25. Orrin to Son Benjamin, January 3, 1865, Densmore and Family papers, MNHS.

26. Orrin to Son [Daniel], January 18, 1865, Daniel to Dear Father, January 28, 1864[1865], Densmore and Family papers, MNHS.

27. Daniel to Benjamin, February 26, 1865, Daniel to Benjamin, March 11, 1865, Benjamin to Father, March 28, 1865, Orrin to Son [Benjamin], April 2, 1865, Densmore and Family papers, MNHS.

28. Benjamin to Father, April 16, 1865, Densmore and Family papers, MNHS.

29. Benjamin to Father, April 23, 1865, Densmore and Family papers, MNHS.

30. Orrin Jr. to Daniel, May 13, 1865, Benjamin to Friends, June 28, 1865, Densmore and Family papers, MNHS; Special Orders No. 142, Hd. Qrs., Post of Columbus, Kentucky, 20 June 1865, Orders, 4th U. S. Cold Heavy Art., Regimental Books and Papers USCT, RG 94, NARA; Special Orders 173, Hd. Qrs., District Western Kentucky, Paducah, Kentucky, August 20, 1865, Orders, 4th U. S. Cold Heavy Art., Regimental Books and Papers USCT, RG 94, NARA.

31. Orrin to Son [Daniel], May 14, 1865, Orrin to Son [Benjamin], June 10, 1865, Benjamin to Dear Friends, August 15, 1865, Densmore and Family papers, MNHS; Capt. B. Densmore to Maj. Gen. L. Thomas, September 30, October 31, 1865. D–244 1864, ser. 360, CTD, RG 94, NARA. Capt. B. Densmore to Col. C. W. Foster, November 4, 1865, D–244 1864, ser. 360, CTD, RG 94, NARA.

32. Benjamin to Father, October 31, 1865, Densmore and Family papers, MNHS.

33. Margaret to Dear Brother [Benjamin], February 7, 1866, Martha to Benjamin, October 2, 1865 [Aunt Martha's letter to Benjamin is included in Martha's letter October 2, 1865], Martha to Brother Benjamin, October 29, 1865, Densmore and Family papers, MNHS.

34. Orrin to Son [Benjamin] December 3, 1865, Orrin to Son [Benjamin] December 10, 1865, Daniel to Brother [Benjamin], November 28, 1865, Densmore and Family papers, MNHS.

35. Orrin to Son [Benjamin], November 7, 1865, Orrin to Son [Benjamin], December 3, 1865, Densmore and Family papers, MNHS; Special Orders No. 278, Hd. Qrs., Post of Pine Bluff, Ark., December 11 1865, Special Orders No.1, Hd. Qrs., Post of Pine Bluff, Ark., January 2, 1866, Orders, 4th U.S. Cold Heavy Art., Regimental Books and Papers USCT, RG 94, NARA. The 6th Minnesota Infantry was stationed at Helena, Arkansas, for a little more than four months in mid-1864. During this time, seventy-two men died of disease and six hundred were hospitalized. Kenneth Carley, *Minnesota in the Civil War: An Illustrated History* (St. Paul: Minnesota Historical Society, 2000), 202; Frederick H. Dyer, *Compendium of the War of the Rebellion*, 2 vols. (1908; Dayton, Ohio: National Historical Society in cooperation with the Press of Morningside Bookshop, 1979), pt. 3, p. 1721.

Conclusion

1. Aunt Martha to Nephew Daniel, November 16, 1862, Daniel to Friends at home, June 14, 1863, Benjamin Densmore and Family Papers, 1797–1955, Minnesota Historical Society (MNHS); Daniel to Aunt Martha, April 24, 1863, Civil War Letters of Daniel Densmore, 1833–1915, and his Family in the Charles V. Hibbard Papers, 1811–1954, Wisconsin Historical Society (WHS).

2. Lisa Tendrich Frank and LeeAnne Whites, eds., *Household War: How Americans Lived and Fought the Civil War* (Athens: University of Georgia Press, 2020), 1–4, 8, 118–33.

3. Leslie A. Schwalm, *Emancipation's Diaspora: Race and Reconstruction in the Upper Midwest* (Chapel Hill: University of North Carolina Press, 2009), 41–42, 66–68.

4. [Daniel Densmore], "History and Genealogy of the Family of Orrin and Elizabeth Densmore," 26–27, Densmore and Family papers, MNHS; Franklyn Curtiss-Wedge, ed., *History of Goodhue County, Minnesota* (Chicago: H. C. Cooper Jr., 1909), 757–58; William D. Erickson, "'Something Must Be Done for Them': Establishing Minnesota's First Hospital for the Insane," *Minnesota History* 53, no. 2 (1992): 47; Frederick L. Johnson, *Goodhue County, Minnesota: A Narrative History* (Red Wing, Minn.: Goodhue County Historical Society Press, 2000), 82–83.

5. [Daniel Densmore], "History and Genealogy of the Family of Orrin and Elizabeth Densmore," 6–7, 31–32, 36, Densmore and Family papers, MNHS; "Representative Norman Densmore," Legislators, Iowa Legislature. Accessed, July 8, 2022. https://www.legis.iowa.gov/legislators.

6. Orrin to Son [Benjamin], January 7, 1866, Orrin to Son [Benjamin], February 15, 1866, Densmore and Family papers; Johnson, *Goodhue County*, 82–83; Paul A. Cimbala, *Veterans North and South: The Transition from Soldier to Civilian after the American Civil War* (Santa Barbara, Calif.: Praeger, 2015), 37–39; Brian Peterson, Carrie Conklin, Char Henn, and Steve Kohn, *Footsteps through Historic Red Wing: Three Walking Tours of Red Wing's Historic Architecture* (Red Wing, Minn.: Red Wing Heritage Preservation Commission, 2009), 7–8, 11, 20.

7. Daniel to Benjamin, June 25, 1865, [Daniel Densmore], "History and Genealogy of the Family of Orrin and Elizabeth Densmore," 33, Densmore and Family papers, MNHS; Nina Marchetti Archabal, "Frances Densmore: Pioneer in the Study of American Indian Music," in *Women of Minnesota: Selected Biographical Essays*, ed. Barbara Stuhler and Gretchen Kreuter (St. Paul: Minnesota Historical Society Press, 1998), 94–115.

8. "Last Tributes to an Honored Life," *Red Wing Morning Republican*, January 30, 1913.

9. Daniel to Benjamin, November 7, 1865, Densmore and Family papers; Andre Fleche, "'Shoulder to Shoulder as Comrades Tried': Black and White Union Veterans and Civil War Memory," *Civil War History* 51 (June 2005): 175–201. In November 1865, the Minnesota State Republican Party's proposal to change the state constitution to allow Black male suffrage was defeated at a state referendum. Male African Americans finally gained the vote in 1868. William D. Green, *A Peculiar Imbalance: The Fall and Rise of Racial Equality in Minnesota, 1837–1869* (Minneapolis: University of Minnesota Press, 2007), 141–48; [Daniel Densmore], "History and Genealogy of the Family of Orrin and Elizabeth Densmore," 35, Densmore and Family papers, MNHS.

10. [Daniel Densmore], "History and Genealogy of the Family of Orrin and Elizabeth Densmore," 7, 38, Densmore and Family papers, MNHS.

11. Orrin to Son [Benjamin], March 26, 1865, Benjamin to Father, April 6, 1865, Orrin to Son [Benjamin], April 13, 1865, Martha to Brother [Benjamin], April 14, 1865, Martha to Mother [Elizabeth], May 6, 1865, Orrin Jr. to Daniel, May 13, 1865, Martha to Brother Daniel, June 5, 1865, Densmore and Family papers, MNHS.

12. Orrin Jr. to Daniel, May 13, 1865, [Daniel Densmore], "History and Genealogy of the Family of Orrin and Elizabeth Densmore," 7, 41, Densmore and Family papers, MNHS Densmore and Family papers, MNHS.

13. Daniel to Benjamin, December 13, 1863, Densmore and Family papers, MNHS.

Genealogical Tables

[Daniel Densmore], "History and Genealogy of the Family of Orrin and Elizabeth Densmore," 1903, in "Densmore (Benjamin and Family) Papers, 1797–1956," Minnesota Historical Society (MNHS); Kathryn A. Johnson, "Densmore (Benjamin and Family) Papers, 1797–1956," St. Paul, Minnesota Historical Society, 1956. Typescript inventory and description of the Benjamin Densmore and Family Papers, MNHS; Find a Grave: https://findagrave.com. Representative Norman Densmore, Legislators, Iowa Legislature, Accessed July 8, 2022. https://www.legis.iowa.gov/legislators.

Bibliography

The Densmore Family Collections

The bulk of the Densmore papers pertaining to the Civil War are in the Benjamin Densmore and Family Papers, 1797–1955, collection in the Minnesota Historical Society. The society also has two collections of papers relating to Frances Densmore, the daughter of Benjamin Densmore, the Frances Densmore Papers, 1926–1939, and Papers Relating to Frances Densmore, [1930–], 1951–1959, 1971, 1994. Frances Densmore became famous for recording and preserving Native American music.

The Wisconsin Historical Society has two collections of Densmore family papers, the Orrin Densmore Papers, 1854–1861, and the Civil War Letters of Daniel Densmore, 1833–1915, and his Family in the Charles V. Hibbard Papers, 1811–1954. The Orrin Densmore Papers consist of letters written to Benjamin Densmore while he was working as railroad surveyor in Minnesota. They were written by his father, Orrin, his brothers, Norman and Daniel, and other members of the family living at Emerald Grove and Janesville, Wisconsin. The Letters of Daniel Densmore consist of Civil War letters written by Daniel Densmore to his uncle and aunt, Russell and Martha Cheney, who lived at Emerald Grove, Wisconsin.

Beloit College, Wisconsin, also has a collection: the Densmore Family Papers, Beloit College Archives and Special Collections. This collection consists principally of letters written before the Civil War, by Daniel Densmore when he was a student at Beloit.

The Goodhue County Historical Society has two collections of Densmore papers. One collection, the Densmore Family Papers, focuses on the family's engagement with the Red Wing community. The other collection, the Frances Densmore Collection, focuses on the work Frances Densmore undertook to conserve Native American music.

Primary Sources

Manuscripts

Beloit College Archives and Special Collections, Beloit, Wisconsin, Densmore Family Papers.

Henry E. Huntington Library, San Marino, California, George W. Buswell Papers, 1862–1888.
Goodhue County Historical Society, Red Wing, Minnesota, Densmore Family Papers.
Library of Congress, Washington, D.C.
- Manuscript Division: "Testimony of Lizzie McCloud", Federal Writers' Project:
  - Vol. 2, Arkansas, Part 5, McClendon-Prayer, 1936. Accessed July 26, 2021. https://www.loc.gov/item/mesn025/.
- Photographic Division: Gen. N. B. Forrest, Gen. A. J. Smith.

Minnesota Historical Society, St. Paul, Minnesota.
- Christopher C. Andrews Papers.
- Charles Bornarth, Diary, Charles Bornarth Papers, 1863, 1865, 1894–1898.
- James M. Bowler Family Papers, 1827–1976.
- George C. Clapp, Diary, June 1863, George C. Clapp and Family Papers.
- Benjamin Densmore and Family Papers, 1797–1955.
- James T. Ramer Diary and Letter, 1862 August 14–September 5, 1865, August 16, microfilm M87.

National Archives and Records Administration, Washington, D.C.
- Record Group 15, Records of the Veterans Administration.
- Civil War Pension Application Files.
- Record Group 94, Records of the Adjutant General's Office.
- Series 360, Colored Troops Division, Letters Received.
- Series 519, Carded Records of Volunteer Organizations: Civil War.
- Series 534, Carded and Medical Records, Volunteers: Mexican, Civil War, 1846–65.
- Regimental Books and Papers, USCT.
- Regimental Books and Papers, U. S. Volunteer Organizations.
- Record Group 393 Records of U. S. Army Continental Commands, 1821–1920.
- Part 2, Polyonymous Successions of Commands.
- Series 2818 Letters Sent.
- Part 4, Military Installations.
- Series 245 Inspection Reports.
- Microfilm Publications.
- M594, Roll 212, Compiled Records Showing Service of Military Units in Volunteer Union Organizations.

White, Jonathan W., and Reagan Connelly, eds. "'Off to Dixie and Adventure': The Dakota War and Civil War Diaries of George W. Buswell, 7th Minnesota Infantry and 68th U. S. Colored Troops," unpublished book manuscript.

Wisconsin Historical Society, Madison, Wisconsin.
- Orrin Densmore Papers, 1854–1861.
- Civil War Letters of Daniel Densmore (1833–1915) and his family, Carlisle V. Hibbard Papers, 1811–1954.
- John Johann Civil War Diary, April 1864–1865, 2008. Typescript.

Newspapers and Periodicals

Columbia Daily Tribune

Daily Missouri Democrat

Goodhue County Republican
Harper's New Monthly Magazine
Harper's Weekly
New York Times
New York Times Illustrated News
Red Wing Morning Republican
Saint Paul Pioneer and Democrat Weekly

Published State and Federal Government Documents

United States Adjutant General's Office. *Official Army Register of the Volunteer Force of the United States Army*. 8 vols. Washington, D.C.: Adjutant General's Office, 1865–67.

United States War Department. *Atlas to Accompany the Official Records of the Union and Confederate Armies*. Washington, D.C.: Government Printing Office, 1891–95.

United States War Department. *The War of the Rebellion: A Compilation of the Official Records of the Union and Confederate Armies*. 128 vols. Washington, D.C.: Government Printing Office, 1880–1901.

Wisconsin Adjutant General's Office. *Roster of Wisconsin Volunteers, War of Rebellion, 1861–1865*. 2 vols. Madison, Wisc.: Democrat Printing Company, 1866.

Databases

Find a Grave: https://www.findagrave.com.

National Park Service, Washington, D.C.

Civil War Soldiers and Sailors System (CWSS). Accessed March 18, 2013. http://www.nps.gov/civilwar/soldiers-and-sailors-database.htm.

Other Published Primary Sources

Anderson, Gary Clayton, and Alan R. Woolworth, eds. *Through Dakota Eyes: Narrative Accounts of the Minnesota Indian War of 1862*. St. Paul: Minnesota Historical Society Press, 1988.

Andrews, C. C. *History of the Alabama Campaign: Including the Cooperative Operations of General Wilson's Cavalry in Alabama*. New York: D. Van Nostrand, 1889.

Basler. Roy, P., ed. *The Collected Works of Abraham Lincoln*. 9 vols. New Brunswick, N.J.: Rutgers University Press, 1953.

Berlin, Ira, Joseph P. Reidy, and Leslie S. Rowland, eds. *Freedom: A Documentary History of Emancipation, 1861–1867*, Series II, *The Black Military Experience*. Cambridge: Cambridge University Press, 1982.

The Bible. New York: Thomas and Sons, American Standard Version, 1901.

Blight David W., ed., *When This Cruel War Is Over: The Civil War Letters of Charles Harvey Brewster*. Amherst: University of Massachusetts Press, 1992.

Ebell, Adrian J. "The Indian Massacre and War of 1862." *Harper's New Monthly Magazine* 27. no. 157 (June 1863), 1–24.

Engs, Robert F., and Corey M. Brooks, eds. *Their Patriotic Duty: The Civil War Letters of the Evans Family of Brown County, Ohio*. New York: Fordham University Press, 2007.

Hamilton, Gail. *Country Living and Country Thinking*. Boston: Ticknor & Fields, 1861.
Old Settler, by an [Joseph Woods Hancock]. *Goodhue County Minnesota, Past and Present*. Red Wing: Red Wing Printing Co., 1893. Nabu Public Domain Reprints.
Pryor & Co. *Red Wing City Directory*, 1876/77.
Reid, Richard M., ed. *Practicing Medicine in a Black Regiment: The Civil War Diary of Burt G. Wilder, 55th Massachusetts*. Amherst: University of Massachusetts Press, 2010.
Wood, Alley and Company. *History of Goodhue County: Including A Sketch of The Territory and State of Minnesota*. Red Wing, Minn.: Wood, Alley & Co., 1878. Kessinger Publishing's Legacy Reprints, 2009.

Secondary Sources

Adams, Michael C. C. *Living Hell: The Dark Side of the Civil War*. Baltimore: Johns Hopkins University Press, 2014.
Aley, Ginette, and J. L. Anderson, eds. *Union Heartland: The Midwestern Home Front during the Civil War*. Carbondale: Southern Illinois University Press, 2013.
Alotta, Robert I. *Civil War Justice: Union Army Executions under Lincoln*. Shippensburg. Pa.: White Mane, 1989.
Anderson, David. "Dying of Nostalgia: Homesickness in the Union Army during the Civil War." *Civil War History* 56 (January 2010): 247–82.
Anderson, Gary Clayton. *Little Crow: Spokesman for the Sioux*. St. Paul: Minnesota Historical Society Press, 1986.
Anderson, Gary Clayton. *Massacre in Minnesota: The Dakota War of 1862, the Most Violent Ethnic Conflict in American History*. Norman: University of Oklahoma Press, 2019.
Angell, Madeline. *Red Wing, Minnesota: Saga of a River Town*. Minneapolis: Dillon Press, 1977.
Archabal, Nina Marchetti. "Frances Densmore: Pioneer in the Study of American Indian Music." In *Women of Minnesota: Selected Biographical Essays*, edited by Barbara Stuhler and Gretchen Kreuter (St. Paul: Minnesota Historical Society Press, 1998), 94–115.
Attie, Jeanie. *Patriotic Toil: Northern Women and the American Civil War*. Ithaca, N.Y.: Cornell University Press, 1998.
Ballard, Michael B. *The Civil War in Mississippi: Major Campaigns and Battles*. Jackson: University Press of Mississippi, 2011.
Beard, Mary. "What Made the Romans Laugh?" Background Briefing, Radio National, ABC, broadcast, April 19, 2009.
Beck, Paul N. *Columns of Vengeance: Soldiers, Sioux, and the Punitive Expeditions, 1863–1864*. Norman: University of Oklahoma Press, 2013.
Bell, Andrew M. "Trans-Mississippi Miasmas: Malaria & Yellow Fever Shaped the Course of the Civil War in the Confederacy's Western Theater." *East Texas Historical Journal* 47, no. 2 (2009): 5. Accessed July 21, 2021. https://scholarworks.sfasu.edu/ethj/vol47/iss2/6.
Berry, Stephen W., II. *All That Makes a Man: Love and Ambition in the Civil War*. New York: Oxford University Press, 2003.

Billings, John D. *Hardtack and Coffee; or, The Unwritten Story of Army Life*. Boston: George M. Smith, 1887.
Blassingame, John W. *The Slave Community: Plantation Life in the Antebellum South*. Oxford: Oxford University Press, 1979.
Blight, David W. *Race and Reunion: The Civil War in American Memory*. Cambridge, Mass.: Harvard University Press, 2001.
Blount, Jackie M. *Destined to Rule the Schools: Women and the Superintendency 1873–1995*. Albany: State University of New York Press, 1998.
Brasher, Glenn David. *The Peninsula Campaign and the Necessity of Emancipation*. Chapel Hill: University of North Carolina Press, 2012.
Brooks, Ross A. *The Visible Confederacy: Images and Objects in the Civil War South*. Baton Rouge: Louisiana State University Press, 2019.
Brundage, Fitzhugh. "Race, Memory, and Masculinity: Black Veterans Recall the Civil War." In *The War Was You and Me: Civilians in the American Civil War*, edited Joan E. Cashin, 136–56. Princeton, N.J.: Princeton University Press, 2002.
Burton, William L. *Melting Pot Soldiers: The Union's Ethnic Regiments*. Ames: Iowa State University Press, 1988.
Bushman, Richard L. *The Refinement of America: Persons, Houses, Cities*. New York: Alfred A. Knopf, 1992.
Carley, Kenneth. *The Dakota War of 1862: Minnesota's Other Civil War*. St. Paul: Minnesota Historical Society, 1976.
Carley, Kenneth. *Minnesota in the Civil War: An Illustrated History*. St. Paul: Minnesota Historical Society, 2000.
Cashin, Joan E., ed. *The War Was You and Me: Civilians in the American Civil War*. Princeton, N.J.: Princeton University Press, 2002.
Cashin, Joan E., ed. *War Matters: Material Culture in the Civil War Era*. Chapel Hill: University of North Carolina Press, 2018.
Chambers, Lee V. *The Weston Sisters: An American Abolitionist Family*. Chapel Hill: University of North Carolina Press, 2014.
Cimbala, Paul A. *Veterans North and South: The Transition from Soldier to Civilian after the American Civil War*. Santa Barbara, Calif.: Praeger, 2015.
Cimbala, Paul A., and Randall M. Miller, eds. *Union Soldiers and the Northern Home Front: Wartime Experiences, Postwar Adjustments*. New York: Fordham University Press, 2002.
Cimprich, John. "The Fort Pillow Massacre: Assessing the Evidence." In *Black Soldiers in Blue: African American Troops in the Civil War Era*, edited by John David Smith, 150–68. Chapel Hill: University of North Carolina Press, 2002.
Clark, Christopher. *Prisoners of Time: Prussians, Germans and Other Humans*. Dublin: Penguin Random House, 2021.
Clark, Christopher. *The Sleepwalkers: How Europe Went to War in 1914*. London: Penguin Books, 2013.
Clark, Clifford E., Jr. *The American Home, 1800–1960,* Chapel Hill: University of North Carolina Press, 1986.

Clarke, Frances M. "So Lonesome I Could Die: Nostalgia and Debates Over Emotional Control in the Civil War North." *Journal of Social History*, 41 (Winter 2007): 253–82.
Clarke, Frances M. *War Stories: Suffering and Sacrifice in the Civil War North*. Chicago: University of Chicago Press, 2011.
Clemmons, Linda M. *Dakota in Exile: The Untold Stories of Captives in the Aftermath of the US–Dakota War*. Iowa City: University of Iowa Press, 2019.
Clodfelter, Michele. *The Dakota War: The United States Army versus the Sioux, 1862–1865*. Jefferson, N.C.: McFarland, 1998.
Cogan, Frances B. *All American Girl: The Ideal of Real Womanhood in Mid-Nineteenth-Century America*. Athens: University of Georgia Press, 1989.
Cott, Nancy C. *The Bonds of Womanhood: "Woman's Sphere" in New England, 1780–1835*. New Haven, Conn.: Yale University Press, 1977.
Coultrap-McQuin, Susan. "Legacy Profile: Gail Hamilton (1833–1896)," *Legacy* 4, no. 2 (1987): 53–58.
Critchley, Simon. *On Humour*. London: Routledge, 2002.
Curtiss-Wedge, Franklyn, ed. *History of Goodhue County, Minnesota*. Chicago: H. C. Cooper Jr., 1909.
Davison, Eddy W., and Daniel Foxx. *Nathan Bedford Forrest: In Search of the Enigma*. Gretna, La.: Pelican, 2007.
Dixon, Chris. *Perfecting the Family: Antislavery Marriages in Nineteenth-Century America*. Amherst: University of Massachusetts Press, 1997.
Dobak, William A. *Freedom by the Sword: The U.S. Colored Troops, 1862–1867*. Washington, D.C.: Center of Military History United States Army, 2011.
Duncan, Russell, ed. *Blue-Eyed Child of Fortune: The Civil War Letters of Colonel Robert Gould Shaw*. Athens: University of Georgia Press, 1992.
Dyer, Frederick H. *Compendium of the War of the Rebellion*. 2 vols. 1908. Dayton, Ohio: National Historical Society in cooperation with the Press of Morningside Bookshop, 1979.
Emery, Lynne Fauley. *Black Dance: From 1619 to Today*. 2nd ed. Princeton, N.J.: Princeton Book Co., 2017.
Erickson, William D. "'Something Must Be Done for Them': Establishing Minnesota's First Hospital for the Insane." *Minnesota History* 53, no. 2 (1992): 42–55.
Escott, Paul D. *The Worst Passions of Human Nature: White Supremacy in the Civil War North*. Charlottesville: University of Virginia Press, 2020.
Etcheson, Nicole. "No Fit Wife: Wives and Their In-Laws on the Home Front." In *Union Heartland: The Midwestern Home Front during the Civil War*, edited by Ginette Aley and J. L. Anderson, 97–124. Carbondale: Southern Illinois University Press, 2013.
Faust, Drew Gilpin. *This Republic of Suffering: Death and the American Civil War*. New York: Alfred Knopf, 2008.
Fitzharris, Joseph C. *The Hardest Lot of Men: The Third Minnesota Infantry in the Civil War*. Norman: University of Oklahoma Press, 2019.
Fleche, Andre. "'Shoulder to Shoulder as Comrades Tried': Black and White Union Veterans and Civil War Memory." *Civil War History* 51, no. 2 (2005): 175–201.

Foner, Eric. *Reconstruction: America's Unfinished Revolution, 1863–1877*. New York: Harper and Row, 1988.
Foote, Lorien. *The Gentlemen and the Roughs: Violence, Honor, and Manhood in the Union Army*. New York: New York University Press, 2010.
Fox-Genovese, Elizabeth. *Within the Plantation Household: Black and White Women of the Old South*. Chapel Hill: University of North Carolina Press, 1988.
Frank, Lisa Tendrich, and LeeAnn Whites, eds. *Household War: How Americans Lived and Fought the Civil War*. Athens: University of Georgia Press, 2020.
Franklin, John Hope, and Loren Schweninger. *Runaway Slaves: Rebels on the Plantation*. New York: Oxford University Press, 1999.
Fraser, Rebecca J. *Gender, Race and Family in Nineteenth-Century America*. London: Palgrave Macmillan, 2013.
Fredrickson, George M. *The Inner Civil War: Northern Intellectuals and the Crisis for the Union*. New York: Harper Torchbooks, 1968.
Freemon, Frank R. "Detecting Feigned Illness during the American Civil War." *Journal of the History of the Neurosciences: Basic and Clinical Perspectives* 2 (July 1993): 239–42.
Gallagher, Gary W. *The Union War*. Cambridge, Mass.: Harvard University Press, 2011.
Genovese, Eugene D. *Roll, Jordan, Roll: The World the Slaves Made*. New York: Vintage Books, 1976.
Gerteis, Louis S. *Civil War St. Louis*. Lawrence: University Press of Kansas, 2001.
Gienapp, William E. "Nativism and the Creation of the Republican Majority before the Civil War." *Journal of American History* 72 (December 1985): 529–59.
Ginzberg, Lori D. *Women and the Work of Benevolence: Morality, Politics, and Class in the Nineteenth-Century United States*. New Haven, Conn.: Yale University Press, 1990.
Glatthaar, Joseph T. "Duty, Country, Race, and Party: The Evans Family of Ohio." In *The War Was You and Me: Civilians in the American Civil War*, edited by Joan E. Cashin, 332–57. Princeton, N.J.: Princeton University Press, 2002.
Glatthaar, Joseph T. *Forged in Battle: The Civil War Alliance of Black Soldiers and White Officers*. New York: Free Press, 1990.
Glymph, Thavolia. *Out of the House of Bondage: The Transformation of the Plantation Household*. Cambridge: Cambridge University Press, 2008.
Green, William D. *The Children of Lincoln: White Paternalism and the Limits of Black Opportunity in Minnesota, 1860–1876*. Minneapolis: University of Minnesota Press, 2018.
Green, William D. *A Peculiar Imbalance: The Fall and Rise of Racial Equality in Minnesota, 1837–1869*. Minneapolis: University of Minnesota Press, 2007.
Greenberg, Kenneth S. *Honor and Slavery: Lies, Duels, Noses, Masks, Dressing as a Woman, Gifts, Strangers, Humanitarianism, Death, Slave Rebellions, The Proslavery Argument, Baseball, Hunting, and Gambling in the Old South*. Princeton, N.J.: Princeton University Press, 1996.
Gutman, Herbert G. *The Black Family in Slavery and Freedom, 1750–1925*. New York: Random House, 1977.
Hall, Richard H. *Women on the Civil War Battlefront*. Lawrence: University Press of Kansas, 2006.

Halttunen, Karen. *Confidence Men and Painted Women: A Study of Middle-Class Culture in America, 1830–1870*. New Haven, Conn.: Yale University Press, 1982.

Harper, Judith E. *Women during the Civil War: An Encyclopedia*. New York: Routledge, 2004.

Harrison, Simon. *Dark Trophies: Hunting the Enemy Body in Modern War*. New York: Berghahn Books, 2012.

Hemphill, C. Dallett. *Siblings: Brothers & Sisters in American History*. New York: Oxford University Press, 2011.

Hess, Earl J. *The Union Soldier in Battle: Enduring the Ordeal of Combat*. Lawrence: University Press of Kansas, 1997.

Hess, Earl J. "The Material Culture of Weapons in the Civil War." In *War Matters: Material Culture in the Civil War Era*, edited by Joan E. Cashin, 99–122. Chapel Hill: University of North Carolina Press, 2018.

Hixson, Walter L. *American Settler Colonialism*. New York: Palgrave Macmillan, 2013.

Hooper, Earnest Walter. "Memphis, Tennessee: Federal Occupation and Reconstruction, 1862–1870." Ph.D. diss. University of North Carolina, 1957.

Horowitz, Murray M. "Ethnicity and Command: The Civil War Experience." *Military Affairs* 42 (December 1978): 182–89.

Humphreys, Margaret. *Intensely Human: The Health of Black Soldiers in the American Civil War*. Baltimore: Johns Hopkins University Press, 2008.

Hurst, Jack. *Nathan Bedford Forrest: A Biography*. New York: Vintage Books, 1994.

Irwin, Gregory J. "Introduction: Warfare, Race, and the Civil War in American Memory." In *Black Flag over Dixie: Racial Atrocities and Reprisals in the Civil War*, edited by Gregory J. W. Irwin, 1–18. Carbondale: Southern Illinois University Press, 2004.

Iowa Legislature. "'Representative Norman Densmore,' Legislators." Accessed July 8, 2022. https://www.legis.iowa.gov/legislators.

Jimerson, Randall C. *The Private Civil War: Popular Thought during the Sectional Conflict*. Baton Rouge: Louisiana State University Press, 1988.

Johnson, Frederick L. *Goodhue County, Minnesota: A Narrative History*. Red Wing, Minn.: Goodhue County Historical Society Press, 2000.

Johnson, Frederick L. *Uncertain Lives: African Americans and Their First 150 Years in the Red Wing, Minnesota, Area*. Red Wing, Minn.: Goodhue County Historical Society Press, 2005.

Johnson, Kathryn A. "Densmore (Benjamin and Family) Papers, 1797–1956." St. Paul: Minnesota Historical Society, 1956, 1–23. Typescript inventory and description of the Benjamin Densmore and Family Papers.

Jordan, Daniel W., III. *Operational Art and the Campaigns for Mobile, 1864–1865: A Staff Ride Handbook*. Fort Leavenworth: Combat Studies Institute Press, 2019.

Jordan, Weymouth T., and Gerald W. Thomas. "Massacre at Plymouth, April 20, 1864." In *Black Flag over Dixie: Racial Atrocities and Reprisals in the Civil War*, edited by Gregory J. W. Irwin, 153–202. Carbondale: Southern Illinois University Press, 2004.

Joyner, Charles. *Down by the Riverside: A South Carolina Slave Community*. Urbana: University of Illinois Press, 1984.

Keller, Christian B. *Chancellorsville and the Germans: Nativism, Ethnicity, and Civil War Memory*. New York: Fordham University Press, 2007.
Knowles, Mark. *Tap Roots: The Early History of Tap Dancing*. Jefferson, N.C.: McFarland, 2002.
Kolchin, Peter. *American Slavery, 1619–1877*. New York: Hill and Wang, 1993.
Leonard, Elizabeth D. *Yankee Women: Gender Battles in the Civil War*. New York: W. W. Norton, 1994.
Linderman, Gerald F. *Embattled Courage: The Experience of Combat in the American Civil War*. New York: Free Press, 1989.
Litwack, Leon F. *Been in the Storm So Long: The Aftermath of Slavery*. New York: Vintage Books, 1979.
Luke, Bob, and John David Smith, *Soldiering for Freedom: How the Union Army Recruited, Trained, and Deployed U.S. Colored Troops*. Baltimore: Johns Hopkins University Press, 2014.
Lystra, Karen. *Searching the Heart: Women, Men, and Romantic Love in Nineteenth-Century America*. New York: Oxford University Press, 1989.
Manning, Chandra. *Troubled Refuge: Struggling for Freedom in the Civil War*. New York, Vintage Books, 2017.
Manning, Chandra. *What This Cruel War Was Over: Soldiers, Slavery, and the Civil War*. New York: Alfred A. Knopf, 2007.
Marten, James. *Children and Youth in the Civil War Era*. New York: New York University Press, 2012.
Marten, James. *The Children's Civil War*. Chapel Hill: University of North Carolina Press, 1998.
Matt, Susan J. "You Can't Go Home Again: Homesickness and Nostalgia in U.S. History," *Journal of American History* 94 (September 2007): 469–97.
McDowell, Robert E. "Bones and the Man: Toward a History of Bones Playing." *Journal of American Culture* 5, no. 1 (1982): 38–43.
McPherson, James M. *Abraham Lincoln and the Second American Revolution*. New York: Oxford University Press, 1991.
McPherson, James M. *Battle Cry of Freedom: The Civil War Era*. New York: Oxford University Press, 1988.
McPherson, James M. *For Cause and Comrades: Why Men Fought the Civil War*. New York: Oxford University Press, 1997.
McPherson, James M. *Ordeal by Fire: The Civil War and Reconstruction*. New York: Alfred A. Knopf, 1982.
Miller, Randall M., and John David Smith, eds. *Dictionary of Afro-American Slavery*. Westport, Conn.: Praeger, 1997.
Minnesota Board of Commissioners on Publication of History of Minnesota in the Civil and Indian Wars. *Minnesota in the Civil and Indian Wars, 1861–1865*. 2 vols. St. Paul: State of Minnesota, 1890–93.
Minnesota Legislative Reference Library. "McLaren, Robert N." In Legislators Past & Present. Accessed July 17, 2014. http://www.leg.state.mn.us/legdb/fulldetail.aspx?ID=13825.

Mintz, Steven. *A Prison of Expectations: The Family in Victorian Culture*. New York: New York University Press, 1983.
Mintz, Steven, and Susan Kellogg. *Domestic Revolutions: A Social History of American Family Life*. New York: Free Press, 1988.
Mitchell, Reid. *Civil War Soldiers: Their Expectations and Their Experiences*. New York: Viking, 1988.
Mitchell, Reid. *The Vacant Chair: The Northern Soldier Leaves Home*. New York: Oxford University Press, 1993.
Moore, Kenneth B. "Fort Pillow, Forrest, and the United States Colored Troops in 1864." In *Trial and Triumph: Essays in Tennessee's African American History*, edited by Carroll Van West, pp. 128–44. Knoxville: University of Tennessee Press, 2002.
Murray, Donald M., and Robert M. Rodney. "Colonel Julian E. Bryant: Champion of the Negro Soldier." *Illinois State Historical Society Journal* 56, no. 2 (1963): 257–81.
Murrell, Amy E. "Union Father, Rebel Son: Families and the Question of Civil War Loyalty." In *The War Was You and Me: Civilians in the American Civil War*, edited by Joan E. Cashin, 358–91. Princeton, N.J.: Princeton University Press, 2002.
Nacy, Michele J. *Members of the Regiment: Army Officers' Wives on the Western Frontier, 1865–1890*. Westport, Conn.: Greenwood Press, 2000.
Namis, June. *White Captives: Gender and Ethnicity on the American Frontier*. Chapel Hill: University of North Carolina Press, 1993.
Nappi, Kylie. "When Johnny Comes Marching Home: One Hundred Days in the Ohio Volunteer Infantry during the Civil War." Ohio History Connection. Accessed August 29, 2023. https://www.ohiohistory.org/when-johnny-comes-marching-home-one-hundred-days-in-the-ohio-volunteer-infantry-during-the-american-civil-war/.
Neff, John R. *Honoring the Civil War Dead: Commemoration and the Problem of Reconciliation*. Lawrence: University Press of Kansas, 2005.
Öfele, Martin W. *German-Speaking Officers in the U.S. Colored Troops, 1863–1867*. Gainesville: University Press of Florida, 2004.
Osman, Stephen E. *Fort Snelling and the Civil War*. St. Paul: Ramsey County Historical Society, 2017.
Ostler, Jeffrey. *The Plains Sioux and U.S. Colonialism from Lewis and Clark to Wounded Knee*. New York: Cambridge University Press, 2004.
Ott, Victoria E. "There's No Place Like Home: Gender, Family, and the Confederate Alabama Household." In *War Matters: Material Culture in the Civil War Era*, edited by Joan E. Cashin, 176–97. Chapel Hill: University of North Carolina Press, 2018.
Paludan, Philip S. *"A People's Contest": The Union and the Civil War*. 2nd ed. Lawrence: University Press of Kansas, 1996.
Peterson, Brian, Carrie Conklin, Char Henn, and Steve Kohn. *Footsteps through Historic Red Wing: Three Walking Tours of Red Wing's Historic Architecture*. Red Wing, Minn.: Red Wing Heritage Preservation Commission, 2009.
Plant, Rebecca Jo, and Frances M. Clarke. "Studying Underage Enlistment in the American Civil War." *Journal of the History of Childhood and Youth* 2 (Winter 2018): 47–52.

Pratt, Dorothy O. "Bounty System." In *Encyclopedia of the Civil War: A Political, Social and Military History*, edited by David S. Heidler and Jeanne T. Heidler, 256–57. New York: W. W. Norton, 2000.

Rable, George C. *Damn Yankees: Demonization and Defiance in the Confederate South.* Baton Rouge: Louisiana State University Press, 2015.

Rable, George C. "Hearth, Home, and Family in the Fredericksburg Campaign." In *The War Was You and Me: Civilians in the American Civil War*, edited by Joan E. Cashin, 85–111, Princeton, N.J.: Princeton University Press, 2002.

Randall, J. G., and David Donald. *The Civil War and Reconstruction.* Boston: D. C. Heath, 1961.

Reid, Richard M. *Freedom for Themselves: North Carolina's Black Soldiers in the Civil War.* Chapel Hill: University of North Carolina Press, 2008.

Rhoades, Nancy L., and Lucy E. Bailey, eds. *Wanted—Correspondence: Women's Letters to a Union Soldier.* Athens: Ohio University Press, 2009.

Richard, Patricia L. *Busy Hands: Images of the Family in the Northern Civil War Effort.* New York: Fordham University Press, 2003.

Robertson, James I., Jr. *Soldiers Blue & Gray.* New York: Warner Books, 1988.

Roediger, David R. *The Wages of Whiteness: Race and the Making of the American Working Class.* London: Verso, 2007.

Rogers, Laurence D. *Apostles of Equality: The Birneys, the Republicans, and the Civil War.* East Lansing: Michigan State University Press, 2011.

Rotundo, E. Anthony. *American Manhood: Transformations in Masculinity from the Revolution to the Modern Era.* New York: Basic Books, 1993.

Rotundo, E. Anthony. "Boy Culture: Middle-Class Boyhood in Nineteenth-Century America." In *Meanings for Manhood: Constructions of Masculinity in Victorian America*, edited by Mark C. Carnes and Clyde Griffen, 15–36. Chicago: University of Chicago Press, 1990.

Ryan, Mary P. *Cradle of the Middle Class: The Family in Oneida County, New York, 1790–1865.* New York: Cambridge University Press, 1981.

Schwalm, Leslie A. *Emancipation's Diaspora: Race and Reconstruction in the Upper Midwest.* Chapel Hill: University of North Carolina Press, 2009.

Schwalm, Leslie A. *A Hard Fight for We: Women's Transition from Slavery to Freedom in South Carolina.* Urbana: University of Illinois Press, 1997.

Schwalm, Leslie A. "'Overrun with Free Negroes': Emancipation and Wartime Migration in the Upper Midwest." *Civil War History* 50, no. 2 (2004): 145–75.

Scott, Anne. *Hannah More: The First Victorian.* Oxford; Oxford University Press, 2004.

Seager, Robin. *Pompey the Great: A Political Biography.* Oxford: Blackwell, 2002.

Shaffer, Donald R. *After the Glory: The Struggles of Black Civil War Veterans.* Lawrence: University Press of Kansas, 2004.

Shively, Kathryn. *Nature's War: Common Soldiers and the Environment in 1862 Virginia.* Chapel Hill: University of North Carolina Press, 2013.

Silber, Nina. *Daughters of the Union: Northern Women Fight the Civil War.* Cambridge, Mass.: Harvard University Press, 2005.

Silber, Nina, and Mary Beth Sievens, eds. *Yankee Correspondence: Civil War Letters between New England Soldiers and the Home Front.* Charlottesville: University of Virginia Press, 1996.

Sledge, John S. *These Rugged Days: Alabama in the Civil War.* Tuscaloosa: University of Alabama Press, 2017.

Smith, Elbert B. "Frémont, Jessie Benton (1824–1902), Political activist," and "Frémont, John Charles (1813–1890), Union general, politician." In *Encyclopedia of the Civil War: A Political, Social and Military History*, edited by David S. Heidler and Jeanne T. Heidler, 785–88. New York: W. W. Norton, 2000.

Smith, John David. "Let Us All Be Grateful That We Have Colored Troops That Will Fight." In *Black Soldiers in Blue: African American Troops in the Civil War Era*, edited by John David Smith, 1–77. Chapel Hill: University of North Carolina Press, 2002.

Smith, Michael Thomas. "The Most Desperate Scoundrels Unhung: Bounty Jumpers and Recruitment Fraud in the Civil War North." *American Nineteenth Century History* 6, no. 2 (2006): 149–72.

Smith, Shawn Michelle. *American Archives: Gender, Race, and Class in Visual Culture.* Princeton, N.J.: Princeton University Press, 1999.

Steiner, Paul E. *Disease in the Civil War: Natural Biological Warfare in 1861–1865.* Springfield, Ill.: Charles C. Thomas, 1968.

Stevenson, Brenda E. *Life in Black and White: Family and Community in the Slave South.* New York: Oxford University Press, 1996.

Stevenson, Louise L. *The Victorian Homefront: American Thought and Culture, 1860–1880.* Ithaca, N.Y.: Cornell University Press, 2001.

Taylor, Amy Murrell. *The Divided Family in Civil War America.* Chapel Hill: University of North Carolina Press, 2005.

Taylor, Amy Murrell. *Embattled Freedom: Journeys through the Civil War's Slave Refugee Camps.* Chapel Hill: University of North Carolina Press, 2018.

Taylor, David Vassar. *African Americans in Minnesota.* St. Paul: Minnesota Historical Society Press, 2002.

Teters, Kristopher A. *Practical Liberators: Union Officers in the Western Theater during the Civil War.* Chapel Hill: University of North Carolina Press, 2018.

Tilley, Heather Anne. "Sentiment and Vision in Charles Dickens's *A Christmas Carol* and *The Cricket on the Hearth*." *19: Interdisciplinary Studies in the Long Nineteenth Century* 4 (April 2007): 1–22.

Vida, István Kornél. *Hungarian Émigrés in the American Civil War: A History and Biographical Dictionary.* Jefferson, N.C.: McFarland, 2012.

Volvo, Dorothy Deneen. *Daily Life in Civil War America.* Westport, Conn.: Greenwood Press, 1998.

Weddle, Kevin J. "Ethnic Discrimination in Minnesota Volunteer Regiments during the Civil War." *Civil War History* 35 (September 1989): 239–59.

Welcher, Frank J. *The Union Army, 1861–1865.* 2 vols. Bloomington: Indiana University Press, 1989.

Werner, Emmy E. *Reluctant Witnesses: Children's Voices from the Civil War.* Boulder, Colo.: Westview Press, 1998.

Westwood, Howard C. *Black Troops, White Commanders, and Freedmen during the Civil War*. Carbondale: Southern Illinois University Press, 1992.
White, Deborah Gray. *Ar'n't I a Woman: Female Slaves in the Plantation South*. Rev. ed. New York: W. W. Norton, 1999.
Whites, LeeAnn. "The Civil War as a Crisis of Gender." In *Divided Houses: Gender and the Civil War*, edited by Catherine Clinton and Nina Silber, 3–21. New York: Oxford University Press, 1992.
Whites, LeeAnn. "Written on the Heart: Soldiers' Letters, the Household Supply Line, and the Relational War." In *Household War: How Americans Lived and Fought the Civil War*, edited by Lisa Tendrich Frank and LeeAnn Whites, 118–34. Athens: University of Georgia Press, 2020.
Wiley, Bell I. *The Life of Billy Yank: The Common Soldier of the Civil War*. Baton Rouge: Louisiana State University Press, 1978.
Wilson, Keith P. *Campfires of Freedom: The Camp Life of Black Soldiers during the Civil War*. Kent, Ohio: Kent State University Press, 2002.
Wood, Forrest G. *Black Scare: The Racist Response to Emancipation and Reconstruction*. Berkeley: University of California Press, 1968.
Wyatt-Brown, Bertram. *Honor and Violence in the Old South*. New York: Oxford University Press, 1986.
Wyatt-Brown, Bertram. *The Shaping of Southern Culture: Honor, Grace, and War, 1760s–1880s*. Chapel Hill: University of North Carolina Press, 2001.

Index

abolitionism, 36, 40, 80, 116, 120, 181–82; of Hamilton, 69; manhood and, 76, 79; Republican Party and, 13; temperance and, 47; USCT and, 4–5, 55
Acton Township, 18
Adam and Eve, 237n21
Adams, Charles Francis, 4
Adams, Charles H., 46, 191
Adams, John, 1
African Americans, 3–4, 36, 43, 58; as childlike, 83; culture of, 118; enlistment by, 3, 40; equal rights for, 70; as inferior, 34, 37, 41, 45–46, 55, 85; labor of, 46, 53, 123, 126–28; male suffrage, 241n9; progress of, 92; recruitment, 4, 40; refugees, 38, 40–42, 46, 52–54, 167; rights denied to, 45; as servants, 46, 49, 52–54, 77, 90; society role of, 57. *See also* Black soldiers
agriculture, 40
Algiers, Louisiana, 146
Andrews, Christopher C., 154
Andrews, Edwin E. (Dr.), 118–19, 191
Anglo-American culture, x
antebellum period women, 61
antiquarian tradition, 150
antisemitic stereotyping, 114
Apple Creek, 33, 36
arms, right to bear, 69
Army of the Potomac, U.S., 111–12
ars moriendi (art of dying), 49
artifacts, Indian, 30–31
Asboth, Alexander Sandor, 40, 47, 191
assassination, of Lincoln, 175
Australian and New Zealand American Studies Association Conferences, xiii

Banks, Nathaniel, 32
Beaver Orssk, 28
Beecher, Harriet, 4
Beecher, Lyman, 4
beliefs, core, 6
Beloit College, 14, 47, 55, 185, 187; Archives and Special Collections, xii
benevolence, feminine role of, 62
Benton Barracks, 16, 74, 83, 104
Berlin, Ira, ix
Betcher, Herman, 86–87, 90, 191
Bible stories, 237n21
Big Mound battlefield, 33
Birch Coulee, Dakota territory, 30
Birney, James Gillespie, 4
Black enlistment, 3, 40
Black labor, 46, 53, 123, 126–28
Black male suffrage, 241n9
Black recruitment, 4, 40
Black servants, 46, 49, 52–54, 77, 90. *See also* Priest, Mary
Black soldiers, 4, 104–5, 147, 149, 154, 164, 181, 187; Christmas for, 110, 121; contributions from, 171; Densmore, B., on, 41–42, 58; Densmore, D., on, 81, 100, 113–15, 160; Densmore, O., on, 75–76; dependency of, 76; education of, 173–74; executions of, 225n28; fighting qualities of, 37; at Fort Pickering, 103; health of, 81, 100; as inferior, 43; manhood of, 76, 85; negative views of, 41–42; payment of, 239n20; progress of, 151; protection of, 75; public execution of, 108; self-reliant citizenship of, 58; superior performance of, 88; sword-fighting contest for, 113; training capacity of, 89

blood flux, 99
Board for Examining Officers in the Colored Troops, 56
Board of Examiners, 43, 59
Board of Supervisors, 14
bones, rhythm, 227n20
Bouton, Edward, 73, 80, 100, 191
Brice's Crossroads, 79
Brockaway, Betsy Ann, 126
Brown, John, 116
Buell, Don Carlos, 16, 17, 191
Bull Run, 24
Bureau of Colored Troops, xii, 3
Buswell, George W., xii, 57, 99, 104, 191, 225n19, 225n29; Clendening and, 84; on Indian artifacts, 30

Caesar, Julius, 115
Camp Atchison, Dakota territory, 32
Camp Hayes, Dakota territory, 30–32
Camp Pope, Dakota territory, 25, 28, 30
Camp Slaughter, Dakota territory, 36
Camp Stees, Dakota territory, 33
Canby, Edward R. S., 145, 147; movement of forces for, *148*
Carrollton, Louisiana, 165
casualty rate, high, 63
celebrations, 110, 170
challenge dances, 227n20
charity work, 61, 62, 65
Cheney, Martha, 50, 56, 191
Cheney, Russell, 56, 156, 191
Chetlain, Augustus L., 117
Children's House, 53
Chilson House, 170
Chippewa, 18, 33. *See also* Ojibwe
Christmas, 110, 116–19, 121, 172
church schools, Northern, 159
civilized Indians, 28
Civil War. *See specific topics*
Civil War Roundtable of Australia and New Zealand, xiii
Clark, Christopher, xi
Clarke, Frances m., 86

Clendening, James H., 84, 119, 121, 191
clothing, 137. *See also* fashion
Coelebs in Search of a Wife (More), 162–63
color line, 157
Columbus (servant), 49, 192
Columbus, Kentucky, 38, 41–43, 46, 48, 72, 87–89, 128, 175
Columbus Ordinance Room, 89
combat performance, 76
combat training, lack of, 43
communication: by Densmore, D., 25; forms of, 8; letter writing as, 6–7
community endorsement, 178
community life, 162
community recognition, 71
comradeship, 144
Confederacy, 52, 76, 78, 126, 145, 156, 158
Connelly, Reagan, xii, 225n29
Constitution, U.S., 1
contagious diseases, 83
contrabands (formerly enslaved people), 38, 209n1
core beliefs, 6
Country Living and Country Thinking (Hamilton), 69
courtship rituals, 67, 140
Crary, Benjamin F., 38–42, 46, 192
cricket on the hearth, 220n22
Critchley, Simon, 115
Crompton, Barry, xiii
cruel and unusual punishments, 108
cultural change, humor and, 115
cultural development, 92
cultural values, 131, 136

Dakota (Sioux), 13–14, 33, 79, 134, 205n1; at Acton Township, 18; attitude toward, 80; cultural history of, 30; Densmore, D., and, 23; discontent among, 19; Lincoln and, 24; Madelia raid and, 28; New Ulm and, 25, 27; racism against, 23, 58; savagery of, 23–25, 36
Dakota War, 18, 20, 36, 63, 179
Dana, Napoleon J. T., 102, 103, 113, 192

Index

Davis (Lieutenant), 140
Davis, Dick, 108, 192
Dead Buffalo Lake, 33
Dearborn (Lieutenant), 95–96
death, 48, 99; disease and, 43; Good Death, 49–50; of Lincoln, 175; view of, 101
Densmore, Benjamin, x, 26, 37, 39, 58–59, 163, 168, 192; Adams, C., and, 46; arrest of, 59; on Black labor, 46; on Black soldiers, 41–42, 58; Board of Examiners and, 43; Crary and, 39–40, 42; education and, 173–74; Forrest and, 73; at Fort Halleck, 38–47; gifts for, 65–66; Goodhue County Rifles and, 16; health of, 7, 32, 44, 89, 175; Hundred Days' Men and, 88; personal visits from, 8; as Quartermaster Sergeant, 18; recruitment by, 41; as reserved, 7; white supremacy of, 45
Densmore, Daniel, x, 1, 20, 32–34, 48–60, 73–74, 102, 192; in Alabama, 156–57; antisemitic stereotypes and, 114; on Black soldiers, 81, 100, 113–15, 160; Black women and, 118; Christmas and, 117–18; Clendening and, 84, 119; communication by, 25; courtship and, 67–68; Dakota and, 23; Densmore, Martha, and, 66–68; enlistment of, 17–18; on fatigue duty, 106; at Fort Blakely, 151, 154; at Fort Pickering, 103–5; Fort Pillow and, 73–74, 85; gift exchange and, 8; health of, 36, 98–100, 168; at Holly Springs, 83–84; homecoming for, 171–72; Jones, J., and, 153, 161, 168–69; letter writing by, 6–7; Lincoln and, 112; in Louisiana, 145–46; at Madelia, 28; manhood and, 162; at Mankato House, 27; on marriage, 116, 162–63; on military order, 108; personal visits from, 8; Philleo, W., and, 98; physiognomy and, 158–59; Poillon and, 78, 129–30; postwar career of, 163; racial attitudes of, 36–37, 80; Sibley and, 20, 23; on Southern manhood, 158; well-being of, 6, 31
Densmore, Elizabeth, xii, 7, 9, 123, 125, 192; Black servants and, 53, 77, 124–26, 132; health of, 52; Priest and, 124–26, 130, 132, 163–64; Red Wing Ladies' Soldiers' Aid Society and, 3, 184; white labor and, 125
Densmore, Margaret, x, 2, 11, 25, 49, 51, 185; on citizenship, 101; death of child, 48; difficulties of, 45; on Priest, 126–27; tragic circumstances of, 50
Densmore, Martha, 2, 7, 11, 25, 51, 62, 62, 87, 155, 192; authority of, 8; bereavement and, 49; on Black servants, 54; on Densmore, Margaret, 50; domestic affairs and, 185; dressmaking and, 136–37; on drinking, 67; in Emerald Grove, 65; fashion and, 137–39; Fort Pillow massacre and, 72; gender relations and, 68; Hamilton and, 69; home renovations by, 143; on letter writing, 66; as matchmaker, 67; McLaren, A., and, 131, 134–44; meals served to soldiers by, 63; Priest and, 123, 126–28, 130–32, 165, 167, 182; Red Wing Ladies' Soldiers' Aid Society and, 3, 61, 137, 179; on Taoyateduta, 23; teaching by, 70; Whittleton and, 26
Densmore, Norman, x, 1, 16, 65, 150, 185, 192
Densmore, Orrin, x, 2, 11–18, 24, 64, 70, 87, 110–11, 193; background of, 11; Black servants and, 53; Black soldiers and, 75–76; on Crary, 40; Dana and, 103–4; Fort Pillow and, 73; on Hobart, 38; home of, 143; Lincoln and, 112; manhood and, 79; on McLaren, Robert 134–35; news provided by, 31–32; on Orrin Jr.'s adventure 86–87, 94; photograph of, 12; Mary McElroy (Mary Priest), Black servant and, 45–46, 53–54, 77, 124, 126–29, 132
Densmore, Orrin Jr., 8, 64–65, 112, 193; Black soldiers, servants, 89–90, 91–92; on Dakota, 24–25; on Densmore, Daniel, 34–35, 85; enlistment a pathway to manhood, 86, 90, 97, 187; on Mary McElroy, 127–28, 131; reports to parents, 89–90; tension caused by enlistment prospects, delayed departure, 90, 93–96; visits brothers' camps, 86–96

260 INDEX

Department of Missouri, U.S. Army, 49
Department of the Northwest, U.S. Army, 19, 24
Department of the West, U.S. Army, 111
departures, 166–78
deserters, execution of, 141
"Destuque Waltz," 66
Devil's Lake, Dakota territory, 23, 28, 30
Dewey, Elizabeth, 68–69, 70, 193
Dickens, Charles, 228n22
discrimination, racial, 106
disease: contagious, 81, 83; death rate from, 43
Dobozy, Peter P., 59, 193
Dodge, Mary Abigail. *See* Hamilton, Gail
dog tents, 99
domestic slaves, 122
domestic sphere, for women, 3
domestic work, 77–78, 101, 132
Douglass, Frederick, 4
dressmaking, 136–37
drought, 1
dueling, 112–14
Dunn, Colin, xi
dying, view of, 101

Early, Jubal A., 110
"ebony occasion," 114–15
education, for Black soldiers, 173–74
Educational Sergeant, 174
emancipation, 3; policy of, 75
Emancipation Proclamation (Lincoln), 40
emotional support, 139
empathy, 62
enemy lands, 183
Engineer Corps, 175
engineering skills, 39
enlistment, 1; Black, 3, 40; of Densmore, D., 17–18; underage, 86
Episcopal High School, ix
equality, racial, 80
executions, 225n29; of deserters, 141; public, 108

family honor, 24
family values, 180
Farago, Peter, xiii
farming, 13
fashion, 137–39
fatigue duty, 106
Faust, Drew Gilpin, 49, 101
female friendship, 144
5th Minnesota Infantry, 178
1st Minnesota Infantry, 63
First Brigade of U.S. Colored Troops, 73, 90
First Confiscation Act (1861), 209n1
food, gifts of, 65
Fordham University Press, xiii
foreigners, dislike of, 47
formerly enslaved people (contrabands), 38
Forrest, Nathan Bedford, 16, 17, 72–74, 78–79, 85–86, 193; campaign area of, 82; Densmore, B., and, 73; raid by, 90–91
Fort Barrancas, 147–48, 149
Fort Blakely, 151–52, 154, 156, 172, 187
Fort Halleck, 38–47, 60, 87–88, 105, 120, 172, 181, 185
"Fort Halleck and Stockade at Columbus, Kentucky," 42
Fort Heiman, 26, 38, 39, 185
Fort Pickering, 91–92, 99, 102, 105, 120, 181; Black soldiers at, 103; Provisional Barracks at, 104; as unhealthy post, 103
Fort Pillow, 41, 43, 85, 155, 180; massacre at, 72–74
Fort Randall, 28
Fort Ridgely, 23
Fort Snelling, 26, 36, 48, 131, 134, 140
4th Missouri Cavalry, 46
4th U.S. Colored Heavy Artillery, 210n3; Arkansas, 177, 240n35; combat 88; education 173–75; machines and manhood, 41, 88, 173; nativist discontent 46–47; training 41, 47, 89
Fowle, Benjamin, 126
Fowle, Elizabeth. *See* Densmore, Elizabeth

Fowle, Hanford, 80, 98, 193
Frank, Lisa Tendrich, 179
Freedmen Aid Societies, 52
Freedmen's and Union Refugees Department, 57
Freedmen's Department, 91
Frémont, John C., 14, 55, 111–12, 193
friendship: female, 144; networks, 98

Gamble, Hamilton R., 56, 193
Garden of Eden (Bible story), 237n21
Garrison, William Lloyd, 4
gender: differences, 68; issues, 95; relations, 96–97. *See also* men; women
Genesis, book of, 237n21
gifts, 8, 65–66, 183
Giger (Captain), 153
Gillers, Eleanor, xii
Ginzberg, Lori, 61
Gleason (Lieutenant), 153
Good Death, 49–50
Goodhue County Board of Supervisors, 14
Goodhue County Historical Society, xii
Goodhue County Rifles, 16
Graham, Mary, 140
Granger, Gordon, 147
Grant (Lieutenant), 90, 95
Grant, Ulysses S., 19, 32, 142, 145, 193
Great Northern Railroad, 151
Greenland, Sarah Adelaide, 186
Gurney (Lieutenant), 90

Hale, William D., 41, 43
Hamilton, Gail, 69
Hamline University, 14, 40
Hanford, Charles, 55–56, 77, 194
Hanford, Frederick, 55, 193
Hanford, Mary, 55, 193
Hanford, Susan, 55–56, 194
Hawkins, John P., 145, 147, 154, 156, 194
Henry (runaway slave), 126
Hess, Earl J., 34
Hickman expedition, 89
Hobart, Chauncey, 38

Holly Springs, Mississippi, 83–84
homecomings, 166–78; community endorsement and, 178; prejudices and, 170; rivalries and, 170; tensions with, 169
home renovations, 143
honor, family, 24
Hood John Bell, 145
horse riding, 137
humor, 115
Humphreys, Margaret, 81
Hundred Days' Men, 88, 89
Hungarian immigrants, xiii, 46–47, 182

immigrants, 11, 13, 14; Hungarian, xiii, 46–47, 182
infant mortality rates, 48
inspection visits, 106
instruments, musical, 31
"Interior of Indian Jail," 27
intuition, 62
Irving Block, 91

Jackson, Andrew, 146
Jackson, Thomas "Stonewall," 19
jaundice, 100
Jefferson, Thomas, 1
Johnson, John A., 99
Johnson, Kathryn A., xii
Johnson, Louisa, 53, 99, 125, 132, 194
Johnston, Joseph E., 156
jokes, 115
Jones, J. Blackburn, 73, 93, 99, 103, 106, *107*, 114, 177, 194; Densmore, D., and, 153, 161, 168–69
Jones, Millie (Mrs.), 119, 152, 194

Kappner, Ignatz G., 99, 103–5, 117, 120–21, 194, 225n19
Keller, Christian B., 212n23
Kirby Smith, Edmund, 156, 161
Kurpiers, Ron, xii

labor, 77; Black, 46, 53, 123, 126–28; shortages, 70; white, 53, 125, 127

labor hire, 40
landscape, Southern, 76, 150, 157
La Trobe University, ix
Lee, Margaret, xiii
Lee, Robert E., 19, 156
letter writing, 7, 139; by Densmore, Martha, 66; well-being and, 6. *See also specific topics*
Library of Congress, U.S., xii
Lincoln, Abraham, 2–3, 19, 56–57, 69–70, 75, 111, 194; assassination of, 175; Densmore, D., and, 112; election of, 16; First Confiscation Act and, 209n1; Sioux and, 24
Little Crow. *See* Taoyateduta
Love, Deacon, 98

Madelia, 28, 30
manhood, 40, 63, 86, 96, 162, 173; abolitionism and, 76, 79; of Black soldiers, 76, 85; Densmore, O., and, 8, 79; for former slave, 79; patriotism and, 5; Southern, 158; sword-fighting and, 112–14, Victorian American, 95; willpower and, 44
Mankato House, 27
marriage, 67, 114–16
martial law, 112, 176
masculinity, 134
masquerade party, 64–65
Mayfield expedition, 88
McClellan, George, 19, 111, 112
McDonald, A. C., 115, 116
McElroy, Jenny, xi
McElroy, Mary, (Mary Priest), 78, 122–33, 163–64, 166, 182, 194, 231n24
McFarlane, James H., 168
McLaren, Anna, 67, 127, 195, 231n1; Densmore, Martha, and, 131, 134–44; domestic environment for, 136; dress worn by, *138*
McLaren, Robert N., 11, 15, 48–49, 65, 134, *135*, 195, 203n1, 231n1
McPherson, James, 126

McVean, Archibald, 11, 195, 203n1
Mdewakanton, 33
Mead, George Gordon, 112
meals for soldiers, women providing, 64
medical expertise, self-care as, 43–44
medicines, 44
Memphis, Tennessee, 73, 81, 85, 90–95, 98–99, 145
men: character of, 96–97; public sphere for, 3. *See also* manhood
Meridian Campaign, 56
Meserole, L. C., 136, 139
Methodist Episcopal Church, 14
Miller (Governor), 100
Miller, Harry, xii
Minnesota Historical Society, xi–xii, 150
minstrel shows, 45
Mississippi River Valley, 183–84
Mississippi Valley Sanitary Fair, 57
Missouri Democrat (newspaper), 155
Missouri Historical Society, xii
Mitchell, Maggie, 95
Mitchell, Reid, 201n3
Mobile Campaign, 145–55, *148*
Monash Research Connections, xiii
Monash School of Humanities, Communications and Social Sciences Research Forums, xiii
Monash University, xi
Montgomery, 156
Moore, David, 81
moral authority, of women, 61, 96
morale, 74
moral values, 162
More, Hannah, 162–63
mortality rates, 99; infant, 48
Murfreesboro, 38, 63
music, 66, 91–92, 150
musical instruments, 31

Nachbaur, Fredric, xiii
nation, concept of, 1–2
National Archives, U.S., ix, xii
nativism, 47, 181, 212n23

Navy Yard, Memphis, 93
New Memphis Theatre, 93
New Orleans, Louisiana, 146–47
New Ulm, 25, 27
New Year's Day, 119–20
New York Historical Society Museum Library, xii
9th Minnesota Infantry, 61
Northern church schools, 159

"'Off to Dixie and Adventure'" (White and Connelly), xii
Ojibwe (Chippewa), 13
177th New York militia band, 92
Orphans Fair, 114
Osman, Stephen, xii

Paducah, 106
Panic of 1857, 14
patriotism, manhood and, 5
Peninsula Campaign, 19
Pensacola, Florida, 148–49
Perry, James, 231n24
personal visits, 8
Petroich, Arelle, xii
Philleo, F. F., 15
Philleo, Theresa, 187
Philleo, Will, 98, 195
photographs, 8, 68
physiognomy, 158
Pigeon Wing (challenge dance), 227n20
Pile, William, 74, 84, 195
Pine Bluff, Arkansas, 177
Plant, Rebecca Jo, 86
planter class, 158, 159
Poillon, William A., 77–78, 129–30, 164, 167, 195
political messaging, 110–11
Pompey, 115
Pope, John, 19, 33, 195
Post Hospital, Columbus, Kentucky, 46
Potter, O., 142
poverty, 159–60
power relationships, 122, 131

presidential election (1856), 55
presidential election (1864), 112
Price, Sterling, 111
Priest, Mary *See* McElroy, Mary
private sphere, 3
Proclamation of Amnesty and Reconstruction (Lincoln), 57
Providence Landing, 156, 160
Provisional Barracks, at Fort Pickering, 104
Provost General Headquarters, St. Louis, 56
Public Building Committee, Red Wing, Minnesota, 14
public executions, 108
public schooling, 14–15
public sphere, 142; for men, 3
public welfare, 61
punishments, cruel and unusual, 108

racial differences, 203n13
racial discrimination, 106
racial equality, 80
racial prejudice, 88
racism, 36–37, 45, 47, 58, 167
racist humor, 115
racist stereotypes, 34, 49, 55, 80, 118, 123
Ramsey, Alexander, 19, 24, 55
recruitment, Black, 4, 40
Red Iron (chief), 23
Red River, 165–66
Red Wing, Minnesota: Fair in, 93; Iron Works, 186; Ladies' Soldiers' Aid Society, 3, 61, 65, 137, 179, 184
Red Wing Morning Republican (newspaper), 186
Red Wing School, 173
Red Wing Temperance Society, 184
Redwood Falls, 28
refugees: African American, 38, 40–41; camps for, 102, 209n2; from slavery, 52–53, 77–78
refugee settlement, 40
regulation, "red tape" of, 17

relational war, Civil War as, 179
Republican Party, x, 6–7, 13, 47, 61, 111, 185–86
rhythm bones, 227n20
Richter, Mary, 67
rights: for African Americans, 45, 70; to bear arms, 69; of women, 69
Rock County Historical Society, xii
romantic love, 67
Ronable, Mollie, 26
Rosecrans, William S., 56, 195

Sanitary Commission, 64
Schofield, John M., 56, 195
Schwalm, Leslie A., 46, 167
2nd Minnesota Infantry, 63, 66
2nd Tennessee Heavy Artillery, African Descent, 34, 38
Second Bull Run, 19
self-care, 43–44
self-discovery, 97
servants, Black, 46, 49, 52–54, 77, 90
Seven Days battle, 19
7th Minnesota Infantry, 17, 49, 61, 169
7th U.S. Colored Heavy Artillery bugle band, 91
sewing, 136–37
shelter tents, 102
Sheridan, Philip H., 110–12, 195
Sherman, William T., 56, 145, 172, 195
Shively, Kathryn, 43
Sibley, Henry H., 19–20, 22, 28, 32–33, 37, 195; at Camp Pope, 30; Camp Slaughter and, 36; Densmore, D., and, 20, 23; at New Ulm, 25; routes of expeditions by, 29; at Wood Lake, 23
siege of Vicksburg, 34, 41
Sioux, 18. *See also* Dakota
6th Minnesota Infantry, 142
68th USCT (4th Missouri Volunteers, African Descent), xii, 57–58, 73–74, 92, 99, 100, 105, 113, 148, 151–55, 166; celebrations at Fort Pickering, 110, 112–18; combat, 74, 79–80, 83, 151–55;

discriminated against, 102–8; disease in, 68, 81, 83, 98–100; fighting Gen. Forrest, 73–85; Fort Pillow, 73–74; manhood, 75, 79–80, 113, 153, 161; Mobile campaign, 145–55; occupation duty, 156–61, 165–66; organized, 58, 215n31
Slap, Andrew L., xiii
slave plantations, 158
slavery, 5, 9, 13, 37, 41, 46, 55–57, 122; color line and, 157; contrabands (formerly enslaved people), 38, 209n1; domestic slaves, 122; health and, 81; marriage and, 114–15, 116; refugees from, 77–78
The Sleepwalkers (Clark), xi
Smith, Alvah, 152
Smith, Andrew J., 74, 75, 80–81, 84, 86, 146–47, 196
Smith, Gilman, 50, 52, 79, 101, 196
Smith, James Edwin, 185
Smith, Margaret *See* Densmore, Margaret
Smith, Otis 2, 44, 196; dying, death, funeral, 48–52; illness, contraband labor, 45, 52, 60
social capital, 182
social development, 92
social functions, 137, 139
social values, 162
soldiers. *See* Black soldiers
Southern landscape, 76, 150, 157
Southern manhood, 158
Spring Campaign, 97
Springfield rifle, 89
Stanton, Edwin, 4, 40
State Insane Asylum, 185
State Regimental Papers, xii
State School Law (1861), 15
Steele, Frederick, 147, 151, 155, 196; movement of forces for, *148*
stereotypes, 167, 182; antisemitic, 114; racist, 34, 49, 55, 80, 118, 123
St. Louis Board of Examiners, 43
St. Louis Sanitary Commission Fair, 58, 60, 181
Stony Lake, 33

Index

St. Paul Daily Press, 151, 154
Sturgis, Samuel D., 78
suffrage: Black male, 241n9; for women, 69
Sully, Alfred, 28, 36; routes of expeditions by, *29*
Sumner, Charles, 112
Swanson, Julia, xiii
sword-fighting contest, 113

Talbot (Lieutenant), 153
Taopi (chief), 23
Taoyateduta (Little Crow), 19, *21*, 23, 195, 205n1
Taylor, Amy Murrell, 201n3
temperance, 47
Tennessee Historical Society, xii
10th Minnesota Infantry, 61
Thanksgiving, 48
3rd Minnesota Infantry, 16, 38, 63–64, 169–70, 178
3rd United States Colored Heavy Artillery, 117, 121
This Republic of Suffering (Faust), 101
Thomas, George H., 145
Thomas, Lorenzo, 40
Thompson, Jasper, 231n24
Tink (horse), 129
Trans-Mississippi armies, Confederacy, 156
Treasury Department, U.S., 41
tribal bands, 205n1

unarmed rebels, attacks on, 154
underage enlistment, 86
Union Army, xii, 3, 6; progress of, 32. *See also specific units*
United States (U.S.), ix, 1
United States Colored Infantry (USCI), 57–58, 73, 104, 151
United States Colored Troops (USCT), ix, xi, 47, 56, 60, 72–74, 171, 177; abolitionism and, 4–5, 55; Black soldiers and, 58, 79; First Brigade of, 90; as social experiment, 75
Universalist Church Convention, 174
unmarried women, 68
U.S. *See* United States
USCI. *See* United States Colored Infantry
USCT. *See* United States Colored Troops

values: cultural, 131, 136; family, 180; moral, 162; social, 162
Vicksburg, siege of, 34, 41
Victorian America, 8; manhood in, 95
vigilance, 89
visits, personal, 8
voting, right to, 69

Wabasha (chief), 23
Warner, Susan Melvina, 70, 186
Webster, Belle, 25–26, 70, 117, 140, 195
Welch, Abraham Edwards, 24
Welch, William H., 24
Weld, Theodore Dwight, 4
well-being, 6
White, Jonathan W., xii, 225n29
white labor, 53, 125, 127
Whites, LeeAnn, 179
white supremacy, x, 6, 36, 45, 129, 211n18
Whittleton, Robert, 26, 179
Williamson, Hugh, 1
willpower, 44
Wilson, Ellen, 68
Winter, John, 90, 95
winter quarters, 102
Wisconsin State Fair, 93
women, 134, 179; antebellum period, 61; courtship for, 67, 140; domestic sphere for, 3; fashion for, 137–38; friendship for, 144; moral authority of, 61, 96; public sphere for, 142; rights of, 69; soldiers' meals provided by, 64; unmarried, 68
Wood Lake, 23–24, 37–38, 169

youth, 8

Keith P. Wilson is an affiliate in the School of Philosophical, Historical and International Studies, Monash University, Melbourne, Australia. His books include *Campfires of Freedom: The Camp Life of Black Soldiers during the Civil War* and ed. *Honor in Command: Lt. Freeman S. Bowley's Civil War Service in the 30th United States Colored Infantry.*

THE NORTH'S CIVIL WAR
Andrew L. Slap, series editor

Anita Palladino, ed., *Diary of a Yankee Engineer: The Civil War Story of John H. Westervelt, Engineer, 1st New York Volunteer Engineer Corps.*

Herman Belz, *Abraham Lincoln, Constitutionalism, and Equal Rights in the Civil War Era.*

Earl J. Hess, *Liberty, Virtue, and Progress: Northerners and Their War for the Union.* Second revised edition, with a new introduction by the author.

William L. Burton, *Melting Pot Soldiers: The Union's Ethnic Regiments.*

Hans L. Trefousse, *Carl Schurz: A Biography.*

Stephen W. Sears, ed., *Mr. Dunn Browne's Experiences in the Army: The Civil War Letters of Samuel W. Fiske.*

Jean H. Baker, *Affairs of Party: The Political Culture of Northern Democrats in the Mid–Nineteenth Century.*

Frank L. Klement, *The Limits of Dissent: Clement L. Vallandigham and the Civil War.* With a new introduction by Steven K. Rogstad.

Lawrence N. Powell, *New Masters: Northern Planters during the Civil War and Reconstruction.*

John A. Carpenter, *Sword and Olive Branch: Oliver Otis Howard.*

Thomas F. Schwartz, ed., *"For a Vast Future Also": Essays from the* Journal of the Abraham Lincoln Association.

Mark De Wolfe Howe, ed., *Touched with Fire: Civil War Letters and Diary of Oliver Wendell Holmes, Jr.* With a new introduction by David Burton.

Harold Adams Small, ed., *The Road to Richmond: The Civil War Letters of Major Abner R. Small of the 16th Maine Volunteers.* With a new introduction by Earl J. Hess.

Eric A. Campbell, ed., *"A Grand Terrible Dramma": From Gettysburg to Petersburg: The Civil War Letters of Charles Wellington Reed.* Illustrated by Reed's Civil War sketches.

Herbert Mitgang, ed., *Abraham Lincoln: A Press Portrait.*

Harold Holzer, ed., *Prang's Civil War Pictures: The Complete Battle Chromos of Louis Prang.*

Harold Holzer, ed., *State of the Union: New York and the Civil War.*

Paul A. Cimbala and Randall M. Miller, eds., *Union Soldiers and the Northern Home Front: Wartime Experiences, Postwar Adjustments.*

Mark A. Snell, *From First to Last: The Life of Major General William B. Franklin.*

Paul A. Cimbala and Randall M. Miller, eds., *An Uncommon Time: The Civil War and the Northern Home Front.*

John Y. Simon and Harold Holzer, eds., *The Lincoln Forum: Rediscovering Abraham Lincoln.*

Thomas F. Curran, *Soldiers of Peace: Civil War Pacifism and the Postwar Radical Peace Movement.*

Kyle S. Sinisi, *Sacred Debts: State Civil War Claims and American Federalism, 1861–1880.*

Russell L. Johnson, *Warriors into Workers: The Civil War and the Formation of Urban-Industrial Society in a Northern City.*

Peter J. Parish, *The North and the Nation in the Era of the Civil War.* Edited by Adam I. P. Smith and Susan-Mary Grant.

Patricia Richard, *Busy Hands: Images of the Family in the Northern Civil War Effort.*

Michael S. Green, *Freedom, Union, and Power: The Mind of the Republican Party During the Civil War.*

Christian G. Samito, ed., *Fear Was Not In Him: The Civil War Letters of Major General Francis S. Barlow, U.S.A.*

John S. Collier and Bonnie B. Collier, eds., *Yours for the Union: The Civil War Letters of John W. Chase, First Massachusetts Light Artillery.*

Grace Palladino, *Another Civil War: Labor, Capital, and the State in the Anthracite Regions of Pennsylvania, 1840–1868.*

Christian B. Keller, *Chancellorsville and the Germans: Nativism, Ethnicity, and Civil War Memory.*

Sidney George Fisher, *A Philadelphia Perspective: The Civil War Diary of Sidney George Fisher.* Edited and with a new Introduction by Jonathan W. White.

Robert M. Sandow, *Deserter Country: Civil War Opposition in the Pennsylvania Appalachians.*

Craig L. Symonds, ed., *Union Combined Operations in the Civil War.*

Harold Holzer, Craig L. Symonds, and Frank L. Williams, eds., *The Lincoln Assassination: Crime and Punishment, Myth and Memory.* A Lincoln Forum Book.

Earl F. Mulderink III, *New Bedford's Civil War.*

David G. Smith, *On the Edge of Freedom: The Fugitive Slave Issue in South Central Pennsylvania, 1820–1870.*

George Washington Williams, *A History of the Negro Troops in the War of the Rebellion, 1861–1865.* Introduction by John David Smith.

Randall M. Miller, ed., *Lincoln and Leadership: Military, Political, and Religious Decision Making.*

Andrew L. Slap and Michael Thomas Smith, eds., *This Distracted and Anarchical People: New Answers for Old Questions about the Civil War–Era North.*

Paul D. Moreno and Johnathan O'Neill, eds., *Constitutionalism in the Approach and Aftermath of the Civil War*.

Steve Longenecker, *Gettysburg Religion: Refinement, Diversity, and Race in the Antebellum and Civil War Border North*.

Harold Holzer, Craig L. Symonds, and Frank L. Williams, eds., *Exploring Lincoln: Great Historians Reappraise Our Greatest President*. A Lincoln Forum Book.

Lorien Foote and Kanisorn Wongsrichanalai, eds., *So Conceived and So Dedicated: Intellectual Life in the Civil War–Era North*.

William B. Kurtz, *Excommunicated from the Union: How the Civil War Created a Separate Catholic America*.

Kanisorn Wongsrichanalai, *Northern Character: College-Educated New Englanders, Honor, Nationalism, and Leadership in the Civil War Era*.

Ryan W. Keating, *Shades of Green: Irish Regiments, American Soldiers, and Local Communities in the Civil War Era*.

Robert M. Sandow, ed., *Contested Loyalty: Debates over Patriotism in the Civil War North*.

Grant R. Brodrecht, *Our Country: Northern Evangelicals and the Union During the Civil War Era*.

James G. Mendez, *A Great Sacrifice: Northern Black Soldiers, Their Families, and the Experience of Civil War*.

Gary W. Gallaghar and Elizabeth R. Varon, eds., *New Perspectives on the Union War*.

Paul A. Cimbala and Randall M. Miller, *The Northern Home Front during the Civil War*.

Keith P. Wilson, *Family War Stories: The Densmores' Fight to Save the Union and Destroy Slavery*.

www.ingramcontent.com/pod-product-compliance
Ingram Content Group UK Ltd.
Pitfield, Milton Keynes, MK11 3LW, UK
UKHW041810220225
455401UK00003B/27